HURON COUNTY LIBRARY

O9-BHJ-997

HURON COUNTY LIBRARY

Date Due

HFN Feb85 MAY 1 7 1986			
JUN 7 1986 WALNo 9+			

BRODART, INC.   Cat. No. 23 233   Printed in U.S.A.

49510

910.45   Anderson, Allan, 1915-
And   Salt water, fresh water; over a hundred
         Canadians who work on the water ... pass
         along their vivid stories of life afloat,
         past and present. Toronto, Macmillan, 1979.
           xv, 391 p. illus.

         1. Seafaring life.   I. Title.
         0770518192   0907863

61,Helen

SALT WATER, FRESH WATER

Salt Water, Fresh Water

Over a hundred Canadians who work on the water — fishermen, guides, pilots, divers, rum-runners, whalers, tugboat skippers, and many more — pass along their vivid stories of life afloat, past and present.

ALLAN ANDERSON

Macmillan of Canada
TORONTO

49510

DEC 4 '79

© 1979 by Allan Anderson

All rights reserved. The use of any part of
this publication reproduced, transmitted in
any form or by any means, electronic,
mechanical, photocopying, recording, or
otherwise, or stored in a retrieval system,
without the prior consent of the publisher
is an infringement of the copyright law.

Canadian Cataloguing in Publication Data

Anderson, Allan, 1915 –
  Salt water, fresh water

"Over a hundred Canadians who work on the water —
fishermen, guides, pilots, divers, rum-runners,
whalers, tugboat skippers and many more — pass along
their vivid stories of life afloat, past and
present."

ISBN 0-7705-1819-2

1. Seafaring life.   I. Title.

G540.A54   910'.45   C79-094710-2

The Macmillan Company of Canada Limited
70 Bond Street, Toronto
M5B 1X3

Salt Water, Fresh Water *is for my
father, John Jafferson Anderson (1874-1966),
the finest gentleman I ever knew, or ever
shall know. His boyhood and early youth
were spent in Chatham, New Brunswick.
After I was born, we lived in Calgary and
Montreal, but he always yearned for the sea
and his beloved Maritimes. He told me often
of his days by the Miramichi, and he liked
nothing better than to settle down with a
novel about life at sea. His adult years
were spent inland, but he was a mariner at
heart. It is with the deepest love and
respect that I dedicate this book to him.*

Contents

Author's Preface

There is nothing quite like the dazzle of the sun on the sea on a bright August morning. One such morning, Cassie Brown, the Canadian writer, drove me the short distance from St. John's, Newfoundland, to Portugal Cove and then along the shoreline a bit to St. Phillips. We parked facing the sparkling water of Conception Bay, the gulls wheeling and diving and soaring around us, and porpoises suddenly leaping out of the water and falling back again in what seemed like an expression of playful joy. Across from us, on the other side of the wide expanse of Conception Bay, the massive cliffs of Bell Island plunged from a flat tabletop surface down into the sea. It was a totally delightful day with a kind of energy that lifted one's spirits. I shall always remember it.

Cassie Brown had grown up in an outport, way across on the western flank of the island near Port-aux-Basques, in a place called Rose Blanche. She knew the outport people, she knew fishermen and their ways, and her words were eloquent:

"To the Newfoundland fisherman, the sea is in their blood, in their bones, it is in the very marrow of their bones, it is their very existence. A real, genuine, honest-to-goodness fisherman doesn't feel whole when he leaves the sea. He doesn't feel that things are going well with him. He is never satisfied and happy and completely at one with the universe unless he is right on the sea, doing what he was born to do."

My interview with Cassie Brown, of course, was part of a work-in-progress which eventually became this book, *Salt Water, Fresh Water*. In 1977, my first book, *Remembering the Farm*, had been published, in which people all across the country recalled their days on farms and ranches. Some of them still were farming or ranching. Canadians liked that book: in fact, they put it on the bestseller list for four months. Since *Remembering the Farm* was about people working on the land, the obvious follow-up was a companion volume about people working on the water. In July 1978 I hit the trail again, this time in search of the astonishing variety of Canadians who make their living, in one way or another, from or on or under the water.

I covered the country by plane, train, bus, and car, and, of course, by boat — I was even stranded overnight on Grand Manan Island when the weather was too rough for the ferry to get me off. I started in the Atlantic provinces, poking in and out of communities with the zeal, if I may say so, of a Yankee pedlar of olden times. I spent many fruitful days on the West Coast. I ranged through the Prairies, and, then, finally, Ontario and Quebec. I talked to men and women from the Yukon and the Northwest Territories, until every province and territory was properly represented. All the long winter of '78-'79 was spent editing the cassette tapes, and dubbing them to reel-to-reel tapes, with further editing. The result of all this was that my surprised publisher, Macmillan, was finally presented with a manuscript of over four thousand pages. You never know what will be valuable or useful until a fine editor gets his hands on a manuscript of such immense proportions. It is my considered opinion that only Doug Gibson, whom I have said is the greatest editor in Canada, has the fortitude and enthusiasm to tackle and skilfully edit a manuscript of such epic size. I'm glad to say he survived it!

I was delighted with the variety of people I came up with who worked on the water. They ranged in age from twenty-one to eighty-nine, and one fine old man told me, truthfully, that he had been fishing for eighty years. The list includes fishermen of all kinds (it never occurs to a landsman how many different kinds of fish there are in the sea and in inland waters), tugboat captains on both coasts and on the Mackenzie and other northern waterways, ferry captains, air-sea-rescue operators, coast-guard officers, divers, whalers, river pilots, captains of icebreakers in the St. Lawrence and the Arctic, guides, merchant seamen, submariners, rum-runners of days gone by, cable-layers, bush pilots on float planes, scientists studying the oceans and inland marine archaeologists, white-water trip guides, and men who build or operate oil rigs on the Beaufort Sea. Add to the list the wives of fishermen, those who stay at home and those who go fishing with their husbands, and you have an extraordinary collection of interesting people.

No one knows the number of Canadians employed in all these various operations. The numbers would be impressive, but it isn't just those whose work is directly related to the water, it's all the other people who run auxiliary or back-up services. Let's just take fisheries alone: there are about forty-five thousand full-time, part-time, or occasional professional fishermen in Canada. Then there are the men who build and maintain boats, and nets and other gear, there are the fish-packers, the transportation services, and even the seafood restaurants. Take all the other categories I have mentioned — even take poachers, whom I haven't mentioned, some of whom make a very good living! — and you have a solid mass of Canadians whose work, in its origin, goes right back to the sea or the lakes and rivers of Canada.

Canadians who work on the water fall into three categories. The first is the people who are transporting cargoes by water — from the days of the voyageurs, water routes have tied Canada together, and people and goods, be they Hudson's Bay kettles or giant cargo containers, have been transported by water. The second, smaller group extracts natural resources from beneath the floor of lakes and oceans. The third, and most important, category is the group that can simply be called fishermen. They are the men and women who gather in food from the depths — cod, halibut, salmon, lobster, scallops, oysters, trout, and even eels.

In the individual introductions to the various chapters of the book, I'll discuss people in the other occupations on the water, but here I want to talk mainly about fishermen. In my travels I quickly learned that fishermen have no real love for the sea. A few of them mentioned fine, moonlit nights when the sea was calm, and there was a sense of peace and of the world being right, but most fishermen have no affection for the sea, treating it rather with wary respect, because they know it can be capricious, moody, and unpredictable. They never take the sea for granted.

A farmer can't work the land in bad weather, but if the fishing is good, fishermen have to suffer the elements, and that's that. It's

better now, but men at sea and on the lakes may have to endure
the cold, the wet, and hard, hard work. Everyone knows that a
warm day on the land can seem chilly when you're on the water,
and in winter the cold could be bitter. An old captain told me:
"Down out around there lots of time it would be five below or
something like that, but when we worked up north, I would say
we worked in ten below. Your fingers were freezing and turned
black, turned right black, you know, from the frost. And there's a
man here who had his fingers all froze one time."

Gales, heavy seas coming aboard, the deck wet and slippery
and dangerous: that has been the fisherman's lot, the elements
against him.

The long hours, my God, the long hours! One old dory fisherman told me: "You was turned out in the morning, say at three
o'clock everybody was out and you was out maybe till nine, ten
o'clock that night, working, catching fish, and that went on maybe
sometimes for two or three days till you had your trip. We stayed
out eight days sometimes. If you got two to three hours' sleep out
of twenty-four, you were gittin' a lot of sleep."

After a while, you worked automatically, sleep-walking almost,
accident-prone and pushing yourself to the limit.

Now add to all that, seasickness. Before I started work on this
book, I thought, naively, that fishermen wouldn't be bothered too
much by seasickness. I was dead wrong. Over and over again (I've
spared you most of this in the book) fishermen told me they were
agonizingly seasick when they first went to sea. They were so
tired from the long hours and so weak from being constantly seasick they just wanted to die. They have begged that they would
die and get it over with, they have prayed they would die. Even
when they got toughened up, both younger and older men would
admit that when they went back to sea after a two-week lay-over,
say, they would feel "squamish" (it was never "squeamish"; they
all said "squamish" as in "aw"). Young men, hired on for the first
time as deck-hands, would reel around, dazed and groggy, trying
somehow to do what they were supposed to do, in a way never
wanting to go back, but actually worried that they wouldn't be
rehired because of their dismal performance. What they didn't
realize was that it was a hell common to most young fishermen,

an initiation most of them underwent.

With all they have to contend with, why then do fishermen fish? The answer is simple and straightforward: they want to fish more than they want to do anything else in life. For them, it is the greatest challenge in the world. Fishermen are highly, intensely competitive — even to a degree that surprised me. They always want to catch more fish than the next guy. The best of them will sneak out to sea ahead of the others and then try to pretend he isn't catching many fish when the others check him out with binoculars. In Newfoundland, a fisherman onshore will call out to an inbound skipper, "Ar'n?", which, roughly speaking, means, "Did you catch any? How was the fishing?" The answer invariably is "Nar'n!", which translates more or less as "Nothing much". The boat may be all but sinking from the weight of fish in it, but the answer is still "Nar'n!"

You can use all the fancy phrases in the book and still not exaggerate too much when describing fishermen. They are a rare breed, they are a race apart, they are sturdy professionals. For many of them fishing is an addiction. Fred Kohse fishes 365 days a year on the West Coast. Other highliners, as the fishermen who bring in the most fish are called, work hard, too, but I think even they would say that 365 days a year is a little much. Yet Fred Kohse is curious about world affairs, has books lining the walls of his cabin, and is bouncy and energetic, although he's been fishing for years and years.

I found many fishermen like Fred who are lively and articulate, but not commonly given to long and complicated stories; so, in general, you'll find that the stories in this book tend to be a little shorter than those in *Remembering the Farm*. Perhaps there's some deep significance in this difference between rural and sea-going story-telling styles — perhaps it has something to do with shouting into a force-six gale.

To the fishermen I met, the key word is: challenge. Radar, sonar, loran, navigational equipment of all kinds, fish scanners that practically show them schools of fish swimming below them, have helped incredibly, but an experienced fisherman will still say, "I don't know. I think we'd be better off a couple of miles away from here." Much of the time he's right. Fish follow food supplies, and food supplies drift or move about. Currents and water temperatures will change and the areas where fish are will change with them. One thing that was drilled into me was that fishermen never stop learning.

I chatted with scores of older fishermen who had gone to sea, usually with their fathers, at the age of nine or ten or eleven or twelve. Many of them would be on their own at twelve years of age, teamed up with another boy that age, fishing by hand-line from a rickety boat, and getting next to nothing for the fish they caught.

Like everyone who works on the sea — the widow-maker — fishermen are fatalists. They have to be. Again and again the sea plays tricks, even on men in modern well-equipped boats. The book is full of examples of wrecks and other accidents and dramatic rescues, but let me give one extra example. In the middle of June 1959, the Atlantic salmon were running through the Gulf of St. Lawrence, heading for the Miramichi and the Restigouche rivers. Escuminac is in New Brunswick on an estuary of the Miramichi. On the morning of June 19, the Escuminac fleet put out to sea to meet the salmon run, the best run in a decade. The fishing was good, so most of the boats stayed on the fishing grounds that night. Late in the evening, after crews had set their drift nets, a savage storm came out of nowhere and smashed into the fleet. Nets parted, sails and rigging came crashing down, and twenty-two boats were crushed or capsized by giant waves. By morning, thirty-five fishermen had lost their lives, leaving behind them twenty-six widows and eighty-three children. There was a wind back at Escuminac that night, but no one had any idea of the violence of that storm at sea until the sixteen battered survivors limped in to tell them about it.

It's a tough life at sea, and I gathered that some or many fishermen (take your choice) are hard drinkers. When they stop ashore they drink hard and get the sea out of their systems. They go from pub to pub, drinks on me, and from bar to bar until their money is all but gone. Others, of course, will go home quietly and just rest. But there is no doubt that for all of them, water is their element. I ran into a good number of fishermen who, when they got home, if the weather was good, would head inland for a little lake where they had a pleasure boat, and they and their families would have a great time. You'd think the last thing they would want to see would be more water! Others, when they had idle moments, would whittle ships.

I found in talking to people for *Remembering the Farm* that the great days of the family farm are over. I now know that the great days of fishing are, too. As one man said to me, "It's a commercial venture now. It's not man against nature. Everything is commercial, and they have to get fish to keep the fish plants goin', to give employment ashore. . . . They'll be factories, these new freezer trawlers, they'll catch the fish, process them at sea and freeze them, and bring them in ready to sell." If that isn't the end of the old days, I don't know what is.

Yet there will still be men going to sea in their own boats. That, I'm sure, will never really end. An old fisherman summed it up: "When you're out there you wonder what you're doing there and when you get ashore you want to go back. I don't think anyone loves the sea that's been on it, because they know what it can do, but you can't get away from it and you miss it and you go back again. It gets in your blood when you go so long. It gets in your blood or something, it won't get out."

Allan Anderson
R.R. #3
Tottenham, Ontario
June 20, 1979

SALT WATER, FRESH WATER

ONE

Something Different Every Day

Killer Whales... Up Over the Bow... Swordfish Attack... To Hell With It ... Good, Clean Rivalry... Don't Show Your Hand... An Early Launch... An Eventful Trip for Mr. Jennings... The Biter Bit... Just Push It Through ... The Proper Light Touch... God Help Me!... An Alberta Cash Crop... Highliner Fish... Hope It's Going To Miss You... My God, That's a Woman!... Man Overboard, Man Overboard!... Respect for the Sea... Excuse Me, Is the Lady of the Cabin at Home?... In the Shoes of the Fisherman... The Hooks Caught Him... The Case of the Stunned Halibut ... Creaking... All Part of the Eel Business... Go Out and Make Yourself a Livin'... All Those Shallow Areas... Something Different Every Day

This first chapter is meant to be a sort of preview of the rest of the book and is made up mostly of shorter pieces. I hope that it will give you an idea of the range of the people whose voices come through these pages, and of the range of the stories — tragic, informative, astonishing, or amusing — that appear in the book.

I know that I was surprised by the amazing number of ways in which people make their living on the water, and by the things that happen to them there. I hope that you will be, too.

KILLER WHALES "I've seen whales travel right alongside the boat to get away from the killer whale. You look back and there's killer whales coming behind. But they won't come near the boat, you see, and the whale seems to be aware of this and he stays alongside of you, just floating alongside of you, travelling full speed.

It's a small little whale, only ten, twelve feet, with a big fin on the top, but apparently everything is scared of the killer whale."

UP OVER THE BOW   "In 1935, Davy Wilson got run over in the Bay of Fundy by another boat that cut his boat in two underneath him. Just before daylight, in fog, he come and run right over top of him. Davy jumped out of the boat — he was all alone — and grabbed the anchor and crawled up over the bow of the boat that run him down.

The man that was at the wheel almost took a heart attack because he'd never expected to see a man coming up over the bow, and I guess he was shook up more than Davy was. They turned around, they picked his boat up, in two pieces. And they brought his nets in and he put the boat ashore.

And he went the next week and bought another boat and went back fishin' to finish out the season."

SWORDFISH ATTACK   "Swordfish would attack a dory quite often. We used to do a lot of harpoonin' around Sable Island, you know, shallow water, eight, ten, twelve fathom of water and that was the worst place for them.

One day we had one dory, and a swordfish came up through the bottom three times. It was quite dangerous work. There have been fellows, you know, cut with the swords when they go up through the boat, but none of my crew ever got hurt.

When they come through the dory some swordfish will come out again. But most of them, you have to saw their sword off inside and pound them out with an axe or something. They'll be right in there solid."

TO HELL WITH IT   "One night we were coming into Montreal harbour and we had an old pilot aboard and we were bound for Shed 37 and he was manoeuvring the ship coming into the dock there. He missed his manoeuvring and instead of going to 37 we went to a section across the slip.

So the captain told him, 'We're not going to this section, we're going to 37.' The old pilot said, 'Well, I don't care if you're going to 37, I'm going to this section, I'm all through wid you!'

The captain wasn't allowed to handle his own ship in the harbour, so he asked the old pilot to move him back to the right section. But he said, 'No, I'm through, I'm going home.' He had boarded us at Quebec — there was no relief at Three Rivers like it is today — so it was a twenty-six- or twenty-seven-hour run. He was fed up and tired, and when he missed the right place, the wind took us across to the next section; he was so fed up he told the captain, 'To hell with it, I'm through, I'm going home.'

The captain had to go ashore and call for another man to shift him across."

GOOD, CLEAN RIVALRY "The fishermen in the outports are very competitive and this is what makes you go, you want to beat your neighbour. This is good, clean rivalry. You always want to come in and say: 'How much fish did he get?' and you have to have more or, by God, tomorrow you'll stay out all night and get more fish.

In the fall when you're fishing with handlines on the ground, on the ledges, there's only certain spots where you catch the fish, and the one who gets there gets them, and the one who gets on the tail end gets very little. So you'd get up in the morning early, you wouldn't start your engine, you'd scull or row your boat out the harbour so you wouldn't wake the other guys. And you have an hour's fishing before they get out and you'll be out and have fish caught. Then you just wave your hand, thumb your nose, and say: 'Tough tit, Paddy, I've got the fish, you can have what's left.'

Oh gee that would hurt. Oh my God, if you've got a fellow ahead of you, you wouldn't go near him.

And some fellow that don't know the fishing grounds, he'd be circling around and couldn't get any fish and you'd be catching fish, you know, and he'd come along: 'Any fish?' 'No ... nar'n ... very scarce.' And the fish would be down drowning on your lines, and you wouldn't haul up, no way. You'd get a smoke, you know, or pretend to cook a feed, and he'd say: 'Well, nothing here,' and be gone.

But meantime you had to keep stiff till he was off in the distance, because if you moved he'd know damn well you were catching fish."

DON'T SHOW YOUR HAND   "One night, it was a very beautiful night out, we were laying out there dressing the fish, and I was
cutting open the fish, taking out the insides, and this friend of
mine was scraping the blood out and putting them over the side to
wash them. He had one fish, he dropped it over the side, he went
to lift it up and all he had was the head in his hand.

A shark had just come up and cut the fish's head right off, the
whole fish right off, and left him with the head in his hand. We
looked over the side with the light, and here was a dozen great big
sharks, these blue sharks — some of them get up around six,
seven feet — swimming around the boat. They got teeth on them
like razors: it was lucky my friend didn't lose his hand. So after
that we didn't put the fish over the side of the boat any more."

AN EARLY LAUNCH   "The *Marco Polo* was built in Saint John,
New Brunswick. I don't know exactly the year she was built, but
when she was ready to be launched, she got away on the people
that went to launch her, and she went across the creek in Saint
John harbour and into the earth on the other side of the river. And
it took many men sixteen days, I think, to shovel 'er out of the
earth, to get 'er back out into the water.

Her keel was twisted and they couldn't fix it. But when they put
'er under sail, after gettin' 'er dug out, she proved to be the fastest
ship in the world at that time — the fastest ship in the world."

AN EVENTFUL TRIP FOR MR. JENNINGS   "I can recall when I
was working up the west coast of Vancouver Island leaving Victoria at eleven o'clock one night with a full cargo, a deck-load of
lumber, both holds full, twelve tons of coal in the afterdeck. Anyway, we got out off Carmanah Light, it was just breaking daylight
and the bottom had completely dropped out of the glass. I
watched this and I couldn't believe it, because it was such a beautiful night.

Come daylight all hell broke loose. It was a south-east gale and
I sized the situation up pretty quickly and I said to my mate, 'You
know, if we keep goin', we're gonna founder. She's just gonna
come right over the back end and we're gonna go down with this
cargo we've got on board.' So I waited for an opportunity to turn

around, and we jogged into it, running slow speed into the sea. This was eight o'clock in the morning and in an hour and a half we could have been over into Neah Bay at normal running, but we jogged all day long, and we got over to Neah Bay at four-thirty that afternoon.

There was water everywhere, even up in the wheelhouse, but fortunately we had diesel engines so that didn't bother that old diesel, it just kept plugging away. We found out some time later through a newspaper clipping my wife had saved that the wind at that particular time was gusting to seventy-eight knots, which is well over eighty miles an hour.

Well anyway, on this trip we had a passenger, an old fellow, Mr. Jennings was his name. He had asked if he could go up the coast with us, and of course he came aboard. He was about seventy years old at this time and during the height of all this he had to go to the bathroom, and the door to the toilet was outside — you had to go out on deck and crawl over this pile of lumber to get into the toilet. So he got in there, but he couldn't get out. So he had to stay in the toilet until we got into Neah Bay, which was, you know, four or five hours later.

I don't think he ever travelled with us again after that."

THE BITER BIT "If you know where to catch a lobster across the back and are a little bit careful, he cannot get ahold of you.

One day I stuck my hand in a box of lobsters, a little careless, talking to somebody, not paying attention to what I was doing, and this lobster grabbed me by the thumb and I could not release him at all. But I knew what to do immediately. After he drew some blood and I done a little bit of squealing and hollering, I pinched his eyes and pinched a little bit harder and harder, and eventually he let go, that was it."

JUST PUSH IT THROUGH "In my years of operation I've been very fortunate. I've never had a man fall overboard. I've never had a man get any kind of hook in him. *I* did though, bass fishing.

This was on Lake Simcoe one time. I had four customers and we were fishing away and this fella, I tried to teach him how to set the hook and reel it in; he managed to set the hook real hard and brought it up and the hook went and caught me on the side of the face, right underneath my right eye.

This gentleman, just before that, was telling me that he'd been in the war and whatever, you know, been many, many places. So I asked him to look at it, 'cause I couldn't see, I didn't have a mirror on board. I said just push it through. 'No,' he said, 'I can't do that. Look at the blood.' And nobody else on the boat would do it.

So I had to turn around, push the hook through, and I had a pair of pliers and I cut the hook off the wire and I took it out again and cleaned it up. I held it for five or ten minutes and it stopped bleeding. Any skin that you hold tight enough long enough, it'll stop."

THE PROPER LIGHT TOUCH   "I heard one story, one fellow was telling this other chap about this big codfish that he caught. The other chap said, 'That's nothing,' he said, 'I was fishing and I pulled my line up and there was a lantern on the end. And,' he said, 'it was still lit.'

He said, 'I don't believe that.'

'Well,' he said, 'I don't believe your story but,' he said, 'I'll tell you what to do. You take three feet off of your fish, and I'll blow the light out.' "

GOD HELP ME!   "It was real cold that morning, it was eleven below zero, actually, when we got up that morning, the day after Christmas. But by ten o'clock the weather began to let up a little bit and I suppose the temperature came to about zero and I decided that we would go fishing, just this young lad and me, he was about twenty at the time. We were the first two that went out, as it happened. And I went around to the back of Grand Manan, which was a very rugged coastline, and we didn't really have that much wind, about fifteen miles nor'west wind; the weather in general was pretty good that day.

This young lad, inexperienced as he was, he went up on the side of the awning. I didn't see him when he went up or I would have hollered at him and told him not to go up, but when he come back he was hanging on to the top of the awning with just one hand and he took a step, and made another grab with his hand

again — he had an old tire in the other hand — and when he let go
of the railing, the boat gave a lurch in the sea, and he missed the
railing with his hand. And when I looked around he was about
fifty foot out astern of me in the water.

I didn't know if the boy could swim and there's only three
words I remember saying that day, when I looked back and seen
him in the water, I said, 'God help me.' I didn't have the awning
door open and I didn't have my gaff where I could grab it, and by
the time I swung my boat around and got up alongside of him, the
waves of the boat had pushed him away, so when I reached out
the gaff it didn't reach him, and then I had to make another circle
and come up alongside of him.

By the time I did that, the boat was very close to the rocks, the
wind was pushing us onto the rocks all the time and he was
hauled in under the boat. The boat was roundin' on the bottom,
and he was kind of sucked in under that. And I reached to get
ahold of him and he had his oil clothes on, which is very slippery,
and his hip rubber boots, and I had no way of gettin' ahold of
anything. But I reached down inside of his oil clothes and got
ahold of his belt and hauled him aboard the boat. And I really
don't know yet how I hauled him aboard, because at that time I
weighed a hundred and thirty-eight pounds, and he told me he
weighed about a hundred and ninety-nine, stripped off.

Of course, the deck was very slippery, actually we had two
inches of ice, and when I hauled him in, he laid right face down
on the ice, for a full minute I would say.

I felt that I was quite composed all the time I was rescuing him,
but once I got him aboard the boat, I began to shake and actually
began to cry a little bit.

We didn't have any fire inside the boat at the time, so I took his
clothing all off and wrapped a woollen blanket around him, and
then laid him on the engine box and wrapped him, and he just
kinda curled around the exhaust pipe of the engine and kept
warm that way.

I radioed in that I'd lost a man overboard and that I'd rescued
him and was coming back in. I didn't know whether they had
heard me ashore, nobody answered me, but when I got ashore
there was a considerable number of people on the wharf waiting

for him. He was shivering and in shock, although when I called his mother that night to see how he was, she said he'd gone to the movin' pitchers. So I think I was in worse shape than he was.

He was a right young, rugged, strong lad and a very good swimmer, but I didn't know it at the time, of course. Very few fishermen can swim. I cannot swim myself. It's very doubtful if I fell overboard that I could swim to the boat.

He never took up fishing as a career but he went back fishing, he finished the season with me. Not that anything was said about it very much, we didn't make much fuss over it, just took it for one of those things. Eventually, he gave up fishin' and went out to Central Canada, I think."

AN ALBERTA CASH CROP   "The local fishermen, local farmers who were farming with irrigation, took out licences and fished the lakes in Southern Alberta, mostly for local sale. Some of them sold their fish to people come up from Calgary. The commercial fishing in Southern Alberta did help out farmers by giving them cash, a cash crop in the wintertime when they were idle anyway. In those days they would probably get ten or twelve cents a pound for whitefish and maybe four or five cents a pound for pike they caught, fishing through the ice."

HIGHLINER FISH   "When you talk highliner fish you're talking about best-quality fish and when you talk to a fisherman and you mention the word highliner — and if you talk to any captain he'll tell you the same thing — when you talk the word highliner you think you've got to have your fish so clean that you've got to scrub their teeth with a toothbrush."

HOPE IT'S GOING TO MISS YOU   "I've been in a couple of instances, not towing log rafts but towing log barges, where I've had engine failures. And this is even more traumatic, because at least a log raft would pretty well stop in the water, whereas a log barge just keeps right on coming. If you've got a log barge behind you which is already about twice or three times your size and it outweighs you by a couple thousand tons and you can't get out of its way, well, all you can do is hope that it's going to miss you.

I had a breakdown off the west coast of Vancouver Island one time with a log barge and the log barge missed me all right, but unfortunately I had no manoeuvring qualities left in the vessel, so we sort of drifted alongside each other, and it wasn't a case of two smooth hulls coming together. It was a case of the logs projecting over the side of the log barge playing a little havoc with the tug. You see, the projecting logs, which overhang the side of the barge, are considerably higher than the tug. For example, the bridge of the tug may be twenty-five, thirty feet above water whereas the logs on the log barge may be sixty, seventy feet high.

So, when you're out at sea like that and you have no control over the tug or the tow and you're rolling, if you're rolling in synchronization — fine. But if you're not, then you come together and the butts of the logs may clean off a little bit of your superstructure.

Fortunately we just bounced along the side and took a little damage, but it didn't hole the ship or anything like that."

MY GOD, THAT'S A WOMAN!   "I'd go down with the rest of the men dressed up in oilskins, just like the rest of the guys, and all with their long rubbers on, you know. And I'd go down to go out in the boat and next you could hear somebody: 'My God, that's a woman, there's a woman there!' And it's just breaking day, right early in the morning, and they couldn't get over it, the older fishermen that would be getting ready to go out on the water, they really couldn't get over it. They'd say, 'Look, there's a woman.'

Now my husband has had the most fish down there, and the fishermen say that: 'Well, he must have his charm aboard' — this is what they refer to me as, his charm. Last year, I stayed home a couple of days, and the two days I stayed home they had no fish. So the next day I went down and they had eighteen thousand pounds. So all of the men joked and said: 'I'm takin' you tomorrow.' They all wanted me to go out with them the next day, like.

Our boat is well equipped, and any real heavy work like hauling the main ropes and stuff like this is mostly done by a gurdy. So I haul the ropes along with them, I don't mind. But there is work now that really is too heavy for a woman to do, like when you start haulin' the trap first, to picking up the main ropes and gettin' them across the boat and stuff like this. Well, there is women in Newfoundland could do it, but as you see, I'm not that big. I'm not even five foot tall, I'm four eleven."

MAN OVERBOARD, MAN OVERBOARD!   "Back in 1938 when we had the low water on the Athabasca, it was so low that we just couldn't get out of McMurray with a rowboat hardly. And at that time the delta of the Athabasca was just one big, long mud flat. And so when we took the barges out, we had one tug push and one on a line in front. This was a very small, light tug that we had pulling, and a deck-hand was back there aft, watching the barge, and all of a sudden the skipper pulled her hard over, and that swung the towline around and knocked him overboard.

Well, the skipper came charging down and hollered, 'Man overboard, man overboard!' and threw him a life-ring, and the guy stands up. He's up to about his knees in mud and water."

RESPECT FOR THE SEA   "Well, I stayed out a little bit too long and then she blew pretty close seventy, eighty miles an hour and we were caught out in it. The squalls were coming one way and the wind was blowing like hell from the other way and you just couldn't run from it. You had to stay out there and fight it out. If you ran from it you probably would have foundered and rolled over, and you just had to fight it out, and it was just a matter of having to stay at the wheel until the storm blew over.

You couldn't eat, you couldn't sleep, you couldn't do nothing. You just had to hold onto the wheel and then just watch every wave and every punch that was thrown at you.

I mean this was one time that old mother nature was throwing a bit of a tantrum and we didn't pay attention to it. And this is one thing about being on the sea and dealing with the sea, is having to learn a great respect for its power, because it can crush you at any moment, just like you may take a fly and crush it in your hand. It can do that to you with no problem."

EXCUSE ME, IS THE LADY OF THE CABIN AT HOME?   "This was 1956 or '57. There was a travelling salesman for the Fuller

Brush Company and we met him in Norman Wells and he had a little motor-boat, a little skiff, and he had it loaded down with everything that Fuller Brush owns, and he was travelling just from trapper to trapper, to town to Fort, to whatever. Then we met him again, above the Sans Sault, about three days later, and we forgot all about him till we got into Aklavik, and he was in Aklavik, and he was just makin' a fortune. He was flying out to get supplied and come back in again, one more trip.

Well, we come down the rapids and we met him again at Mountain River there at the tie-up and he didn't know really what in the heck he was gonna do with the rapids, because he had quite a load of Fuller brushes on. And, of course, the rapids are really up raging at this time. So one of us told him to go over to the Mountain River side and to stay on the port shore and run down the shallow-water side and he was quite safe.

So he didn't do that. He went down the wrong side and he got swamped. And for weeks after, people were pickin' up brushes down the whole bloody river.

He rode it out but he lost everything. All he had was his clothes; he wore his pants rolled up here all the time and a pair of old sandals and an open shirt, and that's the way we found him down there at Good Hope or whatever Fort it was. He says, 'That's it.' Wiped out. That was his finish. He got out and he quit. Never seen him since."

IN THE SHOES OF THE FISHERMAN "Usually the smelt are back right in what they call the cod-end of the net. But I have seen the net come up with smelt and it was plugged full right to the front end. So full that you couldn't do anything with it, you just had to let some of them get away.

When you pull that net up, sometimes if it's full of smelts, smelts float, and the net will just pop, it'll actually jump right out of the water. It just looks like a big sausage, you know.

And I have seen fellas — I don't practise it because I don't swim — but I have seen fellas get out and walk on the net, it's so full of fish that you could walk on it. Just for the hell of it, I guess, they'd walk back to the end of the net and pull the cord and then let them go because they just couldn't do anything with it, it was so full of fish."

THE HOOKS CAUGHT HIM   "You're hauling this trawl back at the rate of four or fives miles an hour, which means the hooks are comin' in quite fast, you know, it keeps a man quite busy. If it's snarled up a bit and he can't get it off, this hook keeps comin', the brake on those big reels wouldn't stop them all that quick sometimes. In the time they've got to stop it this big reel would possibly make a whole turn, which would bring in maybe twenty feet of line.

And one fellow, the hooks caught him and just pitched him right over the big reel and hit him on the side of the boat, killed him. Another fellow got caught in the stomach and it ripped him right up till it got up in his rib cage, and just turned him right over the reel and killed him."

THE CASE OF THE STUNNED HALIBUT   "The only time I remember losing an oar was when I was jigging halibut on the north end of Thetis Island and I got a seventy-five-pound halibut. In between the two seats I had built a checkers with covers on 'em, that's where you keep your fish so they won't slither around all over the bottom of the boat and get mixed up in your feet and everything else. So I got this seventy-five-pound halibut on a handline, put him in the checkers, covered him up, and of course the oars were laying on top of the checkers.

All of a sudden, about an hour after I got this halibut, he took off and his tail hit the checkers board, lifted the oars up, and threw one over.

But we always kept a couple of spare oars, you never went out without a couple of spare oars. I couldn't recover the oars that quickly because I always had an anchor out when I was jigging halibut.

I had a club that I used to use and if you hit them in the right place, just forward of the nape, just above the eye, you could stun them and you'd get no more movement out of them. But if you happened to hit 'em a little back of that place you'd probably just stun them for a short while, and this is probably what happened to me this day. He was out for a while but when he came to life he really came to life again, with that tremendous strength they have, and the result was I lost one oar and had a hell of a time holding this halibut down. It was quite a commotion there for a while, he was a pretty good chunk of fish, but I did manage to give him a good club when I got him in the right place, and he settled down this time for good."

CREAKING "We built steamships down here, but still it's not the same as the wooden ones. I don't know, to lay in a bunk and hear the things creaking, you know, you don't get that any more, that kind of sound."

ALL PART OF THE EEL BUSINESS "Eels have to make a round trip around the world, and they come to the Richelieu River in the Province of Quebec by way of Lake Champlain in the States. The eel season is April until October.

Our family, the Thuots, has been in the eel business for 175 years. The catch would be 100,000 pounds a year and they'd sell in the Old Country for $1.70 a pound. The traps were like V's in the river, two-by-twos made out of wood separated to let the water pass through. At the end of each V is a box that catches the eels. A normal-size eel weighs three pounds and is about two and a half to three feet long. They taste greasy unless they're smoked.

One year, 1973, there was a dam up-river to dry up the Richelieu, and we had thirteen bulldozers taking all the rocks out of the river and placing cement slabs for eel traps. My father, Marcel Thuot, was directing a bulldozer and he fell and one leg stuck between two cement slabs. The river was dry when the accident happened, but the valves were opened and the river started rising and he couldn't get his leg free. I was frantic because that water was rising rapidly. I got a steel post and started chipping away at one of the cement slabs, trying to free my father. It was a terrible situation. About twenty to twenty-five minutes went by and the water was up to his shoulders, and I thought he was done for. Then, finally, by hacking away at the slab, I got him free, and just in time, too. He couldn't walk for some time after that, and hasn't fished since.

We overdid it, taking rocks out of the river, and the current ended up being very strong — the rocks used to slow down the water. And later the ice came down the river and broke up almost all the cement slabs.

I was working in the river, and a bulldozer passed beside me and made more current, and I got washed away, maybe three hundred to four hundred feet from where I was. There was ten to twelve feet of water in the Richelieu and I was sure I was finished because I had on big boots that came right up to my arms and the water got in them and I got stuck feet-down with the weight of the water in those boots which kept pulling me down. I thought it was the end, because there weren't any rocks in the river. But there was one we'd missed and I hit on it by good luck, and I grabbed that rock for sure. Some men were working on the shore near by and saw me and they got a boat and came out as fast as they could and rescued me."

GO OUT AND MAKE YOURSELF A LIVIN' "I had been out with my father fishin' when I was a young kid but I went as a man in the boat when I was twelve years old. I was seasick, good and seasick, so seasick at times that I wish I could've died and got it over with, but as the years grew on I got by that, as I got my growth, I imagine.

At seventeen years old my father gave me a boat and a net and gear to go fishin' in the Bay of Fundy and he said, 'Here's a boat, here's a net, now go out and make yourself a livin'.'

I was seventeen years old. I've never stopped since."

ALL THOSE SHALLOW AREAS "One chap followed us from Britt to Tobermory, and he had a fifty-foot boat, oh, one of the old Constellations. And he followed out, and he was dodging around all over the place following in our wake. We were making our straight line across as usual, but he was dodging this way and that, he was going miles out of his way. We couldn't figure it out, so we thought, oh, he's just having a good party!

So, finally, he came into Tobermory harbour just a bit behind us, and he came over and said, 'Boy, you guys in the coast-guard must really know the waters around here! That was something else again, coming across that Georgian Bay!' We said, 'Well, what do you mean?' So the guy said, 'Well, all those shallow areas!' We couldn't understand what he was talking about, because Georgian Bay's a pretty deep bay.

Turned out that the chart was marked in fathoms, of course, but he was reading them as feet, so every time he saw a ten-fathom patch, which means sixty feet of water, he thought it was ten feet of water, and he was dodging out of the way so he wouldn't hit bottom. He thought that we were spectacular, because we could dodge in around all these little clumps and shallow spots, and, of course, we were drawing more water than he was!"

SOMETHING DIFFERENT EVERY DAY   "In our society where people risk boredom, if you're a fisherman I'll be damned if you're going to be bored, because there's always something different every day. Either different problems or a different set of circumstances crop up, and your catch varies, you never know what you're going to bring up — and you get some idea, but you never know for sure — and there's always something new and different and fascinating about the sea. The sea is always restless, and the man who goes on it is as restless as the sea."

TWO

Characters

A Retired Fisherman... Uncle Cy... The Russian Steward... Noah
Fished in the Summer... He Never Complained... If It's Fighting You
Wants!... Storms, Secrets, and Sandy's Sou'wester... A Guy from St.
John's... Streeper's Ark... The Man from Michigan... Paddles and Patrol
Officers... Old Paddy... Fast Work on the Tangles... An Audience for the
Chief... My Father

A good many people who work on the water are "characters". They don't go around thinking of themselves as characters, or developing a ginkiness that will appeal to the tourists
who, in known fishing ports, are waiting to yack with them when
they pull up to the pier on pleasant summer days. They are characters because they were moulded individually. They haven't
been imprinted by the cities, where everyone works in the same
kind of office, sitting behind the same kind of desk. So it isn't at
all odd that they should be quirky, stubborn-minded, given to a
peculiar humour yet quick to put up their fists.

When they are young, they will cut corners and take chances
and yarn about it later in life, but they soon learn the limit to
which they can risk their lives. At sea, when it's part of the job,
they will work five days and five nights without stopping, but on
land they don't like to be rushed. Years ago, an old fisherman at
Torbay North in Newfoundland was grumbling about the hustle
and bustle of modern life, and he said, "It's all hurry up and take
your time." To this day, I do not know exactly what he meant,
except that he was against rushing around.

A RETIRED FISHERMAN "I grew up in a little village at the mouth of the harbour here, and in the afternoons in summer I'd go down around the wharves and listen to the old fellows; they weren't fishing any more and they were more or less retired, I suppose. They'd sit around on the old lobster traps and they'd start telling lies, stories, there were two or three of them that would try to outbeat each other in telling these stories. I used to creep in underneath the wharf and listen to them, myself and some other fellows. The old fellows would get as mad as hell if they found us there and they'd chase us. But it was something to do on a quiet afternoon in the summertime.

There were several old fellows down there, one of them in particular, he was really a little bit strange. He was a retired fisherman, just retired I guess, and he lived by himself in an old house. And every time it would get a little breezy, he used to take this big piece of rope he had stored out in the shed and tie one end around the house and the other end around a big rock in his yard, to make sure that the house didn't blow away. He was a little weird, but he was one of the finest old gentlemen I think I've ever met.

And there was another old character down there who is long gone now; he never did believe there was such a thing as a submarine."

UNCLE CY "Uncle Cy was a fisherman, he'd fished all his life in Raleigh and he was Uncle Cy to the whole community. He'd come and visit me and we'd play Rooks, and he would always wind up the night by telling stories.

He came in this night and we had our game and we had our mug-up and he said, 'Wonderful cold tonight, Tetcher' — he never called me anything but 'Tetcher' — and I said: 'Yes, she's chilly, Uncle Cy.' 'Not half so cold as the time I was up catching rabbits.' 'Is that right, Uncle Cy?' 'Cold,' he said. 'My God, cold, boy, I'll tell you how cold it was. The kettle would be on the front part of the stove boiling like crazy, and the tea pot on the ass end froze solid.' And he said: 'That was the time we was catching the rabbits.' He said: 'You know there was no place in there to make a drop of water and you had to go outdoors. So I woke up this morning and I had to go. I opened the door and here was a rabbit right in front of me. So I grabbed the axe and made a swipe at her ... never touched her, and I took off in the snow after this rabbit. Every time I'd get close and make a swipe at her and she'd jump again.' He said, 'Tetcher, I suppose I chased that rabbit a mile, perhaps a mile and a half, perhaps two mile, and when I come to discover, what do you think 'twas?' 'I don't know, Uncle Cy.' 'Well,' he said,' 'twas a louse perched right between me eyebrows.'

THE RUSSIAN STEWARD "I was in charge of the pilotage station at Les Escoumains. That's the first place where deep-sea ships take pilots, or disembark pilots. It's about forty miles from the Saguenay River between the Saguenay and Father Point. Father Point was on the south shore but Les Escoumains was on the north shore. As you know, we have fog quite often there.

It was the fifteenth of July and a dense fog, and we disembarked the pilot on a Russian ship around ten-thirty in the morning and then he went on his own, going to sea. The Russian ship went full speed into a Norwegian ship coming up. The Russian ship hit the freighter about 150 feet from the wheelhouse near the centre of the ship, midships. The Russian ship was going at least twelve knots; they must make time and usually they just sail with precaution, but anyway.

So after the accident the Russian ship turned back and went on the phone and asked for doctors and everything. Two men was killed on the Russian boat, the third engineer and one deck-hand. The third engineer was on the second deck and he was sleeping, and when the ship hit a second time, stern to stern, it hit so hard, he was just crushed, and the deck-hand was at the same place one deck below, and the same thing happened. Both were killed at the same time.

The chief steward, he survived, but he had injured his leg. So they asked for help and I went out and picked up the doctor at Les Escoumains, a small town, Dr. Tremblay. I said, 'We just have a big accident and they need you on board ship and can you arrange for the ambulance and everything?' He said yes and I went with him and the ship arrived about an hour and a half after the accident. So we went aboard. At that time, all the Russian ships they had their own doctors on board, and Dr. Tremblay couldn't speak a word in English or Russian, but anyway he saw the guy with the leg.

It was terrible to see, and I couldn't imagine how a man could stand that. When I saw him he was conscious and talking to his doctor — and he had a piece of wood through his leg and out the back (it was about one to three inches wide and twenty-seven or thirty inches long, right through him at the thigh).

Now they decided, both of them, not to remove it, so they worked at him, what they could, and so right away they call for an ambulance. Anyway, we disembark that guy on the pilot boat on a stretcher. They send him back to Quebec in the ambulance and he stay there a month and a half. Thirty-six hours after he was disembarked at Les Escoumains the wood was pulled out in Quebec.

The doctor on the Russian ship wrote a letter to Dr. Tremblay a year and a half after, mentioning that the' man was back in his country and he was in good health, limping a little bit, not perfect, but in time he was back on the ship."

NOAH FISHED IN THE SUMMER "I taught school in Point Leamington on the north-east coast of Newfoundland, and of course the Salvation Army was one of the big churches there, and Point Leamington had its town drunk — a typical Newfoundlander — a great guy, drank a lot, fished in the summer, worked in the woods in the winter, but Noah drank a lot. He beat up his wife and he gambled and he ran around a bit — he was an awful character. And one night he went to the Salvation Army and he got saved. Well, the rejoicing was unbelievable. And everybody all week was wondering how Noah's soul was, you see.

Well, as the principal of the school down there I had to go to church, and the next Sunday night I decided to go to church with my wife, and everybody was wondering how Noah did all week, if he stayed saved... you see he didn't swear, didn't drink, didn't play cards. So they get the service open and they had the testimony meeting where you get up and tell what the Lord has done for you. And the first one on is Noah.

He gets up, and I will remember this till the day I die. He said: 'You know, friends, I was a terrible sinner.' And everybody said:

'Amen.' But he said: 'T'anks be to God, I've been saved.' And everybody said: 'A... men.' By this time Noah was getting kind of emotional and as they say in Newfoundland, half on the ball or the wing... half crying. And he said: 'I was just thinkin'... sniff... last Sunday night I was sittin' there in the back with my two buddies.' And everybody said: 'A... men.' And he said: 'I was makin' fun of everybody that come in and everybody that got up and testified.' And everybody said: 'A... men.' 'But I've left my buddies behind now, f--- 'em.' And everybody said: 'A... men.' "

HE NEVER COMPLAINED   "Dad spent many long hours fishing. He'd get up probably four, four-thirty in the morning and he would either walk or go by bicycle three miles to the back of the island, Grand Manan Island, where he'd get his dory and go out to haul traps, and he had to haul them all in by hand. He'd probably get home maybe eight or nine o'clock at night, so you can see that he did put in a lot of long, hard hours.

Oh yes, he was very tired when he got home but he never complained. He'd go to bed again by ten o'clock, ten-thirty at night and he'd, like I said, get up the next morning between four and five and leave home and be gone until maybe eight, eight-thirty, nine o'clock at night again, and do the same thing all over again.

And in all those years that Dad worked in lobster and fished I never remember him ever having to take a day off due to sickness or because he was hurt, or anything like that. He just kept right on working."

IF IT'S FIGHTING YOU WANTS!   "My grandfather is alleged to have killed a man. He was an Englishman this fellow that he allegedly killed, his name was Parsons. He come to Grand Bank as a young man, tried to get in with the fishermen — of course they never accepted outsiders for some reason — and they got into a fuss, as they used to call it, a row over where you could fish. They drew lots, you see, and fished in certain areas. And Parsons came down one day where Grandfather and one of his buddies, Jimmy, were fishing, and he got too close. And Jimmy, who was fishing with my grandfather, said: 'If you gets any closer, you'll catch me cold.' And Parsons got mad... got angry. And when they came in they were splitting their fish and he came up to where they were and he made some remark that he didn't think it was very funny what Jimmy had said. He'd bloody well fish where he wanted to. So that was fine, one word led to another and that there was no man in Grand Bank that he was afraid of with his English accent and Grandfather said: 'I don't know what in the hell you're worried about — there's nobody around you frightens either.'

So with that he went to hit Grandfather, and Grandfather sidestepped and caught him in the ribs and drove him about three feet, knocked him down in the fish. And he jumped up and he said: 'Well, if it's fighting you wants, it's fighting we're going to get.' He was a bit of a bully, was known as a bully, and they stripped off to the waist, stark naked to the waist, and he made another run at Grandfather and he sidestepped him the second time and hit him on the opposite side and knocked him down. And Grandfather was a strong man.

Parsons lay in the fish, and Grandfather said: 'Now my son, it's about time we stopped this foolishness, because if you comes again, I'm going to hit you — I'm going to hit you to hurt you — I've only been playing with you so far.' Parsons got up and he kicked at Grandfather's groin and he caught him in the muscle on the inside of the leg, and the old man reared back and punched him full in the chest, and knocked him out. He was out cold for twenty minutes. They finally got a drawing bucket, hauled up some salt water, and threw it in his face and brought him around.

Within a year, Parsons was dead. The doctor, old Dr. MacDonald, claims he died of an enlarged heart directly attributed to the blow from my grandfather's fist. No charges were ever laid, of course, because there was no autopsy, there was nothing to substantiate the theory, but there is no doubt in the minds of a lot of people that he did kill that man with a blow."

STORMS, SECRETS, AND SANDY'S SOU'WESTER "You'll have a hell of a storm and the whole world just seems to be crashing down on you and you think, 'Oh God, how am I ever going to get out of it.' But then the next day it's beautiful and the next night's beautiful, and it only takes one good night to get rid of all these things that you've just passed through, they just vanish and you just think, 'Oh my God, it's beautiful.'

I think I gained a lot from from conversations with some of the older fishermen, on the beach and when you were tied up due to bad weather. If you were friendly with them they would give you some information. They don't tell you everything — they'd withhold the rest, you know; they had their little secrets and they wouldn't tell you everything. You had to find a little of that out for yourself, as to depth and the like.

I remember fishing with a fellow, his name was Sandy Cook, and he tells a story about going out in Hecate Strait and the gale came along and they lost his sou'wester. He really loved this sou'-wester, you know, it was his pet and he'd had it for quite some time and it was more of a good-luck thing to him. Well, they lost this sou'wester and this really upset him. And then on the next trip out, they set the gear out and they started hauling the gear, and he said, 'You know, Clem, believe it or not,' he said, 'first hook up, what was on the end of it — my sou'wester.' "

A GUY FROM ST. JOHN'S   "We were down off the Cape and this open boat came up behind us, and we were cooking up a feed. We were steaming along, so we slowed down and we tied his boat fast to ours, towing her, and this man and his sons came on the boat with us. He had two more chaps with him and he said: 'You stay out there and have an eye to the boat.'

So I started taking up dinner, and in the meantime one of the guys aboard, a little small guy, I suppose he started to get hungry, the smell of the fish was drifting back past him, so he decided to come aboard our boat. So he started to come in on the rope. Now our boat was steaming along and this rope was quite taut. So he swings down over the bow of the boat and takes it hand over hand on the rope and starts to come in.

Now there was a guy aboard our boat from St. John's that didn't understand what the other guy, Buddy, was doing. 'By gosh,' he said, 'I believe a guy fell overboard.' And my stepson cut the engine, and when he cut the engine, our boat stopped and the rope went slack, and down went Buddy into the water."

STREEPER'S ARK   "I think the most fantastic story in the whole Arctic was Streeper. I first met Streeper when I was mate on the *Radium Charles* at Norman Wells in the late forties and I says, 'What in the hell is this tied up beside us?' He pulled in with something that looked like Noah's Ark. He would leave Fort Liard and come down the Liard River — nobody's ever navigated the Liard River except this old farmer.

He was a Saskatchewan farmer and he moved to Fort Nelson and he built himself a flat-bottomed dory-style barge, put an old truck engine in it and some kind of a shaft to a propeller, with an old wheel up there for a steering wheel, and built two little boxes on top for his family and kids and babies and cows and dogs, and he filled it with groceries, just groceries, apples, oranges, candy bars, pop, and he was gonna make a fortune. He comes down the Liard River and he goes into all the towns selling oranges and apples, twenty-five cents each, all the way down and peddling stuff.

He's a wealthy man today and they're still running boats up and down the Mackenzie, but he started like that."

THE MAN FROM MICHIGAN   "We hardly could believe this ourselves, but we had a chap with about a forty-foot Chris Craft come up to the *Spray* at her moorings there, and request information of how to get over to Britt, and that was about a sixty-mile run across the Georgian Bay there. So, he said, 'Well, would you mind showing me on your maps just where I go?' So, I said, 'Well, fine. I'll go across to your boat, and I'll line it up on your charts, there.'

So, I went across and said, 'Okay, well, bring out your charts and I'll show you how to do it,' and he hauled out a road map, and a Michigan road map at that!

That's all he had on board he used, and so I said, 'The first thing you do is go across the harbour and buy a proper chart for the area, because otherwise you're gonna run aground. You have no concept of where the deep water is and where the shallow water is.'

Well, it turned out that this chap had never really done any boating at all before in his life, and had come up from Detroit for his two- or three-week holiday, and he was proposing to go through all these island areas, the thirty thousand islands of the north shore of Georgian Bay, using a Michigan road map."

PADDLES AND PATROL OFFICERS "This friend of ours was here one evening and we were showing her some movie film that we had taken on a trip we had up to Ontario some years ago. And in one shot, I was paddling my wife in a canoe and this dear old soul was quite amazed that I could handle a paddle. She couldn't think of the word 'paddle', so being an outport woman she thought of 'oar', of course, but from where she came from it came out 'h'oar'. So 'Oh,' she said, 'look how he can handle that h'oar.' And of course I couldn't resist it, I said: 'That's no hoar, that's my wife.'

I told it once in Ontario when I was sort of being looked at over a certain gentleman's nose because of the fact that I was a New-foundlander, and this was at a time when these silly Newfie jokes were just coming out. I said: 'You haven't heard the latest one.' I said: 'You know there was an old Newfoundland fisherman out fishing off the coast about four or five miles off and the patrol vessel came on, and the skipper of the patrol vessel hailed him and he asked him how the fishing was, and he said: 'Very good, sir.' And then he said: 'You got lots of fish in your boat, you know you're fishing in Canadian waters.' And the old fellow said: 'Yes, sir.' And he said: 'They're Canadian fish you've got.' And the old fellow looks at him and says: 'No, sir.' 'Well,' he said, 'how do you know? You've got a lot of fish there. Are those Canadian fish?' 'No,' he says, 'those are Newfoundland fish.' 'Well,' said the skipper, 'how can you tell the difference?' 'Oh,' he says, 'we throws back the ones with the big mouths!' "

OLD PADDY "On the west coast here I've heard a lot of old stories from old-timers. You don't have it among the young fellows any more as much as you did on the old people. Especially some of the really colourful Indian or native fishermen, they have some tales. Like, I remember one old man, Paddy George, and he was supposed to be the medicine man for his tribe, he was an excellent fisherman.

Well, I've seen him call seals. He could call seals to the boat, and I have heard that he could also call deer, and I know he could, or claimed he could, talk to crows for example.

Now, the Indian people never talk about themselves, they always talk about a cousin or a relative of some sort. But this day Paddy George was telling the story that over on the Gulf Islands he met this rich American yachtsman and started talking with him. And then it finally got around, over a little bit of drinking, that Paddy, paddling his canoe in this rough weather, could beat this guy in the power yacht over to Vancouver.

And so the story goes that old Paddy — it was a very rough day that day — old Paddy takes off and the yachtsman takes off. And Paddy comes to Porlier Pass and is met by some sea lions who show him through the right pass and the right channel and everything else, so he makes more time, then he gets out into the open sea and he runs into some killer whales which are, of course, brothers of the Indian fishermen, and they show him the calm stretch of the water so that he can paddle his canoe very safely.

But he had one problem. There was one octopus out in the middle of the straits there in this rough water and this octopus didn't like Paddy because he'd killed so many octopus in the past, for food. And he was feeling around for Paddy, but you know how an octopus is built, he's got his eyes in the middle, he's got the body on the end, and then the arms are attached to the head itself, eh? So he is feeling around to try to catch Paddy, and Paddy's trying to avoid it. And this octopus, as Paddy would say, 'This octopus whas feelin' around up dere. He's lookin' for Paddy, he's lookin' for Paddy but he can't see Paddy because his head is under de water, you know.'

So he goes on and on about this story, and as the story ended up he avoided the octopus, and with the help of the killer whales and the help of all the sea brothers, you know, he finally did beat the yachtsman to Vancouver, and won the bet."

FAST WORK ON THE TANGLES "One of the things that a young fellow does when he's reeling nets, because his boss tells him to, is to get all the snarls, all the tangles out of the webbing, because if a fish strikes a net of fine twine with his front teeth and his snout and then twists around and 'round and 'round, he makes a dandy wind-up in the twine. Fishermen have various names for these snarls, none of them very polite. Anyway, one time back on Lake Erie the young fellow beside me was reeling nets for the first time, and he sure beat me. He had his all done in no time, and he was being commended by the head fisherman, the owner, and the young fellow, sweating a bit, pulled out a red bandanna handkerchief to wipe his brow — and a great mass of little snippets of net fell on the ground when he pulled his handkerchief out.

It turned out that he'd had his knife in one hand, and he would grasp one of these tangles, and simply cut it off, and no problem at all, no time required to untangle the nets. However, when the net was examined, one little tangle cut out leaves about a two-foot circular gap of nothing in the nets, and he practically ruined the nets while almost being commended for his speed at the job.

I thought that was pretty good. The workman's solution to a job is not necessarily the boss's solution."

AN AUDIENCE FOR THE CHIEF "The *Manitoulin* was built in Midland. When we left Midland with this vessel we were invited to go to Manitoulin Island, as a presentation was to be made to the captain, Captain Patterson, and as you know, Manitoulin Island has a community of about a thousand people. These one thousand people somehow or other raised a dollar a head and had a thousand dollars in one-dollar bills which was to be presented to the crew and the sailors of the vessel.

It turned out that the Indian chief on the island was to present the thousand dollars to the crew, and Franz Johnston, the artist, had done what they call a linocut of a shield for the ship. The idea was that the Indian chief would make the captain Big Noise Over the Water, and then a plaque with the design by Franz Johnston would be handed to the Indian, who in turn would hand it to the captain along with the thousand dollars.

However, the Indian chief saw his opportunity with a big audience and decided to say what the British had done to the Indians, and his conversation, which was listed for about five minutes with a small talk to welcome us to Manitoulin Island, lasted for over three-quarters of an hour. There were attempts by senior naval officers and Mr. Johnston to thrust the new crest of the ship into his hands to present to the captain, but not he, he wouldn't accept it. We didn't dare do anything because he had a thousand dollars in cash in his pocket in one-dollar bills.

After this very successful sort of pirate raid of one thousand dollars off Manitoulin Island we told the captains of the other ships and one of them was *Magdalen Island*. So all the captains started writing letters desperately to these islands saying what had happened at Manitoulin, would they do the same thing for them.

Now the island of Magdalen was in very bad financial trouble, and they had a much better idea. They suggested the ship adopt the island, not the island adopt the ship, which meant that *they* wanted money from *us*. So that went out of the window."

MY FATHER "I can go back to six generations in Grand Bank, on the south coast of the Burin Peninsula, about twenty-five miles from St. Pierre and Miquelon. And I always wondered about that tremendous load on my father and my grandfather, and his grandfather, the feeling they had for the sea.

But eventually I went back after I had been away for some time when I was twenty-four or twenty-five, and I was able then to understand what some of these men have. It became evident to me that they were very strong-willed men, first of all. They were very courageous men. I went out fishing with my father, and the things I saw in sequence went something like this.

We were going to go out at four o'clock in the morning, which was his normal starting time, but it was too windy. Now he didn't have a radio on at four o'clock in the morning to know it was too windy, he knew that intuitively. So he said: 'Go back to sleep, my son, there's no point in getting up. She's blowing too much.' So about six o'clock he came and called me again and he said: 'The wind has let up a bit now, we'll go out.' So we went down the stage and we got into the fishing gear, you know, the oilskins, the sou'wester, and the hip rubber boots, and I felt like a diver with all this equipment around me, and he got down the dory, got everything ready, and I was to be the navigator.

We putt-putted out the harbour and got out in about five

minutes, and I looked back at Grand Bank, and it was as if
someone had drawn an envelope of fog around it. Things were
visible, yet they were full of mist, and I had some images go
through my mind, the spire of the church, the steeple seemed to
look down holding some mystic reverence. The water reservoir
looked like an out-of-place cigar; it seemed to me that the houses
were almost huddled together, protecting themselves from the
cold and the dampness. Dad said it was going to take us thirty-five
minutes to get out to where we wanted to fish. By the time we got
halfway there, I looked at it again and everything had changed.
The fog let up again, and it was clear, you could see everything.

We got out to where he wanted to fish, he called it the Bagger —
it was a rock that he knew — and he said: 'Okay, throw the jigger
over.' So I threw the jigger over and let it go down till it touched
bottom and I pulled it back and I suppose there was thirty
fathoms of water there, 180 feet, and I pulled it back a couple of
feet and I started tugging the jigger, and of course I hit a fish, a
codfish, pulled it up, and it was about three and a half feet long; I
was absolutely elated. God, it was the greatest thing that had ever
happened to me, and I pulled that one in and dropped the jigger
over again and went through the same process, and this time, I got
two. So that went on, and eventually he looked at me and said:
'We're not in the right spot, we've got to move.' And I looked in at
the town and it was encased in that envelope of fog again. Things
kept changing.

And there is an aroma to the sea, a smell, there is a feel to it,
and I started to feel it. I got very comfortable because my father
was a very strong-willed man and for a long time I lived in his
shadow. I never felt that as men we could identify, but I suddenly
got very comfortable with him. And we moved a bit and he
started to jig and I was a raw rookie by comparison. He was pulling the codfish in faster than you could think about; he had two
jiggers going. But we didn't get too many, not enough to suit him;
we maybe got a hundred and he said: 'Let's check the salmon net.'

So we putted up the cove about four and a half miles up across
the harbour diagonally, and we got seven or eight salmon. And
while we were sitting there, we had a mug-up, home-made bread,
strawberry jam, molasses mogs, hard molasses cookies. And it

was then that I started to find out what kind of a man Phil Stoodley really was.

He started to talk to me in a way that we had never communicated before. And I said: 'Why do you do this? You know you've been almost fifty years out here? You've had countless opportunities to work on the shore, because you're a good worker.' 'My son,' he said, 'there's a freedom out here, a freedom. I don't answer to nobody but me.' And I said: 'You've almost drowned out here.' 'Oh a few times.' 'But isn't that important to you? Were you ever afraid?' 'Oh, a couple of times, you know a lope, a big wave, come over; I was a bit worried about it, and you bailed like crazy and you come out of it. But nobody has ever told me that I gotta be to work at eight o'clock in the morning, and nobody is not going to tell me, either. If I want to get up at three o'clock in the morning and go fishing I'll get up. Nobody ever called me. Never going to have to call me.'

And I said: 'Well, what about the dogfish and the hazards and the sore hands and all that?' 'You takes that as it comes, that's part of it, part of the kind of life that I chose to live. I brought up five children, educated you all the best I could, and I take some satisfaction in that I was able to accomplish that without ever having to take the dole.' And he said: 'There's somethin' about being out here that is so wonderful that I can't put it in words. I can tell you when she's gonna blow; when it's gonna be good weather. I can tell you when there's gonna be fish and when there's not gonna be fish. I can get out here in a fog bank and I'll find my way home; all I needs is a compass.'

That's the kind of challenge I suppose that he saw.

I know that for fifteen years Phil Stoodley, my father, and Phil Riggs, they were first cousins, got more fish than any other fishermen in Grand Bank. They worked harder at it; they knew the fishing grounds better. I'm prejudiced, but they were top-liners all the time. They fished together for fifteen years, and they never had a disagreement, which is something of a record in itself.

Yes, they talked a lot, they talked to each other; they talked in short conversations. They talked about the weather; they talked about the conditions that they were fishing under. They seldom if ever talked about their own problems, their personal problems, their family problems. That was their own business. They may have talked about how much money they thought they could make, but all of their conversations I think were basically about what they were doing. And my father sang a lot of hymns — he's a very religious man, and that's what Dad used to do, he'd entertain Phil singing hymns.

In the height of the fishing season, they would be up at three in the morning. They would have their breakfast, would go get caplin, a little small fish that they used for bait, and then they would go to the trawls and they would haul their trawls, thirty, forty, fifty lines, whatever; or they would handline or they would have a floating trawl — a trawl on deep ground as they called it would be on the bottom of the ocean. The floating trawl would have floats on it to keep it up in the water so the fish, if they were moving, would get the bait that way and get caught.

They took lunch with them, for a mug-up about nine or ten o'clock in the morning. They used to take a thermos of tea, always strong black tea usually with molasses in it as opposed to sugar, maybe a drop of cow's milk, because they kept cows (and horses and pigs and all that, they were fishermen farmers), and they'd usually get in around two o'clock in the afternoon from the fishing grounds. They'd start to clean their fish, and they would probably work till six o'clock in the evening, five, six o'clock before they got home for supper. Now that was their main meal of the day, and they ate tremendous, horrendous amounts of food by that time. Supper-time was the big time, everybody was home for supper-time, you had better be home for supper-time. That food would run from fresh fish to almost anything you could imagine, home-made bread, home-made pies, home-made tea biscuits, baked beans was a family favourite — these were the kinds of things.

They'd have supper at five or six o'clock. The rest of the chores that had to be done around the house usually were done, and Dad was in bed by nine o'clock and dare anybody make a sound. He would be so tired I can remember as a boy going upstairs and seeing him — he always said his prayers, knelt down and said his prayers before he got into bed — seeing him sound asleep on his knees, from absolute fatigue.

Another thing I can remember is he'd get squid juice on his hands, and if you have any kind of an allergy to it, your hands become very sore and they bleed. And I can remember him telling me my mother used to dress him in the mornings — his hands were so sore that he could not button his shirt. And the only cure for that was to urinate over them, and that's how he started his day. Once you got the salt water over them, they were functional again, you could use them. But the only relief to the excruciating pain of squid hands was your own urine and salt water. There was nothing you could do for that. You couldn't wear mittens or rubber gloves, it got in the pores of your skin, squid juice, and it devastated your hands.

We never saw my father from May till September other than for meals and on Sunday. They never fished on Sunday. I remember one time he fished on Good Friday and they almost drowned and he said the Lord was going to get him for that, and he never fished again on Good Friday. In the wintertime he was always home, see. And he was getting his trawls and his nets and his gear ready for next season. So they had a lot of time in the wintertime; he went and chopped firewood, of course, worked incredibly hard, but he loved it.

And I said to him one time: 'Don't you ever get tired?' He said: 'I don't know what it means, boy, to be tired, what's dat?' My father is still alive — he'll be seventy-four years old in November — and it wasn't until he was well into his fifties that he ever expressed a feeling of being tired.

I saw him do something one time that Barnum and Bailey would have loved to have had in their circus. He had a pig-iron killock mooring, weighed three hundred pounds. Anyway, he came in with a three-hundred-pound pig-iron killock, and it was low tide and he had to get the damn thing on the stagehead, so he reached down, picked it up, and he threw it fourteen feet in the air and it landed on the stagehead. And it took four men to carry it from there into the stage. That's how strong he was physically ... and his spiritual personal strengths are unlimited.

Dad fished till he was almost seventy on a continuing basis, and then he decided to retire, get the old age pension, you see. He figured he'd put fifty-two years into it and it was time to quit. So he quit working full time. Now he works part time. I was talking to him not too long ago — he still has a salmon net, still goes out and jigs enough codfish to keep himself for the winter, salt fish. And loves it as much now as he did when he was twenty-five years old."

THREE

Catching Fish

A Game of Checkers... Fascinated by Herring... Balls of Herring... A
Guide Speaks... Jumping Ropes for Shrimp... All by Dates... Gill-net
and Seine... Staying with Your Age Group... Salmon Navigation... The
Salmon Mortality Rate... Getting Salmon... Tuna Fish and Porpoises...
A Rustle in the Water... Harpooning Swordfish... Swordfishing Fever...
A Chance for the Fish To Bite... The Squid-Jiggin' Ground... Whaling...
A Blow Off My Port Bow... The Right Wind for Codfish... Fishing the
Oysters... The Shape of the Oyster... Holy Mackerel!... Really Excited

F ishermen are eager learners. They learn early how to outwit
and catch fish and they keep on learning. If I heard it once
on my travels across Canada, I heard it fifty times: "Every day
you learn something new. If I live to be a hundred, I'll still be
learning something new about catching fish."

If you're going to be any good at it you have to learn "to think
like a fish". You have to learn the ways of fish, the meaning of
depth of water and currents in relation to moving schools of fish,
dates when you could expect fish to arrive in certain waters. You
have to learn to monitor the elements: the smell of the air, a sudden slackening of the wind, an unnatural calmness, the look of
the sky, the feel of the wind, the tattle-tale news the clouds bring.
All this coalesces in their senses and in their minds and they become fishermen.

How do fishermen catch fish? Well, in simple terms, they use
lines with hooks on them strung out behind the vessel, they have
purse seines that surround fish and trap them, they have gill-nets
the fish get caught in, they drag the bottom of the ocean for scallops, they "farm" oysters by placing immature oysters on trays
under the water or on a rocky bottom. Fishermen catch fish in
every way they know. The only thing they don't do is jump overboard and catch fish in their bare hands; if that would work,
maybe they'd do that too.

Perhaps what it boils down to is a fifth sense. All the experience, all the sophisticated techniques and gear, can't and don't make up for the fact that the best fishermen just know that a mile or more away the fishing is better than where they are.

A GAME OF CHECKERS   "It's kind of like a game of checkers, you know — that's why I like gill-netting better than I do trawling. Trawling you go out there and you drag your net until you fill it up with fish. But gill-netting you have your little spot where you think the fish come every year and you go and you put your net there and you try and out-think the fish, you know. It's kind of like playing checkers. You make a move and the fish makes a move and you go out the next day to see what his move was, you know, it's kind of a game.

Gill-nets you set on the bottom of the lake with a marker buoy on each end and the fish comes along and sticks his head in 'em and gets caught. This time of the year, right now in the spring when the water is cold, you can leave them a week, and they'll be nice and fresh. We're starting to bring some of our nets up because the water is warming up, but up until last week we had a gang of nets for each day of the week. Like, Sunday we pulled the gang that we pulled last Sunday, Saturday we pulled the one that we pulled the week before. We had seven gangs of nets in. By the first of July you'll have to pull your nets every day, the same nets every day, because the Lake Erie water temperature comes up to seventy."

FASCINATED BY HERRING   "I'm fascinated by herring, yes. You can't predict the movements of the immature herring that much. They could be here today and somewhere else tomorrow. It's hit and miss, you never know."

BALLS OF HERRING   "Especially in the spring runs, we have things that we call balls of herring, a school of herring that is completely balled up, into a tight ball. This usually happens when you have predators such as spring salmon and dogfish — dogfish, by the way, is a small shark — feeding on them. They very very tightly ball up, not allowing the predator to penetrate. If the predator did penetrate, it would probably be smothered by the large body mass of this particular ball.

It's very easy picking for a bait fisherman. When a person wants to go out and catch live herring to supply his cod fishery, then these balls are sort of heaven-sent."

A GUIDE SPEAKS "This is just a thing I learned from experience. Weather is very important when you're fishing. I believe in the pressure, I believe in the winds. I'm not saying certain winds you can't catch fish, but I believe, in the east wind — you've got problems. You can use all your techniques and you might be able to get a fish, but the east wind is very bad for fishing. But a northwest, a west, you can get fish.

It mostly depends on the pressure, what the barometer is doing. If it's steady or going up it's good. I believe in that. I believe in the pressure which all nature, all animals, all fish or mammals, go by — the pressure, the atmosphere. Most people don't but I do."

JUMPING ROPES FOR SHRIMP "The habitats for the different species of shrimp vary. Now, for example, what we actually call a shrimp here on the west coast is actually a prawn species. But here, the pink shrimp that we have is a cocktail shrimp and it's found on muddy bottom. The pink shrimp we catch in trawls very easily at about thirty fathoms simply because of their habitat preference being on muddy bottom and sort of fine sand, eh? We have a sole rope on the front of the trawl. This causes the shrimp to jump over the rope and into the net, so the net's slightly off the bottom, maybe a few inches. You see, they're trying to avoid that sole rope that happens to be tickling the bottom. It's a very soft rope and it just follows all the nooks and crannies on the bottom, and as a shrimp comes along and feels this thing he just naturally jumps, swims backwards very rapidly, and then he settles down again and by the time he settles down, he's right inside the net."

ALL BY DATES   "Well, I was taught in a very early part of my fishing career that there's a peak in every area, you know, like the Skeena, there are certain dates the fish are there. That's how I base my fishing, is learn all these dates that each area will peak for salmon.

I was taught that from a man from the fishing company. He said, 'If you want to make money,' he says, 'come back here in a week, for the coming season; I'll have everything for you,' and that's what he did and he explained to me that if you want to make money in this business this is what you have to do. As far as I was concerned it worked out fine 'cause that is my system, it's all by dates."

GILL-NET AND SEINE   "Basically the way a gill-net operates on a particular species of fish — salmon, for example — the fish sees an opening in the webbing and feels it can go through the webbing and finds itself lodged and tries to back out, and of course the gills then become entangled and the fish is held fast. This is the method of gill-netting.

And the other methods of catching these fish are seines, for example, where the fish are surrounded.

The seine operates on moving fish that are fairly deep sometimes, very heavily schooled fish, whereas the gill-net operation can operate on fish that are sparsely distributed and are moving, spread over a large area, because you're sort of filtering the water with a gill-net. With a seine, you're surrounding a specific school of fish."

STAYING WITH YOUR AGE GROUP   "Fish tend to travel in age groups rather than a mixture of ages. You have fish, salmon, for example, the ones that would have been spawned in 1974, these fish pretty well stay in one school most of their life unless they're broken up by natural disasters or perhaps a heavy fishing operation. Basically they stay in one age group. You don't find too many age stocks mixed."

SALMON NAVIGATION   "A lot of people talk about celestial navigation that fish may use. That's been studied extensively, but basically it seems to be triggered by the chemical sensitivities. They seem to be able to sense the chemical output of their various river systems and they home towards this. This is the way at least myself as a fisherman would look at it, and it doesn't take them long before they orient themselves to the best route to go.

Now when they get towards the river, of course, then they take a holding pattern, usually some area in the middle of the Gulf greatly influenced by weather conditions. They can wait there for a month or a month and a half until the conditions become right for them to start migrating to their home streams. This usually depends on whether there is enough rain, enough water up in the spawning grounds for them to go up the river — and they seem to be able to sense all this.

I don't think there's anything like sonar involved in this, I think it's basically a chemical sensing device, they can probably sense by the amount of chemicals that are being carried in the stream itself or in the water as to what the flow in their native streams are."

THE SALMON MORTALITY RATE   "The salmon mortality rate is fantastic. Basically they figure that for every two parents that go up and spawn — and the female, for example, averages from three thousand to four thousand eggs — if the return for those two parents that went up is three, then we have a bumper crop, and if it's only two, then there's a lot of conservation measures have to be applied in order to protect the fish itself. So you can see, the survival rate is pretty low."

GETTING SALMON   "As soon as they come up over the stern, I have a club there which is a piece of oar sawn off, and the first thing I do is get ahold of him in the net and I hit him on the back of the head. You've gotta hit them on the top, back top, of the head. No sense hittin' him around the gills or anything, but you hit him right on the very top of the head out and into the nose, right up here. Just one good clip like that and he just stiffens out like that. I kill the fish right immediately — I don't let him beat around, don't let him thrash around, because he'll bruise himself up — and then I take him out of the net. I have a fish-box in the boat which usually has ice in it and he's laid in there and taken care of. I lay him on top of the ice, cover him up, keep the sun off him. You take the very best care of him as a good fisherman always does take the very best care of his fish because we want a good product.

We usually wear a pair of canvas gloves or a pair of rubber gloves that has a rough face on 'em, you see, and if you grab ahold of 'em with that by the tail — the salmon, you can get a great hold around his tail. I can take one twenty pounds livin' in the water and if I get ahold of his tail, I can hang onto him. He's not gonna go anywhere if I can get ahold of him and get me hand around him. And soon as you club them, you pick 'em up by the tail like that and then you take the net off them and put them away.

But I have seen people get salmon that they didn't kill. They'd leave 'em thrash around, you know, take them out of the net and they'd thrash through the boat, and about all they do is bruise themselves up and they bruise the meat up.

In the Bay of Fundy fishery we landed our fish every day. Our fish was all landed every morning, they were put on a truck and trucked in to the city market every morning between six and eight o'clock."

TUNA FISH AND PORPOISES   "I was navigator on a tuna-fishing boat for fourteen months. The idea is to find a school of porpoise, you know, with the binoculars, and the tuna fish are just underneath the porpoise in the daytime. The tuna fish come up in the morning about nine o'clock, but they leave the school of porpoise again about three or four o'clock in the afternoon, you see, and the whole idea is to get the net around the porpoise and, of course, you trap the fish as well and that can be quite exciting.

We're very very careful not to harm any of the porpoise because they mean a living to us. So you come astern about half speed on the engines and that drags the net away ahead of the ship and ninety-nine per cent of the porpoise'll jump right over the head of the net, you know, and they're gone, and then, of course, the tuna fish is left behind, left in the net."

A RUSTLE IN THE WATER   "When you fish for tuna, you

equip your boat with a chair, a belt, big huge pole, a hundred-and-thirty-pound test line. You put a steel leader from your hundred-thirty-pound test line, twelve feet. You fasten six mackerel on a steel leader. One of those mackerel we'll sink a hook in, the rear one, all sewed in, out of sight, and that's trolled behind your boat. There's two other dummy lines with six mackerel on each line, with no hooks, this's a teaser line, to attract the fish, to get them up near your boat. So, all those fish are trolling on the surface and there's a rustle in the water, eh? You can turn sideways and you hear the great rustle of all the fish coming along behind your boat, sixty feet behind your boat. So, the tuna fish can hear at least a hundred feet under water, they can sound the rustle, they don't see, they come to the rustle. And when he gets there, he don't take long to make up his mind which fish he's going to take. Fast, he makes a tremendous commotion, then he's got your hook, then the guy in the chair is away for a two-and-a-half-hour fight, three hours.

I have fought them for six hours and ten minutes, one fish. And nine hundred and eighty-two pound, I believe, was the biggest I landed here. At the end, boy oh boy, you're a sore man, you're very sore. Every muscle in your body is used."

HARPOONING SWORDFISH "For catching swordfish we used to harpoon them. We'd have a stand or a pulpit out from the bow of the boat where the harpooner would stand and the harpoon was a pole about, oh, twelve, fourteen feet long with an iron spike onto it about, oh, eighteen, twenty inches which the dart went on with a rope. When you harpoon the fish this dart slipped off the pole, you'd have a hundred fathom of rope or buoy line which was attached to a keg, and when you harpooned the fish it would take off and you'd throw all this rope overboard and the keg after it. After the keg was in the water there'd be a man go in the dory and he'd pick up this keg and he'd pull this fish back. He'd pull until the fish died. Sometimes it only takes fifteen minutes, though I've seen as high as three hours to get one fish. Some of them will run as high as four, five hundred pounds."

SWORDFISHING FEVER "It's fever, it's fever. Like this fella, this Captain Jack Howe, you know, telling me, goddamn the swordfishing, he's never gonna go at it again. Hell of a nice man, he was, he was well up in the air force when the war was on, you know.

So anyway, it was only a matter of next year and I see him down there swordfishing again, getting ready again. I said, 'Jeez, I thought you told me you was never gonna go at that goddamn swordfishing again?' He said, 'It's a fever,' he said. 'When the time comes you gotta go, whether you want to or not.' "

A CHANCE FOR THE FISH TO BITE   "There was five men on a gill-netter, four crew members and my dad, he was skipper. Two men on each dory and one man on the boat. Well, you'd get in the dory and you'd set your trawl, oh, would take possibly an hour and a half to set your three miles of trawl, and then you'd go back aboard the boat again and you'd have a lunch, mug-up we'd call it, and rest around maybe for two or three hours, you know, give a chance for the fish to bite.

And then you'd get back in the dories and pull the gear back. On some days with a lot of tide it would be hard work, it took you a long time. But usually you'd have it hauled back in two hours and a half, three hours, something like that. Well, at that time, you know, if you got four or five thousand pounds, that was a fairly good catch.

We used to bait the trawl in our fish shed at the wharf and you'd bait it after you'd get in in the evening. Say you got back from a trip at five or six o'clock, well then you'd bait your trawl that evening again, for the next day. You would be working some nights nine, ten, eleven o'clock and maybe leave two o'clock or something in the morning to go back out again. You didn't have too many hours off."

THE SQUID-JIGGIN' GROUND   "You'd lower your jiggers over and you'd jig two hundred squid for your bait the next morning, to put on your trawl. When they comes first, they're very near the boat, you jig them up just like this, just up and down that way, two hands, as fast as you could pull it in, down the other one and just as fast. They squirt all over your face and you're black as tar, and sometimes you swallow it, but it doesn't sting, not too much.

So you go out in the mornings and cut your squid for bait — a squid can make four good baits. You had a big old knife in the dark; you take the squid out of the bag, some are fresh and some are stinking day-olders. You put them down in the dark and you chop; you cut the bait an inch long, you cut the squid around, not up and down, you cut it clear across in round baits, and you can do it in the dark. And you smell your hands and oh, good God, you asked me would I eat a squid . . . not on your life. I can still smell them stinky bastards now. I wouldn't eat one, not on your life, never eat squid, because the smell comes back and I can throw up almost, you know. It was a sweet, sickly smell, and it was nauseating, and now just upon your hands it would take days . . . well, you'd never get it off your hands. The smell is on your hands all day long.

Now just fancy cooking on board that boat. You had to cook your own dinner; you cooked fish, and you have this smell on your hands and you're cooking that fish, but anyway you had an appetite like a horse, and a dog stomach.

Well, your trawl is out in the water fishing now, all night fishing; you had your bait all lined up in a box, cut up in wee little pieces, oh, a big box, maybe two boxes, what you could handle. You went out to the trawl, you had a big buoy sticking up and you haul this big tall stick aboard, and you haul this 180 fathom of rope and you stuck the trawl with the fish on it; you haul it in, took off the fish and immediately started to bait up, hook the hook into these little baits and put it in your tub again."

WHALING "We'd leave Vancouver in April and go up to Coal Harbour, take on our harpoons, equipment, and head out for the outside of Quatsino Sound fifty miles and go over as far as the Queen Charlotte Islands. My ship was the *Boba III*, specially built for whaling. A high bow and all the steering is done outside and you run down this ramp and the harpoon is right on the bow. The skipper shoots the gun and he directs the mate, who's steering from just about midships, which way he wants them to go. If you want a little more speed you tell them 'a little more speed', 'half speed', or you might say 'slow' when you're comin' up on the whale, you see. At the bow of the boat the gun is standing right there with the harpoon in it, about twelve feet above the water. The harpoon is a hundred and thirty-five pounds with a detonator screwed on the end of it that goes off ten seconds after the gun is fired. So the harpoon goes into the whale and then this detonator explodes inside of the whale and tears it all to pieces. Kills it.

Now, attached to the harpoon we have a nylon line they call the foregoer. It's a nylon line, it's light and it's about two hundred feet, and then it goes onto the main line which is ordinary manila line, and it's maybe about four inches in diameter. Quite a big line, four to five inches in diameter. And then when the whale runs, they very often run and take out quite a bit of line sometimes, maybe around about three, four hundred fathoms. And you keep stopping them all the time, keep holding them tight, you see, the line is on a spring so you don't get too much of a jar, and they keep taking the line out, taking the line out, till finally you get them to stop. You do sometimes lose them if they happen to foul the line up or you just stop them too hard and they'll pull the harpoon out or break the line. The line is all coiled up below decks and coiled up very carefully. But there is an odd time, but very, very seldom, that it'll bunch up and won't come up through the holes, you see, and it'll snap the foregoer.

The skipper generally does the harpooning, sometimes within forty feet, sometimes at a hundred and fifty yards. You miss now and again. The boat's jumping around and you miss now and again. If you miss you have to coil everything up again in the pan and that takes about, oh, half an hour, to get another harpoon ready.

If you get him, if he's dead he'll naturally sink, but he'll not go far if you start hauling him in right away. But if he's not killed he'll usually go off along the surface of the water and keep blowing and keep taking out line and taking out line until you finally get him stopped. Sometimes they'll take a dive and go right straight down, and we have had them hit the bottom, then go slack. You start to pull them up, usually when you bring them to the surface he's dead. To stop them from sinking we have an air hose, that's a spear, a piece of pipe sharpened on the end with little, fine holes in it and there's a hose connected to this. We put it into the whale and turn on the air and it inflates them, brings them right up to the surface. It fills them with air and they float, then they plug the hole with a little piece of cotton, oakum usually, and plug the hole where you pull the spear out and they'll float indefinitely, I guess.

When you go to do some more hunting, we have a flag with a sharp spear, like a long bamboo pole with a flag on it, and we just put it into the whale with a light on it. If it happens to be dark when you're picking up the whale you can see the light, you pick up the light. And then when you pick up the last whale, you come around and pick them all up, maybe six or seven, and tow them alongside the boat, with chains around the tail."

A BLOW OFF MY PORT BOW   "The way we found whales was we saw them blowing. We started off at five in the morning and then we'd work until dark. Whenever the lookout in the crow's-nest seen a whale he'd report down to the bridge the direction of the whale; he'd say, 'I see a blow off my port bow' or 'starboard bow,' whatever it may be. We'd just turn the boat and head right, and he tells you when you're dead on it. The harpoon gun is not ready to go, you gotta load it every time, gotta put a new harpoon in every time, you see. There's two or three on the bridge all the time with binoculars. I think that's what ruined my eyes is looking through those binoculars. And then I had to wear a hearing aid, too. You see, I was standing right over that gun off the port, you know, and it's like a little cannon going off, and if you use ear plugs you can't hear what the fella's telling you from the crow's-nest. He can see the whale coming up before you can ever see it, so he can tell you 'He's starting to come up, he's starting to come up' and then you're right ready for 'im the minute he breaks water.

They come up at different times, you see, I mean they don't all come up to the surface at the same time. You know, if there's a bunch of them around, you might see two or three blowing at a time. But, as I say, if there was ten or fifteen whales around, you know, there'd be some down when others would be on the surface.

You gotta do a certain amount of hunting for each whale, you've gotta get up on it, you see, you don't run right up on a whale, sometimes you might take an hour and a half to two hours to get close to that whale because you gotta time them, how long he's staying down, which way he's travelling, how far he goes every time he goes down.

You can see 'im blowing and you go straight and he'll go down for eight minutes, so just when you figure he's about to come up, you get a little speed on your boat so that you're close to him, and when he comes up he's right in front of you. A finback will never change direction on you. The humpback does, he'll probably turn and come up astern of you. Some of them are very hard to hunt, they're a shallow whale, great big barnacles all over them, and they know where the boat is all the time. He'll turn around and, oh, just drive you crazy trying, you just gotta go away and leave him.

April to September, an average year you might get around about a hundred whales a year."

THE RIGHT WIND FOR CODFISH "With the trapping of cod-fish, we need the sou'west wind, and the wind a little bit on the shoreline. If you get the winds off the shore, like nor'west wind, wester wind, and north-east wind, it seems to turn the cod away from the cod trap, turns 'em away from the shoreline. If the wind is up from the north-east, even if it's not too strong, you can get out and pull your traps, you won't get very much fish."

FISHING THE OYSTERS "We fish the oysters in an oyster skiff, or we call them in this area a dory. These are approximately four-teen to eighteen feet long and usually powered by a small out-board. You stand in the bow of the dory where we have a culling board — a flat board on each side of the bow — you stand in the bow and you use a set of rakes which consists of two long handles crossed approximately two-thirds of the way down and have two rakes on the ends. They kind of close together like a pair of scis-sors. What you do is grope for the oysters, and you close these tongs and gather up the oysters on the bottom.

It's hard to tell small rocks from oysters, but you can mostly tell rocks because they feel harder and they're lumpy, you know. It's hard to explain but you can tell it.

Okay, after the oysters are taken off a the tongs and put on the culling board, we throw back the old shells, dead shells, bits of seaweed, could be anything come up on your tongs, mud, stones, whatever, and pick out the oysters and just place them in boxes to be graded. In the spring of the year I would get approximately three to four boxes of five-peck boxes, which are approximately a hundred pounds to a box, a day. That'd be about anywheres from three-fifty to four hundred oysters in a box. After the oysters are taken ashore we take them in our grading house and they are graded for shape and also for size."

THE SHAPE OF THE OYSTER "At the time when my father started the oyster business first there was no grading at all. They were just simply breaking the oysters apart and shipping them as they were, in large barrels that contained around twelve to fourteen pecks. Then it came down to a smaller barrel which held ten pecks, and then the grading system came in. Now that grading meant grading for size and for shape.

The top grade of oysters that we supplied to all the clubs in Upper Canada we called them, the top grade, "four-X". Four X's were stamped on top of each barrel. That meant the top grade. The next grade was a little different shape. It wasn't quite as round an oyster and we called that a three-X. That was for cheaper trade. The next grade we called a two-X. That was more for restaurant trade. It was open in glasses and sold in glasses and towards cheaper trade. The next grade was a one-X, and we didn't sell very many of them, that was sold mostly to be opened up and to put in stews, where people wanted an oyster stew.

Now, the meat and flavour in that low-grade oyster was identical to the meat and flavour in the top-grade oyster because they're grown on the same grounds, they're grown in the same water and consume the same food, so there was no difference in the meat and flavour. The difference was the shape of the oyster."

HOLY MACKEREL! "You anchor a trap by four anchors — it's about the size of a house, only it's made out of twine — and fastened to that you've got a leader, leading through the doorway of this open trap to the shore. And fishes swim up and come up to this leader and they follow the leader into the trap, and when they get inside the trap, there's nothing to lead them out, so the fish just stay in the trap. And when you go to haul the trap, the first thing you do is lift up your rope and close the door off, so that the fish cannot get out of the trap; they're trapped inside the trap.

Now in one trap we had forty thousand pounds mackerel. Now mackerel is not like a codfish. A cod is very quiet. You can get codfish and haul them up and they don't make no noise, but you start hauling a mackerel trap, they'll bore down and they got a leader, and once the leader starts going down, all the rest of them form in a circle and follow and push down. They follow that leader down and it makes just like a whirlpool in the water with the speed of them swimming down, going in circles to go down, and they're really wild, and all you've got to do is hang on to the trap.

And when they start to relax and swim around again, you'll haul them up. And when you start drawing them up, and there's not that much water in, they'll leap right over the twine, back out into the water and get away. They're really wild."

REALLY EXCITED   "When they start hauling up the trap, you don't know exactly how much fish is in it. You just watch, and as more of the line gets taken in, the fish gets pushed back to the back of the trap all the time. And you watch, and you say: 'Oh, there's a bunch there, and look at them over there! How much do you think is in? 'Oh, there might be a couple of thousand pound.'

And when you haul it a bit further, you say: 'Oh, there's more than that — there's three or four thousand.' And as it starts to get drawed right up, you really, really get excited and then the dip-net is lowered, and you dip the net into the fish that's out in the trap out beside the boat, and swing it in over the boat and undo the bottom of the dip-net and it falls down in the hold of the boat. And I just sit there countin' the dips, that's one dip, two dips, how many pounds is in a dip? Two hundred pounds in a dip, well that is four hundred pounds.

And I like things like that — I like to watch the fish."

FOUR

The Old Days

*Now I Can Only Wish You All Goodbye... Brave Days in Yarmouth...
Sailing Out to Sea... A Cabin-Boy on the Lakes... Stone-Hooking... The
End of the Marco Polo... A Pair of Oxen... Swilin'... Their Beacon...
Building a Stage... A Family Affair... On the Labrador... Still Hanging
On... Octopus Weather... The Canadian Merchant Marine... Half the
Village... Closing Up the Outports... No More to Safe Harbour*

The days of the sailing ships were great days: nothing finer
than the sight of a noble vessel with all square sails billowing and the spume blowing as she ploughed through the waves.
Great days, but they were also extremely hazardous. The hidden
reefs of Grand Manan, the entire coastline of Sable Island, in
fact the shorelines of all the Atlantic provinces, are graveyards
for countless numbers of sailing ships. Fog, navigational errors
at night, submerged reefs — the sailing ships were at the mercy
of the elements and of man, and both could be unpredictable.

In St. John's, Newfoundland, an old-timer, Captain Albert
Blackwood, told me: "We used a sextant when we were on the
Grand Banks, but we'd probably be out there for ten days and
get only one sight, we had a lot of fog and that. You had to do a
lot of dead reckoning...."

If you think of a desperate, bedraggled sailor, clinging to the
rigging of a hulk resting at a crazy angle on the rocks below, with
only the tops of the masts above water, and the shore a mere
hundred yards away, your mental picture is more likely to be a
fact of the sailing days than fiction. A companion picture is that
of a man, chilled and almost out of his senses, hanging on de-
spairingly to a loose plank, hoping against hope for rescue that
never came, and finally scrawling a brief farewell on the plank
before slipping into the sea and away forever from a harsh
world.

Fishing, in the old days, involved the whole family. In New-foundland, in the thousand outports, men went to sea to catch the fish, brought them back to be cut and dressed by the women and older men, and then cured on the stages that had been built to dry the fish, the stages that clung precariously and yet tena-ciously to the rocky edges of the outports. It was a picturesque life, from our vantage-point, and the people had a grace under duress, "civility without servility" in the accurate words of Joey Smallwood. But it was a risky life, with danger and death al-ways tugging at your elbow.

NOW I CAN ONLY WISH YOU ALL GOODBYE   "They were in Georgian Bay in a storm and they disappeared and some of the bodies were found, of course. And a bottle was washed ashore at Goderich, with a note in it. No way it was a hoax at that time, this was in the 1800s, and it read something to the effect of, 'Dear Wife, we are now in Georgian Bay. We signalled the Steamer Buell,' that's an accurate name.

And he said, 'They came close to us and I can talk to them but then they went away and left us. Now I can only wish you all goodbye. Give my love to the boys. Get my insurance policy from Cronin.' And, 'signed, your loving husband'.

And they all disappeared, they all died. The ship went down."

BRAVE DAYS IN YARMOUTH   "Yarmouth, at one time, had the highest per-capita tonnage of shipping owned at any port in the world. This was in the nineteenth century — around the 1870s to '80s — and many of the ships that were built never returned to Yarmouth after they'd been built, unless they were returning for refit, because many of them were large ships — when I say ships, I mean, barks and barkantines, brigs and brigantines — and they would bring too much cargo of one item to come back to Yarmouth. But nevertheless they were owned by Yarmouthians and they were sailed and crewed by the Yarmouthians in so far as the captain and officers were concerned; generally, however, when I say Yarmouthians, I mean people from south-west Nova Scotia.

And they sailed all over the world, until eventually steam caused them to gradually die out. We had our own marine insurance companies here, and it was really a maritime centre. Many of these ship-owners and masters, who often became part owners or owners of vessels, built large and attractive homes in and around Yarmouth and with fine gardens and beautiful hedges that were often rounded, and they were very well kept, and then they had large trees, growing all around the place.

Well, they went to the west coast, they went to China, they went to India, they went all over the world."

SAILING OUT TO SEA "The *Hestia* went down on the ledge, the old Proprietor Ledge, just around the turn of the century, and they thought there were no west ledges just off of the Nova Scotia coast so they sailed to the east in lifeboats, thinking they would come to Nova Scotia very shortly.

And two people stayed aboard, they wouldn't go, they climbed the mast and lashed themselves to the rigging. At daylight next morning, somebody saw a mast sticking out of the water and they went out and they rescued these two people.

And the remainder, thirty-odd people, I think, were never found, they died at sea. And along with them there was a dozen or so very prized Clydesdale horses, lost in the same wreck."

A CABIN-BOY ON THE LAKES "My father's name was John Wesley Young and how he became involved in sailing was that his father and mother sent him to Port Milford to pick up a few staples when he was twelve. At Port Milford, of course, the harbour and docks were filled with vessels ready to sail over across to Rochester, Charlotte, and Oswego to pick up coal. And being a young lad and interested in vessels, he got on board of one of the schooners and the captain happened to see him, and he needed a cabin-boy and he asked him if he would like to take a trip across the lake. My dad's only concern was what his father and mother would think, so the captain told him, he said, 'Well, we'll see that they're notified.'

He went, and he never got home with the staples till late in November. He got taken on as cabin-boy and he enjoyed it and he went to Charlotte, and from Charlotte they went to Hamilton and then to Kingston, and he may have had an opportunity to get off the vessel in Picton or Milford but I think he was a little bit afraid of what his father and mother would do to him, so he waited till fall when the season closed and then he had to go home.

The captain of that ship was a very well respected man, and as soon as they found out who he was with, well, they didn't have any worries.

After he'd been out on the schooners a couple of years he got to be wheelsman and from there he went on up to first mate. Even years after he retired, and he told me this about a month before he died, he said when you're sailing at night and there's a nice breeze and you're just skipping along there, you know, and there's no noise except the wind in the sails, and the ropes creaking, it's hard to believe what a peaceful situation it is.

The last ship he sailed on was one that they burnt in Toronto in 1934, the last sailing vessel on the Great Lakes. I was in Toronto the night that it burnt up, and when I came back and told him what had happened, he was quite a hard man in his own way but boy, the tears were right out of his eyes. Just imagine, the last vessel on the Great Lakes and they burned it, ten cents' admission."

STONE-HOOKING "Stone-hooking was rather a unique trade in that it existed in western Lake Ontario and nowhere else on the Great Lakes. The trade lasted roughly from about 1820 to 1920, and for about, oh, maybe sixty years of that period there'd be upwards of twenty to forty schooners working in the trade at any one time. This trade supplied pretty well all of the early building stone for Toronto — the stone for walls, the stone for sidewalks, pavement.

The vessels used a long-handled rake with two tines on it. The men would stand on a scow and slip the tines underneath the stone on the lake bottom and then raise the rake in a quick hand-over-hand movement and then swing the stone onto the deck of the scow. From there, the scow was pulled over to its attending schooner and the stone was tossed aboard the schooner. Physically it certainly was hard work. Of course, the stone when it was under the surface of the water was not so heavy, but once it broke the surface of the water, you were dealing with quite a weight and in its later years they had to lift larger pieces of stone with a winch and then break them with a sledgehammer into smaller pieces.

The stone itself was then taken down to Toronto and unloaded on the docks and it was built into rectangular walls, six feet long, twelve feet wide, and three feet high, called a "toise", and if you were a builder in those days you would come down with your team of horses and you would buy those piles of stone, ten tons each."

THE END OF THE *MARCO POLO*   "The *Marco Polo* came up the north side of the Gulf of St. Lawrence here with a load of lumber in 1883. The swells were quite heavy and the Captain decided he would come in offa Cavendish and lay to. But the sea got worse and he decided he would start out to sea. So he started out to sea and he found she was leakin' so bad he would turn 'er and let her come to the beach. So she grounded in thirty feet of water.

And then they had to get the crew off, so many farmers, around a hundred people from the surrounding area, French River, Stanley Bridge, Cavendish, they all went down to rescue the crew, offa the *Marco Polo*. So, they took the seine boat by land from a cove at New London Bay, carried it by land to Cavendish Beach. They went out and they lashed oil drums on the side of the seine boat; they couldn't make it, they were droven ashore and the seine boat filled with water. So they tried many times and eventually they got to her, by evening. And all the crew got aboard of the seine boat but one man, who was left on the *Marco Polo* to guard the lumber, she was loaded with deal. So, they got them all ashore but one man.

They left him about six days, and the *Marco Polo* stayed above water. Forbes Kennedy was the captain and he belonged to the east end of Prince Edward Island, so he decided to go home, and he paid all his crew off on the dining-room table of John F. McNeil's in Cavendish. From there he left and went home.

Then the insurance company, Hyman and Company, took over the *Marco Polo*, and they got many people surrounding the district, North Rustico, they hired those men to salvage all the lumber on the *Marco Polo*. So, after six days this captain from North Rustico that was on the *Marco Polo* was asked to come ashore because there was a bad storm coming. And he wouldn't come ashore. He said he was put on there to look after the ship and he was gonna stay. So, they went back ashore and night was comin' on and they decided 'We'll go out and we'll take him and that will be it.' But they went out and finally told him if he didn't come off, he was done, he wouldn't get any pay. So, he went to jump from the *Marco Polo* to the seine boat and he was drowned, he went between the two and his life was lost.

The bad storm come and threw the lumber all over Cavendish shore. The insurance company got some of it, but very little. And there's houses built in Cavendish out of the *Marco Polo* lumber, windows, doors, many things was built out of the lumber of the *Marco Polo*."

A PAIR OF OXEN "I think the people around Tancook was pretty fortunate with their boats, you know, there wasn't many, if any, that was lost, totally lost. Different ones came ashore, would part their moorin's and come ashore.

In them days there was no wharves to lay the big boats to, no breakwaters like we have now, nothing like that. It was just little stages and we had to land right on a rock beach, and after a storm we'd have to go down and pick the rocks out one way and the other for to come in.

And we had no motors in them days, no stationary engines to haul up the dories. We had to yoke a pair of oxen, you know, hook fast and haul up your dory up to the shore."

SWILIN' "Well, the sealing industry in the days when I was a boy, and even in my father's day, it was quite different from what it is today. There was no such thing as quotas on seals then, you could go out in a ship and kill so many seals, you'd be right. In St.

John's there would be around two to three thousand men constituting the seal fishery. My uncle, my father's brother, was eleven years Master of the *Imogene*, and he brought in the biggest trip in the history of Newfoundland, fifty-five thousand seals one spring ... fifty-five thousand ... he had a crew of 280 men.

The seal hunt would open around the fifth or the tenth of March, it would be around then that the seals would pup. In them early days, you wouldn't have to go so far north as they go now. You'd only have to go down here about thirty or forty miles north of the Funk Islands. Usually the ships would get down twenty-five or thirty miles north of that island and would strike the seals. But now the last years the ships have to go away down off the Hamilton Bank to get seals.

For the seal hunt, in a ship like the *Imogene*, we speak about one particular ship, you have about 230 or 240 men, and they would be split up in watches, and a master watch would look after thirty or forty men, when you go on the ice.

Say I was appointed as a master watch, I would have thirty or forty men under me, and another master watch would have thirty or forty men, and we would have different directions to go to kill the seals, and we would have to look after the men. If the weather got bad we would have to know when to go aboard that ship. The captain would give us orders what to do.

The food conditions in them days wasn't too good. And your sleeping quarters would be in the same hold where the seals would be coming down. You'd be sleeping on the side in berths here with the seals coming down only about six to ten feet away, and the odour would be pretty high. Some officers aboard had quarters, and the captain wouldn't be sleeping there.

When we'd go on the ice, for our lunch we'd carry some raisins with us, and dry rolled oats, we carried that in a knapsack. We'd have a gaff you know, with a hook into her. The gaff was long enough to take you from one pan to another, about seven or eight feet in length, and then we'd have a knife for pelting the seals and a knapsack on our back to take our lunch in, then we'd walk away from the ship on the ice. You'd be all day walking from the time you leave in the morning until you get back in the evening, seven or eight miles.

You can't imagine how hazardous it is to be at the seal fishery
unless you were out there yourself. It's a job for you to believe
what a person would tell you. When I told you that they threw a
mitt in the water to reach the other pan, it may seem funny to you
to understand that, but to me it is not. You see, the men usually
wore mitts, what you call woollen mitts. If the pans were too far
apart and they had to jump across, they would pull in a little
small piece of ice, or some fellows often threw their mitt down in
the water, to break their jump. And when you go to jump to the
other pan you would jump on that mitt and that would give you a
break... just to say there is something in between there.

As soon as you reach the seals, you get out and kill, pelt the
seals, then you dragged them all on pans and pulled them up, and
put a flag on the pan. Everybody would carry a flag on a pole and
the name of the ship would be on the flag, if it would be the
Neptune, it would be the letter N or the Imogene, I, on the flag.
And you'd stick that flag on the pan and the captain would steam
up to the pan and pick up your seals. If he couldn't get to the pan,
you would have to pull them, drag along three or four at a time.
You'd lift them up on a hauling rope and you'd jump from pan to
pan and haul them across.

But it wouldn't be always loose ice, you know. Out to the seal
fishery, there's times you could walk miles and it would be like a
frozen... just as flat as my concrete walk out there. It wouldn't be
all so dangerous that you'd be falling in every minute, though you
would fall in occasionally, but not too often. The captain would
usually be alert on the job and if he saw that the weather was getting too bad, he would be blowing the whistle, you know, sounding the whistle for them to come aboard.

Well, I've heard my father say that he had killed 125 and pelted
them himself in one day. I know in the Imogene with my uncle
that was captain he had over two hundred men, I know they
killed and panned fourteen thousand seals one day. Now you're
talking about a big crew of men and every man they can spare is
on the ice and only a skeleton crew left aboard that ship. The
skipper would be manoeuvring all day up alongside the pans with
the seals on 'em, then the skeleton crew would be hoisting them
aboard and hoisting them down below. They'd have a spyglass on

board where they would be spying the flags in different directions. Probably there would be five or six different ships in that area, and the captain would have to know his own flag and steam towards it and pick up his seals."

THEIR BEACON   "The old original churches you would find in the outports were usually built on high prominent locations, so they could be seen, and they were always built with a high steeple. Now, you must remember that these people would go out to sea without so much as a compass, so that they had a marvellous instinct of direction, but still that church steeple when they were coming back in was their beacon. So the church to them meant more than just the religious context, it was a thing of safety and life and death to them, so the church played a very prominent part in the thinking of the Newfoundland fisherman. Because not only was it a place where he could worship his God, but it was also a beacon for him to guide him back to shore."

BUILDING A STAGE   "Every fisherman had to build out what they call a stagehead, a wharf, what you call it, but it wasn't a wharf with rocks in our place because the sea was too high, it would knock it all down. You'd build this in May... April or May. About Easter-time I would quit school for a week and go up every day with my father over the ponds to cut stage material.

This would be stuff thirty feet long, garden rails, garden stakes, and beams for flakes for drying the fish on, and beams for our stagehead or our wharf. And we had to cut a lot, in the back of Heart's Content. We couldn't haul this home, we'd haul it out to the waterfront, out to the nearest harbour, Hants Harbour or Neuchelle or New Melbourne, we'd haul it out there, we'd store it up on the bank of the coastline, right by the water. Now when the ice would move off in March or April, we'd launch out the boat, get the engine in, steam up there nine or ten miles, and load the stuff aboard the boat and bring it back. We call this cruising the wood back.

We'd have six or seven boatloads, you see, of wood, and we'd haul it back and we'd take the bark off it, then we started in. You had to build your stage out over the water, drive the sticks down you see, so they were just sticking up in the air. It was a weird-looking, clumsy thing, and it would be about twelve feet in the air, because the sea would come in and run underneath it, so it wouldn't knock it down. And when you came to the boat to unload your fish, they were all pitchforked away up, twelve feet up to this landing, you see. Then you cured it up there, you dressed it, cut it, and the women would work up there too, salting it. You salt your fish first for about, if it's pickled fish in barrels, for about four or five days or ten days, or salt them about a month. It's struck we call it, cured. You take it and wash it then, and then you spread it on the flakes, the flakes you build up on the land with rails on them, made of wood, framework. You put boughs on top of it and then you spread the fish face up, you see, on this and air would dry it, and then you put it in your storage after it got dried."

A FAMILY AFFAIR "Come fall you take your gear in and you put it all away for the winter, haul your boats up, put them in store for the winter. Everything was dried out and put away. On the bad days you had to dry your fish, spread your fish, wash out your fish and dry it. When you're out there fishing it is a family affair, your mother would look after it for you, your sister would dry it for you, your grandfather would dry the fish up while you're out fishing.

If the grandfather was an old man, at sixty-five or seventy, he retired ashore at five dollars a month if he lived that long. He was the boss of the shore plantation, he stayed ashore and looked after the women. He would put the flag up to come out and spread the fish, and then the wife and the daughters all arrived out, spread the fish. And they had to wash the fish, this was salted in barrels. They'd take it out and wash the salt off it, and when you're fishing codfish in the summertime, you get a lot of fish; you get twenty, thirty, forty quintals in those days, the boat was unloaded three times a day. They came down to wash on the stage, to cut throats, gut fish, take the livers out, then salt the codfish. Like my grandmother, she was the height of a barrel, but she salted every bit of fish that grandfather caught.

And if you're ashore you dry the fish, no dull moment at all.

You dig your potatoes out of the ground, about sixty or seventy barrels of potatoes, and you take up your turnip and your cabbage, put it in the cellar for the winter. You didn't get paid for your fish until the fall, so just before Christmas you go up to the merchants who buy your fish, Mr. Hopkins or it might be Moores, Frank Moores' father, and you'd go and you'd wind up.

He'd look up what your account was, your food and your twine and all your salt and your oil and your gasoline and you'd look at all that you owed, put that on one side, your debit, and here's your credit and the balance. Sometimes it would be zero from zero, naught from naught, you're just straight, nothing left. Sometimes you have $100 left or $200, so then you say, Okay, I want so many barrels of flour, twelve barrels of flour, so much beef, so much sugar, so much pork, so much tea, so much soap. You bought all that there, and you brought it home, and put it in your storehouse, that's for winter's food. You didn't go shopping every day, you bought your stuff from them, and that was enough till next fall. If you needed it, he would give you the full nine months' credit, nine barrels of flour, a barrel a month, sugar, tea, and so on."

ON THE LABRADOR   "My first time taking charge of a fishing vessel was in 1934 for the firm of W. & J. Moores of Carbonear, and in these days there were a lot of codfish on the Labrador; there was no problem in getting a load of fish. We had a crew of ten men, myself as master and nine more besides, and we started off about the first of June from Bonavista Bay to go on the Labrador, and we would arrive home somewhere between the middle of August and the first of September with about 1200 to 1500 quintal of codfish. Now a quintal of codfish was 112 pounds — and that would be two days sun-dried.

In them days there was about 250 to 300 vessels going on the Labrador. They would sail down on the Labrador, leaving around the twenty-eighth of May and sometimes around the fifth of June, depending on the ice conditions. If there was heavy ice, we wouldn't start off before June. I have been nineteen days ice-bound in Quirpon, which is the most northerly point in Newfoundland, not being able to get out of the harbour for nineteen days on our way to the Labrador. There would be probably twenty vessels in the harbour and we'd go back and forth from one vessel to another in the morning. We'd go up on the hills and look out over the harbour and out over the straits of Belle Isle because you could look right across the straits and see if the ice would loosen up and give us a chance to get across. We played cards and we'd go ashore and we played ball and we'd go out with the girls and ... all that goes with it.

And then we'd get loose ice all the way down the Labrador, and probably we'd have to go about six hundred or seven hundred miles up north, right up to Cape Mugford. I'd say there was about 250 to 300 sailing vessels going on the Labrador in my day, and there was no problem, there was no such thing as scarcity of codfish on the Labrador, no problem with salmon we'd get in the cod-trap or any of the varieties of fish.

When we went on the Labrador first there was quite a lot of Eskimos. They were friendly, you know, but they lived in their own environment and they weren't too interested in fishing. We wouldn't associate very much with them because when we were fishing we were fishing, and when we give up in the evening we were too tired to go ashore.

But they would usually come out aboard in a boat. They'd want to see what a boat was like and they'd sit down on the deck. They'd have a meal with us, and have our lunch. The Eskimos are great musicians, you know; no matter what you had, if you had an accordion aboard your ship or anything at all, nearly every one of them could play that, all the family — music, no problem.

There was no such thing as catching bait, because we were fishing with a cod-trap. Now a cod-trap is about sixty fathom on the round, and about ten fathom deep, ten to twelve depending on where you're going to set your trap from the shoreline. And you extend your trap out from the shoreline about thirty or forty fathom. Yes, I think it's almost as easy for the fish to get out as to get in, but when the water is full of fish, we'd get so high as fifty, sixty quintals of fish all in one cod-trap.

Now, there has been accidents in the fishing industry on the Labrador. My father's first cousin was lost and all hands on Cape Bonavista after coming off the Labrador with his load of fish. He'd come up to St. John's and discharged it, and on his way home he was lost on Northern Head. He had three sons on board and himself and nine crew, and they were all lost except one of his sons. He went ashore in a gale of wind, with snow, in the month of December on his way back home, he ran into the land and they were lost, but one jumped from the bow of the vessel when the sea was running out and he jumped ashore and he climbed up a cliff, probably a hundred or a couple of hundred feet and he was saved — the only one out of all of them. So there has been accidents on the Labrador during the fishing industry."

STILL HANGING ON "Back in 1917 Samuel Ferguson and Howie Galbraith was fishin' together. It was a salmon skiff which they had in those days, they were built for sailing and rowing. And they were drifting in that night and it come quite a breeze of wind easterly, was a bad storm, and a lot of the boats made shelter on different places, but they didn't get to home. They turned over and swamped their boat and they got her back on her feet again, up on her, or mouth up, which is back on her bottom again. But she was full of water, they couldn't get the water out of her, and they hung onto the centreboard from four o'clock in the morning till five that evenin'. And when the wind come the next day, it blew hard from the nor'west and there was people that did go out to look for them but they didn't find them. They wrote on the centreboard in pencil that they were still hanging on at five o'clock in the evening but would soon be gone because they were played right out, they couldn't hang on any longer.

Them two men were drowned and that is two and I only know of three in all my lifetime that has been drowned out of Lorneville.

When they brought the skiff boat ashore they took the centreboard and it is still in the church hall in Lorneville yet, with the writing on it of the two men that were lost at that time."

OCTOPUS WEATHER "We fished for octopus in a different way to what they do these days. They use traps, I think, mostly now, but we did it with a spear, two men in a rowboat. You'd bait the beach at night at low tide, put bait along the beach, herring, you know. With a bucket of herring you'd walk along the beach at low tide, this is in the wintertime too, and then hope that the weather doesn't come up overnight to make visibility poor. Frosty weather is great for this because frosty weather is usually quiet weather, it's not stormy, you know, or ripply.

So you put two fish-hooks back to back on the end of a pike pole, a pike pole's about eighteen, twenty feet long, you see, and you row along over where you had the bait. Of course, it attracts the octopus and of course you can see them feeding on the bait. You've gotta row very carefully, very slowly, because they're very timid. They'll run away, you know, if they're scared at all, and they can move very rapidly, and they'll throw out this brown sepia dye that makes a sort of brown cloud, and they get away in the cloud.

So you row very, very carefully and then the man with the spear, when he gets right over them — he's giving his signals all the time, we even have lard on the oars and that, and wrapped in cloth so there's no noise at all — he drops this thing straight down over the top and just touches it on the back, light, just a little touch on the back, then they'll start to run. That's when he grabs them. Because if you went and just put it right down there and grabbed it, you'd never get it, because he'd stick onto the rocks and you can't pull them off. You know, they've a massive number of suction cups and they just cling to the rocks and you would never get them. So you have to get them when they're moving. Touch it on the back and it'll start to run and as soon as it starts running you've gotta pick it up quick before it latches on."

THE CANADIAN MERCHANT MARINE   "I started to go to sea in 1919 and sailed until 1972. I was a bo'sun for twenty-five years. My father went to sea before me since he was sixteen years old, and my grandfather went to sea before him, I don't know what age.

I didn't like it at first. My father got me a job on a ship of the Canadian Merchant Marine and I made a trip up to the Mediterranean and back to Canada with Christmas fruit. When I got back to Canada, they asked me if I wanted to go to sea again. I said yes I wanted to go back again, and the A.B.'s (able-bodied seamen) on the ship give me a hard time, very hard time, to try and drive me off the ships, but I wouldn't go back off. It was no life in them days, today it's a gentleman's life. They wanted to help me get a job ashore, they wanted me to better myself and stay ashore. But I was determined to stay, I guess it was the Irish in me.

I worked two years as a deck-boy on the ship, two years as an ordinary seaman, before I become an able seaman. We had open fo'c's'les, all the seamen lived in one big room. Maybe there was twelve seamen and they all had bunks in there, iron bunks. You were too tired for snoring — four hours on, four off. When you come off the deck you just flopped into your bunk, no wash, no nothing. You didn't have showers or anything like that in them days.

When you left port you were given one blanket, a double blanket, no pillow. There was a bale of straw out on the deck — they give you a mattress cover and you go and fill that full of straw. That was your mattress. You had a knife, fork, and spoon, and if you lost one of those it cost you a day's pay, fifty cents.

Because Canada was a young nation on shipping, they didn't have the officers, the men for to run these ships. It was all Englishmen, Scotchmen, Irishmen, Australian, and what have you, that was undesirables in their own country. So they get jobs out here because Canada wanted them. There was no Canadians, I was one of the first Canadian boys on the ship. When I first started I made fifteen dollars a month and I went up to twenty-five dollars a month and then I went up to forty-five dollars and then fifty dollars a month — later seventy-five.

The old saying that a sailor has a girl in every port — that's a lie, because if every sailor's got a girl in every port then every girl has got a boy on every ship.

In port, you'd always head for the first pub. But I never missed getting back to ship, no matter how drunk I was. In later years I used to black out, so I stopped drinkin' and I stopped smokin'.

We didn't have to eat hardtack, but it was issued to us when our bread run out. Of course, there was no frigidaires in them days, we couldn't freeze anything. Everything was just fresh. When the cook in the morning wanted to go into the fridge to get something, he would go in and one man would stand at the door and shut the door of the icebox, and he would get what he wanted or what the chief steward told him to get for the day, and if he forgot something he would never get in again, 'cause you had to preserve your ice. I remember one ship where there was no such a thing as running water. You had to pump it up from the tank. It'd be open a certain time of the day for the cooks to draw enough water to do the cookin', and if you were lucky you could sneak in then and get a bucketful of water, if you pumped enough water for the cook — helped him out. There was no spare water of any kind, and to stop us drinkin' that water, or gettin' a bucket of it to go and wash, they used to put handcuffs on the pump.

When you couldn't get any water from the pump you had to go right down into the engine-room — it's about two storeys down, iron ladders all the way down — and go to where they make the fresh water. You'd dip your bucket in — and it's boiling water and you take that and you lug it up them two storeys, get it on deck, and lug it aft where you belong, and you sit down there and you watch that bucket coolin' off. Because if you took your eyes off that bucket somebody would swipe it.

And when you were in port, you used to take your bucket out to the steam winches and drain off the water. That was for washing. When your water was cool enough in the bucket you'd go into the washroom, you had showers in there, but it was only salt water. You'd take your bucket in there and wash yourself all over and when you were finished you'd empty your bucket on your head — that was your shower."

HALF THE VILLAGE "In the gale of August of '26 there was a number of vessels lost with all hands aboard, some as high as three and four in the family, father and two or three sons. In Blue Rock, which is a small community about four or five miles east of Lunenburg, half the village was wiped out, their men. I know the girl that works in the fishery office, her father was lost in the gale in August of '26 and she was born in December, so she never saw her father. And the whole crew, he was captain, the whole crew was lost."

CLOSING UP THE OUTPORTS "When men began to come to

this island from England and from Ireland, mostly England, they settled on the great headlands, where the island of Newfoundland at a number of points jutted out into the Atlantic Ocean forming great headlands. The settlers moved into those headlands so as to be near the great bodies of fish which were always found in the headlands, not up in the bays, not up in the indrafts, not up in the fjords, but out on the great headlands, and that's where they settled in the sixteenth century, in the seventeenth century.

Now, as the population grew a bit on those headlands, the towns of Bonavista and Bay de Verde and so on, there came to be too many people, too much congestion. Number one, there wasn't enough land, there was not enough land. When a family had ten sons, where were they going to build their homes? There came to be insufficient land on these headlands and there came to be insufficient fish off those headlands for the growing population. So, what happened? What happened was that the people began breaking away. First, this young man said, 'I've had enough of this!' and up he goes ten miles up the shore, inside the bay away from the headland, and he builds himself a little hut and starts fishing. He's soon followed by a brother. He's doing better. He's living a little easier. He's followed by cousins, and before you know it there is a new settlement.

And that process went on for a hundred years, from about the year 1750 to about the year 1850, and in that century about a thousand new harbours and settlements and coves were founded and all of them were up in the bays and away from the great bold headlands. They were isolated. They were as remote in one of those coves as if they'd lived a thousand miles away — completely remote.

They could live very simply. They lived very humbly. They lived very meanly. They'd have one suit of clothes maybe throughout a whole life, once in a life a man would have a suit of clothes. For the rest of the time, he wore a canvas jacket or a moleskin or a sheepskin wrapped around as a sort of apron, and they lived on rough food and humble. There were no schools or very few schools. There were no doctors. Well, that was all right! They were willing to do that, they were not discontented. There was no yardstick by which they could measure the standard of their living. That was all they knew. They knew nothing else. They heard of nothing else. They read of nothing else. Nobody told them of anything else. They were lost to the world, in every individual cove and harbour of that kind, a thousand of them, stretching over six thousand miles of our coastline, a thousand settlements containing two-thirds of our population.

Well, the coming of radio and TV has acquainted them with the fact that there is another world that they haven't had, that they haven't known, they haven't enjoyed. It's not only radio and TV that did this. There were two world wars in each of which thousands of men, including young fishermen from those settlements, went to war and travelled all over. And they've come back, and it all put together has created a divine discontent. Indeed, without that discontent there would have been no Confederation. Now, Confederation did come and this has added enormously to the discontent.

What's the cure? There's got to be a cure or there'll be trouble. There is a cure and the cure is to evacuate seven-tenths of these settlements, evacuate them, close them up, and help the people to move into larger places where they have decent schools, where they can have hospitals and doctors and nurses, where they can have recreation, where they can have so many things that they can't possibly have. No government, even the rich government of Canada, could bring all these amenities into every one of those little far-off, remote, isolated harbours and coves and settlements. It can't be done. It can be done, to move them. The Canadian government have come in and joined with us in this and have raised it to a maximum of thirty-two hundred dollars a family to help them to move. And already a couple of hundred places have closed down, but there's still four or five hundred that need to close down.

Of course, there's no compulsion. We don't force them. It's got to be completely voluntary. The people have got to be completely willing to move, but if they are willing, then the two governments, St. John's and Ottawa, are happy to help them, pretty substantially, to move.

I think we are seeing the last of a generation that was here for nearly five hundred years, and those of us in Newfoundland who love the marvellous story of Newfoundland's past are stricken in heart over the loss of so many of these great qualities of quiet courage, of civility without servility, of gentleness and of politeness and of that God-fearing simple humility. The disappearance of these qualities or even the marked diminution of them will be a pretty bad blow to our Newfoundland civilization.

But then we have a very fast-growing population. What are they going to do? They're not going to make their living at hand-line fishing half a mile off the shore of their own harbour. They can make part of a living at that. Some of them will continue doing that, a few, and they'll get work in the woods, cutting pulpwood for the pulp-and-paper mills and getting odd jobs at construction on the roads and at the construction of large buildings — but this is how they've lived for the last fifty years and longer. Some will continue doing that. A great many will go to the vocational training schools and get trades and become qualified tradesmen. A good many will go to the fisheries college and become qualified seamen, deck-hands on modern fish-draggers, and then work their way up to captain, going through the various stages. And the captain of a dragger today represents the restoration of the Newfoundland aristocracy, which always was the skipper man, the master of his own vessel. The captain out at sea has always been the true aristocrat, and that aristocracy is coming back by means of the draggers, the deep-sea-fishing vessels that are now operating and increasing rapidly in number to supply the rapidly increasing number of modern fish plants that are getting to be dotted about the coastline."

NO MORE TO SAFE HARBOUR "We went back to Safe Harbour last week, my husband and son and myself, and at first I had to stand and wonder where everything was. I couldn't even visualize where our house was, and where my mother's house was. The settlement had been abandoned, oh, years ago, about fifteen or twenty years ago, and now the whole place is overgrown with brush and trees and everything. I didn't feel too bad until I went to the cemetery. My father is buried in the cemetery, and his grave was overgrown and I couldn't even find his headstone, so I said: 'Oh, I just can't leave the cemetery until I find Dad's gravestone.' I was really getting upset, so everybody started to look, then finally they found it in a mound of brush.

Well, I felt really sad ... I felt really upset. We did the best we could. We cleared away the brush, but there wasn't much we could do because we didn't have anything there, because I didn't think it would be in that condition.

I wouldn't want to go back, never. I don't want to go back any more to Safe Harbour."

FIVE

Hard Work, Long Hours

*Just Working, Working... Keep At It, Boy... Nobody Slept... Drifting Off
to Sleep... Night and Day... Long Hours... Making Lobster Traps...
Hauling Traps... Everybody Had Rowboats... Working for the Cannery
... Bait for the Halibut... The Survival of the Fittest... Building a Net...
Oiled Nets... Some Cold... The Night My Daughter Was Born... Late for
School... Double Your Money*

This chapter shows that a man, if he is hardy enough, can get used to almost anything. The captain of a scallop-dragger, for instance, told me he had learned to get by on two or three hours' sleep a night. But for most men, the hard, ceaseless work and the lack of sleep eventually left them walking around in a harsh dream. Some fishermen told me that the agony of getting up after one or two hours' sleep was almost more than they could bear. Self and time and place melted into a dull unreality.

And the work was hard: hard on the hands, hard on the muscles, hard on the back. Hauling nets onto the open deck of a side trawler in all kinds of weather, or hauling lobster-traps out of the water and over the side, trap after trap, as heavy as a man could lift, hour after hour — that took all the strength a man had. Rowing a dory until the land or the mother ship was out of sight: that took effort in the rough seas. Making nets, caring for the gear, working with sharp hooks in a tossing boat — it was all endless work.

I remember, years ago, talking to two quiet, well-mannered dory fishermen at Witless Bay, outside St. John's, Newfoundland. Henry Yard was one of them. He and his partner left home at three-thirty in the morning in their dory, boiled their kettle of tea and had something to eat during the long hours fishing, and got back to Witless Bay at about four o'clock in the afternoon. I asked Henry if he had it to do over again, would he be a dory

fisherman? There was a moment's silence. "No," he answered, in
a slow voice. "Why not?" I asked. "Too long of hours, too hard of
work," he said.

I've always remembered that. It epitomizes the way of life of
the fisherman for me. Too long of hours, too hard of work.

JUST WORKING, WORKING   "The shares those days, with
those long-liners that started in the forties, got around about
forty-two hundred dollars a man. We were four men on these
small boats and that's the closest thing I guess to communism
there is.

There was no time to smoke or anything, hardly. You just got
yourself whipped up into a frenzy early in the morning and kept
that way all day, just working, working, and at night when you
lay down, every bone in your body was aching and you'd swear
that you'd never be able to get up again next day. But a few hours'
sleep and you woke up and you felt fine. I've seen us work for
thirty-six hours. But this is not good, this is very stupid. When
you're younger you do these sort of things, but it's not good to
work yourself like that.

I know of a young fellow, a fellow in his thirties, the doctor told
him 'If you hadn't come in, you would've lost your leg.' His leg
had turned black from standing for thirty some hours at the side
of the boat, hauling gear and not exercising. And this can very
easy happen. When the fish are running, fellows will push themselves and sometimes have accidents."

KEEP AT IT, BOY   "We were living in Lunenburg and when I
worked in the woods I found out I couldn't make enough money
to keep things going, you know, there was seven in the family and
my father was sick. So that's when I made up my mind — I would
try fishing. I had a buddy I kind of grew up with, and he got into
fishing and he was making all this big money, and I decided I

would try it. It just so happened that he was going to take a trip off, and I had talked to him at different times, you see, about making a stab at trying to go fishing to make some of this good money, so he came to my door to see me and ask me if I'd go out in his place for a trip. I was dressed up with a suit on, I was going somewhere, taking a girl to a dance or something, and I said, 'Well, yeah I'll go.'

So, I went home and I told my mother and she got some clothes together and I told the girl I was going fishing. The boat was supposed to be sailing at seven o'clock that evening. So I got my things together and he took me in his car to the boat. I still had my suit on. I was thirteen but I was big for my age, so he goes down to see Captain Ray Corkum. He's dead now, but he was a highliner, so when you sailed with him you had to work to keep your place, because there were a lot of guys standing on the docks waiting to take your place. So anyway he says, 'Look alive,' and away we go.

Well, I was thinking over in my mind what the hell did I get into here. The side-draggers at that time used to carry a crew of seventeen, eighteen men, and when I took my gear down below, there was a few of the guys aboard that I knew from around the local area, like down from Liverpool. I can still remember that first trip because it was in April, when you get a lot of blowy weather, and when we left the dock they were giving the forecast out for thirty-five- to forty-mile-an-hour winds. Well, I went down and turned in my bunk and we were about eight to ten hours steaming away from the wharf and I wasn't really sick but I felt sick. And first thing the skipper, he sings out, 'Shoot away,' so all hands get up, and I get into my friend's oil gear, it was a little bit big for me, but that was okay.

So, I was up with the rest of them and the one fella says, 'Hey, you ain't on this watch. You'd better turn in, you're on the other watch.' I didn't know what he meant so I went down below and I got curious of this bang, bang, bang, and I said, 'I've got to go up and see what that is.' So I went up and stood in the doorway and just kind of watched them and I couldn't get no sleep, you know — and then she finally hit me. I was up on top of the boat-deck and there I was, feeding the fish, and I never stopped for the whole darn trip.

I threw up every day. I used to eat dry crackers and oh, they used to play tricks on me, trying to get me to eat all kinds of fatty meat, like corn beef with fat on it, you know, 'That'll settle your stomach,' and 'Eat lots of buttered bread,' stuff like this, and 'Drink lots of water!' Oh yes. They used to do that to a greenhorn, you see, so I went along with it — I was so sick I'd have tried anything anyway. When you get seasick you don't give a darn about anything. At first I was scared, you know, hanging on to the rail, scared I was going to fall overboard, and here's the boat rolling around, you know, and rough water flying over, and I set there with the water flying over me and everything. But after a while I'd never hold on to the rail, I just sat there, and I wouldn't care what happened to me.

Fishing, you've got to learn everything the hard way, you see. That's the way it used to be, everything you had to learn the hard way, so it would sink in and you wouldn't forget it. I guess that was the whole idea of it. We've got what you call a niggerhead aboard the boat to bring in the net, you took turns around the niggerhead and you pulled on this rope, you see. One guy stood on one side of the niggerhead and one guy stood on the other side of it, and that was my job when we hauled the net back. Or one of my jobs. And there was two guys on the after dory and two guys on the far dory, eh, and well, the guy that you worked with, he showed you what you had to do. He showed you a number of times and then he stood there and he told you what to do, and you did it at the time he was telling you.

Well, that was all right, but after we got the fish dumped out of the net and we got the gear all shot away again, and we started cutting these bloody fish with the blood coming out of 'em — and seeing all these guts and stuff, did I ever get sick. Ohhhhh! And it was pretty choppy and I'd try to do it, you know, for a while and oh, I was so sick I said, 'I'm going to die.'

'Keep at it. Keep at it, boy,' that's all he'd say, 'Don't stop.' So I hung on, I kept at it, trying to get the watch through. The second-last day of fishing, I was so done in and so worn down I went back and I wrapped my arms around that niggerhead and held on

to that. I can see it yet, and I just wished I was dead. I just wished
I was dead and I can hear yet the old fella, the captain, he opened
the window up and yelled up, 'Hey boy, what are you standing
holding on to that for? You can't get work done that way.' I
thought in my mind, you old bastard, and I stood there and
looked at him and he yelled, 'Come on, boy. Get to work. Lots of
work to be done.' So I went back up with the other fellas and I
was staggering around and falling around, same as a man drunk.

But I got through the trip and then the gang was telling me that I
was only getting a half-share. I wouldn't get the full share, you
see, because I couldn't do a man's work I suppose. But I tried, you
know, I really tried.

So when we come into the dock and I got my two feet on the
wharf, I was just the same as if I had still been aboard the boat yet
with the boat rocking. When I came in and stood on the wharf I
couldn't control my feet and legs at all, I was all over the place. So
anyway, I came around after a while and I said, 'No more. No
more. I'll starve to death before I'll go on board one of those
bloody things again. No more. This is it.'

But you know after I got the full share, a hundred and forty-two
dollars, this is what turned it, you see. When I found out how
much money I'd made I said, 'Gosh, that's a lot of money. I've got
to go and try that again. Maybe this time I won't get sick.' But then
I didn't know if he'd take me or not because this other guy only
had planned on taking the one trip off. So after I made the trip in
his place he decided he'd take another trip off, you see, so I made
the second trip in his place. So this second time he went and
asked the skipper if it was all right for me to go in his place. 'Yes,'
he said. 'If the young fella wants to go out again, I'll take him.'
And he laughed and I thought maybe I can do a little better this
time. And I just had about the same kind of a trip that I went
through the trip before. No change, still seasick, still discouraged
as ever. So we came in and that trip there, I did better, I made
over two hundred dollars that trip.

Well, I said, now this is it, the other fella's coming back this trip
for sure. And sick as I was, you know, it was good money, and
this was the only racket that there was any money in for a young
fella like me. I had no education, nothing. I wanted to go back the

next trip but I figured that my friend, he was coming back, and he must be a good hand for the skipper to let him take a couple of trips off, and if he goes back, then there's no place here for me because everybody else was staying. So I went down to the boat and the skipper was down there and I went down and started getting my clothes all off the boat and the skipper yells down, 'Hey, young fella, where do you think you're going?' I said, 'Well, I'm just getting my clothes together and I'm going to take my gear home.' 'Well, what do you want to do that for?' he said. 'Well,' I said, 'I was only out in this man's place and he stayed home two trips and he's coming back and none of the other crew is staying ashore, so I guess there's no chance for me.' He said, 'Well, young fella,' he said, 'if you want a chance the chance is yours. You put your gear right back where you got it from — and that fella there can go and keep on going.'

He wouldn't take him back. I guess he just wasn't that good of a worker. That's the way it was in those days. He was mad but he couldn't do nothing about it, not a goddamn thing you could do about it. I felt real bad about it. Yes.

So anyway, the captain said, 'Come on up a minute.' I went up and now he said, 'How are you outfitted for gear?' So I said, 'Well, I had his oil gear and now I've got no oil gear.' 'That's okay,' he said. 'You go up to the store and you tell him that you want a whole new outfit. Tell him you want a sou'wester and an oil jacket and oil pants and boots.' So I went up to the store and I told them. 'Who are you?' So I told them, 'Well, we don't know you. No, you can't have it. You've got to have a slip of paper signed by the skipper.'

I went back down and he said to me, 'Where's your oil gear?' I told him they wouldn't give me any. 'Wouldn't give you any? What do you mean he wouldn't give you any?' 'Well,' I said, 'I told who I was and who I was with and he told me I had to have a paper signed by you.' He tapped me on the shoulder, 'Come with me, young fella,' he said, 'I'll see about this.' So we went in the store.

With the door half open, 'What the hell is going on here,' he said. 'I sent this young fella up here to be outfitted,' he said, 'and you never gave him one. What the hell is the reason? What's going on? When I send a man up here for gear I want him to have gear. Now I want this young fella fitted out right away,' he said. And the fella scurried out from behind the counter and goes and gets what I want, you see. Well, that was on tick, that was written down on tick, you see, and then when you come in from the next trip and settle up it was taken out of the settlement because the supply-goods store was the firm's, you see. It's all one. I'd say it cost around forty-two, forty-four dollars for all the gear. That was for a pair of boots and oil pants and an oil jacket and a sou'wester.

I was thirteen when I started fishing, you see, it was April 21 when we left the dock and April 26 was my birthday, so I had my birthday out at sea, sick as can be.

I stayed with Mr. Corkum for four and a half years. He used to be after me all the time, you know, he used to want me to come up to the wheelhouse and try to learn it. I used to go up sometimes. By this time, after this four years and a half, I knew how to mend twine, and splice wire and splice rope. This here you could learn because it was there, you were doing it every trip, every day, you see, but the electronics in the wheelhouse, you had to find spare time to go up there to learn that. By the way, the first trip that I made he had me at that steering wheel. You had to steer the boat. Everybody stood watch, a regular watch, and you had to steer the boat. There was no putting it on automatic pilot and letting her go. You steered, by compass course. If you didn't know the compass, he stood you in front of the compass, you see. Now, he'd say the course was maybe, he'd say 'sou'west by west' and you'd have to repeat it after him, you see, and he'd say, 'What course did I tell you?' 'Sou'west by west.' 'Next time when I tell you the course you repeat the course.' Just like that. Then he'd try a little later on. 'Let her go west, sou'west.' Well, you'd say, 'Yeah.' He'd shout, 'What the hell did I just tell you a while ago?' But he says, 'Now, while you're here I want you to learn that compass.' And he'd come in and go around the compass just a few times, you see, you started right then and there, and you just go around and you say the main points over and over in your mind because you had to memorize it. Just looking at the compass wasn't good enough. You had to memorize it, and he wanted you to learn the compass so you could box the compass, name off every point on the compass right off the top of your head.

Everybody, you know, is kind of alike when it comes to an old skipper like that. You get in situations where you respect him, you've got to respect him, you know, because he knows what he's doing and he always uses better judgement. When he tells you something it's for your own benefit, that's the only reason. He'll never tell you something to make a fool of you, you know. Well then, there's times, like when you're up long hours and you're working hard and a lot of times maybe you thought it was really unnecessary for you to be up that long and you cursed him, not that he heard you, but you cursed him.

I can't say that in that four years and a half, I can't say that I got to really like the sea. I liked my job, I liked fishing, but I didn't like the sea. I didn't mind the work and I liked the money, and I got so that I didn't mind the long hours much, either, because I figured I could stay as much as the next man and that was it. I just got more stubborn. You had to be stubborn and pig-headed because that's the only damn way you could stand it.

What really turned me on to leave, the captain's nephew had come aboard. He was a greenhorn the same as I was when I started, but the only trouble was the captain, he fancied him a lot; of course he was a relation, too, I suppose, but I thought, you see, that if I stayed there for any period of time I might be able to work my way up. But he used to take him up in the wheelhouse all the time and tried to learn him and show him and he was telling him things all the time. So anyway, after he came in I guess I fished about three months, but I saw what was going to happen. I saw there was no chance for me to work my way up, or I thought so. So I just quit, just like that. I saw another skipper and I asked him for a chance and he just happened to need a fella. 'Yeah, sure,' he said.

So I went and made this trip with Anthony Kelly, and after I made the first trip with Kelly, we got in like today and the next day the old boat that I was on came in, you see. And going along, walking along the wharf, who did I meet but my old skipper. 'Well,' he said, 'how do you like it on the other boat?' I said, 'Well, it's all right I suppose.' 'It's all the same thing, anyway,' he said. I said, 'Well, I suppose.' 'Yes,' he said, 'and you left at one wrong time. That was one big mistake you made.' I said, 'Why?' but he wouldn't tell me. And I just walked right past him and I saw one of the deck-hands and I said, 'Did you fellas change any men?' 'Yes, we got a new mate and a new bo'sun.'

I probably would have been bo'sun-man. That's what he meant but he wouldn't tell me."

NOBODY SLEPT "When you was turned out in the morning, say at three o'clock, everybody was out and you was out in your dory maybe till nine, ten o'clock that night, working catching fish — and that went on maybe sometimes for two or three days, maybe even eight days, till you had your trip.

And if you got two to three hours' sleep out of the twenty-four, you were gittin' a lot of sleep. When you were workin', when you were fishin', everybody was up, there was nobody slept."

DRIFTING OFF TO SLEEP "I've seen me leave home on Monday morning and not be back till Friday night. And I've seen weeks that you'd only got in maybe twenty or twenty-five hours' sleep for the whole week. I've seen me go seventy-two hours and never get an hour's sleep, but I never fell aboard. I fell overboard out of the tenders at home, and the only time I done that was just bein' careless and not payin' attention to what I was doing.

If I'd get real tired and have to have a couple of hours' sleep, well, being a fisherman, you've got to know where you're gonna drift and what's gonna take place in the next two or three hours that you're gonna have a little sleep, and I've had times that I've slept five and six hours at one stretch out there, have had real good sleeps.

But one night, I went into Musquash Harbour when I was out salmon-fishin' and it was a night was no good for fishin', so I thought I'd go in and tie her onto a weir stake there and have a rest, have a sleep, and go fishin' the next morning. And I lay down, went to sleep.

And the next morning, I heard this loud motor alongside the boat and, crash, a fellow jumped aboard the boat and while layin' in the bunk, I was thinking, well, what's going on? There must be somebody coming in here to see what I'm doing here. This other fisherman come aboard and he said, 'What are you doin'?' he says. I says, 'Oh, I'm havin' a sleep.' He says, 'Do you know where you are?' I said, 'Yes. I'm tied to a stake on Musquash.' He said, 'You are not. You're about a hundred feet off Dipper Harbour ledges,' he says.

At some time in the night, I think probably when the tide turned around at one o'clock in the morning, the line lifted up over top of the stake, and I went out to sea and went adrift and I'd been driftin' all night. And at six o'clock the next morning I was about six miles down the coast from where I had tied the boat up."

NIGHT AND DAY "I can remember when we had a hundred fishing boats in the Bay of Fundy, a hundred small fishing boats, anywheres from thirty- to forty-foot fishing boats.

You'd be out day and night, you'd fish twenty-four hours. Years ago, before we got into nylon nets, we had to fish at night because they wouldn't strike the old nets in the daytime, but since we got nylon nets you can catch fish in the daytime now and it's been mostly in this last year or two that we got down to fishing mostly fifteen hours a day, all the daylight hours."

LONG HOURS "After you've been working long hours on a fishing vessel for a few years you get to relax a bit more. If you know you have to put in a full twenty-four or even thirty or thirty-six or forty-eight hours, you've got to pace yourself so that you're not gonna fold up and say to hell with it and go to bed.

Yes, I've been very tired, but if you are catching fish and things are doing well it seems to buoy you up, just like having a shot in the arm. It just seems to keep you going, but when it's over you sometimes think, you know, what the hell am I doing this for, I must be stupid, I'm gonna get a job ashore where I can go to bed all night."

MAKING LOBSTER TRAPS "When I was a young fella, eight or nine years old, my brother and I used to set lobster traps before we went to school, maybe twenty-five traps. We usually made them ourselves, you know, we were little fellers but we'd learn this stuff seeing our older brothers doing it, or our dad making traps, and of course we'd get help from them.

For a start we'd go in the woods and cut our boughs, you know, small spruce sticks or trees to make boughs out of, and we'd go to the lumber mill and buy our lath and our strapping for the bottoms, and then you'd go around the shore and gather up flat rocks for ballast, then you'd buy twine and you'd knit all your headings yourself.

I suppose you could make outright, with your headings and everything, about three or four traps a day, that's about all.

My brother and I set a hundred and sixty traps out one year, and the next day after we set them there came a storm, and all we had was ten left out of a hundred and sixty."

HAULING TRAPS "Each fisherman fished in the vicinity of three hundred and fifty traps at that time and there were traplines as we called it, and that line was set out on the 26th of April and was never taken in until the 26th of June. Each one of those lines contained one hundred traps, and those lines were pulled by hand, the hard way.

And there isn't any question about it, when the fisherman finished hauling his traps he had to make shore the best way he knew how. If the wind was a slow wind my father happened to have a motor-boat at that time and he would have to go outside of the harbour and tow each one of his boats in individually in the warm weather in order to save the lobsters from dying.

I don't think we ever had any problems that they really had to quit fishing, but they've had sore backs, there isn't any question about that, from pulling those traps, because those traps were bedded or set in around eight fathom of water and that's quite a pull up from the bottom up to the top of the boat. You see, those traps weigh anywhere from seventy-five to eighty to a hundred pounds."

EVERYBODY HAD ROWBOATS "I was twelve years old when I moved up there to the Sayward district from Victoria. There was a lot of fish there in Johnstone Strait, and I got interested and started rowboat-trolling when I was thirteen. Even though we were right in the heart of the Depression, salmon were still fifty cents apiece, which was a lot of money in the Depression because your wages were down to two dollars and seventy-five cents a day, the minimum wage, and you were lucky if you ended up with one dollar a day. So if you could go out during the summer and get ten salmon at fifty cents apiece, that was five dollars, and that was a lot of money.

Everybody there in those days had rowboats, that was the thing, you either built one yourself or bought one, this was the mode of getting around. The loggers used to row from one camp to the other for their jobs. Some of the old-timers stayed at our farm, in some of the old shacks, for three dollars a month. Lots of them were fellows up sixty, seventy, and they were telling me stories of logging Granville Street in Vancouver in the early days with oxen. Their history went back a long way. During the summertime, if the camps were shut down for fire, fire hazard, forest fires, they would all go out rowboat-trolling and pick up the odd salmon and make a few dollars that way.

With rowboat-trolling we didn't use any nets, just a single line and a spoon, a lure called a spoon, and that was the cheapest method of going out and fishing. We just rowed two to three miles away from home and in summertime we'd be out there right at break of dawn, three o'clock in the morning, in the fall a little bit later, but that was the best time to be out there, early in the morning, and the evening usually fishing on the tide. Starting in with the rowboat-trolling and starting to make a few dollars, it sort of gets into your blood, the fishing, it's kind of an adventurous life.

And the one year, this was 1931, I was eighteen years old then, a chap came in and started telling us stories about the big sockeye fishing in Smith Inlet and saying that was the place to go. We were listening to this chap's stories about this great fishing and the money to be made up there, so we weren't doing too much work on the farm and finally my dad said, 'You fellas better take and go, you're not doing any good here.'

So we took our sixteen-foot rowboat and the two of us rowed to Smith Inlet, oh, it was a distance of well over a hundred miles, and we rowed out there. We were four days getting up there bucking westerly winds and when we got up there, we ran into a

Russian chap in a skiff, and he had something like ten dollars' worth of fish, which we thought was a fortune. So we rowed into the Inlet, went up into Margaret Bay, and we went to the cannery, and Mr. Trotter, who was the manager then, one of the old-timers up there, gave us a net and a skiff to go out, and we went out and started fishing.

We fished for the whole month in this skiff, just a real big flat-bottom skiff, twenty-six feet long, quite a bit of beam and a little sail in the centreboard, and we attached ourselves to a chap who used to do quite well there, and whenever he set his net, we set, and when he hauled, we hauled. And we were there for just a month and we made a hundred and ten dollars apiece, which was virtually a fortune at that time, around 1931, that was a lot of money.

And we rowed back home with the rowboat, to give father a hand to put the hay in."

WORKING FOR THE CANNERY   "During the days, you would fish in Rivers Inlet because the salmon seem to rise up on the surface in the daytime, but at night you would go outside, practically out in the open Pacific, and set out all night. In the morning you would haul up and go inside again, and we'd fish right around the clock that way.

Every day a small packer came around, about a fifty-foot packer, and in those days all up and down the coast there'd be canneries. There must've been, oh heavens, thirty or forty canneries. Every little hole had a cannery and you'd fish for that cannery. They had a store there, they had food there, and gasoline, and you'd go in there on the weekend and mend your nets and have a bit of a rest and fool around and so on. But this small packer, he would carry the fish in there and they would can them in that cannery."

BAIT FOR THE HALIBUT   "My husband went out on halibut two years. The first year he had another man with him and the second year I went with him. Well, what an experience! That's something I wouldn't want to do again. We were up at four o'clock in the morning putting bait on hooks, oh, hundreds of the darn things, and my hands would be so cold I couldn't even feel them. There must have been four or five miles of line, I guess, and the hooks were six feet apart, so there was lots of baiting to do. Gradually in working my hands would warm up, but for the first hour I just didn't know I had hands."

THE SURVIVAL OF THE FITTEST   "One time, this was before the war when there was no mechanical drum to help you bring in the net, it was all hand-picked, we fished five days straight, day and night. The survival of the fittest. There was only two days of grace. Saturday we mended our net and we bluestoned our net on Sundays, loaded it up on Sunday evening, and back to the wharf again on Monday, and we fished right through five days. You have to be tough to be a fisherman."

BUILDING A NET   "There's different kinds of nets. Like when I first started fishing we used gill-nets, and they're just a fine webbing strung on a line with a weight and a float on one side, but in 1960 they got into the trawl. When we first started trawling on Lake Erie, nobody knew anything about trawls at all, but I made up my mind that somebody built them nets and I was going to make them, and I was going to fix them. They sent a fella here from the west coast, name of Wes Johnson, and I learned to build nets from him.

You have to shape a net. It's got to be shaped; it starts big at the front and it tapers back until you come to the part where the fish end up, they call it the cod-end. You see, you drag the trawl along about two and a half, three miles an hour and it just scoops the fish into it, something like the idea of pulling an ice-cream cone through the water. And when the fish all are in the cod-end, you just pick it up and pull a string and the fish all fall out on to the boat.

The nets we've used around here for smelt, actually we started out with a shrimp trawl in the Gulf of Mexico, but we changed then and we tried different nets, a Texas net, nets from the west coast. And we tried patterns of our own and after trying about ten different types we've ended up with a couple of nets right now that would be covering an area on the bottom of about eighteen feet high and probably, possibly sixty feet wide. There's one called a two-singer, it's just a fisherman name, and there's another called a wingloxi.

I've never really built a net that was actually my own. I've modified 'em. I take a pattern that is working pretty good, you know, and I'd do something to it that I think would make it work better.

One man working on a trawl, it's about a fifty- or sixty-hour job to build it. It takes a good hard week's work. The way we build them, the webbing itself comes from Korea or Japan and it comes in big barrels, maybe fifty pounds in a barrel, and you buy so many barrels that you want to make a net, different sizes, and then you cut a section out of each one and you sew that together. For instance, one net there, the front section of it is around maybe three hundred and some meshes across; well, you start with that and gradually it goes back until maybe at the end of the net the end of the section is maybe only seventy-five, or something like that. And you'd have anywhere from a dozen to twenty pieces that goes into a net. It takes about sixty hours to sew these together and then you have to put the seams down the sides and you have to put what they call rib lines which takes the strain off the web. If you towed the web without anything on it it would tear, so you put a rope down to take the strain off it. Then you put it on a piece of cable; right now we're using what they call a poly-cable, it's still cable but it's wrapped with tar so that it's not slippery, and you'd use about two hundred feet of this cable to hang the net on.

Yes, it's kind of a challenge to make a better net, you know. If you can build something that's better than the other fella's, well, then you're going to make more money."

OILED NETS "Well, nowadays, of course, it's all nylon nets, nylon gear. In those days it was all Irish linen, brought over from Ireland. And they were oiled nets, that was a big job in the spring. The men went up early and they oiled all these nets with linseed oil and then you would use bluestone, steep them in a bluestone tank, during the summer to keep them clean, and also it made the linen sharp. But you had to look after those nets, because if you didn't take them out of the boat and put them in bluestone once a week to clean all the slime off, they would rot on you. There was a lot of work to it which very few of the fellas do nowadays, they all fish nylon, nylon gear, nylon lines, everything."

SOME COLD "You didn't mind the cold so much, you know, you were working hard, and that kept you warm. I know a few years back I had a boat of my own out lobster-fishing in the winter, and you come in some days and your outer clothes would be covered with a half an inch of ice.

And fellers would say, 'You must be some cold.' But you didn't mind the cold, you were used to it."

THE NIGHT MY DAUGHTER WAS BORN "I was fishing twelve miles nor'west of the *Lurcher* Lightship when my daughter was born, and Hurricane Edna hit upon us that afternoon. I was fishing in a fifty-four-foot vessel, without a radar, having never been in Yarmouth before by vessel, thick fog and blowin' about forty, forty-five at that time, going in between the shoals to go into Yarmouth. That was a very hairy experience being a relatively new skipper and having no radar, and only the compass and the sounder to go by.

I'd received word from my father-in-law about my daughter's birth, and everything was fine at home and I was very happy and elated that way, and I'd received congratulations from Yarmouth radio. However, I had other crew members aboard my vessel that I was responsible for, and I had my father's vessel that I was responsible for, and I was very nervous as to the conditions that I was presently in. I knew that something was coming that the weatherman wasn't giving. He was giving light winds and we were well above light winds at this time — and as it turned out we had Hurricane Edna.

It certainly seemed like an eternity until I got in around the Yarmouth light heading up the harbour where I was within the protection of the land, because the seas were building, and although I had a fifty-four-foot boat, a sort of a Cape Island style vessel, the only one at that time in this area, but she was open, and if seas broke over we had the water into her, and it made it a little hairy.

When I did land there was no way that I could celebrate because we had a boatload of scallops and along with my crew members I had to shuck these scallops out and get them to market in a fresh state, which took most of the night. We arrived in Yarmouth just about dusk or shortly after and it was thick fog as I say, and then we laid to for the night and we shucked and cleaned up our scallops and got 'em in ice and bagged and whatnot so they wouldn't spoil.

I got to see my daughter about three, four, or five days after that. I wouldn't want to pinpoint a specific time but within a week after that."

LATE FOR SCHOOL "I was supposed to be in Grade Six that September but now I was a full-fledged shareman, getting a full share, and had to be up in the morning at two o'clock and go out and dig squid and the like and go fishing, and that's where I started as a young fellow. Well, I was as tough as a gad — that's an expression in Newfoundland to say you're tough — and with big thick hands, fisherman's hands. But I could just reach over the gunnel, the edge of the boat, with my chin. We were fishing with long-lines, trawls with hooks on them, and we had about twenty lines. Now a line is fifty fathoms long, so we had twenty of that, about a mile and a half long. We would put this out in Trinity Bay in deep water, 180 fathoms, and we had to haul it all by hand in 180 fathoms of water — no gurdies in those days to do the hauling for you — and the fish was on the hooks, you see, the weight of that coming up, and the boat was drifting, and the fish were four feet long, big. I would just get the hook in them and get them aboard, gaff them in. My job was just on gaffing fish, you see. My uncle was hauling, I was on gaffing; my cousin my age was pulling in and my dad was baiting. We'd haul it in, put it in the tub, bait it, and then we'd go set the lines again.

I remember one day people had gone and we were the only ones out there, and the wind had come down and was blowing us hard and we two young gaffers were sayin': 'Let's go in....' They'd say: 'Look, we were here first. The wind came after, we were here first and we'll leave when we're ready.' So the boat was a good thirty-foot open boat — she was a good sturdy, good rough-water boat, and we fished.

And one day we were out there and we drove out, driving with the wind, cripes, we drove out about eight miles. But this was good, because as we drove over the grounds, the damn trawlers was fishing, and all that was running was coming over the bottom, with fish all over the place, and all the fish were getting on hooks and we were loading the boat down, and my uncle said: 'Boy, we've got a lot of fish, now, we won't have to fish today.'

So he took the trawl in and he said, 'Now let's set up the trawl again and head for home' — and the wind was about forty miles an hour. A schooner went along by us, a schooner going north, with double-reefed canvas, and she was putting the waves right up on her canvas, and we were out in this old boat. It was foolish, you know, but we knew she would take it, and we knew the engine was good, an old Lunenburg eight Acadia. So we head her home.

And this is the cute part about it. My uncle, he loved to smoke his pipe, and come hell or high water he smoked. It was blowing like hell, but he gets his pipe out and his old tobacco, crumpled it off, and got the oil jacket over his head, trying to get his pipe fired. The wave broke on the boat and over she went, and this fellow should be steering to keep it into the wind. So Father looked back and shouted, 'Jim, you so-and-so fool, you're gonna drown us all!' And he just didn't care, he got his pipe lit, and went up to the wind and she came back and we went on up the bay.

And setting the trawl, my cousin was sitting up in the front of the boat on a thwart, and came a wave, it was away high, oh gee, it must have been twenty feet up, and when she came down fast, he was up in the air and the boat shot ahead and he went back in the trawl tub, where the trawl was, and the hooks went into his backside and he was stuck on the trawl. Gee, we've got to untangle him from the tub and from the hooks in his rear end. They said: 'Don't you move, don't you move, don't tip over the trawls,' you know, you're anxious to get fish, see, and the hell with the fellow with the hook in his backside. 'You sit, don't you move, don't you move, don't upset the trawl tub.' But my uncle slowed the engine and said, 'Let's untangle the poor fellow.' So we got all the hooks out of him, and then we threw the trawl overboard and ran down the bay and set the trawls. See, it's baited, you have to set it, or no fish tomorrow. So we just took the hooks out of his bottom, and it was just tough luck if he tore his skin, tough luck. But anyway we pulled him out and he had a lot of iodine on his backside the next day and it cleared up... so we did well that day.

Anyway, when we came in that fall, the 4th of November — I was supposed to go to school. Remember, in Grade Six — it's November and I haven't started school yet.

But we ended up that fall, we had two hundred dollars a man. I was a man and I got a man's share, I got a full share. Now, I didn't get a damned cent — Dad kept that, of course, but when we were paid off, I was paid off two hundred dollars. I immediately passed it over to my dad because I was only a kid."

DOUBLE YOUR MONEY "You turn around and look at the average scallop fisherman, and you say, that can't be too hard work, look at the big healthy-looking fellows.

But, if you was to take some big trucks and load them trucks up with rocks and gravel and mud, whatever you'd haul up on board in a normal watch of scallop-draggin', and if you was to take and put a bunch of shells all in through this, and then come over here to the fish plant and pick the highliner scallop boat and tell the crew, say, that you'd give them double the money that they'd make aboard a scallop-dragger, for, say, ten days: 'There's scallops all in through this guck, we'll pay you double for the time you work here on land and you'll be doing the same thing for the same period of time' — and see how many would do it. See how many would call you crazy, or damn fool or somethin'. "

SIX

Strange Sights and Superstitions

There's No Rocks Here... Paddy Parr's Light... That Ship Is There... In San Mateo Bay... Ghost Ship... In God's Pocket... Piles of Rock... Superstition and Mythology... These Old Fellows... Mirages... Not Alone on the Sea... Superstitions and Bibles... Don't Whistle... Just Flapping Around... A Forty-Ton Shark... Death of a Whale... A Big Sea Lion... A Load of Herring... Dolphin's Wake... Some Queer Serpent-Like Creature... The Ogopogo

L ook at a fisherman as a fisherman and you see a diehard pragmatist. Look at a fisherman as a person and you see an optimist, a gambler, in essence a romantic. The old romantic tales of the sea, tales that are still told from time to time, perhaps in earnest, perhaps in disbelief, summon up a legendary host of ghost ships, mysterious lights at sea, fire ships that suddenly burst into flames and sail, burning, towards the horizon, vessels that appear luminously out of the fog and sail through the nets without damaging them, the muffled sound of warning voices, bells tolling.

I listened to these stories, and because I wanted to believe in them, I did. Laugh at me as you may. Many modern fishermen will pooh-pooh them, yet these same men will tell you of strange sea creatures following a ship for a day, or a day and a half, creatures as long as the ship itself. An experienced pilot who has flown many, many hours of rescue missions, and is now in charge of air-sea rescue operations for Atlantic Canada, swears that he has seen Ogopogo.

Monsters and mirages, sailors and superstitions. It may all seem strange to a landlubber — but do you walk under ladders?

THERE'S NO ROCKS HERE "Well, there are some mysterious things. Now, I'll tell you what happened one night. There was actually four of us aboard. A man and his wife was in the stern of my boat, sleepin' in the tent, and we were in the cabin. And we were coming down the outside of Texada Island. We were going to Egmont, as a matter of fact. So it was a beautiful night, sort of moonlight, it wasn't full moon but it was quite light, maybe a two-thirds moon.

And there we go and by golly, you know, right ahead of us — and this is night-time, remember — there's a big rock. It's a big long rock, real long rock, and there was an Australian fellow with me in the cabin and I said, 'Gosh,' I said, 'that rock, I don't know anything about that rock, there's no rocks here. Not really, not supposed to be.' He said, 'Well, there it is. You can see the water went up high.' Seaweed come back, you know, the water went up, it wasn't rough but it was enough swell to work the seaweed back and forth. Yeah, clear you know, and a fairly long rock.

So this fellow at the back there, this Ernie Silvey, he was born and raised in that country, in Egmont. So I hollered for Ernie. I said, 'Ernie, take a look out here.' In the meantime, I slowed right down, because I didn't want to hit this rock, you know. And so there it is. There's your rock out there and by this time I've stopped, just pulled the clutch out. So he come out, he stuck his head out there, and he looked at it for a little while.

He says, 'Head right for it.'

I said, 'You're crazy.' He said, 'Go ahead. Really. Head right for it.' So I put the clutch in, headed for it. Sure enough, it just took off and disappeared.

He said, 'My dad's told me about that. You know, I've never seen it before. It's a mirage. It happens on a certain moonlight night.'

Obviously it's not a rock, you know. But we saw it there, just as clear as a bell, four of us, so I mean there's something that takes a little explaining. His dad had told him that there was a rock showed up there. He had told him about it and there wasn't a rock there at all, it was a mirage."

PADDY PARR'S LIGHT "Before a storm people say they saw a

light come in. It was a harbour, this was, but you had to come in a
tickle to come into Safe Harbour; and there was a rock there, Ben-
burry's Rock. They said there was a ship lost, and the captain of
the ship was Paddy Parr. But after that, before every storm, there
was a light, just like a ship's light, that would come in, take perhaps three or four minutes to come in, come right in to this rock.
I've seen this light come in, maybe a motor-boat, a boat come in
or something, but we'd run. 'Oh, that's Paddy Parr's light,' we'd
say. We were frightened to death of Paddy Parr's light. We could
see it coming in, and we would all run for home."

THAT SHIP IS THERE   "My mother was a schoolteacher and
the first school she taught was up at the west point, that's up,
straight out to O'Leary, it's O'Leary Road. Now there was certain
evenings they'd go up to the rails at O'Leary, right to the edge of
the bank, right to the shore, and looking off to the west'ard they'd
see this here ship, four-rigged schooner, two-masted schooner,
just as plain as could be, and that was the ghost ship, because at
one time there was a ship burned right out there in the same area.
And that ship, many is the person seen that ship there since —
and a certain air, the wind has gotta be a certain way and the
sky's gotta be clear, and that ship is there."

IN SAN MATEO BAY   "One night there were a few fishermen,
among them one of my friends, an old, old fellow that I've learned
a lot from in my life, he was mentioning about this ship that came
through and they felt they'd seen. It was very foggy that night in
San Mateo Bay and they seen what they thought was an outline of
a ship and they swear on a stack of Bibles that this freighter went
right through their nets, they felt the wake and everything else, yet
the nets weren't cut, you know, so it was a ghost ship."

GHOST SHIP   "We were runnin' out of Saint John here one
night, we were fishin' for hake out on the Yankee Bank, which
was a four-hour run from Saint John. We had a thirty-five-foot
Cape Island boat and we were about six miles out, and it was a
nice clear moonlight night. I was in the cabin there and Ken Lewis, an old fellow from Nova Scotia, Ken called me and he says,

'Look at the big ship comin' down on us.' So I got out, we looked at the ship. There you could see the silhouette of the ship coming through, the lights on her and everything, a big merchant ship, and he kept comin'. We kept alterin' course, but no matter where we altered course the ship was alterin' course the same way as we were.

So we were standin' there tossing all around and all at once it disappeared, like that. As we looked at it, it disappeared before our eyes. We seen it on two different occasions and both times on moonlight nights, for five or ten minutes we seen this big merchant ship coming right at us.

I was mentionin' it to some of the older people around home and I've mentioned it to one of the pilots in Saint John and he says, 'Yes, we've seen it,' and he didn't go to elaborate any further, but he says, 'we've seen it, we've seen the ghost ship out there.'

It was just one month later, in the licht moonlights, on the full moon, we seen it again and in the same area. And Ken and I was fishin' together at that time and we both seen it, I know that, and myself, I've gotta see it before I believe it. I don't imagine these things and we weren't drinkin', either one of us, we never had a drink, that's for sure. When you run into something like that and it's quite a phenomenon, you see it and after a while, after it disappears, you begin to think well, am I goin' off my rocker or is there something there that isn't there or what's taken place, and then when you turn around and talk to the other fella and he's seen the same thing, well, both of us can't be going off at the same time, that's the way I would look at it.

The thing was, every time we altered course to go clear of it, it altered course. And this was the first thing that comes into your mind, what's the matter with that fella, is he crazy or are we crazy? And it gives you quite a little start at the time. But goin' along with fishin', I guess you take everything in your stride and you don't pay too much attention to it, it's just somethin' that happens while you're there."

IN GOD'S POCKET   "There's a story about an old Indian ghost up in Christie Pass, in a place they call God's Pocket, and this ghost has a dislike for Orientals, and for a long, long time a lot of

Japanese fishermen just wouldn't tie up in God's Pocket at all, you know. And strangely enough — and this is going to sound like a lot of malarkey, mind you — when I was younger and I had my first big boat, I went up to God's Pocket and we tied up there. And I had a French-Canadian kid with me, and Paddy George was telling this story to us, and this French-Canadian friend of mine, Bob, he didn't know about this story.

So anyway, later on that night, he was sleeping in the next bunk, and I heard him choking. I got up and I said, 'What's the matter? What's the matter?' And he was screaming, he said he felt hands around his throat and imagined himself being choked, and he was actually choking, he was just choking and gagging and everything else, it was just like somebody had him by the throat, you know.

We got him up on deck and we got him calmed down and everything. But then the next time coming back down from Rivers Inlet, going through there, there was no way he wanted me to stop in God's Pocket."

PILES OF ROCK   "I was goin' up the Bay of Quinte one night, takin' a boat up. It was a dark night and I had the courses down fine and I was lookin' at the radar and my position seemed perfect, see. And all at once, ahead of us it looked like piles of rock not too high out of the water. I said to the wheelsman, I said, 'What the deuce, there's something wrong here someplace. I'm lookin' at it on the radar,' I says, 'and it looks to me like a pile of stones,' I said, 'and we're headin' right on it.'

You know what it was? A flock of geese."

SUPERSTITION AND MYTHOLOGY   "You go back to history and superstition is the traditional thing among many people. Wherever you go in the Atlantic Provinces, you will hear stories of ghost ships. There's the fire ship in the Bay of Chaleur; there is another fire ship that is broken down in Northumberland Strait. A fire ship was supposed to be a ship that is sailing along completely in flames; it was burning, but she never seemed to burn up. Of course, one of the things that seamen fear the most at sea is fire, and fantasy is born of this. Maybe it's generated by some freak of nature like a mirage or something. You'll find this all through history — it's a traditional thing with the maritime people that they see ghost ships. They see these fire ships, or ghosts looming out of the fog.

The story of the old fisherman coming in out of the fog and finding this ghost ship that guided him off the rocks and saved his life, how do you explain it? I don't think you can. And there's all kinds of things about the sea, of course, that are much more interesting than the land, because actually man knows very little about what's in the sea. We're just scratching the surface. Yet the marine biologists, many of them think they know all the answers. 'They ain't seen nothing yet,' as the saying goes; they're just scratching the surface.

They talk about seeing sea monsters. Well, there is the giant squid. It has been seen with its great tentacles. In fact, I've seen one that was over sixty feet long. It was found — it was dead when it was found — up near Conche up towards St. Anthony on the north-east coast. We had it refrigerated up there in one of our bait-freezing units and brought down to the university here because the marine biologist was looking for it, but it's the real McCoy. For some reason unbeknownst to scientists or anybody else, these creatures in the ends of their lives come to the surface, and they drift in.

Whales have been caught with marks on them where the tentacles of these giant squid have fastened on to them and left scars, and the whale is one of the prime enemies of the giant squid. This they know, and they have been seen in conflict. But these are the sort of things about the sea that could cause all kinds of mythology to generate... all kinds of mythology."

THESE OLD FELLOWS "A lot of people had a superstition in my father's day — like my father would never leave harbour, say, turning against the sun in the sailing ship. If he was getting his anchor humped to go leave that port, and she was going to fall against the sun, he would drop his anchor again; he would never turn the ship in harbour against the sun. Nor would he leave home on a Friday to go down the Labrador to go fishing. There were certain superstitions that they had like that. I don't know if there was too much wrong with it. These old fellows had a lot of ideas.

You take today with all the technology you've got aboard a ship, and all the electronic equipment, and you take that away from some of these fellows that are commanding these ships, they wouldn't take her out from the wharf.

Whereas these fellows in my father's day, they had none of that at all — it was only their own practical knowledge, and looking at the weather, being up early in the morning and seeing the sun rise and seeing the sun set, they had an idea of whether it would last — and that's the way they operated."

MIRAGES "'Of course, in the Gulf you see lots of mirages, especially in the summertime. You see beaches lifted away up and you see boats comin' long before they even arrive, and then they go out of sight and then you finally see them come in. You know what I mean, you see them lots of times right out of the water."

NOT ALONE ON THE SEA "I heard an old fisherman saying one time that he was coming home and he wasn't sure if he was heading in the right direction, it was dark, and when he came around this point in this darkness, he couldn't see nothing, he couldn't see where the boat was at. Well, a ship had went aground at the very same spot eighty or ninety years previously. And he saw this boat loom up in the dark, and he steered clear of it. And when he went around it he saw that where this boat was, now this was rocks, it was shoals, and if he had not steered around it he would have went aground, been up on the rocks. And he went on into St. Paul's and went safely home.

They don't be scared. It gives them courage, and it seems like these ghost ships they see is a good omen. Yes, they believe that this is there to protect them, the fishermen that are gone are trying to protect them from something. They feel confident that they're not alone on the sea."

SUPERSTITIONS AND BIBLES "If you came aboard with grey mittens they didn't like it. White mittens was all right. Now, if you had grey socks they was good, but if you had white socks they didn't like it.

We was sailing alone one time and we wanted a piece of some twine, and this other schooner was right alongside of us and we didn't put a dory out but came close enough and he said, 'Throw something back.' We had to throw a penny back before he would throw the ball of twine to us. He wouldn't give anything, you know, he was afraid he'd give us his luck.

Oftentimes today they still try to launch a vessel so her bow will head towards the sea. It's bad luck, you see, if the stern goes in, and they'll put a drag on one side so that she'll drag a certain way and turn towards the sea, then they'll put a line on her quick and make sure she's heading out there the right way.

And I was with captains that wouldn't turn around, they stayed here in the harbour; if they couldn't turn with the sun they'd never go out, they'd come back to the dock and tie up. I still try my damnedest to turn with the sun when I back away from the dock.

These superstitions lasted a long time, right up to the thirties. Once they got schooners with power in they fished every day, but when I went we didn't fish on Sunday. When twelve o'clock came Saturday night we were all through, and we didn't touch a thing till Sunday night twelve o'clock. If a man came up on deck on a Sunday, nice fine day, and tried to take a fish, if the captain heard him he'd come up and make him throw the fish back in the water. 'Get the hell below. Whadda you wanna be up here catching fish for today?'

And the first captain I was with, they'd have singsongs at night. I was only a kid — only twelve, and we had to stand watch up till nine o'clock in the evening, and the captain and five or six other men would be in the cabin with their hymn-books, singing. No music or anything, just singing. They were real singers. Captain Harry Winters was one. That was Bob Winters' father. He was the first captain. You always had your Bible. When I first went fishing, every man had his little Bible. Don't know how many does now."

DON'T WHISTLE "Most skippers were superstitious as all hell, you see. They believed in all kinds of things. Like, this was a favourite habit of mine was whistling. And when I went aboard the ship and I was standing there thinking of something and I started whistling, never even realized I was whistling, and I heard the skipper bellowing, 'Who in old hell is doing that whistling? What are you trying to do? Do you want a hurricane to blow up?'

I said, 'What's he talking about?' and the one old fella said, 'Don't whistle. Don't whistle,' he said. I said, 'Don't whistle? Why?' 'Shhhh! Don't talk about it.' 'Well,' I said, 'you've got to tell me why, or I'll keep on whistling.' 'No, never ever whistle aboard a boat,' he said, 'because when you whistle that's a sure sign you're whistling for it to blow.'

Another saying was 'pig', they didn't want you to say the word 'pig' on board of a boat. There are a lot of skippers who might even go so far as to not want you to say 'pork' aboard the boat, it's just a superstition. Another favourite one of his was, a hatch cover that goes over the hold, and when you come in to take the fish out — don't lay that hatch cover upside down. Oh, there'd be hell to pay if he saw that hatch laying upside down. Oh, that was bad luck, yes."

JUST FLAPPING AROUND "I've often been fishing on the Grand Banks when we've been surrounded by very large whales when they'd been mating, and it would be very dangerous. They'd come right out of the water right by the side of the boat, the female and the male, and, you know, they'd be making funny noises and it would be dangerous using a small boat because they would flap around making a big wallow of the tails.

I've often been surrounded by man sharks, when we've been lying to at night with the lights on the boat, because usually fish go for light, and you'd see sharks running on the water. The man shark is only about seven or eight feet long, but he's a very dangerous fish. And we've often pulled in live sharks on the deck, those big blue sharks, twenty-five or thirty feet long. I always heard when I was a boy that you can do what you like with a shark, cut it up, it will never die before the sun goes down. We found out that to be true. When we had that shark on deck, we had to cut that all up in pieces in order to get it off deck, and that flesh would be alive. It's no joke."

A FORTY-TON SHARK   "While I was fishin' in the bay here drifting for salmon one night, comin' on daylight it was a nice calm morning with no sea, no wind, and I was windin' the net and I wound up to a shark, a big baskin' shark. He was just laying there on top of the water, the net was wound around him. My boat's thirty-two feet long, ten-and-a-half-foot beam, and that shark was at least ten feet longer than my boat, and I would say he was two feet wider than my boat. And I got up alongside him, he was layin' on top of the water, he was higher than my boat, which had a three-foot draft, and I had to cut my net clear. I cut the net and then I went to the other side and cut the net off and let him go with the net, and I would estimate that that shark probably if it was on the land would weigh forty ton.

A baskin' shark wouldn't attack the boat, but we have one here in the bay which we call the whiptail shark and he's a very vicious shark. They grow to thirty feet long or bigger and up to four or five ton, and when you get one of them in your net the best thing to do is keep right clear of him, because he could hit the side of the boat and kill you or probably knock a plank off the boat, that's how vicious they are. And we have encountered a lot of them in the bay. When they get wound up in your net, after they have two or three hours thrashing around in the net they'll drown themselves and maybe you can do somethin', maybe get your net off them if they're not wound up too bad."

DEATH OF A WHALE   "I seen a whale being beat by a thrasher shark and I don't know too much about it except that the thrasher shark has a long tail and he'll get on top of a whale and beat the whale till it kills it. You'll wonder why the whale doesn't dive and get away from it, but while this is happenin', swordfish get under the whale and keep stickin' their swords in him and won't let him dive, and the two fish gang up on the whale. For what reason I don't know, but it happens. You'll hear about it.

Now I seen this one once and when this is happenin' there's water goin' in the air from the whale and the thrasher slappin' their tails in the water with water flying in the air like you just wouldn't believe. Well, I shoulda had pictures of that because it's hard to describe that to anybody, and it's not somethin' that I'll probably ever see again."

A BIG SEA LION   "In the skiff I was able to make twenty-five miles a day. We'd start out at daylight and try and catch before the wind; usually in the summer the westerly wind came up and we always rowed while the wind was down, rowed, then when the weather got too bad we'd tie up and wait till the wind went down. Often I'd row till quite late at night, and I'd never bother going in to pull up the boat at night, I'd just sleep right in the bottom of the boat — you'd wake up sometimes and you're laying in water, soaking wet — and tie up alongside of the kelp.

One night I was tied alongside a bunch of kelp and a big sea lion came along and stuck his head into the boat and scared the daylights out of me. He just put his head in, he was inquisitive what was going on, but it scares you to have an animal with a head on him like the size of a horse stick it over the side of the boat. I got up quickly and started rowing and didn't stay there any more."

A LOAD OF HERRING   "I can recall one time when I was hand-trolling at the south end of Thetis Island, oh, fairly early in the morning and there was just acres and acres of herring clipping in the water and I was just rowing along, and all of a sudden I heard a whoosh and out came this huge whale, and tons and tons of herring went in his mouth. He just came up once and took this load of herring and disappeared.

Just fantastic. I could've taken my herring rake and touched his back, he was that close to me.

That's the only time I can recall that I was ever somewhat afraid that maybe he'd come up again and be under the boat, but you never ever have any trouble with whales or even basking sharks. In Barkley Sound in the summertime you see basking sharks and you can go out to them and hit them with the boat and they'll flip their tail, but they won't hurt ya."

DOLPHIN'S WAKE "Oh, sure there's dolphins, we see them all the time. When you're running they love to play along the bow of the ship and they'll dart in and out, and just touch the hull, maybe scrape a barnacle or two off; they're very playful and we always enjoyed them. I always used to like to go up on the bow and just watch them. They're so graceful, they're just fantastic.

Their capability of navigation must be fantastic 'cause, you know, you can take them right almost into the entrance of the harbour. I remember one time we were goin' to the boat harbour and we took them in with us right to the entrance of the harbour, and then all of a sudden, bang, they knew that this was the time to quit, so they just took off."

SOME QUEER SERPENT-LIKE CREATURE "This was in the Gulf right here, another fellow and I were running up to go fishing, it'd be about one or two in the afternoon, and I looked around and by golly, there's this funny head stuck out there. It was more like a horse's head really, but hairy, sort of. Very hard to describe. I could even say, well, more like a camel, but more hairy than any of them though. In other words, a camel or a horse, that's the shape.

And it just came out, well, maybe say two or three feet and I was hollering to my partner to come and take a look at this thing, for maybe half a minute, and then down he went and that's it. Never come up any more, but that was definitely some queer serpent-like creature. It was sort of followin' us, you see. It came out of the water about I would say a couple of feet, and I saw it quite clearly, eyes and everything. But that's it and away he goes, but I never heard of it or never seen anything like it since. And the trouble is, the other fellow never got a chance to look at it."

THE OGOPOGO "I'm from Kelowna, British Columbia, the reputed home of the Ogopogo. One day in 1957 or '58 — I'm not exactly sure of the year but it was prior to the floating bridge being built across the lake — my father and I were on one of the ferries from West Bank to Kelowna. We were on the upper deck of the ferry when we noticed, towards Penticton, what appeared to be three distinct humps moving from left to right in the water. I immediately looked around to see if I could find a motor-boat that had gone by to make waves, because sometimes a running wave will look like it is humps, but there was no other vessel in the area.

By this time there would be about twenty or thirty people on the upper deck of the ferry watching it. As we approached you could see three distinct humps, and the humps were green and sort of rough texture. You could see through the humps, so they were real, and the overall length would probably be about thirty-five to forty feet long. Now, we didn't see the head of this so-called beast, but it went by at probably two knots, maybe one knot, until it disappeared around the end of the area where they were building the fill for the bridge. So we had a good clear look at it for probably ten minutes before it disappeared, at a distance of a mile and a half to three-quarters or half a mile away.

Everybody on the boat was very, very quiet. I remember somebody saying: 'Has anybody got a camera?' and nobody had a camera, but they were very, very quiet and nobody said much, and when it disappeared, everybody sort of looked at each other as if to say, 'Did we really see what we saw?' And I think a lot of people really didn't believe what they were seeing. They might have thought: 'Oh, it's an illusion or something else rather than a beast.' I think it was some kind of a water creature.

The stomach part of it and the round part that we saw would be almost the same girth as perhaps a fifty-gallon barrel, or perhaps a small hippopotamus, around the stomach that way, about that thick.

I just remember going home and saying to my mother, 'I've seen it. I've finally seen the Ogopogo.' "

SEVEN

Skippers and Men

Able To Catch Fish... Intuition... To Keep the Men in Their Place...
Tight Boots... All Hands on Deck!... The Foremost Man... Afraid of the
Old Man... From St. John's... It Wears You Out... A Bad Egg in Every
Crew... Through the Lower Decks... Good-Living Fellows... No
Problems with a Quart a Day... Give and Take... Somebody'll Git Hurt
... A Little Squirrelly... Onion Thief!... Hook, Line, and Sink...
Punishment at Sea... Other Fellows Depending on You

The old captains I met all fascinated me. Some were bluff and hearty and carried with them still an obvious air of authority. Some were very quiet men, almost shy. A few amazed me: they were men of courtly, aristocratic bearing, fine-featured and well-spoken, a Canadian's concept of an elderly, internationally respected British scholar. Yet they all shared two characteristics: they knew how to catch fish and they knew how to handle men.

They were retired now, and they missed the sea. I met some of them in Lunenburg, Nova Scotia, and we boarded the Theresa Connor, the last of the side trawlers, a museum ship now, explored by waves of curious tourists. The old captains and I sat in the galley, and they yarned about the sea, and sensed it was a past irretrievably gone, and yet they spoke of it with the freshness of memories of yesterday.

What gives a man authority and power over other men? What makes him a leader? How were these captains able to control rough-and-tough seamen and gain respect from them? Some younger captains mentioned from time to time a certain Captain Ray Corkum, and they talked of him with a mixture of fury and admiration. Captain Corkum was hard-bitten and ruthless. He worked his men so hard he took all the spit and fight and energy out of them. He worked them when it wasn't necessary to work them — when they could have rested instead. Yet, while they *cursed him in private, every last one of them realized that Ray Corkum knew exactly what he was doing all the time. If he gave an order, it made sense. If they were in the wildest of gales, they knew that if anyone could get them through it, that man was Corkum. They had more than grudging respect for him, they took pride in working on his ship.*

Some men, like Captain Abram Kean, were so feared that the men were actually afraid to talk to him. This led to a terrible tragedy, an unnecessary tragedy, when scores of men died on the ice during the seal hunt.

Captains showed the way. They worked hard themselves and expected others to do the same. A number of them worked out techniques of give-and-take — the men were treated fairly, and, in return, they did their best.

On both coasts, and on inland waters, captains and crews worked together because it was in their collective best interest to do so. Sooner or later, there would be a crisis when they would have to depend on each other. This, it seems to me, is why men on boats work well together. The other fellows depend on you, and you depend on them.

ABLE TO CATCH FISH   "The biggest thing a skipper or captain has to have, number one — he has to have the ability to catch fish. That is number one, if he can't catch fish, he's gone.

Now, I think most skippers start basically the same way. If you ask most fishermen, 'How did you start fishing?', 'Well, couldn't do anything else.' Usually fourteen, fifteen, sixteen years old. That is still the case here. These guys, by the time they're in their twenties, if they did show a bit of leadership tendencies, they should be mate by their twenties, right? If they stick with one company eventually a boat will become available and they will be picked as captain.

The captain picks his mate, the crew, the whole bit. It's up to him. Basically he picks people he knows. That could be good or bad. If he makes mate, chances are pretty good that he will become skipper, but not too many guys make mate. There's only one captain and one mate on, let's say it's a scallop-dragger which has a crew of about fourteen, so basically you have two men in authority, so of the fourteen you only have two."

INTUITION   "I think that you can get the feeling of the weather. That just seemed to come on you, you know, by itself, and you get the feeling where the fish run, or should run. But they sometimes don't agree with you and they'll run somewhere else, but I think some men have a higher sense of that than others. I think some men really have an intuition as to go to the right spot at the right time. We always called them lucky buggers but, I mean, there is certain men who have it and certain men who haven't got it.

I figure that I was pretty well average. We had some damn good years and we had some poor ones. We made out very well."

TO KEEP THE MEN IN THEIR PLACE   "It's surprising, you know. If you were to take eighteen men and just put them in a room where they wouldn't have too much to do, well, boredom would set in. You'd have a riot, you know. Or if you took eighteen men and put them in a room and gave them all kinds of booze to drink, you'd probably have a fight or a riot or something take place.

But when you've got eighteen men working, you see this was the whole idea, this was the skipper's idea, you see, about putting all those hours in. A lot of them hours that we put in really were unnecessary, but it was to get you tired so that he had control all the time. That was to keep the men in their place. If you were tired and played out when you get in the bunk you're going to sleep. That was the idea."

TIGHT BOOTS   "Aboard this one, all you took off was your boots and your sweater. Your shirt and your pants and your socks was on. That's the way you slept.

I shipped with one fellow, for nine days he slept up in the peak, this was in a schooner named the *R. B. Bennett.* Never took his boots off for nine days, wore a pair of leather boots and, well, they was kinda tight and he couldn't get them off. You could always see his feet stickin' out with leather boots on.''

ALL HANDS ON DECK! "When you're sailing with a guy like Captain Ray Corkum you very seldom see watches of six on and six off. You very seldom see six off anytime. Because when you weren't getting a lot of fish you were going around trying to catch fish on hard bottom and you was getting tore up and rim-racked. You might lose all the gear that you had shot away with, and then you'd have to put all new gear on. So, when you weren't dressing fish you were stowing gear.

We did strike the fish one time, small haddock, and all hands were up thirty-six hours steady working, working steady thirty-six hours. Anyway, in thirty-six hours we had all the fish dressed down and it was just around meal-time so all hands get time to get a good meal. It was our watch below and we had just gotten out of our boots and laid down and we heard this, 'All hands on deck.'

So we had to get up again, and we were up another eighteen hours. We had to put all new gear, we'd lost the whole net. We had the spare gear ready made up to put right on, but after we put this on and got the gear back in the water again, you see, we had to make up new to replace that. That was the policy, see, and we probably had six spare nets up underneath the bow altogether, but just because we lost that net then, we had to replace it.

That was his way of doing it. Now another captain might say, 'Oh well, we have five or six spare nets up there and you boys were up thirty-six hours, go down and turn in and we'll have a watch maybe tomorrow after you've had a rest.' But that was his way of doing it, and that's the way it had to be done.''

THE FOREMOST MAN "I never saw any problem with crew members going against skippers because the skipper worked with them. All hands would work — it wouldn't be any such thing as the skipper lying down and the crew working. The skipper would usually be the first man in the boat. He'd never miss. He'd be in the boat — he'd be the foremost man, and there never was too many problems.

If you went back in my grandfather's day I have often heard tell of mutiny on board a ship to the seal-fishing. That was for some particular reason, you know, living conditions."

AFRAID OF THE OLD MAN "As an example of the ruthlessness of the captain, if you want to call it that, there's the 1914 sealing disaster when seventy-eight men froze to death on the ice ... actually seventy-seven froze to death and one died later in hospital. The 1914 sealing disaster involved Captain Abram Kean, and his son Captain Westbury Kean. Westbury Kean was in an old, old ship, the *Newfoundland*, an old wooden ship. She was caught in the standing ice. She was there for weeks and had only three hundred pelts aboard, and because she had no wireless, Captain Abram Kean had said to his son Westbury, 'When we get to the ice, if I get to the seal herd first, I'll give you a signal and let you know, and then you can give me a signal if you get there first.'

Well, the *Newfoundland* got trapped in the ice, got nowhere, and Captain Abram Kean, in his steel ship, the *Stephano*, he got all kinds of seal. Now, after two weeks the seals had drifted down the coast off the Funk Islands, which was where the *Newfoundland* was trapped in the ice, and seeing his son's ship back there about four or five miles, he gave him the signal that they were in the heavy seal herd, the main packs of seal, hundreds of thousands of seal. Well, the next day, Captain Wes sent his men over the ice, and it was a fine and lovely day, so fine and warm that the steam was flying out of the wooden decks of the *Newfoundland*. Consequently, the men weren't very well clad, but as they walked over the ice, the weather deteriorated and when they got to the *Stephano*, it was beginning to snow. Captain Westbury Kean had told his men that they were to stay aboard his father's ship for that night and he would pick them up the following day; they would stay up there and work the seal.

Now, he gave these orders to the mate. And when they got over to the *Stephano*, old Abram Kean wasn't told this. The old captain said to the mate: 'I'm going to take you back a couple of miles and put you onto a patch of seal, and when you kill the seal, you can go on back to your own ship.' What the mate should have said then was, 'Captain Wes said that we should stay aboard of you for the night' — but he didn't say that, because he was afraid of the old man. Everybody was afraid of the old man, even his sons were afraid of him because he was a very stern and very strict man.

So old Captain Kean put the men out on the ice. And just as all of them went back on the ice, after travelling from seven in the morning until eleven-thirty that day (and they were only twenty minutes aboard the *Stephano*), the storm came on. The snow came on in a real blizzard, but even Kean did not try to pick up the men. His own men he had dropped earlier on the ice farther north, and he went gradually to pick them up. He didn't dash up there to pick them up, he just went up slowly, picking up seals on his way.

Now, to get back to the *Newfoundland* men, here they were out on the ice floe, poorly clad and in a blizzard. So they started back for their own ship and lost the way of course, following their trail from the morning. But what with the current underneath and the wind and the storm moving the ice around, the trail got all jumbled and disintegrated, and they went past their ship.

And so they spent two days and two nights out on the ice. And their own captain, having watched them get aboard the *Stephano*, was sure that they were safe aboard. It snowed all the night and all the next day until the middle of the day, and the wind was so high that the snow kept drifting for the rest of the day, and nobody saw them on the ice. Two ships came near them, turned around and sailed away. Nobody saw them. And they were out there for two days and two nights, and they froze to death in all kinds of awkward positions, grotesque positions. They died kneeling, they died walking, they died singing, they died praying, they would lie down just to sleep for a few minutes and never rise again.

The survivors themselves laid the blame squarely on Captain Abram Kean, but it was the lack of communication that was to blame. The men feared the captain, they did not speak up — they should have spoken up, they should have raised their voices, and nobody did. And the old man went on quite blissfully unaware of what was happening. I don't know if he was aware that every-body was so terrified of him, but he was a very stern man. The Court of Inquiry actually decided that he had done everything that he thought was best for the fishermen, and that it was an Act of God."

FROM ST. JOHN'S "You wouldn't have any crew from St. John's. You wouldn't carry a man out from St. John's, he wouldn't be any good for that job. You have to go to a fishing village where people were brought up by the sea. These men would come from the outports, and all these ships and all these sealing captains that went on these ships came from Bonavista Bay. They didn't come from St. John's, very few skippers ever came from St. John's. If you're going to look for a crew in St. John's, you're in trouble."

IT WEARS YOU OUT "Well, you'd get your gear out say at ten o'clock in the night and you always had to stand your hour, or some nights a two-hour watch, so then you got up again at three-thirty in the morning and got your breakfast. So you didn't have too much time for sleeping. I'd sleep most nights, you know, that's most days, I'd sleep possibly four to five hours, from about ten o'clock till possibly three. You'd get up at three-thirty, cook would have our breakfast ready for three-thirty in the morning.

It wears you out, it wore me out, just from tension. They took me off the boat down on the Grand Banks on a stretcher. I couldn't even sit up. It near killed me."

A BAD EGG IN EVERY CREW "Bein' a captain has good points and it has bad points. You have to let the men know that you're master. You have to let 'em know, if you can. Nowadays a lot of the young fellows, they don't want to work and ain't goin' to work. But years ago there was no such things, it was work till the work was done. If it was eighteen hours, was forty-eight, you would work till the work was done. Sometimes you'd have your hands full to keep them in line but a lot of times they'd respect you for it.

The little experience that I had, there was always a bad egg or two in every crew and that's all it takes to cause trouble, they can get the other ones to join in some easy. You can easy get rid of 'em when you get back to land, but you've got to put up with 'em for that trip, do the best you can with 'em."

THROUGH THE LOWER DECKS   "In the crew of a trawler you don't find the strong definition between upper decks and lower decks and between the skipper and the few officers, such as the first mate and engineer, and the remainder of the crew as you will find aboard a commercial passenger ship, or as you would find in the Navy. Not at all. They work really very closely as a team, and for all a fisherman's independence they all have the ability to co-operate very impressively as a crew.

In the trawlers I'm speaking of, which are run out of Nova Scotia and out of Newfoundland, the trips last from twelve to eighteen days approximately. The crew, when they're fishing, have no time for off-duty amusements; for the most part, they are either sleeping, eating, or fishing. However, at times when they're not fishing, sailing to the fishing grounds or back again, their off-duty entertainments are pretty slight and not very unusual. They read, usually most of the cabins aboard the trawlers are full of pocket books; they do play cribbage. In the trawler I was aboard, one of the rooms was used almost exclusively for playing cribbage or various card games. They simply sit and talk a lot, yarn to one another. They often have radios or tapes and play whatever tapes they happen to be entertained by. On radio, when we were on the Banks, the only station we could pick up on the little transistor radios was a station out of St. John's — it was playing country and western music and this was ringing throughout the lower decks most of the time."

GOOD-LIVING FELLOWS   "You wouldn't fish on the Labrador on a Sunday. A lot of the men would rest and they were fairly good-living fellows. They used to be singing hymns or have a church aboard their own vessels that go out. Yes, I've known fishing on the Labrador where you'd see fellows from one vessel going aboard this certain vessel where they had the church aboard. And on Sunday nearly everybody would sing a hymn, because most Newfoundlanders were very familiar with them."

NO PROBLEMS WITH A QUART A DAY "You've gotta let them know that they're not gonna walk onto you and you've just gotta put your foot down. Either you've gotta run the boat or they're gonna run you — you'll go for a time, but after a while they're gonna get the best of you.

It hasn't been like that all over the years because I know we went to the Cape North under Captain Tom Pitman and from 1947 to '51 we never changed a man, so that'll show you the difference in types of men.

There wasn't much of a problem with the men being drunk. Some ships did have trouble, there was a little drinking done, but not all that much. There's sometimes we used to take rum. You know, we could take rum on the trip with us but it was allow-anced out, we would just give them so much at the time, and they never caused any problems. There was one fellow that drank his quart of rum every day and wasn't drunk and he's still livin'. Just whenever he felt like it, he'd go and have his drink and he would put through a quart a day. That's when we was gettin' it at sea.

Not everybody could get the liquor. You had to be out for twelve days, through the bond — we had bonded stores, you know — and the skipper would allot it out to each fellow, so much. When his would get out, why, he'd buy it from the other fellow."

GIVE AND TAKE "Being the skipper, you know, you've got to give and take. I've always found that, sure, you can get the men to work, sure, they'll work hard and work long hours, but eventually you sense when they start getting sloppy and they start dropping things and the hook just barely misses the scow, you know that they're getting tired.

So what I used to do was knock it off and give 'em a rest for three or four hours and then we'd get back to it and they can do twice the job. You know, you can only push a person so far. You try to go along with 'em and do what you think is right so that it's not gonna hurt them, physically or mentally — and the mental part of it when they get tired is the most important thing that I found. And you know when they're getting tired mentally and physically, and so you just say, 'Okay, boys, let's have a cup of coffee and a sandwich and we're gonna have a rest for a few hours and then we'll come back to it.'

Then, in another case you'll find when you really have to push and you wanna get that extra few thousand pounds offa that fish camp or off that boat, you wanna get it and you wanna get going. So, you'd load that and you'd say, 'Okay, let's get the hatches battened down; you go to bed, I'll take the wheel for three or four hours and you guys have a sleep.' This is the way I always found out was best. You know, you'd give and take and if you'd give a little bit, they're gonna give you a lot themselves."

SOMEBODY'LL GIT HURT   "Well, normally when we go out there we'll work twenty-four or thirty hours, but that's when the weather's good. When the weather's bad, after eighteen or nineteen hours you pretty well wanna be knockin' off or somebody'll git hurt. They work automatically after when they get tired, men that are good at it, but when it gets rough they're not alert enough. It's all right to work automatic when things have slowed and everything, but when the boat's slottin' around a lot you don't want to be doin' it, you know, you want to have your wits about you."

A LITTLE SQUIRRELLY   "You go out on the tugboat for a month and a half, two months at a time. It was like everything else. It was just a job and it could get a little monotonous after a while. We would observe various crew members and we would say, 'Well, this one is going a little squirrelly.' He's starting to stare straight ahead at nothing, sort of thing. You know, 'So-and-so is beginning to look a little squirrelly, I guess. We better get this thing into port pretty soon, or he's going to be climbing a wall.' "

ONION THIEF!   "We had to have two dining areas for staff and ship's officers, and so the main dining area for staff and ship's officers was down below and then we had a small room up top called the smoke room where four of us used to eat. And down below they used to put a lot of pickles. You know, when you go to sea they're very, very generous with pickles; you have mustard pickles, bread-and-butter pickles, you name it and they've got it.

940   PORT DALHOUSIE, A WELL KNOWN RESIDENT.

The illustration above, like all of the illustrations in this section
(with one exception) comes from Allan Anderson's private
collection of postcards of the Edwardian era in Canada.
Selected postcards from this extensive collection have already
produced one successful book entitled GREETINGS FROM
CANADA (published in 1978). As the following pages
reveal, these postcards give a delightful flavour of
life on the water in the old days.

Lunenburg Harbor, N. S.

SEINING A WEIR AT WHALE COVE, GRAND MANAN, N.B.

Hauling Cod trap.

Bringing in the Mackerel—Yarmouth, N.S.

43. Battle Harbor, Labrador. Spreading the fish.

Newfoundland Sealing Fleet ready for Ice-fields.

Ce Bergs in St. Johns Harbor, Nfld.

Quebec   The St. Lawrence River in Winter.

A Shipping Scene at Selkirk, Man.

(31) A & A CO. S.S. DISTRIBUTOR. THE LARGEST BOAT ON THE MACKENZIE RIVER.

Salmon Trap
near Vancouver,
B. C.

Caught in a Salmon net. River's Inlet.

Courtesy of the Provincial Archives of British Columbia.

Scene in Vancouver Harbour, B.C.

THE SALMON FLEET, FRASER RIVER.

VANCOUVER. B.C.

So they had a lot of pickles on that cruise, like a lot of onions, small onions and round onions, and everything was going fine for about three weeks and the next thing there is a great kiyi down below between two hydrographers. What had happened, one fellow had accused the other fellow of stealing all the onions from the pickles.

And this was a very serious thing. They were on the outs for about two weeks after that — they wouldn't speak to one another because of this incident. So that's how things can get out of hand, how people get on other people's nerves in the course of a voyage."

HOOK, LINE, AND SINK   "This Captain Thomas had a pretty fair temper, you know, he could explode pretty quickly. We were going through Metlakatla Pass and Dan Healy had been down to have lunch and I guess he had left all the dirty dishes in the sink and a real mess down in the galley. So Healy relieved him at the wheel and Thomas went down to have his lunch and all of a sudden he came up out of the forepeak and said, 'There'll be no more of this.' I was in the wheelhouse with Healy and we didn't know what he was talking about. He went down to the engine-room and got a couple of wrenches, a pipe-wrench and a monkey-wrench, and went down forward again and pretty soon up he came with the sink in his hand and he said, 'There'll be no more damn dirty dishes here,' and he threw the sink right over the side, right in Metlakatla Pass.

We just had to use a basin from then on. He just didn't like the idea of having a sink that was going to be made available to us for leaving dirty dishes sitting in it. He was a real character."

PUNISHMENT AT SEA   "I remember a tale that my father-in-law told me and I remember this exquisitely because this happened many years ago and I've heard him speak about it different times. And this is a true story about an individual who had apparently been put aboard a raft or a small boat type of thing during a storm and drifted ashore somewhere in the vicinity of Sandy Cove, Bay of Fundy. And apparently after the storm had subsided, some of the local inhabitants came across this man, who was legless. His legs had been amputated at sea apparently by the people who put him ashore, for some terrible act that he had done himself, and in their punishment to him they amputated his legs and put him ashore. He was legless, and the local inhabitants who found him on the beach tried to find out his name, tried to find out where he was from, anything they could, and the man never spoke.

He wouldn't speak a word and he lived in that area for many years, and occasionally, as the story goes, the odd occasional time he might say something to the effect that he had been punished for some mischievous thing that he had done which was the cause of the loss of his legs.

Through those years they cared for him in the Sandy Cove area and then in later years he was moved from that area to some other people down what we call the French Shore, which is just across St. Mary's Bay. And apparently he died in that area and was buried."

OTHER FELLOWS DEPENDING ON YOU "As you know, boats do capsize, they get out in storms and founder and things of that nature, but most people who follow the life of the sea acknowledge that it's one of the fates that some people are goin' to face and we just go back and do our thing again and accept it. Most people feel that way. I know in my case that when I was away my wife used to worry about it, especially when we had a family of six children. And she always says, 'Well, I practically raised them by myself 'cause you were never home. You came home and hung your pants on the bedpost and then I was pregnant again, so then I had to do the rest, I raised them.'

But I think wives in general do worry about their husbands and, as you say, the husband is out there and he's too busy to be worried about anything else, especially during a storm. Your mind has got to keep active, you know you got several other fellows that are depending on you. You've got to make sure that these guys get home safely to their families as well as your own."

Ice

When I started work on this book I knew nothing about winter fishing through the ice. It's as rugged and demanding as any sea-going fishery. Sometimes the men would be as much as ten miles out on a lake, and when the weather thawed, there was always the chance of a break-up of the ice. This was true in northern Manitoba, on Lesser Slave Lake in Alberta, or on any of the remote lakes that fringe the northern borders of the three Prairie provinces.

The men were often of Icelandic origin or native Canadians. Icelandic wives kept busy knitting wool underwear, sweaters, scarves, socks, and mitts for their husbands. In the early days the men took with them to the ice a bag containing twelve pairs of mittens, each pair being used for two nets and then set to dry slowly. Sheepskin-lined jackets with wide collars were common. Felt caps with earlaps were later replaced by fur caps with laps tied under the chin. Then parkas became common. Boots, moccasins, or shoepacks were worn. Sometimes hide was sewn to the sole of socks and up the side of the socks.

Fish camps were often made of rough logs with a roof of saplings set side by side covered with hay or straw with clay on top. The logs were chinked with moss. A slush of snow and water might be slapped on the outside walls to form a sheath of ice.

The men ate beef or pork (usually salted), beans, bannock, but little fish. Potatoes were the only vegetables. Then came rice

111

pudding or prunes, washed down with tea and evaporated milk.
The cooks were usually young fellows of sixteen or seventeen,
who often knew as much about cooking as they did about Tas-
mania. One of them was so flustered by the bannock he made, he
tried to hide it under the mattress until told to bring it out.
Another lad dumbfounded the fishermen by stewing prunes in
juice drained from pickles.

I knew about Arctic ice, of course, since I have always been in-
terested in the Arctic, and one man I very much wanted to meet
was the famous Captain Paul Fournier, who had captained a
succession of Northwest Passage icebreakers over the years.
When I was in Halifax, he graciously took a morning off and
came in from his country place to see me. He's retired now, and
has had enough of the Arctic, but from him, and from Stan and
John Mortensen, who drove in fifty miles to my hotel in Vancou-
ver, I got vivid accounts of icebergs, the changing colours of ice,
finding channels through the ice, surviving in the Arctic, under-
standing Arctic conditions, and stories of Eskimos.

The Arctic, like the Mackenzie, is a world apart. You can't go
there bumbling around in top hats and carrying fine silverware
the way Franklin and his party did. If you're a captain in the
north, you have to learn the nature of that icy world, and you
have to learn it fast.

TEN MILES OUT "The fishing was all winter fishing through
the ice, and we always lived in cabooses or shacks. A caboose is a
building of about ten by twenty, depending on how many fishermen you have employed. On Lake Manitoba, we'd take the
cabooses, a combination of sleeping quarters and a cookhouse,
the whole works, out with us and live right at the net.

We'd haul the cabooses out there by horses and we'd haul the
fish in the same way. We'd have a barn for the horses, close to the
living quarters, with hay and oats, and they'd live just as comfort-

ably as the fishermen. Oh, it was all very well planned. We'd have a little settlement ten miles out on the lake, from early November till the spring.

Traditionally, this is the way of the lake, with the people along the lake, say, from 1910 to 1940."

A COLD LIFE "The tents were all heated by what they call an air-tight stove, that's simply an oval stove made out of sheet iron and, of course, a tiny draft at the front end and a stove-pipe up the back end. When you close the draft, there's absolutely no air can get into the stove. So, that's the reason they call them air-tights, and when you opened the draft, it was just like a little blast furnace going. And, of course, the whole stove would turn red if you left it on long enough. It didn't matter how cold it was outside, it would heat the tent up. Many of the fishermen had milk and eggs in their tent that never froze even though it was twenty or so below outside.

It was a cold life, but fishermen accepted the fact that it was rugged. They were a mixture of white people and natives, it didn't seem to make any difference as to what race they were, they accepted the cold as being part of the occupation. Fishermen generally gathered up two or three outfits together so that they had somebody to talk to in the evenings. Their tents would probably be about twenty, thirty feet apart, maybe two or three fishing outfits, then there'd be a space of about four, five miles to another outfit."

THE MARVELLOUS JIGGER "To set nets these fishermen would drill a hole, insert an instrument called a jigger into the ice, and they would jigger their line under the ice for a hundred yards. Then they'd step it out and walk on top of their jigger and listen to it. Then when they was out a hundred yards on top of the jigger they would drill a hole and pull the jigger out, then they would have a line under the ice for a hundred yards.

The jigger is an instrument that's wooden, like a wooden plank about seven or eight feet long, with a dog and a couple of runners under it, and when you pull the line the jigger goes ahead and then you release the line and the dog comes back, and then you pull it again and the jigger advances again. It's a little device that is very hard to explain, but really works under the ice.

In most of the lakes north of Lesser Slave Lake, each licensee or each fishermen had six nets. They would jig in six nets and the next day they would come and lift those six nets, take the fish out, and if they had a poor set they would move that particular net. They might catch anything from two hundred to a thousand pounds in the six nets, say, a hundred to five hundred whitefish per day."

THE SASKATCHEWAN FISHERY "Well, commercial fishing in Saskatchewan extends from just north of Regina and Last Mountain Lake up to as far as Lake Athabasca in the north. We have had a volume as high as near thirteen million pounds in the past. Commercial fishing here started at least in the twenties because they hauled fish all the way down from La Ronge to Prince Albert by sleigh and team in those days. At that time fish was a back-haul. There was no roads in that country and they used to follow the lakes and the rivers up to the north, up to La Ronge, and they would take dry goods and non-perishables such as flour or sugar and so forth up to the northern communities by horse-drawn sleigh. To make it a paying proposition they would back-haul fish, frozen fish, in the wintertime.

La Ronge by road now is a hundred and fifty-five miles and that's a recently constructed road so it's fairly straight. I understand it used to take them ten days to two weeks, and they had their own provisions with them for stopping over. It was what they called a winter road which could be used in the wintertime but it couldn't be used in the summertime because of open water and unfrozen muskegs. There would be a number of sleighs and the horses would be in tandem, you might have four-horse teams or six-horse teams, depending on the weight of the load. They had staging areas and in there they had log shacks where they could look after the horses. They were very careful, apparently, about looking after animals at that time. You couldn't work them too hard in the severe temperatures where it would get forty, forty-five, and sometimes fifty below zero, that's Fahrenheit. If they worked them too hard the horses would breathe so hard it would freeze their lungs and they would die. It would just kill them instantly and apparently in severe winters the trail was marked with dead carcasses, dead horses."

WARMER THAN ON THE PRAIRIE   "I've talked to some of the old-time fishermen and they've said that they used to have a canvas parka and that was the days before eiderdowns, I guess. They'd wear a canvas, big canvas parka over everything else, and that would keep the wind out. And they maintained they dipped their feet in the water to get a coat of ice on their boots, and that served as insulation too. And then they had a tent or a sleigh with a stove in it and they fished with woollen mitts. And they'd put their mitts in a tin of hot water on the stove and then they'd wring them out. They'd be warm and then, of course, they'd freeze on the outside, but you're dealing with water, and you'll never freeze because as long as it's water, it's not below.thirty-two Fahrenheit. Well, the minute they went out, the mitts would freeze on the outside again and form ice, but they'd stay warm on the inside. You couldn't pull wet nets with anything else, really.

They said they'd rather be on the lake than on the prairie. I suppose in the extreme cold days there's probably not too much wind. Of course, frostbite was always a threat, but they had their parkas that extended out and some of them fur-trimmed."

TIME FOR TEA   "We got married and we went to Big Grindstone for our honeymoon, to go fishing for the winter. The ice was melting and there was a bay that froze over. Well, we were crazy enough to set out on ice and we did. We set six nets out and I said to the boys, 'Let's go to shore and make tea.'

And we were just making our tea and I looked up and four of the nets were gone, there were two left on shore. It could be an Act of God that I mentioned to have tea. The ice broke up in small chunks and, there, we would have gone with it."

WINTER FISHING   "It's a very, very historic lake, La Ronge was one of the early producing lakes. The winter fishing and the summer fishing are two very far removed methods. In the wintertime you have to cut through the ice and string your nets out one, two, three hundred feet and possibly ten, twelve feet deep, and you string them out with leads on the bottom and floats above so the top of the net is at the underside of the ice and the lead pulls the net down taut and the fish come along and get caught in the nets.

To chop a hole in the ice the average fishermen used what they called an ice chisel and a lever bar, and that was an instrument with an iron handle and a broad blade, say two and a half to three inches wide and honed razor-sharp. By driving this into the ice you cut a hole, possibly as big around as a ten-gallon gas barrel or let's say two feet across, until you had a hole there to put your nets down in.

It would freeze over but you would pile a big heap of snow and a little bit of spruce boughs or brush and it would retard the freezing. Once you had it open, the water is warmer than the ice, and by covering it up at night, in the morning you'd only have to cut a little bit of ice and you'd lift your nets every day.

You'd catch similar fish summer and winter. But in the wintertime you had to put those nets underneath the lake, use this jigger device, and all the time you're fighting winter and frostbite. But in winter all you had to do was lift your nets, pull the fish out, gut them, rub them with your mitt, lay them in a big, long line, and in an hour and a half they'd be all frozen. They packed them in boxes, hundred-pound boxes provided by the fish buyer, brought in in a knocked-down state and made up, and then you'd box your fish and a Cat train would come and get them, or they'd haul them in with horses on some of the lakes."

GOOD SPORTS AT LESSER SLAVE   "One of my duties when I first started as a fishery guard at Lesser Slave was to patrol the ice from Canyon Creek to Slave Lake, a distance of approximately sixteen miles during the winter ice-fishing. I used to walk down the lake and check nets on the way down to Slave Lake, and stay overnight there and then come back, walking, on a different route the next day, checking nets.

Usually the fishermen had tents, and in some cases part log cabins, maybe they had a tent roof. They always were very generous, good sports, and it didn't matter whether you picked off a net of theirs and prosecuted them, they'd still offer you a cup of coffee, feed you."

EARLY BREAK-UP "On Lesser Slave Lake, in 1953, fishermen started fishing on very thin ice first of December. We had very mild weather for two days to two weeks, and by approximately the middle of December we had a two-day Chinook, which is warm wind coming from the south-west. The wind increased in velocity to approximately seventy, eighty mile an hour, and one morning, all of a sudden, the ice started to give way on the east end of Lesser Slave Lake and in about two hours, half of the east end of Lesser Slave Lake was wide open. The ice had all gone under, gone under and over, and, of course, the waves started to break it up.

When the ice started to break up, there was twenty or thirty fishermen out there. A few of the fishermen who were trying to get their gear out were stranded on moving ice and some of them came leaping across ice that was, you know, channels in the ice. Fortunately everybody reached shore. But in that disaster, as far as the lake was concerned, about fifteen hundred gill-nets were lost."

MOUTH TO MOUTH "I lost my arm in 1927, June 4, in a saw-mill accident. I got caught in a belt, and it tore the left arm off, and the right arm is all crippled up. I went through a period of recuperation, I would say for two years, till 1929 or '30, then I went out on the lake and fished one-armed. I went out with my brothers and pulled in the nets that was under the ice. It was cold, especially on my arm that I lost, it was colder. That usually froze.

I took an awful lot of fish out with my mouth in them days, I'd grab the net with the fish in it, and place the mouth of the fish in my mouth, and I took the fish out that way, and I flung the fish into the box with my mouth. It's a rather unusual occurrence that a one-armed man should be out fishing, but I'd rather do that than take welfare, which I never took. I always felt that I was on top of the world. I never let this handicap pull me down."

FISHING BY DOG TEAM "They fished anywhere from a hun-

dred yards to a half-mile offshore, and initially they used dog
teams and sleds to haul their fish back into their home base at the
end of the day. The dogs were in teams and they just lay down in
the snow while the fisherman was lifting his nets, and then they
would go to the next hole and lay down in the snow again. They
would have from three to seven or eight dogs in a dog team,
depending how big a sleigh they were hauling and how big an
outfit they were. Some of the dog teams were a mixture of husky,
the odd half-wolf. The fishermen fed them rough fish, ling, suck-
ers, some small pike, and so on. They only fed them once a day, in
the evening, after they were all through their work. At feeding-
time the dogs would snap and snarl, but while they were in as a
dog team, they didn't make too much noise, they were working
too hard to make noise."

CAT TRAIN OVER THE ICE   "In the late forties and fifties, they
were hauling fish to Flin Flon from Reindeer Lake and Wollaston
Lake; it was about four hundred miles by Cat train from Wollaston to Flin Flon, and they'd start out, usually between Christmas
and New Year, for the first trip. And the Cat train was, well,
Caterpillar tractors hauling four or five sleighs, one behind the
other. Once they got a trail and got rolling on the lake, it might
take two Cats to pull them, you know, whatever string they
pulled. Once they got out on the lake and got a trail, why, they
could go along with one.

There were some went through the ice too, occasionally. I guess
there's still some Cats, tractors, at the bottom of Deep Bay on
Reindeer Lake that never did get brought up again. But they used
to send divers down, they used tripods and brought some of them
up again.

They had hatches in the roof of the Cats so the drivers could
hoist themselves up and pull themselves out and jump clear. I've
known of several Cats that went through the ice, but I've never
known a sleigh to go through, although it could have happened,
and I've heard that the boxes of fish would float. Also I've heard
of trucks going through the ice. I know one fellow, the rear end
went through the ice and pulled the driveshaft out of the truck
and he went scooting on ahead so that he didn't lose the truck."

THE ICE WAS STARTING TO CANDLE "Ed Tripp and me, were on the north side of the Severn River, and his camp was on the south side of the Severn River, and we had to get across. We had pouring rain and we had sunshine and the ice was starting to candle, and this candled ice, when you stepped on it, it was just like candlesticks, two-feet sticks would jump out. But we had to get across, approximately three-quarters of a mile.

We started out, and in between there, about half of the distance, there was a small island. So we started out, the two of us. Ed was walkin' in front of me with a stick, and pushing it down the ice, then waving me on. I, in turn, was walking behind him, pulling a smaller hand-sleigh that we also had with us with a few supplies and our sleeping-bags and so on. He had a stick about eight foot long, just a pole, and would go along and try the ice, he'd have this goin' in front of him so he wouldn't go through.

Anyways, we're going along. He hammered on this ice and waved me on. I come, and down I went, I was in the water. The only thing that kept me from going right down, I guess, was my moose-hide parka and this rope of the sleigh, under my arm, behind my neck. The sleigh is up on the ice, and I'm in the hole, hollering.

In the meantime, there was some open water above us, and there was a few gulls, and Ed was walkin' ahead of me, and I'm hollering, and he thought it was the gulls yelling. Then he turned around, and after it, he said, 'All I could see was your nose stickin' out.' So he got down on his knees and crawled back, took this stick that he had, and held it out, and I got ahold of it, and that's the way I got out.

My clothes, by the time we got to the shore of the island from where I was in the ice, they were just frozen solid. We spent the night on that island. He built a big fire, and I dried off, much as I could. I was cold as could be, but luckily we always carry a bottle or two of rum with us, so with some hot tea and rum, I got right into the sleeping-bag.

Well, it rained that night. It rained all night, and here we were on that island, and we still had to cross maybe the same distance, a little better than a quarter of a mile over to the other shore, and the ice was getting worse. What we did, we cut four big long poles, and that's the way we went, on our hands and knees. And where it looked like it was too weak you pushed these poles, and kept going across, crawling.

We started out early in the morning and it was about four o'clock in the afternoon before we got to the other side. We were soakin' wet, because there was water laying on the ice, slush and water, and we were soakin' wet by the time we got there. So we got undressed and got a fire going right away and spent the night, and the next morning, we walked."

CASTING WHITEFISH ON THE WATERS "I worked at a hatchery at Lesser Slave Lake, whitefish hatchery, which is approximately one hundred and eighty miles north and a little bit west of Edmonton, Alberta. The hatchery operated only during the winter.

When we were ready to put the eggs in the lake we drove right out on the ice, of course, with the truck and the trays, drilled holes in the ice, and then deposited the tray in each hole we drilled. The holes we drilled were approximately eighteen inches in diameter, and the ice would be anywhere from two feet to three and a half feet deep. The needle bar is a pointed bar that mounts on the ice that will penetrate maybe six inches at a time, and you make the ice fine and then shovel it out by scoop shovel, until you reach the bottom of the ice. Which was hard work.

On many of the lakes when we arrived with the eggs, fishermen would join up with us and drill holes for us and assist us. The number of holes we drilled in a lake depended on how many eggs you were putting in. One case held, I think twenty-eight trays, which was—twenty-eight trays at fifty thousand eggs to the tray—would be one million, four hundred thousand eggs. For a large lake, if we were planting four or five million eggs, there would be a hole for every tray, which would be fifty-six holes. Usually if we were planting that many we had fishermen help us."

WHEN THE ICE GOES OUT "We try and bring all our tugs and barges back to Hay River for pull-out so we can check them and do maintenance. But the larger vessels are wintered at Tuk Harbour, frozen in the ice, and we'd have no compunction of freezing in one of the tugs. But you don't leave them on the river, because when the ice goes out you'll break up. It takes everything in front of it. There's just no place on the Mackenzie River that you could safely leave equipment."

RIDING THE SPRING BREAK-UP   "In the fall of 1945 I was the skipper of a tug called *The Slave* and we were going north with two barges. For various reasons we got an awful late start; this was the last trip of the season and by the time we finally got under way and on our way down the Mackenzie we shouldn't have been going at all. It was just too damn late, it was in October and we were making for Norman Wells. So anyway we continued north with these two barges, but a day before we got to Fort Ridley, which is a good two hundred miles from Normal Wells, we ran into ice, ice cakes started coming down and it was getting difficult to steer. When I finally got to Fort Ridley we had some freight to unload so I tied up there for the night, but by the time morning came we realized it was hopeless, there was no way we could go. The river was just jammed full of ice and we realized we had to leave the ship there for the winter.

Now this was on a wide-open river and no protection of any kind and the chances of that tug and two barges being there in the spring were almost nil. They were bound to be somewhere down the river, you know, and maybe up on the banks someplace too, or, God knows, inland somewhere, wherever the ice would take them in the spring. But anyway we had no choice, we were stuck, and this little place of Fort Ridley, fortunately there was an airstrip there and we eventually flew out, and this was late in October.

We all flew in there early in the spring, the later part of May. The ice goes out late May, early June, so it was sometime after the middle of May that we went in there. Break-up varies from year to year. And we also took a crew of men in with us, and a ship-yard foreman, Andy Johnson, who was a very resourceful fellow. It was decided that we were going to try and get these ships, the tug and the two barges, up on the beach somehow, and that way when the ice let go in the spring it would push us further up and not take us away down the river. There was a small bulldozer at this airport that we were able to use.

The boat and the two barges were quite a distance away from the shore because the water was so low in the fall that we couldn't get in close, so they dynamited a channel in to the shore so we could get the tugs right along the beach. Then they cut down all kinds of trees and made timbers out of them and we shoved this underneath the tug. We put some heavy cables ashore and then we hoped that when the ice let go of her, the first rush of ice would push her sideways. All we did with the two barges, we put extra-strong lines on them. They were light, they were only drawing about a foot each, they were empty, you see, and we figured that they might just ride over the ice.

When the ice comes down the river, you know, it's three or four feet thick and it comes down with such force that it doesn't just go straight down the river. The river is coming up at the same time, so everything is spreading out, not only down the river but sideways as well. So, what we wanted to happen did happen. The tug was pushed sixty feet up on the beach and of course we were all watching, and as she came up we put more timbers underneath. One of the barges wound up in a great big cake of ice about twenty feet up in the air, the other one was upon the beach.

We were just lucky, you see; it should have just crushed us, but we managed to get away with it. There was no damage. We had to be very careful to shove her back in again because the water kept coming up and going down, you see. Sometimes an ice-jam would form down-river and then the river would come up and the tug would go further up and then the water would start dropping suddenly, then we'd have to shove her in again with the dozer. This went on for two or three days until finally she was clear in the water.

Now, once everything was back in the water and the barges were clear we loaded all this freight ourselves. Then we carried on down the river. The first place we stopped at was at Black-water River. There's an old trapper there by the name of Amos Schellenberger, and he was a bit of a joker, this guy. He was a trapper and a trader. We had a fair amount of freight for him, and do you know what he said when we came in? He said, 'Hey there, young fella. You're a little bit late aren't you?' "

IN THE ARCTIC'S GRIP   "Well, the Mackenzie didn't get a grip on me, no, but the Arctic did. I mean the Arctic is another ball game again. Now that calls for more skill again. I've seen 'em take skippers, one skipper in fact, right out of there in a stretcher. He got in the ice floe and he panicked and didn't know what in the hell to do with his boat on the ice.

Well, you get up there and you get them icebergs come chargin' at you, I mean it's a different ball game. There's tricks to the ice. If you're out in the Arctic in an ice floe, you have to remember what you're on. Well, the *Radium Dew* was a semi-icebreaker, they had reinforced it for icebreaking. She was built for the ocean, she was built for the river, she was a versatile boat could be used anywhere. We were fortunate we were on this·boat. Like, there's a lot of boats, there's no way would I take them out there. First of all, when you get out in the ice, you don't break ice with these boats. They're not made for breakin' ice. But what you do is, if it's flat ice and you can bang away at it and then get a crack in the ice, you can follow the crack and keep goin' and keep breakin' through the crack or break your way through it. Now, in the mush ice, there's no way through mush ice, you know, in the fall. I mean it just packs and you're stuck. We had to dynamite our way out.

But, now, you get into the icebergs. Now there's a different story again. Now you're movin', they're movin'. Them icebergs move and they move up to two knots. Well, you've heard that yourself, and they probably move faster in the Atlantic, but in the Canadian Arctic they have been known to move over two knots with the currents. And the only one time that I was ever a little scared was, I was just gonna take over being skipper on the *Radium Dew* and we went through between two icebergs and all I said when I left the bridge is, when you go through that God-darned iceberg, just remember, there might be one coming the other way on the other side. Because you don't see, you know, all you see is a hole between two icebergs, but another dangerous part is they might be joined together and there you are, crunch.

Well, between these two there wasn't very much space, but we got through with our two barges and tug. But as fate would have it, this time as I spoke and I changed my mind and come back on the bridge, Christ, there was another iceberg coming right at us on the other side from the blind—you know, like we went through the gap and there was another one there.

Well then, that was game over if we'd have kept going. We just come around, right around it, you know, hard over, and got the hell out of there, because if they'd have come together we'd have been crushed right there.

I was trapped in the ice in the Arctic for about twenty-one days, I guess. But we weren't really trapped. We kept ploughin' away at it and we dug a hole in the big blue ice to where we had the ice over top of us and were diggin' a tunnel through it with the tugs and barges."

ICEBREAKER "I captained the *C. D. Howe*, which was a supply and an auxiliary vessel, and I captained the *Montcalm*, which was a cargo and icebreaker, and the *John A. Macdonald*, which was an icebreaker, and my last vessel was the *Louis St. Laurent*, which was the biggest icebreaker in the country.

My feelings of the Arctic is it's a good country to stay away from. You know, I never dreamed of going in the Arctic, but I fell into the icebreaking near the Gulf of St. Lawrence, the year I was in that icebreaker as chief officer, and I was transferred to the new vessel, the *C. D. Howe*, then I was on my way to the Arctic and a new experience altogether.

I found it fascinating, really fascinating. To survive in the Arctic, you have to have great respect for it, because it won't respect you. You don't try to push it along, because you're not going to survive. At first I was kind of anxious, you know, and it kind of got me. You know how it is when you want to get somewhere and you're not getting anywhere, and the ice is in there. But once you learn about it, you change your mind altogether, you really accept the ice as it is, and you say, well, we'll wait and that ice will open.

The *C. D. Howe* was the only Canadian vessel that we had that could go up to the High Arctic, so if you damaged her so she couldn't go any more, or if you got caught in the ice, you knew

you were there for the winter. There was nobody to come and rescue you. So you had about 155 people on the vessel, and they
were your responsibility, so it was always a worry. The navigation season opens in Hudson Strait around the 23rd of July, and
the nice weather is very short at that time of year, we only have a
twilight in those places, at night. But we had to chop through, you
know, and take your time so that you don't push beyond your vessel's capability. If you push too much, you damage your vessel on
the heavy ice, and by that time you get the year-round ice, down
from further north, and some of that ice is ten feet thick. It can be
broken but it's closed, and you have to push on it.

One time I remember I was in a storm off Frobisher Bay, and I
had to stop. And this growler came alongside of us, and we could
see it from the wheelhouse window. It was bobbing past the
wheelhouse window and you know the wheelhouse was fifty feet
up from the water. And this iceberg was going up and down and
right in my face, so I'm telling you, I was glad when I could get
clear of that."

ICE FIELDS AND ICEBERGS   "When you are coming to the ice
field, you see, the weather is clear; when you're standing in the
cockpit, the first thing you look for is a way to go around that ice
field. You go around even if that's twenty more miles, you save
time by going around it. You can use a helicopter to go ahead
about twenty miles and survey it, but I would not need a helicopter because I knew where the ice was after so many years, I knew
exactly where the ice was. You learn by experience.

You know that there's very little change in the pack of ice, you
know, from year to year. And then the main thing is the temperature, and then it depends on the wind, which way the wind blows.
Then you can work out the way to go. Sometimes you go south
towards the land and sometimes you go off the bank—it depends.

We have winter ice, as we call it, and year-old ice, that's blue,
and down the Labrador coast you have the ice coming down from
the High Arctic, polar ice, and the current brings the big icebergs
from Greenland. Some of these bergs coming from Greenland,
I've seen some of those bergs there about a mile square—a mile
long and a mile wide and about 150 feet high—and they look like

an island. If you see them from far away, you'd say that's an island that's come up.

Those bergs, you know, they are beautiful because they're wavy; they are not flat. Some of those wonders have broken off the shelf into the ocean, and they're like an island, and they're wavy, and with the sun on them—the sun is never very high in the Arctic—the sun on them creates shadows, you know, and it's beautiful, lovely, lovely."

NINE

You're a Fisherman

You're a Fisherman... The Salt of the Earth... Since the Hanseatic Wars
... Gamblers and Good Businessmen... The Attraction of the Life... The
Money Resolves Itself... A Different Adventure Every Day... Everybody
Did for Everybody Else... Thinking like a Fish... In My Blood... Good
People, Good Neighbours, Good Fishermen... Manitoba Fishermen...
Still Some Pride... Almost a Disease... Everybody Will Go Look... A
Hell of a Thrill to It... A Challenge All the Way Through... Any
Fisherman... Still Fishing

Beecher Court lives in a plain but cosy house at Rustico,
Prince Edward Island. The entrance to the path leading to
the house is marked by the jawbones of a whale washed ashore
in a big storm about 1924. I asked Beecher Court how long he'd
been fishing.

"I've been actually fishing for about eighty years," he said. He
was born in 1888, and is tall and straight, with a marvellous,
rough-cast, sharp-featured face: a veritable prototype of an Ancient Mariner. He has sturdy sons. He told me: "I go out mack-
erel-netting with the boys. I go out trawling."

Beecher Court had some thoughts about fishing and hard
work:

"I believe the more we worked, the stronger, the tougher we became. You'd get awful tired sometimes, but you'd rest, and be
well rested, and in the morning you'd be fresh again.

"We used to row out a lot. There were two men in a dory, row
out, then we would trawl the nets as much as two and three
miles out. It was hard work but you get used to it. You get mus-
cled up and that, it would give you a great strength of the arms
and the back, too, because every time you row, see, you move
your back muscles. It was great exercise. A great thing to build
up the muscles of the arms and back. Your hands would get har-

127

dened up, too. It didn't bother me any that way, the hands, and I did an awful lot of rowin' when I was young.

"Fishermen did drink a lot, and there's a lot of drinkin' done yet. But I never drunk in my life, at any time, nor smoked, or used tobacco in any way."

Beecher Court gave me a net needle used in mending nets. I prize that net needle. I like to remember Beecher Court. He personifies the pride that comes through in the words of this chapter title: "You're a Fisherman".

YOU'RE A FISHERMAN "There's no way, sir, you could be bored in fishing—no boredom attached to it. You're hauling your gear and it's different fishing from yesterday, a different spot, the wind is different, the tide is different, and you're matching your wits with nature. You're hauling and you're working and your eye is on the weather, the sun, the clouds, the waves, the boat, the engine. There are so many things that there's no time to be bored. The day goes and you don't know it.

And you're out in the open; you're your own boss, and every fish that comes in, that's another dollar in your pocket, and if one gets away, you're eager for him because that's a dollar gone; by God, you can't lose that, that's a dollar there.

You know, we're independent, proud. We bow our heads to no man, take off our hats to no man. Father taught us: 'Look, you're a fisherman, you work on your own, you're your own boss, you're proud of it, and take your hat off to no man.' "

THE SALT OF THE EARTH "The fishermen are a breed all unto themselves. They're a class of people that's a pleasure to know, they're hard workers and the salt of the earth, I call them, and I never crab about the price of fish when you know what they have to go through to get 'em. Ten dollars a pound is still cheap. Years ago they would only make a couple of hundred dollars a season, you know, but now they're making good money, and they're entitled to it."

SINCE THE HANSEATIC WARS "The fisherman is an independent man, very, very independent, and then, among fishermen, you'll find there are rivals. There are the inshore fishermen, and there's the offshore fishermen. The inshore fisherman primarily fishes from comparatively smaller boats and the offshore fisherman fishes in large trawlers—larger boats. And sometimes they get into difficulties with one another, because the inshore fisherman suggests that lines be drawn and so on, and the offshore fishermen should not be allowed inside, and so they have their private wars.

But this has gone on ever since the Hanseatic Wars over in Europe and years prior to that. The fishermen of Great Yarmouth and the fishermen in Lowestoft, both on the east coast of England, used to actually fight out in the North Sea, board one another and shoot one another up, but of course they made peace many years ago. I think that the fisherman will gripe a lot when he's talking, but nevertheless, if you put him ashore, a great many of them would want to go back to sea again. Of course, they're working quite hard when they're at sea and when you see them they've been out for a couple of weeks or so, and when they come back, they're feeling a bit tired and they may say, well, they don't care very much for the sea.

But you watch, you keep them ashore for very long, and they'll probably be clamouring back for a berth. Their moods are somewhat moods of the sea. I mean that they can be patient, hard-working, put up with a lot of cold, discomfort—and sometimes it really gets rough out there. On the other hand, if they get a little bit of booze or something of that sort, they can get excited. We don't have much trouble with them in *this* part of the Maritimes, fighting and one thing and another, at least not that I hear of. I maintain that it's their right to have a good drink when they get ashore. But they want to behave with it. Of course, very often they drink too much and they don't behave."

GAMBLERS AND GOOD BUSINESSMEN "Fishermen are gamblers. They just love that gamble. They go out, they don't know what they're gonna get but it's just a gamble, just like a horse race, betting on a horse race. They go out there and they're just hoping they're gonna fill that hold full of fish. And if they do, they've made her, but then you can have a broker too, you know, you go out there for several days in bad weather or everything goes wrong and it turns out as a broker.

Fishermen here in British Columbia are good spenders. If they make it they're gonna spend it. They'll go on holidays, they'll go to Hawaii, they'll go trips to Norway or wherever they come from or back east to the east coast. A lot of Nova Scotians and Newfoundlanders here, you know, and they make damn good fishermen.

And they'll get better equipment for their boat or they'll buy new cars or they'll buy a better home or buy an apartment building. There's a lot of fishermen here in British Columbia that own apartments and own property.

Oh yeah, and I know two or three fisherman here that started out fifteen, eighteen years ago and had very little money but, boy, they're pretty close to millionaires now. They just hit it at the right time. They borrowed money from the credit union to go out and build a big boat, and this was a big gamble but they hit everything just right and now they're sitting on top of the world.

Most fishermen in British Columbia, if they're good fishermen, they're pretty adept at handling their money and they watch things pretty closely. They're very cautious and good businessmen all the way around, they know what they're doing. Sure there's the odd guy who's slipshod, but by and large today they're pretty darn smart. Pretty capable."

THE ATTRACTION OF THE LIFE   "I do know that fishing has a great attraction for people; it's not just a way of making a living. Right now it is a way of making a good living if you're lucky, and if you're good at it. The fisherman is no longer a man to be pitied for his poverty. But there's a great deal more to it than that.

I know a man who some years ago, maybe ten or twelve years ago, tried to go back to fishing, having run a small but successful business ashore. And he sold off his business and he invested all his money in fishing gear—and this was quite a bit of money, it amounted to some hundreds of thousands of dollars—and he decided he was going to go back to spend the rest of his life fishing, not that he expected to make a better living as a fisherman, but because of the attraction of the life—he simply wanted to spend his life in a fishing-boat.

And he said to me: 'You know, there were times coming into that slipway'... he lived out here in Bauline, which is a fishing village without a harbour, actually... 'there were times coming into that slipway when I wouldn't have given two cents for my life, but once I was ashore I always wanted to go back to it.'"

THE MONEY RESOLVES ITSELF "This one fella came to my house and he said to my wife, he said, 'I've investigated your husband and he makes quite good money and I want to get a job on the boat.' Well, he wanted to know how much I could guarantee him, and I said, 'Well, I can't guarantee you anything.'

We don't know, we might go out there and not make any money at all, which sometimes happens, but on an average we do better than the fellas do ashore, and I always look forward to coming home, and I always look forward to going out fishing. It's more of an adventurous life.

People come out with me, bank managers and different chaps who'd give anything to go out there. If you go to a dentist or doctor, the first thing when he finds out you're a fisherman, he's asking you all kinds of questions, he's interested. It's a big thing if you like fishing. If you like it to start with, well then the money resolves itself."

A DIFFERENT ADVENTURE EVERY DAY "I left the island in '66, and I went on the draggers over to Halifax and I was over there for a year. I come back and I decided to get out of fishin'. I was gonna go out west. So I went out there and I was out there for part of '69 and '70. I was workin' on diamond drills out there, Kamloops and Williams Lake, but when the spring come I had to go home, you know. Just that fishin' was in your blood. The same thing as if you smoke, you're cravin' for a cigarette, you crave to fish.

It's hard to explain really, you know. It's just that spring comes, you wanna be on the water, eh?

Well, the thing is the longer I can spend on the water, the better I like it. It's more or less adventure, because you don't know what you're gonna do. When you're fishing nets, you never know what's gonna be in that next three feet of net, or you never know what's gonna be in the next lobster pot. You never know, and there's a million things that can happen. It's a different adventure every day, you know. Every single day you get a different experience and you're always learning, and if you fish to be a hundred years old you'd still be learning because there's never a day that you don't learn something new.

I mean, it's different. If you went to a job where you're making tires, well, that's the same routine every day, every day, every day. But when you're fishin' and you find new grounds and you get better fish and some days you get poor fish and some other days you work harder and you get more fish—so it's really and truly an experience, every day a new experience. I've been fishin' on my own for six years but every single day that you fish you learn something new, and every year you can see the new things you've learned."

EVERYBODY DID FOR EVERYBODY ELSE   "People in fishing villages were very dependent directly upon each other. Men worked together—there were things they had to do together. At Bauline, for example, it wasn't possible for a man to land his own boat if there was any sea on at all, you depended on your neighbour to come down and help you get it ashore. Jobs like barking nets in the spring—barking is boiling nets in a big iron kettle, and steeped-out, boiled-out bark was used as a preservative, and the job of barking the nets in spring was something that required the assistance of a crew of men. You had to get together to do it.

When my grandfather built the only schooner he ever built, he built it in his backyard in Carbonear, a mile from the water, and people wondered how it was ever going to get launched. What happened is that every man in Carbonear showed up the day of the launching and they hauled the ship by hand down through the streets of Carbonear and down to the waterfront and launched it.

Of course, there was no pay for this, you didn't expect to get paid for doing this kind of work. Everybody did for everybody else, and you were quite dependent on this sort of community co-operation. Well, this doesn't exist, of course, in the more complex societies. You don't depend directly on your next-door neighbour for assistance of all kinds, but it's one of the things that people found attractive about that kind of life."

THINKING LIKE A FISH   "A fishing executive in Halifax told me that a fishing skipper in a trawler really needs to be able to think like a fish. I suppose it's similar to the farmer's ability to know just when he needs to put his fertilizer on, and just when he needs to treat his crop in whatever way he treats it. It's basically experience, so a fisherman has to know where the fish are. Now, mind you, they have a wide range of fairly modern aids, more sophisticated variations of equipment than was used in earlier times. For example, the last time I was out in a trawler, it was the *Cape Argos* out of Lunenburg, about a hundred-and-fifty-foot trawler. The tail of the Grand Banks are almost due east of Lunenburg and Halifax, about two hundred and fifty miles out, and when we got there the skipper knew that area so well that it wasn't really a matter of wondering where to fish, this was a fishing ground and he let out his trawl.

The wheelhouse of the *Cape Argos* was almost as complex as the control cabin of an aircraft. He had his fish detectors and radio equipment, was communicating with other ships in the vicinity, at the same time running the throttle, that is to say his hand control of the engine, and his helm, which was electronic, with a couple of hands, he was sitting in a chair not dissimilar to a pilot's chair in an aircraft. So this seemed to be sophisticated—the equipment was of use to him, obviously, in determining where the fish were.

But at the same time there was all this long sort of intuitive knowledge and feel for the sea that he had, and the knowledge that he had from being out as a small boy in boats, it was all pulled together and went into this experience of fishing."

IN MY BLOOD   "It's in my blood. I know, my days off if there's

any water in the rivers or lakes, that's where you'll find me, is up
the river with a salmon-rod or fishin'-rod. And every mornin',
regular, I gets up when I'm on layoff at home, have breakfast, and
my wife says, 'Where you going?' I say, 'You know where I'm
going now.' I jumps in the car and I go round the waterfront every
morning."

**GOOD PEOPLE, GOOD NEIGHBOURS, GOOD FISHER-
MEN** "I think the natives here are getting probably more than
half of the fish right now. The company we fish for are very par-
tial to the native fishermen and they are good fishermen and I
found them very helpful. They're good people, good neighbours,
and often we'd cod-fish too at times, and we found them always
very good on the packing too.

They were fishing, rowboat fishing, and they had methods of
catching fish, they used what they call a rake, like a last practically, only long with little tiny sharp nails driven in it, to catch small
fish. Then they'd use them and put them on their spoons, these little fish, and they were real experts at fishin'. They even had their
own type of hooks that they made for catching halibut that the
dogfish couldn't swallow the bait. The type of ordinary regular
hook that's known in the Western world, the dogfish will swallow
the bait, but the Indians had a type of a hook that they could
catch the halibut and not the dogfish.

They were very good fishermen, great on watching the tides.
Another thing they do have is a lot of patience, which is very
important, you know. Just like some fellas say, you can have education, you can have luck, but give a fellow perseverance. Some
of these boys are very good at that. They'll stay at a place and stay
there and fish and eventually come out top dog."

MANITOBA FISHERMEN "There is commercial fishing in
about three hundred lakes in Manitoba, but most of the catch is
made from the three big southern lakes, that's Lake Winnipeg,
Lake Manitoba, and Lake Winnipegosis. From these three lakes
the fishermen catch about seventy-five per cent of the total provincial catch of some twenty million pounds. The balance, from
many scattered and far-flung northern lakes, is caught by some

nine hundred commercial fishermen, but in the south there are about twelve hundred commercial fishermen. So, we have around twenty-two hundred men going out on the lakes with their nets to produce for the market. Most of the fishermen in the south are not natives. They tend to be descendants of the original Icelandic settlers. However, in the past century a number of native people have learned the fishing business and have become very skilled in it, so that in Northern Manitoba a majority of the fishermen are natives.

A Manitoba fisherman is an independent and proud person, who has behind him probably his father's and maybe his grandfather's example of being hardy, willing to take a chance, go out in the weather, be prosperous or to be poor, depending upon whether fish are plentiful or scarce in any one year. The fishermen tell me that that's all they know, that's all they want to do: be a fisherman. They're proud of it and they're not very happy when, in times of fish scarcity, they're offered alternate or make-work projects. They don't like that."

STILL SOME PRIDE "There's a story about this guy, he was a bum, you know, and he come down to the wharf and he hadn't had nothing to eat, nothing to wear. So, the crew took him aboard the boat and they gave him a big feed and give him some clothes to wear and fixed him all up good and one of the gang asked him if he had ever went fishing. 'No,' he said, 'no . . . I ain't sunk that low yet.' "

ALMOST A DISEASE "Look, a man finally decides, or the doctor decides for him, that he's gotta retire from fishing. You'll find that poor man two years later, still daily going down to the wharf and wistfully looking out and saying, 'Well, I wish I was there.' You can't take it away from him. He's grown up as a fisherman, he's spent his life fishing. He still has that desire to be out there, he's not comfortable being ashore.

It's a way of life. A fisherman is a rugged individualist, a person that has to do it his way. He's able to go out there and wrest, tear, grasp, make his living with his two hands out there against nature, wrestle it away from nature. Without that type of daily competition, he's just not a man any more. It's been taken away from him.

He has to be out there. It's almost a disease like alcoholism or workaholism. He's constantly trying to prove himself against nature, against his fellow fishermen. He's got to prove he's a man. He's able to withstand the rigours of being out there in this cold weather, the stormy conditions. He's constantly pitting himself against nature and his fellow man.

It's worse than compulsive gambling, he's got to be able to do it. Yet at the same time he's constantly willing to learn to try and do it better. It's a type of mental activity that most of us don't go through, a continuous mental strain and a continuous mental struggle.

He's not in love with trouble, be it trouble with gear breaking down, trouble with the cold weather, trouble with storms—he's not in love with that. He's out there to wrest a living in competition against his fellow fishermen. He's also looking to the fact that in a short period of time on the island as a fisherman, well, in less than half a year, he has to make a total year's income."

EVERYBODY WILL GO LOOK "I was trawl-fishing one time and we got broke down and we had no engine, we had no telephones or anything, and we drifted three days before anybody found us. But we knew we would be found—we just didn't know when. It was thick fog and if it'd been clear they'd found us the first day, but by it being foggy they hunted three days before they found us. But they did find us, some of the other fishermen. We fished out of Broad Cove at that time and when one boat didn't come home, well, then the rest all went back out lookin' for him, and there was one of the boats found us. We had no worries.

You see, everybody will go look, because they want you to look for them."

A HELL OF A THRILL TO IT "The fishermen that we have on this coast range in nature considerably, I think, but they do have a lot in common. In many cases the fishermen come from fishing families that have been in fisheries for quite a number of years.

First of all, I'd say that fishermen are outdoors men just as farmers are. They have a sense and a feel for what's happening outdoors—their fields are offshore. Hence you'll find that our fishermen tend to be highly individualistic, and this is based purely on the fact that they have to make personal decisions and make them rapidly, usually, and they don't have committees and so forth to develop their decisions. Also, there are the dangers and the opportunities that face them, which come quickly and they have to make rapid decisions on them. So, I think that their individualism is fairly understandable. The hard work, the cold, and the wet and all the disagreeable qualities of being a fisherman, are characteristics of the environment the fishermen have to face. I think actually these need to be documented, but not over-stressed, because the farmers face similar conditions, so do lumbermen, outdoors workers face these conditions.

Yes, it's a cold, rough, tough life, but there are a great many fishermen who would not do anything else but fish. I mean their attitude toward the sea is the challenge. It's the same thing as driving a motor-car at a hundred and fifty miles an hour, there's a hell of a thrill to it.'

A CHALLENGE ALL THE WAY THROUGH "What I liked about the fishin', it's a challenge all the way through. You've gotta be your own navigator, you've gotta be your own businessman, you've gotta be your own mechanic, you've gotta be able to catch fish, you've gotta be able to rig your own gear, knit your own nets, and make your own lobster traps. To be a good fisherman you've got to go from one fishery to the other and still make a livin' at it. If you don't want to live up to the challenge, well, you're not gonna be a good fisherman, so you're not gonna make a good living at it.

And this is one thing about fishin', it's a challenge, and you're learning something new all the time, but if you worked at it for three hundred years, if you lived that long, there would be something new coming up in the fishery that you have to learn."

ANY FISHERMAN "I've been to Scotland, England, Norway, and half of the time I was in those countries I spent on a wharf, lookin' at boats, talkin' to fishermen. It's the draw again, isn't it? I think that you could take any fisherman from any community and

drop him in another one and in a very short time you'd think he'd
always lived there, he could blend in."

STILL FISHING   "We were coming down from Alaska and I was
laying in my bunk and it was the time of the earthquakes up there
in Alaska. We were running along and it had been blowing and
there was a big sea running but not real bad, not dangerous or
anything, and all of a sudden there was a crash on the boat, this
terrible crashing of wood, and I thought for a second that an airplane or something had landed on the boat.

A big sea had caught the boat on one side and smashed the
whole side of the lower housing. Cost fourteen thousand dollars
to fix it up, and two fellows got very badly hurt, had to go to the
hospital. Wrecked the whole side of the house and nearly sunk us.
It was just very, very lucky that we didn't sink—we were about
two hundred and fifty miles off the land. Well, we laid there and
managed to get the boat operating. In the meantime we called the
American Coast Guard and they came out. They were very good
and took the two fellows, put 'em on a stretcher, put 'em aboard,
and ran them into the hospital and sent another boat to escort us
into the safer waters.

And that was quite a close call there. But all that time, I mean, I
never said, 'Well, gee, I'm gonna quit.' I don't think any of the
fishermen ever think that, they have a sort of fatalistic attitude.
This one fellow, it was his third bad accident. An oil tanker ran
him down once on his boat, and he was with me when the sea
smashed in and I think it was his third accident, he was on one
boat that went upside down. This fellow, he's still fishing."

TEN

Under the Water

Ninety Feet under Lake Erie... Don't Hold Your Breath... An Amateur
Would Have Been Dead... Down the Smokestack... Sledding... A Hat
on the Ice... Wrecking the Wreck... Looting... Scotch and Water...
Complete Freedom... Caught in the Propeller... Cable Talk... The
Closeness of the Crew... Shrimp, Fizzy Icebergs, and Mountain Peaks...
As Soon as We Left the Harbour

W hen I was a boy, I had the good luck to spend a couple of
summers at Invermere, in the Windermere Valley, a long
and very beautiful valley between the Rockies and the Selkirks.
In the evenings, I would take off by myself and go down to Lake
Windermere and, swimming under water, would turn over and
look at the first shimmering stars through the translucent water.
It was my only experience with that unique, unreal, and yet en-
chanting world below the surface of the water.

But there are dangers too. Just a couple of days ago, I picked
up a Toronto paper and read this: "Tobermory, Ont.—A diving
instructor almost drowned trying to rescue two scuba-diving
teenagers who died when they apparently ran out of air. Dead
are Michael Zolman, 16, and John Snyder, 18, part of an 11-
member advanced diving class from Fort Wayne, Ind., looking
for the steamer Forest City that sank in 1904." The Forest City is
a three-hundred-foot ship that lies in sixty feet of water in an underwater park now called Fathom Five. In this chapter, there's a
bizarre story about the first death involving diving to the Forest
City, and that story reminds us that working under the water is
extremely hazardous; you have only seconds to act when there's
an equipment failure or an accident, and even cool-headed professionals have all they can do to save their lives or the lives of
others when trouble strikes. And that applies not only to divers

but to all those—including that strange, brave breed of men who sail in submarines—who work under the water.

NINETY FEET UNDER LAKE ERIE "Most people don't realize the extent of the operation out here in Lake Erie. There's the five ocean rigs, big rigs, from the Gulf of Mexico. One of these rigs would have forty men working on it. These are permanent rigs that stay in the lake all the time. We have three floaters—two of 'em are made out of big ocean barges, the other one is a lake freighter that was converted into a drill-ship—and then there's two jack-up rigs, on legs, that go out and jack up out of the water.

Canadians have been drilling offshore in the Great Lakes for many years, this year is the sixty-fifth year of drilling, and we've never had a major accident of any kind. In the very early days of drilling, they would go out and actually build a small island of sheet-piled steel or wooden piling, or rock and cement, in the middle of this, and then drill down through it. That was actually a permanent small island that they would drill through. They have been using what we call offshore drill-ships for drilling-rigs for the last thirty years.

What we produce is a sweet gas. When it comes out of the well it goes right into the pipeline and right to your house. There's no refinery, nothing in between. It is good, usable gas when it's produced. Most of it is used locally. Ninety per cent of the Consumers' Gas would go to the city of Toronto. And it's used anywhere from Windsor to Toronto, every city in between. I would guess that on the lake right now there must be around a thousand gas wells, and they're putting down about a hundred and twenty wells a year, usually from a nine-hundred-foot depth to a two-thousand-foot depth. And I'd guess that the lake would be producing right now around twenty-five to thirty-five million cubic feet a day.

It takes an average of four to five days to drill a hole. When a well is completed—a self-contained well on the bottom of the lake—the rig is towed to another location and drills another hole. There are five rigs on the lake that will drill approximately a hundred and twenty wells this year.

Once a well is completed and it is what we call a "keeper", a proven well that has production ample enough to justify keeping it, it is a completed well-head on the bottom of the lake. This is what we call a "suspended well" until it is piped in to the beach. For that we use the tow-tugs. We weld up the pipe on the beach, and we tow it out in the lake behind the tug and drop it at the well-head. Then the diver goes down, he has to cut the pipe, make up all fittings under water. And this pipe is connected to the well-head. When this is completed, the well is turned on and the water is purged out of the pipeline. Once it comes dry at the other end, it is connected there to a compressor station on shore, and the gas is run through the compressor station, right into your main lines. Realize that there may be a hundred wells connected into one pipeline going ashore.

Now in eighty feet of water, a diver has forty minutes of working time on the bottom before he has to go into decompression. He will decompress in the water anywheres from three to ten minutes, actually hanging on an object, what we call a diving decompression ladder, or a chair hung over the side of the boat, down at the ten-foot water level, ten feet under lake surface. You hang there. This gets so much nitrogen out of your system. Then you come to the surface. Then you have to go into a decompression chamber to complete your decompression time.

One diver should be able to complete a hook-up in an hour, and it never takes more than two divers to complete a well, but sometimes you run into problems with mud on the bottom, that you've got to dig down into the mud. Or you get a bad connection that may not just go together the way you would expect it. Bad visibility makes quite a difference. If you can see what you're doing, you can work twice as hard. In seventy feet of water, usually on a nice day you might have five to eight feet of visibility. Now, if you go to ninety feet of water, you're gonna lose visibility, but a diver is accustomed to working in the dark. He's used to working by the feel.

Ten years ago, in sixty feet of water, you could touch your face mask and never even see your finger. It was completely blackness. Now, because of your pollution environmentalist-type people that have created a lot of stink about this, which is good, they are now cleaning up the lake, and we can see, as I say, five to eight feet in seventy or eighty feet of water, which we never could before."

DON'T HOLD YOUR BREATH   "Sport diving, the outside limit is one hundred feet. Now, when you get down into a depth like a hundred or a hundred and ten feet, you're working against time. When you work out your decompression tables, to do a safe dive, you have fifteen minutes' bottom time. From the time you enter the water at the top till the time you're coming back up, you have fifteen minutes. All right, now most people don't get too worried about that, they can keep that straight in their head, but when they get down in the cold water, not only is it cold and uncomfortable, but their equipment sometimes will malfunction. A regulated free flow is a very dangerous thing and is far more prone to happen in cold water than anywhere else, and when a regulator free-flows, the air is continuously venting out of the tank, it's not as though you breathe on supply and demand, the air just rushes out, like it would rush out from a tire if you cut it. And having all these bubbles blowing out in their face at a hundred feet and not being able to get air, they panic and shoot for the surface.

Now, what kills them is they hold their breath. The last breath they got, they try and hold as long as they can, and as they come up through a hundred feet of water, the pressure gets less and less, and this air that's in their lungs expands and by the time they get up to sixty feet or up through, say, thirty feet, they've had a massive air embolism. It kills them by forcing air into the bloodstream. Usually it just blows their lungs all into froth."

AN AMATEUR WOULD HAVE BEEN DEAD   "It's seasonal here on the lakes. A diver can work anywheres from six to nine months. Right now depending on the weather and everything, a diver can make up to $1,600 a week.

I have twenty-two divers working for me right now, all commercial divers. A diver now, to work any place commercially, has to go to college on a special course for diving. When they come out of there—an average course is about ten months long—then we have to take 'em and re-train 'em to our type of work.

Ninety per cent of your accidents in the world with diving is through lack of experience. All of your accidents, pretty well, are in forty feet of water or less. People just don't know what they're doing, and they panic. Up around Tobermory where they're diving up there, most of the accidents are in thirty-five feet of water. It's clear—the people are down—they look up—they can see daylight—they come up too quick.

We have rules that we go by for commercial divers. Number one, there is a dressed diver on the surface, our safety diver. A diver dives ninety per cent of the time using communications to the surface, so you're in direct contact at all times. It doesn't matter what system this man is diving on, he has a back-up system—a complete different secondary source of air. If anything happens to the first source, he has what we call a bail-out box. He has another source of air, a complete different regulator, everything, so he has a double system on the bottom. Ninety per cent of the time he is supplied by surface air. The air is being pumped down to him, so he has no problem with running out of air. He's in communication with the safety diver on the surface. If he has a problem, it would take less than thirty seconds for the other diver to be in the water and on the way down to get him.

One of my divers last year was in eighty feet of water, and a tubing string, which is the actual producing line from the surface down to the well, swung and knocked his helmet off. He would have been dead, except for the safety diver. As soon as this happened, the safety diver knew about it, because he could hear the water in the helmet. He called to confirm with the diver, 'All right?' and got no response, because after he'd lost his air supply on the bottom, the diver headed for the surface. The safety diver met him halfway down, and found that the knocked-off helmet was still connected to his weight and he'd got tangled up in it. The safety diver just cut him out, and within ten seconds had him back on the surface again. The man was just going unconscious when he got to him, so he was actually unconscious when he brought him to the surface, but before they could even get him

back into the boat, the other diver had him conscious and naturally he was vomiting, bringing up water. But it was that quick
that the safety diver saved the man's life—an amateur would have
been dead. From the time the accident actually happened until
that diver was on the surface was less than a minute, out of eighty
feet of water."

DOWN THE SMOKESTACK   "Sometimes the instructors are
taking students into waters that are far, far, far over their heads,
like way out of their depth range altogether. Like, taking a student
into sixty or eighty feet of water is crazy.

Now, this particular instructor, I don't know who it was, took
them into a hundred and fifty feet of water, and they went to the
Forest City and the instructor got into trouble. He got in trouble
personally, the students apparently were doing all right.

And the *Forest City* is a big ship, it's three hundred feet long
and it has a smokestack and everything. It's an intact steamer and
laying on an incline of about forty-five degrees. So he got in trouble down there somewhere around the mid-section of the ship,
and two students were helpin' him to surface and he started to
struggle and they couldn't handle him, he was too heavy, and they
let him go and they kept going to the surface. And he sank down
and went right down the smokestack—and the smokestack's only
about three feet in diameter—and he went right down the smokestack and into the engine, into the boiler, and the guy that recov-
ered him had to go right down the smokestack and get him.

The chances of that happening are just astronomical, you know,
from sixty feet up, with what current there is and which way you
float and sink, that he would hit a hole that wouldn't be any more
than three feet in diameter. He sank down through fifty or sixty
feet of water and hit the smokestack right on the nose."

SLEDDING   "Sledding is one of the most efficient ways to pick
up a body if you don't know exactly where it went down. We've
had boats overturn and we've found the boat but you can't find
the body. So you'll have two divers a hundred feet behind the
boat, and usually the diver makes his own sled, just a piece of ply-
wood with handles in it and a snap here for your rope, maybe a

couple of other snaps for other things you want to hook on, and you just hold it and the boat pulls you along real slow. The diver can swing out his hundred feet to the side or to this side or up or down and you can work a sled in a hundred feet of water. They can cover a far greater area with very little expense of energy or air because they're not swimming, they're not using their air. A sled search is by far the most efficient."

A HAT ON THE ICE   "I started with the Toronto Harbour Police as a lifeguard in 1929, and eventually I worked up until I became Superintendent in 1954, and I was Superintendent from 1954 until 1975. We always sent patrol-boats out around the harbour, in and out the slips and down the ship channel and the turning basin and through the island lagoons and out the Western Gap, inside the Exhibition seawall and so on.

It's a regular patrol, just as a patrol-car of the City Police would patrol city streets, and quite often we'd be going in one of the slips and we'd find a body in there. It'd turn out to be a body of a man who was destitute, or in some cases a man who had cancer and decided to end it all, and he'd jumped in the bay.

I can recall one time—this happened in the wintertime—one of the chaps was coming to work and he noticed an overcoat on a post at the foot of Parliament Street. He thought that was strange, so he went over to investigate, and saw footprints in the snow leading over towards the water. He went over to take a look, and there was a small skim of ice on the bay, about a half an inch or so, and the hat was sitting' on ice which was only about a quarter of an inch thick. It looked as if someone had left his overcoat on the post, jumped in, his hat had landed on the water, and he'd broken through the half-inch ice, and over the period of time since he'd done this, there'd been a quarter of an inch of ice formed on top. The hat was just sittin' there, indicating the hole that had been broken through the ice. And of course we went down with the rowboat, and dropped the drags, and found the man with no trouble at all.

Committing suicide by jumping into the water is a fairly common occurrence."

WRECKING THE WRECK "This was a very good example of an intact ship going down in fresh water, deep where no currents could get to it and staying very well preserved until diving started to gain popularity and the ship became a focal point of diving in the Tobermory area, after its discovery in 1974.

The problem with trying to preserve a ship like this in that depth of water is the anchor damage. It settled on perfectly level bottom, which is rock-ledge bottom, and the only place to get anchorage is in the wreck itself. Now, the only way they can dive is to anchor into the wreck site. Their anchor will not catch anywhere else other than in the wreck itself. Some of these charter boats are sixty feet long, and when they have twenty or thirty people on them, it can do an awful lot of damage in any kind of sea. If there's any sea running at all, they're always pulling, strain on the anchor, and the wreck has suffered damage.

I know for a fact they've pulled one of the masts right off the ship."

LOOTING "There are indeed government regulations to prevent looting of wrecks, although we have trouble catching people doing it. It's extremely hard. If you're not on the scene at the time they bring the artifact or whatever it is out of the water, then you have no case. If you're not right there when it comes up, they can say they got it outside the park, and there are shipwrecks outside the park, some of them very close to the boundary."

SCOTCH AND WATER "Oh, we've done a lot of wreck diving, that'd be back in the sixties primarily, and what happened is we run out of wrecks eventually. But wreck diving is a lot of fun. We done a lot of salvage work, brass and copper, and the way we removed it was with explosives, most of the time. I've seen us lift, you know, fifteen hundred, two thousand dollars' worth of stuff in a day.

And you do run into a few interesting things like the Scotch that we found, the Scotch whisky and silverware and combs. A lot of the Scotch was still on board and they had a very good time here for several weeks, everybody drinking free Scotch."

COMPLETE FREEDOM   "You have to pretty well experience it to know what it's like, but the bottom there is all cliffs and ravines, it's just something like you'd see in a Western movie, you know, and you'd swim over a ledge and you might have sixty feet below you to the bottom of the lake and you can just let yourself go and you'll just float down. You can go straight up a rock wall that might be sixty or eighty feet high, and nothing limits you other than depth. You have to always keep it in mind not to go too deep or to stay too long, but there are no physical limits that are going to hold you in one spot, you can just go wherever you want, see whatever you want, and it's just a complete feeling of freedom. I would say that it's very fantasy-like—you can float and lie on your back on the bottom or you can swim upside down or do whatever you want."

CAUGHT IN THE PROPELLER   "We were towing her and half-way back across the bay it kept breezin', was rough, and I parted her, broke the towline. So I started to go right around that thing, to come up to get her, and I seen that line just the same time that engine grabbed it, caught in the propeller, stalled her right there. I couldn't get it out, so I just said—'Well, this isn't a very good situation. If we go adrift we don't know what's going to happen, we can be lost. The best thing is to go down there and clear that wheel up.' Nobody made a move, so I started peeling off and Ron Small said, 'Hold on, if you mean that, I'd better go down than you.'

And so he peeled off. I put my clothes on, I was half peeled off then. I put a line on a big sharp knife, he went over the side, and he just got over and that thing beat up and down so he had to come right up. He came up and got his breath and went back again and he couldn't cut it. It was a big rope filled with copperlite. But he went down and he took off quite a lot of turns, and come up and had to get warmed up. He come right aboard that time and went right in the cuddy, and he told me he'd reach down on the other side and get a bite and haul it up. He cut that in two and then reached back and hauled the whole thing right out."

CABLE TALK   "I worked on two cable firms, Commercial Cable and Western Union, and it's a very specialized field because you're working at the bottom of the sea and you're on top, repairing breaks. Fishing-trawlers get into them. They fish, oh, up to three hundred fathoms, that's eighteen hundred feet, and they drag their net near the bottom and it fouls in the cable. The cable doesn't necessarily lay flat on the bottom, you see, the bottom may be rough or corrugated and your cable stretches above the sea bed between the high points. Or if the cable has been repaired you have to drop all the slack and then just pile it up and pile it up on a coil, on a regular coil like a spring, and anything comin' by will hook it.

Sometimes you have undersea volcanic activity or earthquakes. That'll break them. Mudfalls develop, too, and I've seen a cable broken by icebergs in four hundred and eighty feet of water. When an iceberg goes along it just bulldozes along the bottom when it gets in shallow water.

Now, a cable is quite small, about two inches in diameter, and you have charts of the cable and of cross-cables that belong to somebody else, and we use electronic devices to get us within, say, half a mile. They test from both ends, and they know how far the cable is alive and that pinpoints roughly the position of the fault. Now, a cable steamer has large reels or shivs on the bow. They also have them on the stern for laying cable, but usually they work them from the bow and it's through these you put out your grapnel and you drag it across at right angles to the cable and it picks up the end of the cable—you have to pick the both ends if it's broken—and you bring it aboard and you put a buoy out.

First you have to get both ends, and when we start off to repair it, the fault must be cut out. So they have to splice in wire enough to join both ends, and the splice on a modern cable has to be moulded. It takes, in some cases, four to six hours to make a splice. Depends how complicated the cable is, and you need good weather to work the cable, the decks have to be dry. When it's fixed you hang it off and you cut it away, and let it drop."

THE CLOSENESS OF THE CREW   "There are two or three feelings which are prevalent in a submarine once you've been there a little while, and I guess the most rewarding one, and the reason why I really wouldn't have traded my career, sixteen years in the submarine force, for anything, is the feeling of camaraderie and the closeness of the crew. Nowhere have I seen a crew in the navy which know one another better. The captain knows everyone and everyone knows the captain. The steward knows everyone and everyone knows the steward. Everybody knows everyone else. In fact, as the captain, you probably know more about their family life than you do in any other ship. You frequently know the names of their wives. You hear them talking, you hear them on watch.

The submarine is really only one level, as opposed to a surface ship which could be five or six levels, and some people on surface ships live on one level only; basically they work on the level they live on and they hardly ever come up to the bridge, but it's not so in a submarine, where there's a real sense of camaraderie and of belonging.

In a submarine, everybody but the captain and the captain's steward stands a watch, one in three, so everybody in a submarine is important. It doesn't matter if you're the lowliest ordinary seaman, when you get to a submarine you're expected to stand the watch eight hours a day and be responsible for what you do, and there's a tremendous job satisfaction from serving in a submarine. The crew feel that they're important. They know everyone else; they trust everyone else. They're extremely well trained and well qualified and you just have to trust everyone else. It's just one of those facts of life. If somebody makes a mistake, you can lose everyone, as you can well understand, so that it's very, very important that everyone is well trained and does trust one another. And therefore the camaraderie that builds up is hard to explain, but it's very, very close at all ranks, amongst all ranks from the captain right down.

It's a young man's game, submarining, and you have to be prepared to put up with those little hardships, the bunks which are not quite long enough, somebody else's feet just above your nose, and this sort of thing.

I miss it very much."

SHRIMP, FIZZY ICEBERGS, AND MOUNTAIN PEAKS "When you dive in a submarine, you are listening passively for other noises around you, and you use that to tell what might or might not be ahead of you. For example, shrimp make a peculiar crunching noise on the bottom, and you can identify shrimp on the bottom. You can identify certain schools of fish. You can identify dolphins, some whales, that sort of sea life is usually fairly readily identifiable, and if you happen to be amongst a school of those sort of things, they may well black out the noise of the target that you're looking for some distance away.

Another interesting phenomenon, I was up in the Arctic and we could hear icebergs. It sounds like Alka-Seltzer, they're kind of fizzy. We could hear them, depending again on the water conditions, at ranges of ten or twelve or fourteen thousands yards, and that's why I became confident, even if it were foggy, that I could tell where an iceberg was. Now that doesn't mean a small piece of ice—I'm talking about a reasonably good-sized berg.

It can be dangerous navigationally in a submarine if you're in a part of the ocean that is not well charted, because it is extremely difficult to tell passively on your sonar where an underwater mountain peak might be, and I think that there have been cases in the American navy where they have been operating their nuclear submarines in areas which are not very frequently travelled by ships and are not that well charted—and they have in fact hit the bottom on certain occasions, the bottom being a mountain peak sticking up in the middle of the ocean which they haven't been able to detect. And that's an ever-present danger now, and if you were ever to hit a mountain like that hard enough to puncture the pressure hull, the sea would rush in and the hull would collapse inwardly. We're not exactly sure, but this is what may have happened to the submarine *Scorpion*."

AS SOON AS WE LEFT THE HARBOUR "You know, when I was the captain, like every other captain I know I preferred to go down as soon as we left the harbour, and we didn't want to surface again until we got right back in. It's far more comfortable; it's far easier to keep the submarine clean; it's far more comfortable for the crew, far easier for the cooks, it's just easier all around to

operate in the medium you were designed to operate in. On the
surface, you're very clumsy, very slow, very wet. You don't have a
proper bridge on a submarine, you just have a little tower, and it's
just very difficult to operate on the surface."

ELEVEN

Accidents

All Around the Bay... The Trena Louise... Knee Deep... A Sad Christmas Day... Up in the Spider Islands... Four Feet of Water... Landslide!... Seal Finger... Fish Fingers... Trussed Right Up... And the Sea Struck... A Man from Sambro... Somethin' Sticky... She'll Be Gone in Five Minutes... All Afire... She Burned for Days... A Good Tight Cabin Floor... An Hour in Lake Erie... Caught by a Stern Dragger... The Blue Wave

Disaster and death have been, and will be, inevitable events at sea and on the Great Lakes; so, too, are disaster and courageous survival. Calamities happen all the time, any time of year. The eerie part of it is that the sea seems capricious; it's almost as if, one month or one year, a kind of impersonal malevolence lashes out at fishing-boats, tugboats, any vessels on the water at the time.

. For example, 1955 became known as The Black Year on Lake Erie—three dead, at least seventeen hospitalized, and a half-million dollars in losses. The tug Ciscoe pitched and tossed in the worst storm in thirty years. At one point, a freak wave hit her and rushed through the entire length of the boat, bursting windows, twisting the superstructure, and sweeping one man overboard to his death. She survived a terrifying night, but next morning the engine died and a roaring wind pounded the helpless Ciscoe onto a sandbar. Tons of water smashed into the tug Beachcomber, layers of ice encrusted her, and after a hellish journey she managed to slip into a tiny harbour on Old Hen Island. The tug began to sink immediately, and Captain Fuller's ice-sheathed clothes had to be torn from his back so that he could escape through a window. The tug Scuffy II went aground and capsized off Point Pelee. The Beverly R. Goodison was pushed sideways a hundred feet by a single wave. A little more than a month later, a tremendous explosion tore apart the rear *deck of the small tug* Eau J. *One man died, and two others, suffering from severe burns and shock, spent an eternity in the freezing waters. They were rescued and survived. So it went.*

Fire, ferocious gales, freak accidents—the doomsday book of the sea will never be closed.

ALL AROUND THE BAY "We were camped about a mile away from where the fishing station was, and one of the shore hands was scared to go on the boat. He was frightened of any travel on a boat, wouldn't take a boat the short way. So he walked all around the bay, which was about three miles, in the curve, you see, and when he came to the fish station, they asked him to catch a line which was thrown from a skiff. And he fell into the lake, because the motor was goin', and the line got caught in the propeller, and he drowned right there."

THE *TRENA LOUISE* "We were fishing herring at the time in Barkley Sound and it was a disaster year for boats sinking and, you know, people drowning that year, losing fishermen. No explanation. They were all different, they were all a bit different. See, the *Trena Louise*, he had a lot of fish—we call it dryin' up the herring, you start drying up—and the strap broke and the net fell back into the water and then gave the fish a little room to move or something, so the fish just moved and pulled the boat over upsidedown.

Three boats went down that night. Within five hours."

KNEE DEEP "I had one occasion in the Bay of Fundy when I was fish dragging and I thought I was going to lose my father's boat. This particular day was a beautiful fine sunny afternoon, everything was normal, all kinds of vessels were out. But the wind was breezing up sou'west and I was towing to the easter and eventually I called my crew to haul back the net and about two minutes after, before they'd really had a chance to get out of their bunks and get onto their feet, we fetched up, the net caught on bottom.

Now, the wind and the sea had kept increasing and I was running an open boat, a fifty-four-foot open vessel, and being an open vessel and fetched up, the net caught on bottom, the seas were startin' to flop over the stern. Water was coming over our stern and I had a decision, a split decision, to make right there, seconds. Either we cut the cables and lose our net or, hopefully, cut one cable and she would turn around into the wind and into the sea—or we were gonna sink.

I hollered to one of my crewmen to cut the cable and he was reluctant to do so, and I grabbed the axe and cut one cable and at the same time ran back into the wheelhouse and turned the wheel and gave her the power, and she came around practically level with the water. We were well down in the water. With our fish and ice we had aboard and the water that was into her, we were above knee level deep in water.

Now at this point we were bucketing water out over the side but there was no more immediate danger. The only immediate danger then, in a sense, was that if enough water was seeping down into the bilge, it could get into the engine and ruin the engine. But between our pumps working properly and bucketing the water out of the afterpart of the vessel, we eventually got the water level down to where we were in no further danger."

A SAD CHRISTMAS DAY   "On the schooner *Bessemer*, the 25th of December was a fine morning and the trawl dories set out to trawl and came back aboard and had dinner. And there was no wind, it was quite moderate. But in the afternoon, after the dories were out fishin' there came up a snowstorm with winds up to thirty-five to fifty miles an hour, and we all cut our trawls and came aboard. All the dories got aboard, except the one. And it blowed quite hard. We laid around there and waited and searched until it got too much wind, we had to lay to, and after the breeze was over, there was no sight or nothin', we never seen them, and then we left for home.

It was a sad Christmas Day, very sad. The one man was a young man but he was doin' quite a lot of fishin' before this, and the older man was in his forties, he was an experienced fisherman, they were experienced fishermen both of them.

You know what it is, a gang of men, twenty-odd men working together day in and day out and then when you lose two like that, I don't know what you would call it, but there was no long stories or anything any more. Seems like it took the joy out of everything for a certain length of time."

UP IN THE SPIDER ISLANDS "When I was about nineteen I was up in the Spider Islands with my brother. We were out about, oh, eight miles, on a small boat that we had, it was only twenty-two feet long with not much freeboard. And a storm came up and it was a real bad one, the water was just flying like sand. We cut the nets and started off home.

On the way home I lay over the motor so it wouldn't get wet. We had no box over the motor. So I lay there to protect the coils in the motor. If it had quit we were finished, and I lay like that until we got to shore. The boat was half full of water when we got there.

The men on shore said there was no use looking for us, we were gone."

FOUR FEET OF WATER "One guy was found in the river in four feet of water, a friend of mine from Hodgson. He just fell overboard on the side of a big log barge and couldn't make it around the end and couldn't climb up the steep wall and they found him in four feet of water, and that's how he was drowned."

LANDSLIDE! "I've only really been scared once. That was a landslide in Knight's Inlet. That was the ultimate in scariness, being absolutely helpless, you know. I was about halfway up the inlet, and there's a very steep mountainside there, very steep. Rises three or four thousand feet, straight up, I mean absolutely sheer, and in the spring with the heavy rains and that, it is very dangerous. There's rocks on the move all the time, there's slides all over the place.

This was about May and I'd just finished pickin' up my net,

right close to the beach, maybe, oh, I would say I would probably be about twelve feet from the shore, which was straight up and down cliffs. And then all of a sudden there was just a machine-gun effect, right in front of me. Of course, I'm still at the stern of the boat pickin' up my buoy, you see, and the bow is out from the shore. So anyway this machine-gun stuff is right in front of me. It's so realistic, I even looked around and I thought, you know, somebody's doing this with a machine-gun. But no way. And then pretty soon the bigger stuff started to crash down—boulders and stuff.

Now, I had a boat there at that time which was very slow starting. It had what they call an air clutch and you put the clutch in and it would take its own little sweet time to get movin'. Ordinarily it wouldn't bother you too much, but this time it bothered you plenty because there was boulders crashing down by this time, the big stuff was coming now and lots of it. Now, my friend in another boat there, he was watchin' this, from about a half a mile away. He heard the rumble and roar and that and he saw me and he figured, that's it. I'm finished. I've had it. So did I! There was rocks every place.

It's a miracle, you know. They were coming down right by the boat and so much so that you felt they were on the boat. You know, you take something that hits right by a boat, it's so much vibration and that from the water, it's just like it's hit the boat. You're sure you've been hit. There's rocks in front, there's rocks on the side and boulders, you know, some as big as this table, and I'm right in it and I can't get out.

Well, I finally did, of course, but it seemed like hours, you know. But how I didn't get hit, I don't know. But I mean there was the most helpless feeling, to see these big things coming and I couldn't do a thing about it. You know, that's the worst, that's the most scariest thing ever. Gales or anything else, I mean you do have a fightin' chance but not with boulders, you've got no chance at all. Probably a thousand tons there must have been—and not one little pebble hit that boat."

SEAL FINGER "I lost my finger to the seal fishery . . . that's the seal finger. The doctor told me the seal grease gets in the pores of the skin and chews away the bone. The bone give out in my finger and I had to have it amputated. I spent twenty-one days in the hospital when I came back from the seal fishery and I had taken a penicillin needle every three hours, that would be eight a day for twenty-one days, 168 needles.

Your finger would get like a seal, and everyone would know it would be a seal finger—it looked like a seal. My finger got crooked, right red and glassy, swollen, and it looked like a seal. And if you would not have it amputated, you'd have the finger for the rest of your life crooked like that. It wasn't a direct pain, it was a pain gradually getting worse all the time."

FISH FINGERS "One day in 1948 while I was fishing, the fanbelt on the rotary pump run off, and just unthinking—I've done the same thing maybe a thousand times and got away with it—I reached down with my hand to run the belt on my big two fingers, right first and second finger went underneath the belt and it snapped the ends off both fingers. At the time, I was fishing trawl and the boat was about an hour out to sea. I had on a clean shirt, so I just took and tore the shirt up and wound it around my fingers to cut the blood off as much as I could. I was all alone, and I made my way to shore, took me about an hour to get in, and the storekeeper there had a truck, so I got him to drive me in to the hospital. It just felt like somebody had hit your fingers with a hammer. It didn't hurt at that time. I looked for the ends, they must've went overboard I guess, flew in the air and went overboard, but anyway we didn't find them.

About half an hour before I got into the hospital, when I was being driven in by the man in the truck, the feeling started to come back into my fingers and up my arm, and by the time I got to the hospital I was feeling pretty blue, I'll tell you that. I was feeling like as if I had a good seasick spell. When I had to sit around waiting for to git somebody, a doctor there to look after me, I was not in a very good mood at that time, I'm tellin' you. I was sittin' in the office there about three-quarters of an hour before a nurse come along and asked me what I was there for. After a while a woman came down from the office and she said, 'Well, who's gonna pay for this if we look after your fingers?' and

I said, 'Well, I've got about three hundred dollars in my pocket. I suppose that would do,' I says, 'to help get these fingers tied off so I won't bleed to death.' And she got kind of red in the face and apologized and about an hour later they took me up and they had a doctor there and he looked at them and he tied them up and he said, 'Next morning we'll take you up and cut some more off and haul the skin out and tie it down over the ends of them so we'll get some cover over your fingers.' I was in the hospital for seven days and I come home and I was laid up for about, oh, in about two weeks I was back in the boat fishin' again.

When I think back now to the fingers that I lost out there in the boat, I think there may be some fish that had a good piece of tasty meat for dinner at that time, and I never did catch the fish with the fingers in him anyway."

TRUSSED RIGHT UP   "My father and I had a boat sink under us. We were fairly close to shore at that time—but the undertow is very bad in a storm and we had a terrible fight with it. That was the first day of April that that happened, and the water was very cold. We managed to stay with the boat and work it towards the shore and unfortunately my father was wrapped up in the net. You see, just as soon as a boat sinks and you have a net in the boat, the floats automatically come up, eh, and the floats and lines all swirled around him, and his feet and legs were trussed right up, he couldn't move. His arms were free but he couldn't move, he couldn't do anything except cling with the boat. So I, with what strength I had, I worked the boat towards shore. When a wave came I'd help it towards shore and then when the wave left, the undertow would take ahold and all you could do was hold. So, eventually we got on the shore and he got straightened out of the net and then we lay on the beach and there was some sunshine and we thawed ourselves out, but the water was in the thirties, you know, the temperature would be in the thirties. Well, I suppose the total time we were in the water would be about half an hour but we weren't completely submerged all the time, eh? I think if we'd been completely in the water all the time we wouldn't have survived that long."

AND THE SEA STRUCK "Five o'clock that evening, I said, 'I must go back and get the weather report,' and I went from the fo'c's'le back to the wheelhouse, turned on the radio to get the weather report, and while I was there I looked out the window and I saw this great mountain up like that and I just grabbed hold and the sea struck and it ripped, took everything. It took the haulin' house off of us, lifted the wheelhouse where I was in, lifted the roof of the wheelhouse that I could see out through and upset everything. I was wet with blood runnin' from my ear. The boat was completely rolled over but she come back. The compass was upside down and back and everything was full of water. The engine couldn't start, the batteries was upset in the engine-room, and the lifeboats was gone.

She was full of water but we kept her afloat that night till the next afternoon and there still was gale winds and I was on deck. I had tablecloths and blankets, the hammer and saw up on deck to plug up holes and one of the guys out on deck said, 'There's a boat.' I dropped everything. The first fellow came to us, he couldn't put a dory off to do anything, so he sent a mayday out and first thing the plane was out and she dropped two life-rafts. We had a hell of a job to get 'em, they used to blow right upside down. We had one man with a broken leg aboard, we wrapped him up in these blankets and tied them up.

There was seven or eight boats got around us, and one boat laid on the windward side of us and he dropped a dory off and two men come down and took us off.

That night there was a warship comin' from Bermuda and he heard the message and he come back and picked us up. Ten o'clock they tried to get us but they smashed a lifeboat puttin' it over to come for us, so they waited till twelve o'clock, then they got one in the water and came and got us and brought us up."

A MAN FROM SAMBRO "We were down off of Cape Hatteras, North Carolina, one winter fishing, and sharks, you know, chewed all our gear up. It was all in pieces everywhere and we were looking for our gear, and a big sea hit across our boat, and nobody paid any attention to it.

About a half-hour afterwards one of the fellas come in and he

said, 'Where's Earl?' That was one of the crew members, and I
said, 'I don't know. He was here fifteen minutes ago. He came in
and asked me what the weather forecast was.' So we started to
look for him and we couldn't find him. He must have washed
overboard when the sea hit our boat.

Well, we retraced our steps, you know, went right back the way
we had just come, and we looked for him but couldn't find him. I
called the U.S. Coast Guard and within a half-hour they had a
plane out. We searched with four or five other fishing-boats in the
area but we never did find the fellow. So we lost a man. He was a
man from Sambro, he was married, he had four or five children,
only a young fella."

SOMETHIN' STICKY   "I was hurt one time scalloping, I have a
scar right there, you can see it. We was fishin' and we were gettin'
a few scallops and it was rough, and the winch was hoistin' a scallop rig in and he left too much slack go and the hook fell out. And
with the boat roll the tackle was swingin', heavy iron tackle it
was, and I went to turn to get out of the way, and my toe caught, I
couldn't get out of the way, and here come the tackle right at me.

I ducked, I dropped myself to try to get away from it, but I was
right in the way of it, you see. So the tackle caught me there and
cut a gash in my head, oh, probably about three inches. It didn't
knock me right out but it stunned me that I couldn't see and I
didn't know what I was doing, you see. So the damn tackle, after
hitting me, it kept going, and it was coming back at me again. So
this guy, he was hollerin' blue murder, you know, for me to get
out of the way. By this time the blood was running down in my
eyes but I started coming to my senses, but I couldn't see anyway,
and I can remember seeing a blur image and it looked like I could
see a hand on me. I reached and I got ahold of this guy's hand and
he gave me a yank and I got out of the way and the tackle just
missed me. It would have caught me right across here somewhere,
across the ribs, but he got me out of there. That just saved me, I
would have been a goner if it would have caught me there again.

So they took me back in the washroom, and they took some
warm water and they washed the blood away so you could see it.
He seen it was bad and he took a pair of scissors and he cut the

hair off, away from the cut, you see, and he says, 'What are we going to do to stop the bleedin'?' You know, it was a bad cut, it should have been stitched, but there was nobody there to put stitches in. So they took a whole bottle of Friar's Balsam and started dabbing, and I said, 'Don't frig around with putting a little bit on, dump it on,' so they dumped the whole damn bottle. That old Friar's Balsam is somethin' sticky, and it went all in through my hair, and I didn't care, I just wanted to get the blood stopped. And they put a bandage over it, and the blood kind of dried into the bandage, and it stopped bleeding. Otherwise I wouldn't't've been here.

We had three days yet to fish and they wanted me to go down and lay in my bunk, but I couldn't do that, I didn't feel I should do that, so I kept on working. Every time I used to bend over and pick up scallops—I used to try it—I used to bleed so bad, the blood would run down my eyes, and I couldn't see, so, for two watches I didn't bother to go out and pick any scallops up, you see, I just stayed back and shucked. As long as I was standing up straight, it didn't bother me—my head would hurt, I had a bloody headache, but it didn't bother me that much, it didn't bleed. And then during them two watches, it kinda healed some, and then the third watch, I was back in there picking up again.

And when I come in, I went to the doctor with it. 'What a mess, what a mess, what a mess,' he said. 'Oh, that Friar's Balsam in your hair, you'll never get it out, you'll have to cut it all off,' he said. Well, I washed it, and washed it, and washed it, and washed it, and—got it out after that."

SHE'LL BE GONE IN FIVE MINUTES "Me and my brother decided that we would run offshore into deeper water to find some more traps and when I did, my uncle came alongside just before we left and he said that gas was leaking out of his carbure-tor down into the bottom of his boat. Actually he should've headed for home that very time but he hauled a few more traps, and in going offshore to haul my own traps I happened to come across a buoy that I recognized that I hadn't hauled that day. So I stopped to haul that particular trap and my uncle happened to sail out of the fog and he shut his engine off and he said, 'I'm going home because I've got a real bad gas leak,' and then he reached and pressed his starter and when he did, his boat exploded into a great mass of flame.

I went alongside the boat and my uncle came aboard and sat on the stern. The man that was with him grabbed a bucket, he started bailing water on the fire, but being a gas fire they couldn't do anything with it. No doubt had I stayed very long my boat would've caught fire, but he and his man came aboard, and my uncle sat on the stern of the boat, he folded his hands and he said, 'She'll be gone in five minutes.' "

ALL AFIRE   "I had one boat that caught fire. We were scallopin' and at that time we had a gas engine and we carried spare gas in barrels on deck. Our tank run dry so we started to siphon gas over in the tank and we got it runnin' and started the engine back up, and went on and hoisted her drags and picked up her scallop and so on, and in the meantime this gas was still siphonin' in the tank and I guess we was careless, kinda forgot about it. And after we got our scallops picked up, one of the fellers lit a cigarette and threw the match overboard, and when he did we were all afire because the tank had run over and the gas was runnin' on deck and out in the water.

So the side was afire, and the water was afire alongside of us, and the deck was afire, and the top of the tank was afire. So we stopped the engine, took it out of gear, and that let the tide take the gas that was in the water just right away from us, so *that* fire didn't bother us, and we pushed the barrel overboard that the gas was runnin' out of and got clear of that, and then we started with a fire extinguisher and there was so much gas on deck that when you put it out in one place, in another place it was lit right back up again. So then we started bailin' water and we bailed enough water on deck that it washed the fire out through the scuttlers and all it did was scorch the side of the wheelhouse and scorch the paint on the side of the engine-house and things like that. It didn't do any damage, so we were kinda fortunate that time."

SHE BURNED FOR DAYS   "When we were down to British Guiana, the cat had kittens in the lifeboat, and someone threw the kittens overboard. The cat was going around crying on the ship and when we went to look for the kittens they were all gone. We wanted to know who'd thrown the kittens overboard and nobody would say who did it. Well, I said, that's a bad omen—something's going to happen.

This was on the *Canadian Navigator*, and she loaded some sugar and molasses, and somebody stole all the spuds off and we lived on rice coming home. In Trinidad she loaded some more sugar and stuff there—spices, coconuts—and she also loaded gasoline, drums of gasoline. In Barbados something happened, at twenty minutes after one in the afternoon. There was a big bang and we looked down and could see the beams that hold the hatches up, see them fly up and go down the hold amongst the tanks of gasoline. Of course, fire and smoke and everything was coming out.

I slid down the back stave of the mast and run fer to git the hoses out with the rest of the men and put it down the hold. That only lasted for about half an hour, then there were several explosions and first thing we know the whole bridge caught fire.

Six men were killed in the hold—stevedores. We didn't get the second fire out. The British Navy was in the harbour at the time and they made us get off the ship, abandon ship. The navy men came aboard and they slipped the chains, didn't have time to get the anchor up. And she drifted out just like she was sailing, flames burning, all the sugar and molasses burning beautifully. She burned for days and the captain used to go out with the one Canadian man-of-war every day and look at her. By and by, she rolled over off Martinique and sank. She had drifted for many, many miles and burned for a week before she rolled over and sank.

I certainly wish they hadn't thrown them kittens over the side."

A GOOD TIGHT CABIN FLOOR "Another occasion here when I was settin' lobster-traps openin' day of the season, I was going out, I had a load of lobster-traps aboard the boat. There was just enough room left for two men to stand, we were loaded right up, and I had an oil stove in the cuddy for'ard and I had lit it and it overflowed. I'd put too much oil in it, you see, and it couldn't burn, and as we went up on the sea and come down like that, she

went up. Flames comes up and she exploded and the whole front
end of the boat and the cabin all caught afire and the friend that
was with me, I told him, 'Get 'er as close to the rocks as you possibly can and we'll pile her up and get out of her if we can't get this
fire out.' So meantime he had hold of the wheel and he was
floatin' her in as close to the shore as he possibly could and I got
ahold of a bucket and then I had some canvas there and I wet it
down and I threw the canvas down over the cabin floor and I
smothered the fire out.

The only thing that I can see that saved our lives that time,
which saved us from being burnt completely, is that the oil was
on top of the cabin floor and I had a good tight cabin floor which
had an oilcloth on it, and the oil didn't get down through into the
bilge. If it hadda leaked down through in the floor and got into the
bilge and went back underneath the motor and everything, there
would've been no hope for us ever gettin' it out at all, because we
were loaded with traps and where we had to land was a big steep
cliff about a hundred feet high and it would've been a fifty-fifty
chance that we could have ever got out of the boat alive, the seas
were so great that it would've been a fifty-fifty chance. It was
quite hair-raisin' for a few minutes, now, I'll tell you, for a matter
of maybe five or ten minutes, quite a predicament to be in. We
were right off what we call the Highland Bluffs between Tiner's
Point and Negro Head at the time in the Bay of Fundy, and after
we got the fire extinguished we looked the situation over and
things didn't look too bad, so we continued on out and we set our
load of lobster-traps and come back in, picked up the second load
and went out to set the second load, so we completed our whole
set of settin' our traps that day.

It gave you a little bit to think about, all right, but this is stuff
that you run into every once in a while when you're fishing, these
little encounters with gettin' ashore on the rocks and things like
this, and we just take them into our stride as a fisherman. We
don't dwell on them. It'd be dark by the time we finished up that
night, and this had happened about ten o'clock in the morning."

AN HOUR IN LAKE ERIE   "There was a fella out of Port Burwell by the name of Martin and his boat rolled over just outside

the harbour in Burwell about three years ago and they all tied themselves to one of them life-rafts and the water temperature was fifty-five degrees and they drifted ashore. It took them about an hour to drift ashore, and the one guy died from exposure, just in the hour in fifty-five-degree water. And the captain of the boat, the Martin boy, I guess the doctor said another fifteen minutes or so and he would have been gone too."

CAUGHT BY A STERN DRAGGER "Sometimes when they're out there fishing for scallops they'll hook in another trawler's rakes. And occasionally they've hooked into nets of fishing draggers, the big stern draggers, and if they get into a fleet of the Russians—my husband has told me he's counted as many as seventy-five, eighty boats in a five-mile area, with radar—if you get into a draft of boats like that, you don't know which way to turn.

My husband did experience being hauled right in against a stern dragger, and I guess they were nearly smashed to pieces. It hauled the boat right up against the stern. They had a terrible time trying to clear it, because the stern-dragger fellow didn't want to cut and lose all his nets. I guess they have quite a value there, too, probably more than the rakes, and there's thousands of dollars' value in a rake and the gear."

THE *BLUE WAVE* "My home town, Grand Bank, is known as the Town of Widows. And in 1959 my sister became one of them. It was one of the great tragedies of Grand Bank, one of the many tragedies, and we were all a part of it because my brother-in-law was lost at sea and he left seven children.

His name was Charlie Walters, captain of a trawler called the *Blue Wave*, a very talented man musically and kind of my brother in a way—when he married my sister I was a very young boy and he filled a gap. He had been a captain since he was nineteen.

They had gone out from Grand Bank dragging for fish for the Bonavista Cold Storage Plant there in the middle of the winter, and on the night of February 9, 1959, he and fifteen other men were lost. The *Blue Wave* capsized about thirty-five miles off Cape St. Mary, which is on the south-east tip of Newfoundland. I was teaching school in Western Newfoundland, a little place called Woody Point, and I went to a social event in there that evening, and a friend of mine said: 'They had a terrible accident down your way.' And I looked at him and said: 'Yes, the *Blue Wave* was lost this morning with all hands. And my brother-in-law was the captain.' I had not heard anything about the story until I said that.

What prompted that? I'll tell you. I'd gone to bed on Sunday evening, the previous evening, about eleven o'clock, and about five to five Monday morning I woke up. My bed was facing a window and Charlie was standing in front of the window. And I had a conversation with him and the conversation went this way—after twenty years I can still remember it verbatim. He said: 'I've got to leave you and I want you to promise me something.' I said: 'Sure, Charlie, anything. What is it?' He said: 'I want you to make sure that Claire and the kids are going to be all right.' And I said: 'Don't worry about it,' and I blinked and he was gone.

Okay. Fourteen hours later, I'm told that an accident has happened and immediately I knew, I knew what had happened. I sent a telegram home—it was simultaneous—I sent the telegram and they were sending one to me telling me that this had happened, and I left to go home. My dad came down to meet me in Goobies, the place where the train came through, which was the only connection to the Burin Peninsula. When I stepped off the train, Dad was there, and he hugged me and started to cry. I had no sense that he was embarrassed by it. It didn't take him long to regain his composure, but it was devastating to me. I'd never seen him cry before.

A snowstorm came and we just couldn't make it the 110 miles up the Burin Peninsula to get home to see my sister whose husband was lost. But the school year ended in July and eventually I got home. Claire and I had fought from the time I was born, I'm sure from the time I could talk; we constantly fought—not that we disliked each other, it was just a thing in the family. And I walked into her house and of course she started to cry and so did I. And we started to talk about it. And she said: 'Did you see anything the night they were lost?' I said: 'Why do you ask?' She said: 'Because I did.' I said: 'Tell me . . . tell me what you saw.' She had seen exactly the same kind of apparition that I saw with one exception.

He told her that I would look after them, and he bent down to kiss her, and when she opened her eyes he was gone.

The other interesting thing about that is that when he left to go on that trip, he got up about four o'clock on the Monday morning, a week before, and they had breakfast together. And he went up—and he had seven children, from three months to nine years—and he kissed them all and he came down and he kissed her, went out and closed the door, and came back and did the whole process again. And she said she had the funniest feeling that she had seen him for the last time when he left the house. My sister was thirty-six then and she never remarried. Many of these women never remarried. There's something about losing a husband at sea that leaves a scar that I don't know if time ever heals.

On that particular *Blue Wave*, there was one lady, a Mrs. Baker, who lost a husband, a son, two brothers, two son-in-laws, and two first cousins, on the one ship. And the town was in mourning. They wore black, all black, an ancient tradition came over from Devonshire or in some cases from Spain, because a lot of the people that live in that area of Newfoundland are of Spanish descent, Devonshire descent. It was like the whole town had suddenly gone into mourning again. And I've heard some stories of disasters in other parts of this country, of Springhill and Nova Scotia mine disasters, and tragedies elsewhere, and we relate very, very well to these things. We understand the agony and the hell and the terror. You know what it's like to wonder for weeks on end whether your husband or your father is ever going to come home again—they're on trawlers, or bankers as they used to be, or they'd go to a port, take over salt fish in the twenties and thirties, and bring back salt. Some of these ships never showed up again.

The women would worry; you could see time etched in their faces, E. J. Pratt said it that way, I think, in one of his poems. Incredible, you could see the sea and the effect of it, just like granite on their faces. And when the truth finally did come, they were never coming back, there was the quiet, passive acceptance of the reality of the sea."

TWELVE

Partners to the Men

*Partners to the Men... Enough Crying... I'd Just Lay There and Shiver
... You Just Know the Boat's Out There... Spyglasses on the Hill... My
Mother Ran the House... Days Alone... Pure Hell... It Bothered Her...
Their Father Is Away So Much... The Fisherman's Daughter... The
Boat My Husband's On... A Deaf Ear Around the House... Good for
Both of Them... Good To Have Him Home, And... A Big Drastic
Change... Sticking By Their Men... Playing Around... Laying Around
... Six Months Married... A Girl in Every Port*

W hen I met fishermen's wives, it was always at their
homes. They might be there with the children and the
husband far out at sea, or the husbands might be with them, or,
infrequently, the room would be full of family and friends. A few
of them had gone fishing with their husbands in the past, and one
cheerful Newfoundland wife, Doreen Noseworthy, still heads for
the fishing grounds three days a week with her husband. They all
talked to me frankly.

The wives of the old-time fishermen had grown up knowing
full well the furies that faced them—the loneliness, the sleepless
nights, the frantic worry when a gale howled around the house.
Their mothers and their grandmothers had lived the same lives
of frustration and despair. The sea was a widow-maker; Cassie
Brown's phrase "a community of widows" was an apt description for many fishing communities.

Wives could face their situation stoically, or they could beg
their husbands to leave the sea.

A handful of the wives I met were bitter. A few were glad to
see their husbands take off—they didn't want them around that
much anyway. As this chapter shows, opinions on marrying a
seaman—and on the faithfulness of seamen and their wives—
differ dramatically.

However, it's not a dismal picture. There will always be plenty

of hearty, healthy girls to marry young fishermen who, them-
selves, usually are an attractive, capable, virile lot. There'll also
be plenty of kids coming along who, in the words of the bawdy
old song, "will climb the riggin' like their daddies used to do".

PARTNERS TO THE MEN   "The women were partners to the
men. They worried even just for one day out, a storm would come
up and they would really be worried. And sometimes, you'd see
the women down on the headland to see if they were coming in,
and they'd be asking: 'Are they in yet?' or 'Did you see Jack?' or
'Did you see so-and-so?' 'Where are they?' They were concerned,
definitely concerned, if a storm would suddenly come up. You'd
see the wrinkles in their brow from worrying.

But the whole family worried, and the whole community worried if people got caught out in a storm. They would all be looking, and if you got a lot of fog and you're out and they rung the
church bell or something to give you a warning, you know to
come in.

And if you were out sealing and were on the ice, they'd put the
flag up or something: 'The ice is moving off shore, come on in.'
And you watch. So you'd be working at something and watching,
always watching. This is how you survive."

ENOUGH CRYING   "I remember well my grandfather telling my
grandmother never to cry for him once he'd gone. She had done
enough crying while he was still alive, worrying about him being
on the high seas.

But anyway, once my grandfather had died—he was eighty-six
when he died—she cried anyway, so she disregarded his wishes."

I'D JUST LAY THERE AND SHIVER   "My father was a skipper,
he had a Labrador schooner. My mother was always worried,
whenever he was at sea she was worried. Well I know she walked

the floor and looked through the window, all night long she'd be up, from one window to the other, and she'd tell us it was a terrible night, and I wonder where is Dad through the night.

I married a man who was also a skipper... Albert Blackwood. I felt the same way my mother did. I worried an awful lot. I followed the same pattern she did. I was up nights and watched, looking through the window. At nights it was worse than the day. You would seem to notice it more, you'd hear the wind howling more at night than you would during the day. You'd look at the weather to see if it was improving or getting worse, or you'd just watch if they were out to sea to catch a glimpse of them coming home.

I can remember one time in Safe Harbour I knew he was ready to leave St. John's, and, oh, it blew a blizzard, and rained all night. So when I looked through the window in the morning, the waves were just rolling in the sea, the breakers were everywhere, and there was no sign of anything. I could see the sea just rolling in on the land, so I watched and watched and I saw a schooner coming in. First I thought it was him, but it wasn't, it was another schooner from Safe Harbour. I was disappointed, really disappointed, but then I was happy that these people were safe. And then, not far behind, I saw him coming.

I didn't sleep all night especially when it was a storm; I'd just lay there and shiver, and I used to be there alone with just small children in the house ... nobody to speak to. It was hard on my nerves, I tell you I used to be so upset all the time. I think it was because of my worrying that he gave up on the water and came ashore, because I'd be always sayin', 'Why don't you give up and come ashore, get something to do ashore?'

I didn't look at the sea as an enemy, but I don't know, I always worried, I thought of things that could happen. The fire could take place on the boat, even if it wasn't stormy. And in a storm, they could run ashore in the fog... well everything went through your mind, and when he come in, I'd forget about it. I'd be happy and forget about it."

YOU JUST KNOW THE BOAT'S OUT THERE "You never really get used to the fact that he's away in bad weather. If there's gale warnings given, marine warnings on the TV or radio, you do worry. I have had sleepless nights that I have woke up ten, twelve times. You hear the wind howling here; you just know the boat's out there tossing and they're only ninety to a hundred feet long, and you can just imagine the torrents of water that pile in, just like mountains, really. You just keep waking up."

SPYGLASSES ON THE HILL   "I wouldn't say the women would worry too much about us. You know, they expect us when the time come around, September, and usually in the small places they would have spyglasses and they go up on the hill and they watch the vessels coming up, and they would know the different vessels."

MY MOTHER RAN THE HOUSE   "The women were the business managers in a lot of ways. A lot of people don't realize that, but my mother ran the house. She was boss of the house; most of the women that I knew in Grand Bank were the boss in the house. They looked after the money. The fisherman brought it home, gave it to his wife; she made sure that the supplies were in, the food was there, the family was clothed—there was enough to bury them. That was the important thing. The house was kept inside in good repair, and the men were responsible for the exterior. They had the children, they brought them up. Father was the disciplinarian; mother was the person they confided in. She was the Coffee Dan; father was the Governor.

And that was true in our home—it was true in many, many of the homes of the people that I knew ... not to say that the fathers weren't approachable or you couldn't communicate with them, but there was something austere about the Newfoundland men as opposed to the women. But they were as strong-willed and as full of fun as the men ever were, and I think in many cases were a lot stronger emotionally than the men."

DAYS ALONE   "Well, I would just have to say that any woman intending to marry a fisherman, she'd have to be very, very sure that she was capable of handling days alone and trusting her man away from home. Otherwise she won't be very happy about it. Be very self-reliant. That's what you have to be."

PURE HELL "We were married in 1967—and in March of 1968 we had our first baby girl, and she took ill in May, and Russell was at home when we'd taken her to the children's hospital, and about three days after he had gone back to sea, she became very seriously sick, and the boat had to be called home to port. I mean, you could imagine the anxious moments, it takes seventeen to eighteen hours for the boat to get home.

Well, then in '69 the whole thing was repeated again. We had a second child in April, and this child was watched very carefully. We had a few anxious moments with it because we looked for the same things to happen, and, unfortunately enough, they did, in October, and my husband was again at sea when the little boy had to be taken to hospital. And while he was in hospital, once again my husband had to be called back from sea, and this time they were fishing on St. Pierre bank, down handy to Newfoundland. They took him to Louisburg, which was the handiest port, and I had to drive there to pick him up, which was a good six-, seven-hour drive from Lunenburg. My sister had gone with me, and once again, you could imagine what a trip it was to come back, and he had just been back, oh, he was back I guess about a week—a week to ten days—and that baby passed away, too.

Those eight to ten days were just pure hell, so I mean this is another ordeal to go through as a fisherman's wife; you're alone with a sick child, and the agony of it. But also, on the other hand, your husband's at sea, and he doesn't know if it's worse or getting better; you know, he's there without word at all. It's even harder on the fisherman in a way, because he's out there not knowing anything."

IT BOTHERED HER "I look back on 'em as good years. The only thing that bothers me a little bit is that I was away from Winnipeg quite a bit and I was married when I was twenty-one and I left my wife every time I went on one of these trips. It bothered her and it bothered myself, plus the fact that she brought up my in all these years. But outside of that I ... of it."

...AWAY SO MUCH "The children are six ...'re understanding more where he is, but ...er five, my little girl used to think he was ...cked and aboard the boat there.

... every man; they seem to have a liking for ...hat their father is away so much. Especially ...s to men very easily, she just seems to adore ...d I attribute this to the fact that her father is ... was under two, she called just about every ... She'd just look at a man on the street, and it ...sing at times."

... DAUGHTER "I am the daughter of a ... all his life until he retired, oh, when he was ...d say. We lived in Lunenburg all our married life. ... ve been married eleven years and Russell has fished ever since we've been married. And before we were married I knew he was a fisherman, and I knew it was going to be a lonesome life. I understood this and my dad, on one occasion, did say to my husband, if he thought anything of me he wouldn't go to sea. And that struck pretty hard at him and he discussed it with me quite a bit, and after about five years of marriage I tried to persuade him to get a land job, a job on land. But the big thing with fishing is the money. Where on land can you work and make the wages that they make? I didn't argue with him. I just said I preferred to have him on land, especially with small children. And he said, 'Well, where can I make this much money on land?' He didn't have too many choices."

THE BOAT MY HUSBAND'S ON "My husband's a scallop fisherman. He's mate, which means he spends most of his time in the wheelhouse. He's home more often, especially the last two years, than he has been. When we were first married they were gone fourteen days routinely. They stayed out to sea, no matter how many scallops they caught. Now the government has the quota, which brings them in sooner, and they're home a bit more often.

You don't like to see your husband go away angry, or you don't like to argue with him just before he's gone to sea, because, well, let's face it, you never know whether he's going to return or not. That's just a fact of life, I mean, you just don't like to think about it, because it would drive you crazy if you did.

But this is one of the things you think about, and I can't watch a boat leave the harbour, especially the boat my husband's on. I never stay on the wharf when my husband is going away the day he sets sail; well, I shouldn't say sets sail, but the day they leave for the fishing banks I never stay on the wharf to see the boat back out and leave. I just, I just can't do it. I'll drive him down to the wharf and I'll give him a kiss goodbye right there, and I'll leave for home. We leave right then and there."

A DEAF EAR AROUND THE HOUSE "A fisherman's wife hasn't got the easiest problem in the world. She is left at home to look after the kids and look after the house, look after everything while the man is away fishing, and definitely she is going to worry about him, whether he's safe, whether he's in trouble, or what takes place while he's not at home or while he's not around to account for himself. There has been times known, I guess, that in some areas fishermen's wives is known to come down with mental strain and end up in a mental hospital. It has been known that there is high-strung women that will get to the stage that they'll continually worry on top of worry that it will put them in the position where they have to have medical treatment.

But I don't have that trouble with my wife. I don't know sometimes when she knows I'm out whether I'm out fishing or whether I'm ashore or not because I've got a pretty deaf ear around the house anyway and she might talk sometimes for half an hour before I hear what she says, and if I don't want to hear it, I don't hear it. So this is the way I've been livin' for this last thirty-three years and it seems to work out all right."

GOOD FOR BOTH OF THEM "Actually that's why a lot of fellows go to sea. You know, a couple of days home with the wife is just enough. A few days away is good for both of them, you know, and then they have a nice time for a few days and then they get away again."

GOOD TO HAVE HIM HOME, AND... "Yeah, well I'm a fisherman's wife and sometimes, you know, he's away for two months at a time fishing. It's always good to have him home, and it's good to see him go, too. He needs to be away on his own; we get on each other's nerves."

A BIG DRASTIC CHANGE "A lot of young fellas today, now, in the last few years, that's going fishing, they've been married before they started fishing, and it never worked out, they split up. They couldn't take it, they wasn't used to it, you see, and it was a big change. But the guy that wants to really hang on is a guy that is fishin', then he goes and gets a girl and gets married. Kinda lasts, I think, because she's brought into the fishin', you see, it's something she gets used to right from the start. But, when you are married for a couple of years, then it's a big drastic change, you see, there's a big change.

There's women fishing inshore, on the inshore boats, just the odd one that goes out and fishes with her husband, you know. And probably you take down here in Blue Rock, there's a fisherman down there, his wife goes out with him, I think, just about every day, helps him to haul his nets. She looks pretty healthy, ha, ha, ha. She looks really healthy."

STICKING BY THEIR MEN "I know some fellows that spend as much as ten months away fishing but then the big mistake they make is, when they come they spend the two months that they're home in the bars, and the woman doesn't get to see them anyhow. So the next thing, they're out looking for something that can be around a little more regularly.

In Steveston we have a very large Japanese population and the Japanese women are exactly opposite to this. They stick right by their men and they don't have this problem. They are out at sea for long times as we are but when they come home they still have their families and their house, and their women are still there

waiting for them. You don't have them messing around like Cau-
casian women will do, although I'm not condemning women at all
because some women have a need that they feel has to be satisfied
all the time, and then there's other women that are capable of
sticking by their men."

PLAYING AROUND   "I think it was a very small minority of fellas that played around when they were away from home, the
majority of them were pretty darn solid guys, at least the ones that
I had ever been mixed up with, and they were true to their wives
and their families. Sure, there's no doubt about it there was some
of it went on, but I think nowadays there probably will be more
fishermen's wives playing around, yes I do, because it's just a
totally different picture today than it was years ago. We were
pretty staid individuals, the old fishermen and their wives, and
some of them were pretty religious, you know, and they were, you
know, pretty solid."

LAYING AROUND   "Some women just can't do without being
with a man for long periods of time, and they do cheat on their
husbands, and eventually, I guess, they will find out, and it will be
the cause of a marriage break-up. I can easily see this happening.
Not necessarily younger women—I'd say women of all ages. And
then, some just aren't satisfied to live alone, or even after their
children, say, are grown and gone, it would get pretty lonesome
then. I mean, I have that yet to face. But then I would think that I
would have a job or a part-time job myself to keep myself busy.

I would say there's quite a percentage of fishermen's wives
have boyfriends while their men are at sea. I don't like to point a
finger on any great number, but I'd be safe to say a third of them,
because I know personally quite a few, and, oddly enough to say,
in quite a few cases the men know it, and so it just doesn't make
too much trouble, which I think is quite foolish, really, on their
behalf. Why should they work and bring home the money, and
build a house and supply the food and furnishings for someone
else to live in them? Oddly enough, some of these men that lay
around with the fishermen's wives don't even have jobs, they just
sponge off the fishermen. I know of two different situations where

the men will move right in with the wife, and the fisherman will go to sea, bring home the money, just drink it up and have a big party while he's on land, and they seem to accept it. I mean, I can't see it myself. I know one thing, my husband wouldn't accept it; I'd be one of the ones that'd be kicked out. But it is done."

SIX MONTHS MARRIED   "At Port-aux-Basques, when the men go to sea, they'll be out at sea for a full month and then home for a month, so when the wives are asked if they're married, if they have boyfriends when their husbands aren't there, they'll say yes, they're six months married."

A GIRL IN EVERY PORT   "This old saying about a sailor that he's had a girl in every port, well, I think it's quite true. It's a good variety. When you're sailing around you've probably been to sea for two or three weeks and you get into a port, usually the first thing is either you go look for a girl or go look for a bottle of booze and both of those together. So I've had some good times. I was in the Navy on North Atlantic convoy duty for three years and nine months, then in the merchant ships—to Rotterdam, Antwerp, London, Liverpool, down to Italy, and down the Med. I'll truthfully tell you that I've had some experiences being in different ports and some places we've been in that wouldn't be very good to put in the book or very good to put on tape. It'd make good readin' but a lot of people mightn't agree with it, though —but the experiences that I've had!

We run into Rotterdam and Antwerp and them places, well, that was right after the war, in 1946 and '47. Well, the country was all blew to pieces and there was nothing there that you could—there was lots of girls there and lots of, well, lots of booze, but anything else, you couldn't. I've seen me walk into a place over in Belgium, and for a package of cigarettes you could get anything you wanted in the store. You could get a quart of liquor sometimes for a package of cigarettes. They didn't have no cigarettes and a pocket comb, well, it was worth about two or three dollars' worth of drinks of beer because they couldn't buy it. And one of our fellows aboard the ship used to carry a good supply of silk stockings and women's pants, which was verboten, and any night at all he had one or two of them lookin' after him.

Antwerp is right on the border of France and we always took the bus and went out to Paris for a weekend. Two or three of the crew would go out there and we'd get a room in a hotel and we usually used the bathtub to keep the booze in. We never took too many baths, but we poured the water in the bathtub and kept the booze in there and you wouldn't be there very long and there'd be some girl come up to the door and ask you if you weren't looking for some entertainment, and bein' as a sailor away from home you always were lookin' for entertainment and we usually took in all the entertainment that was offered, and maybe a lot that wasn't offered."

THIRTEEN

Towing and Being Towed

A Tugboat Master... Pushing Down the Mackenzie... Sandbars on the Athabasca... Everybody Was Working... Anything Can Happen Aboard Here... Towing Coal... Surging on the Line... The Island Sovereign and the Sudbury II... Davis Rafts in the Hecate Straits... Breaking Up... Holding Up for Weather... Torpedoes from a Log Boom... A Barge on the Rampage... In the Beachcombing Business... Sinking the Barge... Being Towed—and Not Being Towed... Tugs Versus Nets... Towboat Men and Fishermen... Shotgun

T ugboats are tough and the men who command them are resourceful. I have a portfolio of maps, lent me by Stan Mortensen, water-stained and worn, forty-two pages of them, showing every twist and turn as well as the shifting sandbars and the islands of the great Mackenzie River. I think Stan made those charts himself, or had a hand in them. Thumbing through them, all the way from Great Slave Lake to the Beaufort Sea, on a scale of two miles to one inch, I find that these primitive maps have a stark quality that makes you wonder how in the world a pioneer tugboat captain like Stan Mortensen ever managed to push loaded barges 2,514 miles down that tortuous, often very shallow river.

The map references recreate the pioneer era. Here, going down-river, are some of them: "cabin", "Indian cabins", "Cache Island", "this channel usually buoyed", "boulders", "Ghost Island", "small rapids", "shallow with rocks", "submerged rocks", "steep banks", "Old Fort Island", "valley banks rise to 300 feet", "old coal mine", "very flat along this section", "keep close to shore", "keep tall tree and point in line to clear rock", "The Ramparts", "Indian grave", and, then, incredibly, "Little Chicago", "trading post", and, finally, "Tuktoyaktuk" and the Beaufort Sea.

Tugboats ranged far out to sea to go to the aid of ships in dis-

179

tress; they towed log booms through the treacherous Hecate Straits off the Queen Charlotte Islands; they got into heavy seas and lost their tow; and tugboat captains, as I say elsewhere, engaged in continuing guerrilla warfare with fishermen whose nets snarled their propellers.

Scrappy little tugs are still around and I hope always will be, but the dangerous days in the logging business, when the small tugs did all the towing, are over. It's a long way from a little tug to the Kingcome Navigation Company's Haida Monarch, designed by a North Vancouver firm and launched in 1974. The Haida Monarch is 423 feet long and is the world's first self-propelled, self-dumping log carrier. Loading cranes lift the logs aboard, and the ship tilts to dump the logs. At a mill, logs can be unloaded in an hour, instead of the days that were needed to break up a Davis raft. The Haida Monarch—and there is now a newer version of her—shows how quickly the technology of seagoing industrial-use vessels can advance under the prod of necessity.

A TUGBOAT MASTER   "The tugboats, they're a very interesting job. I'd stay on the tugboats if it was my choice. I think a tugboat master is the most satisfying job that any man can do, any seaman, because of the different variety of things you run into. There's no stabilized base to it. You're doing everything. You're moving barges, you're towing ships, you're assisting in undocking and docking ships, you're towing barges coast-wise, and there's just no limit to the things that you could be involved in from day to day or month to month."

PUSHING DOWN THE MACKENZIE   "The Mackenzie River is one thousand and eighty-six miles inclusive, that's of navigable water straight down to just below Reindeer Station. At the Sans Sault Rapids it's only a hundred and twenty feet wide, other places it's five miles wide. And it can be three to three hundred feet deep.

On the Mackenzie we didn't pull barges, we pushed 'em. We used tugs with a pushing bow on 'em and you'd secure yourself with your bow inside of what we call the paul-posts or the pushing-posts in the back of the barge and your bow fits inside of these two hardwood posts and then you run your wires from port and starboard sides of your hull, and the wire goes onto the bollards and sterns of the barges. For four barges you'd add one on each side of the tug, and for six there'd be two on each side, and so on.

So that's your first barge, dead ahead, then your next barge would be dead ahead of that. Your first barge has a six-by-twelve bow-piece that fits into the pushing-posts on the barge ahead, the same as a tug fits. Steering is not as hard as it looks, really. Going down-river is a little more difficult to turn than going up-river. Down-river you have the flow of the current and you have the weight of the barges. Like in the rapids, in some rapids it would be virtually impossible to swing eight barges and six barges, so you'd break down to three barges. But, to turn these barges, these ships are all twin-screw, some are triple-screw, and they have tremendous power and they have four rudders on these tugs.

Say you were gonna turn to the right, which is starboard; you would stop your starboard engine and leave your port engine full ahead and your starboard engine full astern, which would give it the turning motion that way, and vice-versa to turn it the opposite direction. Throw one astern and one full ahead and that will turn your barges, pivot them right around in a circle for you."

SANDBARS ON THE ATHABASCA "The end of steel was at Waterways, Alberta, which was approximately three miles south of the present town of Fort McMurray. These fish had to be taken across Lake Athabasca, approximately eighty miles, and then up the Athabasca River, another hundred and eighty miles, so you're looking at approximately two hundred and sixty miles of marine travel to get these fish to the railroad. And in the course of the years, boats had to be built, tugboats put on the river with barges which had to be refrigerated to keep the fish cool so they wouldn't spoil.

The Athabasca River was treacherous due to the fact that there was low water-cycle years those days, and there was quite a few sandbars. You used to get piled up in the sandbars, and it would take you quite a while to get off them, but it never really hurt any equipment. If we had a two- or three-barge tow, normally one barge might be loaded heavier than the other, and of course if it hit the sandbar it would come to a stop; the other two barges would still be floating and their momentum would break the line and they would maybe go drifting down the river and get hung up on other sandbars. If the tug happened to get stuck, all you could do is keep going in forward position or reverse position. If that didn't help, you just more or less turn the engines in slow speed and dig a hole with the wash of the prop and then keep backing into this hole and dig yourself out to the main channel, which may take you three hours. Or you could spend three days too.

But there was a very good esprit de corps on the river. If anybody was hung up badly, you more or less tied up your tow and then went and helped the other fellow get off, because sooner or later they were going to have to help you get off. So this way, everybody didn't get hung up too long."

EVERYBODY WAS WORKING   "On a tug, usually at that time you would have the skipper, the mate, two engineers, first and second engineer, and two deckhands and a cook, and some of them had an oiler too. There were firemen at that time. So there'd be a deck-hand and the mate in the wheelhouse at one time and the next watch'd be the skipper and the deck-hand. But many times the skipper would take the wheel or the mate would take the wheel and the deck-hand would be out painting or, you know, doing these kinds of things.

Plus when you were tying up, everybody was working then. You were tying up the barges and at that time you had big couplers between the barges, ten-inch manilla rope about a hundred feet long and then big wires on the end."

ANYTHING CAN HAPPEN ABOARD HERE   "I hadn't been with the towboat company very long when they called me up one day and said, 'We have a ticket for you at the airport, we're sending you to Goose Bay, Labrador.' I was to pick up a tug that was there in Goose Bay and bring her to Halifax. 'You'll be gone two weeks,' he told me and I'll never forget those words. That was the longest goldarn two weeks that I've ever spent in my life.

I got in Goose Bay and we got the tug, and we left Goose Bay about three o'clock in the afternoon. Around the middle of November up the Labrador coast the weather in that area is getting pretty snooty, let me tell you. But it was a beautiful night that night, and we got out of Goose Bay out into the Labrador Sea. There was a gentle rolling swell when we got out, you know, but nothing ravishing or anything and we were headed for Hare Bay, Newfoundland. So anyway, we got going along and we got down as far as Battle Harbour when we ran into a snowstorm. The idea was to shelter. Now, we had a chart of Battle Harbour but there was a piece missing. The chart didn't take in where we had to go, so we had to go blind in around a cape there for about a half an hour, and it's one of the most eerie experiences that I've had. Battle Harbour itself is a very narrow channel going in there. If something happened there and you went broadside your stem would be in the cliffs on one side and your stern in the cliffs on the other, it's that narrow. It was snowing and you could see very, very little, but we got in all right, without grazing anything, which was a miracle. We got her in and got her tied up.

Now, we didn't know what to expect when we got in there. We could see that there was houses up along inside but not a light, not a dog barking, not a bird, nothing, just absolutely nothing. So, we were wondering about this, but it was late at night so we just turned in and had a little rest. We got up the next morning and here's a small community with houses, oh, I would estimate around twenty-five or thirty homes there, drapes and everything up to the windows, but not a soul there. It was just the same as a ghost town, really. It was a feeling that is hard to describe, it seemed like everybody had just deserted the place, you know, you had a feeling that you were in another world. We didn't know at the time that Battle Harbour is a place that the fishermen go and they fish in the summertime and in the winter they pull up stakes and go back to the mainland.

But anyway, the next day it was still blowing hard so we were still stormbound, so we went up looking around. We'd go around, we'd look into the windows of the houses, and radios and every-thing sit up there, you know, they had those battery radios, eh, but the doors are all nailed up, so of course we didn't want to van-dalize any of the homes. So we went to the church. I don't remem-ber what denomination the church was, but they had the church door locked and they had a key hanging right beside the lock, so of course we opened her up and we went in. They had a little organ there and our second engineer used to play the organ so he played the organ for a little while in the church and there was a collection plate there with some money in it, and we took up a lit-tle collection up amongst ourselves and put it in the plate.

From there we went to the cemetery and we were looking at the cemetery at some of the headstones and it was very, very interest-ing. You know that place dated back to the 1800s. In that little cemetery there was some headstones back in the 1800s.

So anyway, after a day and a half or so there stormbound, we got under way and got out of there. There was no problem getting out of the channel because it was daylight and we could see where we were going and we had a very pleasant trip from there down to St. Anthony. And then we went and we picked up a barge in a place called Main Brook, which is about thirty miles from St. Anthony.

Usually when we pick up a barge we have a surveyor, a marine surveyor that comes down and signs papers saying that the barge is okay, it's seaworthy in other words, but up there we just had orders to go in and pick up the barge and tow her out. So, I didn't see no marine surveyor. I didn't know what the hell we were tow-ing, so we had no choice but to pick it up, our orders were to pick it up so we picked it up. The barge was a fair-sized barge, it was about a hundred feet long or hundred and twenty feet long, some-thing like that. So, we left with it.

Everything going smoothly we got up around Cape Bauld, that's the most northerly point in Newfoundland. We got up around Cape Bauld and we hauled her down for Cape Norman and the winds started to breeze up to the sou'west, right head-on. So the barge was rising and falling in the swell, eh, and by the time we got to Cape Norman she was ascreech in a gale wind and the barge was really working, coming up and falling down in the swell.

After we passed Cape Norman it started to snow. Now, we were towing the barge a thousand feet beyond us and I didn't see the barge no more until we got down off of Bay of Islands, which is outside of Corner Brook, and I could notice the tow-rope was moving back and forth very slowly and when that happens there's something wrong back with the tow, you see. I said to the chief engineer that morning, I said, 'There's something wrong back there,' I said, 'there's no way we can find it out,' you know, you can't stop and take in the towline, it takes too long.

About an hour later the snow slacked up a little and we could see the barge for the first time in about thirty-six hours and here, the damn thing, the water was shovelling right in over the top of it and going right back over it. In other words, the damn thing was sinking. I very quickly gave the orders to haul her into the Bay of Islands or Corner Brook. We were about thirty miles from Corner Brook I figure at that time and I had to slow down because when we slowed down it would bring the barge up a little. So, I slacked up on her, reduced speed, and the barge came up a little bit, and I radioed in and I told them what trouble we were having and they arranged to have one of the pulp tugs here in Corner Brook to stand by and meet us out as far as he could.

We could see her settling in the water more and more all the time and it was a race against time to get her in there, you see. I had a fella standing by the towline to cut it in case she sank. So, anyway, we got her in there and the small tug came and took over and they took her up to Humber Mouth, which is a cove up on the northern side of Corner Brook there and they beached her. I would estimate another twenty minutes and she would have sunk.

I didn't feel like coming out of there, the hell with it, and although they told me they wanted the tug in Stephenville I told them they were going to have to wait. So we stayed in Corner Brook that night, and the next day it was still blowing hard. But we came out the next day and we came on to Stephenville with the idea that we were going to take the tug off charter there and come on home to Halifax. But lo and behold when we got to

Stephenville they had other news for us. They had a barge waiting there for us to take to Montreal.

So, of course, we weren't too happy about that, the crew wasn't
too happy and neither was I. I wanted to get back home and it
was getting up now late in the year, and really we had no navigat-
ing equipment on that tug. We just had a compass and a radar,
which is no navigation equipment for crossing the Gulf at that
time of the year. So after a lot of grumbling we took the barge and
we headed out for Montreal.

We got out in the middle of the Gulf and we ran into a north-
east hurricane. We managed to get her in the lee of Anticosti
Island up there, and that's about the only thing that saved us, they
registered eighty-nine-mile-an-hour winds on Anticosti Island
that night. We just jogged back and forth, back and forth, for
thirty hours and I figured that we'd never save the barge, you
know, the towline would chafe off. Well, we had to keep it moving because we couldn't anchor. All the anchor chains were frozen up, and it's not a good idea to anchor anyway because you'd
be in bottom probably that the anchor wouldn't hold and you'd
be in more trouble than if you didn't anchor. So what we did is
we kept moving back and forth in the lee of the island, just along
the shore, back and forth, and I kept wondering all that night
what in hell would happen if the radar gave out, because that's all
we had was the radar. I was thinking that if the radar did give out,
what I would do was go slow until I eased her right into shore,
you know, ease her right in on the shore dead slow. But it never
happened, I didn't have to do that.

While we were jogging back and forth we heard this ship calling for help. We couldn't figure out where he was at, but he was
calling for help. Of course, we couldn't give him no help, we
needed help ourselves. So when it cleared enough we got straightened away and we got down around Cape Henry and there's a little place called Port Menier, it's a little harbour up there on the
west end of Anticosti Island. I would see range lights there. So, I
figured, if there's range lights there, ships must go in there, although I could see the water wasn't very deep. Anyway, after
about an hour sizing the situation up I decided we'd go in, so we
started in on the range lights, lining up the range lights, with the

barge a thousand feet behind us. We got in far enough where you could see the wharf with the glasses, you could see there was boats in there, small fishing-boats. When we got about halfway in I had glanced at the compass, I was looking at the range lights and I glanced down at the compass, and when I looked back up again there was no range lights. The god-darn range lights had gone.

I panicked for a moment, you know, just momentarily, but I had just noted the course on the compass, so I kept her on the same course and we inched our way in. We got in and we tied up and we found out later that the power went off, that's why the range lights went out right at that crucial moment.

It took us about a day to straighten up everything, you know, fix up the towline and get the barge straightened up again, and in the meantime this fella that we had heard hollering for help was a ship that had been loading lumber in Grand Valley, which is a place on the Gaspé coast up there and the wind had come north-east and he had stayed there until he got trapped there. She broke her lines and drifted ashore in the cove and she really smashed up.

Now, then, the company in Halifax got ahold of us and they wanted us to go across and see what we could do, find out if we could leave the barge where we were and steam across to the Gaspé coast and see if we could assist the ship. Well, there was a small French town and there was a chap there that run the general store, he was the mayor, I think he was everything, the butcher, he was the only chap there I believe that could speak any bit of English. So, we asked him and he said, 'Yeah, you can leave the damn barge there as long as you want. I don't care.' So, anyway, we left the barge there and we went across to Grand Valley where this ship was. We got across there and it was still blowing a little breeze to the north-east. It had calmed down some, but it was still blowing and the wind was right on that shore, you see, causing quite a bit of sea.

When we got in there, I couldn't believe it. There was nine-inch hawsers there that that ship had broken, big bollards that she had tore out of the wharf, literally tore out of the wharf.

So, we got in there and we tied up and, of course, one look at this ship and you could see that it would take about fifty tugs like

us to tow that off, she was right up on beach and she was damaged quite badly. I went ashore to see if I could call the company,
and all the phone lines were down. So, we had to stay there overnight.

The crew of the ship was all ashore, they got ashore. They put a
rope ladder overside of her to walk to shore, she was up that far
on the beach. So, we couldn't do nothing about that, so we got out
of there the next morning.

The fella from Fox River Radio, one of the radio stations on the
coast, called and he said, 'Do you have the ship in tow?' I said,
'Hell no, we don't have the thing in tow. It would take fifty of us
to tow that off from where it's at.' So he said, 'What are you going
to do?' I said, 'I want to telephone the company in Halifax and tell
them that we're going back to pick up our barge and continue our
trip to Montreal.'

So, we went back and we picked up the barge and we started
out for Montreal. We weren't out for more than twelve hours
when we ran into another breeze of wind and it took us ten days
to tow that barge from Stephenville to Montreal. Well, I was
never so glad to get up to Escoumains, that's where you pick up
the river pilots. It's on the north shore of the river and we picked
up the pilot there. We had a barge a thousand feet beyond us and
I knew damn well that we should shorten up that tow, but we
took the pilot on in Escoumains and he looked at us and, you
know, said, 'How's she towing there, Skipper?' and I said, 'She's
towing fine.' 'Good,' he said. 'Pull away for Quebec City.' So I
relaxed then; I thought, hell, you know, a pilot aboard, what the
hell, I'll relax. Before we got into Quebec City we got into a breeze
of wind up there and snow again and it was like that when we
dropped the pilot in Quebec City and picked up another pilot for
Three Rivers. When the pilot came aboard in Quebec City he
asked the other pilot who was getting off how was she towing and
he told him she was towing good. That little bit of French I could
understand, I knew the drift of the conversation. So he said, pull
away, you know, and here's the damn thing still a thousand feet
beyond us and we're getting up in the river now, you see. We
dropped the pilot off in Three Rivers and another one came on
there to take us to Montreal. The same thing happened, you see,

'How's she towing?' 'Fine.' So, we started up to, what's the name of the lake there, Lake St. Pierre, and he made a gentle turn and he cut it a little bit short and I could see the barge was going to go over on the top of one of the marker buoys and I said to the pilot, I tapped him on the shoulder and I said, 'Pilot. The barge is going to go over on top of the buoy.' 'Ha, it's okay, okay,' he said. He never even looked back, but she went right over the buoy and I was expecting maybe she might have put a hole in it, you know, I was expecting the damn thing to sink.

Now, up in the river the ship coming down has the right of way. For good reason. They can't stop. There's no way they can stop. There's about a four-knot tide running there continuously and if they stopped they'd go broadside and they'd be ashore. There's no way they can stop, so they've got the right of way. Now, we got up into Montreal with this barge about a thousand feet behind us and here's this young French pilot and he asks me, he said, 'How long is it going to take you to take in that barge?' I told him, I said, 'About forty minutes, about twenty minutes if everything goes well.' I said, 'If it don't go well, you know...' 'Well,' he said, 'what can happen?' I said, 'Anything can happen aboard here. It pretty well has since I left.'

So, he got her lined up, he got up into Montreal there, and he put her up into what they call a basin and he said that we had so many miles to drift while we're taking the barge in. 'Now,' he said, 'it'll have to be done quick', and I said, 'Okay, we'll do it as quickly as we can.' First thing happened, when we slacked up on her, we were going to take the tow-rope up around to the capstan, it got caught underneath one of the tires on the side of her. It took us fifteen minutes to get it clear, and here's ships coming straight at us coming down the river, you know, and there's no way they can stop, and this pilot, he's jumping from one side of the wheel-house to the other, yacking away in French about a mile a minute. So I said, 'We'd better call for a tug to help us here.' So, he got on the radio and he called for a tug to come down and before he got there, I figured, well, we've had it, you know, because here we were drifting right out in the middle of the channel now and ships going by us like crazy. The tug came and he got ahold of the barge and we got things under control, and we got tied up there. And we sort of had a rest for about a day and we went ashore in Montreal the next morning and we did some shopping and one thing and another, a little bit of Christmas presents for the family and what have you, and then we left to come back down.

It took us three days to cover the same territory that we had taken ten to do before and now we were going to come home to Halifax, you see. But no, we got down the river and everything, the river was beginning to freeze up now and I was afraid we might get trapped up there, you know, because you could very easily get trapped in one of those tugs up there.

Anyway, we got down off of the Gaspé coast and lo and behold the radio cracked and here was a message come in from the office in Halifax there, telling us to go back to Stephenville. I would have liked to tell them to take the tug and stuff it at that time, I'll tell you. I had seen enough of it. But anyway, the hell, we went across to Stephenville and here's another barge waiting to be taken to Yarmouth.

But anyway the wind came to the south-east and I decided maybe we should go to the north side of Cape Breton and get a little bit of lee up there on the north side. So, we got up there and we came down through the Canso Causeway and we got into Port Hawkesbury in the Straits there and we got straightened away again, and the rest of the trip from there was quite uneventful. We left Port Hawkesbury and we went on to Yarmouth and we got back here in Halifax I think a couple of days before Christmas. And the first thing I did was, I went up to the operations manager and I told him what I thought of his goddamn two weeks, and I threatened him never to send me to Goose Bay again. We were away for I think something short of two months."

TOWING COAL "When I started out with Victoria Tug the major job that they had was towing coal. They owned a lot of wooden barges—thirty barges to be exact—and they towed coal from Nanaimo, and Union Bay was another place, to Seattle and down here. But coal was the big item, towing coal, because everybody burned coal in those days. They were wooden scows and they weren't built like the steel scows they have nowadays. You know, the scow would start to leak on the barge and the rolling would give the barge a list and, of course, as more coal went over, any water in the barge would run down to that side, which would give it a further list. If it got bad enough it would just push the boards out the side and dump the load. You see, the coal would be peaked. I mean it wouldn't be loaded flat in the barge. That's why you have to watch the weather.

I remember one day when we were comin' down from just Union Bay and it become daylight in the morning and we looked back and one barge was right upside down. You see, being wood they didn't sink, they'd just turn over. The coal was gone and so we just kept up. Naturally, it was a very hard tow, then, when you get an upside-down sunken—she don't sink to the bottom, she sinks to the water's edge, and so we had to pull into Nanaimo and get rid of that one."

SURGING ON THE LINE   "Twenty-five hundred feet may seem like a long towline to a lot of people, but if you get out in any heavy weather, the action of the vessel towing and the vessel being towed are completely different. The tug would only be maybe a hundred and thirty, a hundred and fifty feet long, weighing around five hundred ton. The vessel being towed, in this case a log raft, is three, four hundred feet long and would weigh maybe thousands of tons. So, naturally, you have two actions to the vessels.

Consequently, the long length of the towline acts as a spring between the two of them so there isn't a jerky motion on the part of the tug, with its surging ahead and then coming up short on the towline, coming to a practical stop and then surging ahead. If that happens the first thing you know you're going to part your towline, and that's about the worst thing that can happen to a towboat man, for him to part his towline. Now, that's a steel towline, what we call solid core. It's a number of steel strands all interwoven and wrapped around one strand, which is in turn wrapped around several strands, so that the diameter would be around two and a half inches—and, as I said, it's about twenty-five hundred feet long.

Experience was what taught you if there was too much surging, as we call it, on the line. You know, you can see the line as it goes over the stern from the towing-winch, it passes over the stern over top of the roller, the horizontal roller and the vertical roller. Under normal conditions, the line might stretch out, oh, thirty or forty feet before it disappeared under the water. In surging conditions you might see it come up to fifty or sixty feet behind the tug. You'd know then that you've got a problem. As it came up to fifty, sixty feet and then it dropped down to maybe twenty or thirty feet you knew then that you have a *real* problem and you better start takin' the horsepower off and slowin' things down a bit or you're liable to part this line."

THE *ISLAND SOVEREIGN* AND THE *SUDBURY II* "In the sixties I was captain of the *Island Sovereign*. She was a tug a hundred feet long and had twenty-four hundred horsepower. So, we left here and went down to what we call off Nitinat, on the west coast of Vancouver Island, right out on the ocean, to go out and rescue this Norwegian ship.

Her engine had caught fire in the engine-room. She was anchored off there in the heavy weather, a heavy swell was blowing and a gale of sou'west. We backed right in close to her and shot off the rocket gun—and then we put a light line on and then we put a heavier line on, and then we had a pennant, a four-hundred-and-fifty-foot pennant, inch and a half wire. We gave them that and then they put that around their bollards and fo'c's'le head. She couldn't get her anchors up, so someone had to go down to the chain locker and knock out the pin and let the anchors go right into the chuck.

And then we started in with her at half speed and we got in, oh, about just off Cape Flattery there when the wire broke. So we got another line back up, and we just jogged in with her. We were getting rolled around and tossed around just like a bumblebee out there, and they sent another tug, the *Island Navigator*, from Victoria out to assist us, and we got her in to Esquimalt.

Later, the poor skipper on the *Sudbury II*, he got sick and they put me on there for relievin' until they got some other deep-water man, and I was on there for about three months. But it was all the difference in the world being on the *Sudbury II* or bein' on the *Sovereign*, because she was twice the size of the *Sovereign*. For handlin' and for pickin' up things you had twin screws, a diesel electric, and you could just back up and hold her right in there while they passed the line up to you, even in heavy weather.

On the *Sudbury II* we used to be on the rock run, towin' big barges from Blubber Bay to the Columbia River to Portland. They were big barges, the *Island Exporter* and the *Island Importer*, and they carried ten thousand eleven hundred ton of limerock. So we went down with this barge and she'd be doin' around seven or eight miles an hour. We got down off the Columbia River bar and we run into a south-east gale. And, of course, the bar there breaks for a quarter of a mile wide. And you can't go in. They got bar pilots there, and even the deep-sea ships couldn't go in.

So we're out there for two days, steamin' out twenty miles, twenty-five miles back and forth, waitin' for it to moderate. Two days, and it was blowin' up to eight miles an hour. An' that ship there, we never even had to lash anything down anywheres, she never even rolled. That was the first time I'd been out in the *Sudbury II* in a gale. It didn't bother her."

DAVIS RAFTS IN THE HECATE STRAITS   "On the B.C. coast here, of course, log-towing by water is the cheapest method of transporting logs. We've always had the problem of transporting logs from what we call the outside areas—the Queen Charlotte Islands, the west coast of Vancouver Island—down to various places in the lower mainland where the mills are located. And, of course, the transportation of logs from the Queen Charlotte Islands specifically has always been quite a problem, mainly because of the Hecate Straits, which is the body of water in between the Islands and the mainland. The Hecate Straits has a particularly bad reputation for sudden storms. The area itself is quite shallow, and so any type of wind at all that comes up we immediately get a violent reaction, wave waters. So, it's always been a problem.

In the early days they started out rafting, Davis rafting they called it, from the Queen Charlotte Islands. In Davis rafts the logs were all bundled together in sort of a big cigar shape. In other words, they'd start out putting a layer of logs in the water, wrapping huge wires around it, and then building up successive layers of logs on top of that, and then tying the whole thing together with huge wires. These were fairly stable; they were sunk fairly low in the water. But they were hard to move. In other words, we used to move them at maybe one and a half to two knots. And travelling a distance of five hundred-odd miles, that takes a little bit of time. Plus the fact that they could only survive so much weather conditions, they couldn't tolerate just any conditions. The rafts would be various sizes depending upon the species of wood. They would be what they used to call four-stick rafts or five-stick rafts, a side stick being a log of about sixty-five feet in length. And so the raft itself would be four sticks down one side or five sticks down one side, so that the raft might contain as much as two and a half million board feet of wood. And to tow from the Queen Charlotte Islands over to the mainland, a large tug would usually only take one raft. He'd have enough problems getting over to the mainland with one raft.

Our big problem, of course, getting a Davis raft across was we had to wait for weather. Our weather-reporting facilities weren't as good twenty years ago, of course, as they are today, and the master of the vessel would pretty well have to rely on whatever skimpy government meteorological reports were available to him, and he would also have to rely a great deal on his own local knowledge. No man is right always.

You'd start out and things would look good and, oh, the jump-across spot at its narrowest is just over twenty miles, and its widest around fifty-five miles, depending upon which camp you're towing from. So you'd start out and things would look great and then all of a sudden about halfways across you've got another twenty or twenty-five, thirty miles to go, up comes the weather. So now you've got to decide, do I keep going, do I turn back, what do I do? If you keep going, well, you think it's going to moderate, perhaps it will, you hope it will, but it doesn't moderate. Then you're watching your raft as you're coming across and waves are gettin' a little higher, and then all of a sudden the raft starts to get a little flatter. In other words, it's just the action of the waves beating against these logs that are tied together by wire which can't be absolutely right, and the first thing you know the thing starts getting a little smaller and smaller and flattening out.

Providing the weather is moderated sufficiently, you're able to get it across. Then you have to take it into some sort of secluded cove and tie it up and have some loggers come over with some machinery from the Queen Charlottes, and they'd have to try and tighten it all up for you. If you didn't manage to get across, well, all you had was a bunch of loose logs floatin' around in Hecate Straits.

Of course, that's the worst possible thing that could happen to you. I was fortunate never to be on a complete loss, although I have been on rafts where they were in pretty sad shape by the time we got 'em across. It's just a case of once it starts working loose and if it got sufficiently loose the whole thing just started to disintegrate. And once that process started, of course, all you had was a towline left."

BREAKING UP   "Davis rafts would break up; if you ran into too much head sea the logs would start to work. Nobody could tell why it would always come out the front end, always against the wash of the tug, but you'd see one stick up. And when one log would stick up on end you'd know then that you were in trouble because you were goin' to lose them. I know once there's three or four got out gradually, the wires would all slacken up. If you kept goin' you would lose the whole thing. Because the more it comes out, the slacker the wires get. You'd lose them all, and all the wires would be hanging on to these big side sticks. There'd be over a million feet in one raft. And the gale come along and throw 'em up on the beach someplace, in Rowe's Spot, or in Alaska."

HOLDING UP FOR WEATHER   "I think the all-time record for a man holding up in the Islands for weather, waiting to get across the Hecate Straits, was something like three months.

Three months just sitting there waiting for the weather to be moderate enough in his opinion to get this raft across. Mind you, in all fairness to him, the raft was being towed from one of the camps where the jump was around fifty-five to sixty miles across the Hecate Straits."

TORPEDOES FROM A LOG BOOM   "In 1939 I was on my own

and I went out in November, and I set my net in a calm sea for my dark-set, you know, the evening set. And within a few hours there was a howling gale and I couldn't pick my net up, so I just swung it to the bow, you know, so that the bow would be facing the storm. And then the log boom being towed up the Fraser by a couple of tugboats, it broke loose from the boom, and fifteen sections of logs started to come at me.

Here I am with my seven-horsepower Easthope, going back and forth, dodging the logs, you know, and I thought for sure that night was my end. I put a big anchor rope on my bow and I had my flashlight on them, and I was just dodging about all night, from about ten o'clock at night till six o'clock. One or two hit me, but luckily no damage. By the morning millions of feet of logs had gone by, beached in the flats."

A BARGE ON THE RAMPAGE   "There was a big log barge tied up just below the Fraser River bridge for repairs and a big southeaster broke it adrift. It came up-river on the flood tide and hooked under the main span and took it right out, clean out. The bridge just sat on the barge and then it dumped the main span in the river, and then the barge carried on up-river sideswiping everything in sight and knocking booms and buildings and everything else all to hell. The main span of the railway bridge, which would be, oh, three or four hundred feet long, went right in the river, but no one was hurt because it was a Sunday morning and I think it was a holiday. No one knew anything about it until the poor bridge-tender phoned up, and he was terrified."

IN THE BEACHCOMBING BUSINESS   "In the beachcombing business you would pick up the loose logs and you would make them into log booms and you would tow them, have them scaled by the government scaler, and you would sell them to the various mills. You would call the various sawmills and see if they were interested in your log boom, and you would tow that boom to whichever sawmill.

We would start off in the morning from where our boats were tied up. I would go up one section of the Fraser and my brother would go up the other, and pick up loose logs. They would be laying up against bridges or up against other booms with the drifting of the tide, and they were usually marked with somebody's stamp. There were dozens of stamps on the end of the logs.

Then in 1951 the government got into the picture and they set up a log-salvage operation and all the owners of these logs would show up on the government scale-sheet and they would be compensated through the sawmill for the loss of that log. It cost you a hundred dollars for the log-salvage licence, and then it was ten dollars a year and you had to have the licence up. You would have a steel wire on your boat with dogs, they call 'em, which is a spike that has a hole in it and the wire goes through this. And as you came on each log you would hammer a spike into it, and you might get six or eight or a dozen logs on this string of wire. Then you would tow it into your own little boom ground—you would grab a few piles somewhere or have some piles driven and make yourself up a little booming ground—then you would haul it in there and make them up into booms.

If you get freezing weather it's very hard to drive those dogs into those logs, and it's really cold, hard, wet work. And if there's other men in the business, you've got to get up earlier than the next guy, otherwise you just can't go out there at noon and expect to find any logs, because they would be all picked up by then."

SINKING THE BARGE "I was loading barges for a big lumber company in Winnipeg, and one time I had my barge loaded with three hundred and fifty cords of wood. This was at Kinowa. And the *Granite Rock*, Bill Flett's big tugboat, was anchored out approximately half a mile away from my harbour, and I started pulling this barge out and I got about ten minutes out in the channel and I couldn't move any more. It was dead calm, but the current was coming in so fast from the north, I couldn't move any more.

I had three barrels of gas on, so I run to shore and dumped the barrels off of my boat as it was starting to blow. And before I knew it my barge lifted out of the channel—the water come up that fast—and whipped around a couple of times and landed on the sandbar. The water was coming up so fast and storming, I got two men with three-inch augers and I drilled holes in the barge, two below the waterline. I sunk that barge so it wouldn't drift any further. And it stormed for two days there and it's a good thing I done that. If I hadn't, we would never have got it off of the beach, because after I sunk the barge, the water still came up another two or three feet.

The tug had to hit out for Macbeth Point to find shelter and it had trouble there when the cable caught in the wheel, three-quarter-inch cable in the wheel, and the storm was so bad that all the coal washed off the other barge. So, Captain Bill Flett, after he'd cut that cable free, had to come all the way back to Winnipeg to get more coal and another flat-deck barge.

So I pulled it alongside this barge I'd sunk and I loaded about a hundred cords off of it onto the flat-deck barge. The *Granite Rock* was approximately over a quarter of a mile away hooked on with a cable, and we waited for another storm to come up. And when the next storm came I had the two holes plugged up with two posts, three-inch posts, and when I plugged the holes up I pumped the water out with two pumps. And when the water raised after the storm the *Granite Rock* started up and pulled both barges off the reef.

So I saved a lot of trouble there by learning from an old fisherman, old P. D. Walker, to carry an auger on the boat and sink it if it catches on fire, to sink it so it won't burn. And I saved the three hundred and fifty cords of wood I had on that barge. Green pulp."

BEING TOWED—AND NOT BEING TOWED "A Japanese chap that had two or three boats, big boats, packers we called them, was looking for gill-netters in Alert Bay to go to Smith Inlet. So we all quit the seining and went gill-nettin' up in Smith Inlet. That was sockeye time, you know. To get to the fishing grounds, to start with, you would go to an inlet and to a camp or a cannery, whatever company you was working for. And on the weekends, there would be posted different areas where the packer, the big boat, would take you—to this area or that area, you know, if you wanted to go up the inlet, or outside or anywhere, there was certain areas and a certain packer would be going to this area. So he would go this route and you'd hook on a towline, you'd just hook on this big towline and get off anywhere you liked.

Okay. He's going up to the head, we'll say, of an inlet. So you could get off anywheres you liked between the camp and the head, wherever you thought you wanted to get off, where you wanted to fish. So the boats'd keep dropping off. They didn't stop to let you off, you know, you had to be careful gettin' off.

Like, here's this big long towline. There may be thirty to forty boats on it sometimes. You might be in the middle, we'll say. Well, you'd put a certain little loop in the towline, then you've just got a loop, just a slip-knot, so you could just pull it and let it go when you're ready to go off to leave the towline. You just pulled that, she would shoot off, then you'd push yourself away and watch out for the other boats coming behind. That's how you got away from the towline.

Sometimes you'd move out to sea, catching the fish as they were coming in, and the packer would come around to tow you all the way back to camp, and would miss you. It's just not a straight street, you know, an inlet. It's full of islands and rocks and different things and you might be somewhere around a little island or something and he misses you. So then there you are, you've got no packer.

This happened to me once really bad. I got way out, way out, you know, in Queen Charlotte Sound and miles and miles offshore, and, boy, you've gotta get in. You'd go to Japan if you didn't do somethin' about it. No engines, no sail, so there's only one way, that's row. In a twenty-four-foot skiff with fourteen-foot oars. So you throw your net out and you row.

I was rowing all night and into the morning, you know, and I didn't have strength to curse. You had to save every little ounce of energy—you couldn't even eat, because if you did you'd go further out again as soon as you stopped, because all inlets are almost always going out. Sixteen hours I was rowing, just thinkin' of how to get back in, that's all. That was a miserable experience."

TUGS VERSUS NETS   "The net fishermen are a nuisance sometimes, especially in the Gulf of Georgia off the sand-heads, that's the entrance to the Fraser River. You go up there sometimes and you see about a thousand lights facing you and you don't know which is the end of their net and which is their boat, and these are just strung out all over. You have to go through those with a tow, you know, and there's no regulations, it seems, for to keep them out of the way. Well, this is just ridiculous, it's thousands of lights, and I defy anybody to go through there without either hanging up on a net half the time or cutting a net.

You get charged for nets, you know, they'll put in a claim for a net. The thing is, at one time all the nets were linen nets, so your propeller would cut them and you would get through, but now they're all nylon and they wind up and then they sort of melt and gum up your propeller. Well, then you're just stuck, you're stalled, and, of course, you know you've got a barge behind you, probably trying to climb up on your stern, and these barges today, I'll tell you, they won't stop. With that big shovel-nose, they just break your housework off if they come over you.

You might be stuck there for two, three hours, before you could get a boat pier and that's if they have a boat available, and all this time you've gotta watch your barge.

You would get the fisherman telling you off in no uncertain terms, and, well, I guess he was worried about his net. But if he was so worried about his net, you would think he might've pulled it in in the first place. See, usually what we do, we're supposed to blast four blasts maybe, and you line up, like you flash your light where you're going through. Well, you know, the odd fisherman will pick up his net. Some of them'll just gradually pick it up slow, but some, they don't pick up at all, so there's no way you're gonna get through them. Oh, we give 'em a blast back but half the time, you know, it doesn't do any good."

TOWBOAT MEN AND FISHERMEN "I realized what these towboat fellas were up against and I usually got out of the way, and not because of a fear of being run down but I thought if you got your net in their wheel you might sue them and get the value of it back, but in the meantime you've lost three or four days' fishing. Some of these fellows that set across in front of a man that has a tow of logs and who can't really get out of the way regardless, I think they're just being stupid and they don't understand his problems.

But there are some towboat fellows I think that really enjoy whacking the end off a net just to show 'em who the hell is boss, you know. They could have gone around the end but they would charge up the middle. But, well, maybe they'd had a fight with their wife that morning, or the boss had given them hell, so they were going to get even with somebody."

SHOTGUN "We were going through Satellite Channel, and the guys had the place all plugged up with god-damned nets and all that, and I think it was old Bill Danner who was on this craft, he was blowin' for to clear the way. He made the mistake of going through a net.

The guy was out courtin' somebody else's wife or something else like that, or having a cup of coffee with the other fishermen, and he had one end of the net tied to the dock or tied to a beach and we went through it. And he came back shortly after he woke up or found out we'd gone through the net, and he come alongside the boat with a shotgun, after the mate up in the wheelhouse.

We quietened him down. He woke me up."

FOURTEEN

Highliners

*Pieces of Silver... Highliners—Goin' All the Time... The Three
Fishermen... The Game of Fishin'... Still Buddies... You Would Cut Off
Your Mother... High Boat... Tit for Tat... Cod-Killers... You're Going To
Have a War... Seiners and Gill-netters... Wildcats in a Bag... The Set-
Gear Stunt... Through the Hulls*

I f you think of fishing as a pleasant, relaxed occupation full of
camaraderie, this chapter will come as a shock to you. For
fishermen, I discovered, are among the most competitive people
anywhere—as one of them said, "It's a hungry, starving, dog-eat-
dog business and you have to face that fact." Another claimed
that you would cut off your own mother to get to the fish.

Most competitive of all are the highliners, the big businessmen,
the top executives of the fishing fleets. They catch more fish than
other men do, even though some of those other fishermen try just
as hard. The highliners I met, some in their sixties, had common
characteristics—boundless energy, imagination, and enthusiasm,
and they looked much younger, very often, than they were. They
were fishermen and technocrats: they had at their command a
massive array of instruments that reminded me of the flight-deck
of an aircraft. The old captains had exactly the same aggressive
drive, but these men joked more easily, their horizons were
broader. Their total concern was fishing, but they also knew
about the world beyond the wide sea horizon they faced day
after day.

The fierce competitive spirit: they all have it. Highliners just
happen to be the best of them. It runs in the blood, generations of
trying to outdo the other fellow.

PIECES OF SILVER "There's one story they tell about one of the highline herring-seiners from Campobello, who actually is a millionaire. They were out fishing four, five years ago, when prices were extremely depressed and the herring they were catching were hardly worth the fuel to catch them. So somebody asked him, said, what the hell are you doing out here for anyway, you don't got to be here, you've got lots of money.

He said, oh yes, he had all the money he wanted, but he said, when he died, when he went through the pearly gates, he wanted to tell St. Peter he killed just as many of the silvery bastards as he could."

HIGHLINERS—GOIN' ALL THE TIME "You've gotta really pay attention and really work. Like there's lotsa guys, I guess I can't mention any names or anything, but there's lotsa guys that are really hard workers and they're just savvy, you know, they work real hard and they're thinkin' all the time about fishin', you know, where they're goin'. You know, you could be getting fish one day but where are they gonna be the next day. You might move down about a quarter of a mile or a mile that night, or eight miles that night, and be right on 'em first thing in the morning —and usually you'll get a bite in the morning or something like that, but then when they go off the bite, the highliners, they still catch 'em.

Well, the average guy, he slows down just about to nothin' if it's springs and that, and the highliners'll haul 'em all day long. Some guys just work at it really hard and they never stop workin' their gear and never stop tryin'. Whereas other guys get a few fish and they're happy enough, or if the bite goes off they don't really bother. While other guys are, you know, goin' all the time."

THE THREE FISHERMEN "There's probably three type fishermen. There's the one man that goes fishin' strictly to earn a livin'. He's quite content to go with somebody else, come to work when he's told, do what he's told, and do his job and do it good. I have one man with me that's exactly like that. He's a good man, I wouldn't want to lose him, but he really never wants to take a boat of his own.

Then you have the other man, or you have two other people
that have boats. You have one man that fishes for money and he
makes a good livin', usually he's an average fisherman.

But then you have another man who is usually the best fisherman, that doesn't fish for money. To him, money is only somethin'
that comes from fishin' but it's not what he fishes for—he fishes
for fish. His main object is to catch more fish than anybody else,
and he'll even go to the extreme of earnin' less money to catch
'em. If it costs him money to catch these fish over and above what
it costs the other feller that's fishin' for money, it makes no difference to him—he'll fish for fish. He wants every fish that's there.
He'd like to be able to catch 'em all and come home and say, 'Do
you know what? I got the last one. There's no more left, I caught
'em all!"

THE GAME OF FISHIN' "I don't think there's a man in our fleet
that wouldn't do somethin' to help the others. In fact, I'm quite
sure that everybody would help the other person out. But don't
ask him where he was fishin' and expect him to tell you, because
he's just not going to. I mean, he'll tell you where, but don't put
too much faith in it if when you git there it doesn't seem to be
what he was gettin', because he's not gonna tell you exactly how
he towed in this 'n' that to get 'em.

I guess we feel that's part of the game of fishin' and I think most
fishermen treat it sort of as a game, as a challenge. Your track-
and-field people, they have a challenge to run fast or to jump high
or whatever. Well, the fisherman has a challenge to catch fish
where he can't see 'em and to be able to catch more fish than the
man next to him. We're all the same, that we like to come home
sayin', 'I done better than the rest.' "

STILL BUDDIES "There was just rivalry between them, between the skippers, you know. Arnold Parks was another wild
and woolly one, and old Foster, and they'd get on the ship-to-
shore phone there and they'd curse and swear over this and
D.O.T. would be listening to them, you know, and they'd threaten
to take their licence from them and it didn't make any difference.

Foster would say, 'Where are you, Arnold?' 'Well, goddammit,

A cold day on the Grand Banks.

Baiting trawl on an old Grand Banks schooner.

Two men to a dory was the usual rule in the old days on the Grand Banks, and the men worked from three in the morning almost around the clock.

A slight swell on the Atlantic.

Hauling in the nets by hand was hard, exhausting work.

This familiar scene on the British Columbia coast shows a net churning with herring as the purse seine is drawn tighter.

A power winch operates the brailer used to scoop the thousands of herring from the net, while gulls hover and swoop down on the catch.

The trawl net is hauled aboard.

Aboard an old side-trawler a good catch of codfish is sorted on deck.

Stewart Rice (left) and Harold Robinson, out of Digby, N.S., sort among the rocks and starfish for scallops brought up by the drag.

Three very different tasks. Top left: A fisherman stows away the long-lining gear after use in the Atlantic. Top right: Doreen Noseworthy relaxes in the door of the fo'c's'le, while "a feed of stew" cooks inside. (Photo courtesy of Doreen Noseworthy) Bottom: A west-coast whaler checks his harpoon gun; note the attached rope coiled beneath the gun.

Checking the catch. Top: Sockeye salmon in a seine net are pulled aboard a B.C. boat. (Photo: NFB) Bottom left: Checking a catch of Atlantic oysters. Bottom right: On the squid-jiggin' ground—"you would get squirted right in your face." (Photo: NFB–Bob Brooks)

Cleaning cod ashore in Happy Adventure, Newfoundland.
(N.F.B.—Chris Lund)

A close-up of a huge tuna being cut into sections in Lunenburg.
(N.F.B.—Gar Lunney)

you can see. If you look out to starboard, I guess I'm over the horizon,' he'd say. 'Any fish there?' 'No, we got nuttin'. Didn't get nuttin' at all today, didn't get a damned thing,' he'd say. Then he'd come in and his decks were loaded and then Foster would say, 'You damned thing, you lied to me. Well, I'm going back again. Well, where was you?' 'Well, don't worry where we was,' he said, 'we know where we was.'

They had a loran then, these old, old lorans they got off the airplanes, they were using them and they'd get a cross-bearing and they knew pretty close to where they were going, but they lied to one another. But still buddies, you know, drinkin' buddies."

YOU WOULD CUT OFF YOUR MOTHER "Fishermen are highly competitive. Friendship ceases once you leave the dock. I mean, even if your own mother was fishing alongside of you, if you figured you would get a few more, you would cut her off.

I don't mean that really, but you just get so that you just can't think of anything else but to get in there to get your share, and maybe a wee bit more, you know. It's a sort of an inborn greed which is all that keeps driving you, and I think that's a good thing too. If you lay back and let the other man have your spot, you're gonna end up on the end of the stick at the end of the season. So, I believe the average fisherman is driven by something that makes him want to come into harbour and say, 'Well, I got five hundred or six hundred and hope to God you, pal, only got three hundred.' And then you feel that life is well worth living."

HIGH BOAT "It's more than money actually, being high boat, you know. That's number one. I mean, a fisherman can come in in the morning with ten dollars' worth of fish, and if he's high, that is, if everybody's got eight or nine dollars' worth, well, he's happy as a clam, you know. He's high boat. Everything's workin' fine. He's number one.

But if he comes in the next day with a hundred dollars' worth of fish, ten times as much as he had the day before, and everybody's got a hundred and fifty dollars' worth, he's the most miserable guy on the beach and he feels really bad about it.

So I mean that's it, it's very strong, competitive. To be high, to be number one, is in everybody's mind. Some won't admit it, say, 'I don't care. I'll just go and tie up if I want to tie up,' and all that kind of stuff, but underneath they do feel bad if they gotta slink up to the packer with a few fish and everybody's unloading big loads, they feel really terrible about it."

TIT FOR TAT   "It's just more or less in your own mind that you can do better than this man, you see. You're always betterin' yourself. Now, you take if I go out fishing lobsters and today I move half my gear on good ground, well, if I come in and told everybody, they'd have all their gear there—and my lobsters, that I could get in the run of a week where I was there all alone, you see, all them lobsters would be shared by the other fishermen.

It's not that I don't like to see the other fishermen make a dollar, but it's tit for tat. Like, you know, if I can get them lobsters before some of them moves there, well, it's more money in my pocket."

COD-KILLERS   "My ambition then was not to go to university, but to have my own boat and go skipper. And be what we call, not a fisherman, a cod-killer, who is a top-notch fisherman. That was the ambition. My grandfather was a cod-killer, and then you had people who weren't so good. But we were from a line of good cod-killers, ambitious, good fellows who always had a good voyage."

YOU'RE GOING TO HAVE A WAR   "We have the squawking and squabbling in Yarmouth here between the gill-netters and the mobile herring fleets. They're both going after the same fish, right, and they hate each other with a vengeance. Gradually they're starting to sit down together and say, okay, there's a resource, how do we divvy it up? and this is good.

There's never that great animosity, really, when there's a lot of money to be made. The animosity comes into it during the hard times. I think if there was no herring here and all of a sudden the New Brunswick fleet showed up, ha, you're going to have a war."

SEINERS AND GILL-NETTERS   "It's always a battle between seine boats and gill-netters. The average gill-netter, he can't stand the sight of the average seine-boat man because he figures that they're just robbing him of his rightful dues, and of course the same goes the other way. I've been in areas fishing where there's a dual fishery going on, like up at Hakai Pass which is near Rivers Inlet, and the seine boats and the gill-netters fish at the same time in the same area together and they don't get along too well there. Of course, it's only a short season and it's a hungry, starving, dog-eat-dog business and you have to face that fact. And once you face it, well, then you live with it."

WILDCATS IN A BAG "Each fellow is his own independent boss and he says, goddamned if any union is gonna tell me what to do, just the same as he's gonna say, damned if any company's gonna tell me what to do. He's gonna sell wherever he wants to sell his catch.

A union would have its advantages, there's no doubt about it, in stabilizing prices not only to the fishermen but also to the processor, because the way it is now, if fish are scarce it can sky-rocket immediately overnight, which isn't good because it shoves the cost to the processors up where he's at that point losin' money. And when the fish are plentiful he's gonna come back after it and he's gonna shove the price way down, so the fisherman isn't doin' too well out of it. So it would serve to stabilize prices, there's no doubt about it. But to get a group of fishermen together, you might as well put fifteen or twenty wildcats in a bag and expect them to get along."

THE SET-GEAR STUNT "One big problem was the local fishermen themselves. You just can't imagine how all these guys around here set and trawl, settin' gill-nets and para-nets and whatnot, and I'm the only dragger, draggin' around these guys, you see. And most of the inshore fishermen around here are older people.

I'll tell you, a young fellow's had it. I'm invading their grounds, you see, so they use all kinds of little stunts. Like, I'm supposed to stay a half a mile away from set gear, that is, any gear that's anchored, or floatin' gear that's anchored, that's set gear. Because they knew I had to stay a half-mile away from them, they sometimes was just takin' buoys and puttin' them down, you know.

There was no bloody net there at all—but just so I wouldn't be draggin' in it, would have no place to drag, you see."

THROUGH THE HULLS "Some offshore scallop-draggers decided they were not getting too much offshore so they decided to come in the inshore grounds, and they came just off Briar Island, which is at the tip of Digby County at the entrance of St. Mary's Bay. And the second that they were there, inshore fishermen were on the bluff with high-powered rifles, shooting through the hulls.

They didn't go back, they played like they weren't there. This is just five years ago, so that animosity is there. But I think they'd shoot their own brother if they thought he was getting their fish."

FIFTEEN

Tasty Bites

A Chowder and a Solomon Gundy... The Way I like a Salmon... In Praise of West Coast Salmon... A Fresh Fish... Out of the Shell... Home Canning and Freezing... The Lobster's Not for Eating... Not Lobster Again!... Squid Is Sweet... This Is It, Eh?... The Japanese Diet... Fresh Meat on the Mackenzie... Whale Meat... Seagull Eggs... Bay Buns and Rabbits... A Dutch Mess... A Molasses Mess... Smoke-tenders... Corncobs...Strawberry Goldeye... Rice and Stove Oil

C anadians have the best fish in the world in the seas off both coasts and in our inland waters, and yet we down a meagre sixteen pounds of fish per person per year. We're notoriously big meat-eaters, yet we're twenty-fifth amongst the nations of the world in per-capita consumption of fish. It's hard to understand. Perhaps, because our population is concentrated in inland areas, we've never really had a chance to acquire the taste. I know that when I first moved to the Ontario countryside thirty years ago, about the only fish anyone saw was canned sardines and whitefish. On a fine summer day, a couple of fellows in an old truck would come along the concessions peddling bad whitefish, which got more rotten as the heat increased and the day lengthened. It was not the sort of thing guaranteed to turn everyone into eager fish-eaters.

Yet, by now we know that, cooked properly—and fishermen will tell you when fish is at its best and what is the right way to cook it, but, unfortunately, their opinions vary—fish can be a delicacy almost beyond an epicure's dream. Mind you, you have to pick your restaurant, from among the scores of seafood places that I'm glad to see have sprung up across the country and you have to pick your fish. I've eaten eel, but I wouldn't rush to a store to buy it again. Then there's squid. Years ago, in this little narrow, long house at Torbay North, I was talking to a tall, gangly old Newfoundlander. I mentioned squid. He said:

"Squid is very messy. If you look overboard, you're gonna get a mess of dirt in your face, you know. The squid is used for bait, handlines, you put it on the hooks. There's people in Torbay ates 'em. My mind wouldn't let me ate 'em. But they say it was sweet. My mind wouldn't."

Well, my mind wouldn't either.

A CHOWDER AND A SOLOMON GUNDY "Fishermen are probably some of the best consumers of fish in the country. I remember going in to visit a lobster fisherman down in Digby Neck one day, and the centrepiece of the entire meeting was a chowder that his wife had made.

The chief engineer aboard the trawler that I was in, who was an old Lunenburger and had fished in the old schooners, was very proud of his ability to make a chowder. He took over from the cook when it came time to make the chowder, and did it himself. Spent the whole morning—this was his time off watch—making the chowder aboard the ship and then later as a special treat made a Solomon Gundy, which is a kind of preserved and spiced herring, as a special treat. And so I would say that the fisherman is probably one of the people who's most keen about fish as a substance of a meal."

THE WAY I LIKE A SALMON "I've ate salmon that was caught all over the world in different places where I've been, and I have never eaten a piece of salmon that ever compared to what a piece of Atlantic salmon out of the Bay of Fundy does, out of the salt water when they come in from the sea into the river to spawn. I don't know how you could explain it, but I have never had anything that I could compare it with. It has very deep pink colour, and on the west coast, they get steelhead out there which look much the same, but that steelhead didn't have the flavour or had the same taste as our salmon does here in the Bay of Fundy.

If you want to get peak flavour out of a salmon, if you catch a salmon, let it sit for twelve to fourteen hours iced down in ice temperature, and it loses its firmness, and the flavour that's in the fish seems to go through the meat, which tastes a lot better. If you was to take one directly right out of the water and cook him in fifteen, twenty minutes' time, he wouldn't have near the flavorous taste as that fish that was laying there on ice for twelve or fourteen hours and with the normal temperatures. This is the way I would cook a salmon, the way I like a salmon."

IN PRAISE OF WEST COAST SALMON "I've always heard it said that Atlantic salmon are better-tasting fish or are better-quality fish because of the colder waters, but I think this is something of acquiring a taste. I've tasted quite a few imported Atlantic fish and I think our fish are much better in taste and quality, and then again it possibly is because I get it fresh and it hasn't gone through the processing."

A FRESH FISH "If I want a fresh fish, just the minute the fish comes in over the side of the boat I cut his throat while he's still alive and he'll bleed—like bleedin' an animal, you'll have a much lighter, much better texture flesh. The average fish is just caught and thrown in a box, and when the fisherman gets a little time he'll shack it—what we mean by shacking is cuttin' and takin' the gut out. The head is left on but it's gutted so that anything the fish has been eating will not burn the insides of the fish."

OUT OF THE SHELL "If I was going to eat fish, and I've ate many pounds of them and hope to eat many pounds in the future, as you can probably see, I prefer a fish taken directly from the water and put in a frying-pan.

Last evening I was on the wharf doing my job collecting log records and statistics from our local fishing fleet and I was picking up some scallop shells for some biological sampling and while doing so I shucked some scallops into one of the fishermen's buckets and I was eating fresh scallops right out of the shell, right out of the water, and I'll take them that way anytime."

HOME CANNING AND FREEZING   "We eat a lot of fish. We're very fond of fish, we eat it twice a week, sometimes three times a week. I especially like cod, that's my favourite, but we eat halibut and a lot of salmon also; I have a deep-freeze and we eat it all winter because I freeze fish and freeze oolichans, the Indians call them candlefish, which are really delicious frozen. I don't know how to explain how they taste. They call them candlefish but actually I don't think they're greasy, oily—when I fry them I have to put fat in the pan. They must be fried very, very crisp to make them good.

I can my own salmon. I have a small canning-machine, and I use a pressure cooker, cook them at fifteen pounds of pressure, and I do any kind if salmon I can get. I don't care for frozen fish bought in the store at all. We never buy it.

When I freeze fish, well, I do some whole and then I glaze them. That is, I dip them in water three or four times after they're frozen hoping it will seal in all the bare flesh in where the head is cut off and so forth, till they get a light glaze over the whole fish. Then, if I am just doing enough for a meal I put the fish in a container and pour water in to cover the fish and then I freeze it. We find that that keeps the fish very well."

THE LOBSTER'S NOT FOR EATING   "I do like the lobster fishery, but I've never eaten lobster in my life. I've never touched one of them. I don't like them. My father before me never ate one and I don't know how many, well, I say I probably caught three and a half million in my lifetime and I love to fish them, but I've never eaten them."

NOT LOBSTER AGAIN!   "At the turn of the century, lobsters were common to the point where the fishermen were paid a dollar a hundred-pound barrel for them. Everyone in the poorer communities, less-well-off people, lived on lobsters, and it was almost a sign that you were plain poor if you lived on lobsters.

So as a result schoolchildren would absolutely refuse to have anything to do with lobsters for their lunches. They wouldn't be seen at school with them, but rather, the parents had to put together jam and jelly sandwiches and the like. You were branded for life if you were an eater of lobsters in your school."

SQUID IS SWEET "We had squid yesterday stuffed and baked, and you use the stuffing the same as you would for chicken, with savoury and bread and onions and butter. And you clean the squid and you stuff them inside, and that's the way I like 'em done. Now some people cook squid and they're really tough; I've eaten them, just like leather. But the way I cook them they're really nice. I had a crowd of men in here yesterday for dinner, that was down workin' on the traps, so I took and baked four squid yesterday, stuffed, and I rolled them in tinfoil and sealed the ends and baked them in the oven, just long enough to bake the dressing, an hour is plenty, and you could cut 'em with the side of a fork.

Squid is sweet, something like the claws of a lobster, very sweet. Some people believe that squid is a scavenger and they feel the same way about mackerel—a lot of people won't eat mackerel. But as far as I'm concerned, if it comes out the water it's good to eat. There's nothing I haven't tried by the water. Well, I never ran across anything yet I don't like."

THIS IS IT, EH? "I caught an octopus in the net one time at Smith Inlet, so I gave it to the Japanese. I know they love 'em, you know. I said, 'I'm gonna give you this on one condition. You've got to give me a little piece when you've cooked it the way you have it.'

So the next day, I was workin' on my net and down came the little succulent mess. It was, you know, a piece of leg about that long, about six inches long, like a wiener, wrapped in seaweed and everything. And they said, 'There you are.' I said, 'This is it, eh? This is the way you have it, eh?' 'Yeah.' 'Well, thanks, you know.'

Well, boy, I'm telling you, you couldn't chew it. I don't know how they eat it. They must have terrific teeth. But just like rubber, really like rubber."

THE JAPANESE DIET "We like all fish, we love cod. We make fish cake out of it, you know. And like sockeye, that's the best canning fish, we can a lot of that, and then springs and steelheads, we mainly eat that fried. You make sukiyaki fish, you know, and different ways of eating it.

We eat a whole variety of fish and we have meat and fish on the table and most of the time I start dinner with the fish, not the meat. Once in a while I like a big, fat, juicy steak, you know, but mainly we go for fish."

FRESH MEAT ON THE MACKENZIE   "On the stern-wheelers going north those days, we would start out with a certain amount of fresh meat, but we had no refrigeration, as we know it today. So there was a lot of canned goods went along with you, and a lot of canned milk and that sort of stuff.

We also carried some livestock on the barges, we had a regular cattle-pen for them, and this was slaughtered later on in the trip, usually by the time you got down to Aklavik and started your return trip. The cook was also the butcher, and we'd take this animal ashore, usually a couple of steers and some chickens, and he'd do the butchering, and then you'd have fresh meat for a few days going back. But eventually, you'd run out. You never had enough to go all the way. So then you'd go back to beans and that sort of stuff.

You looked forward to this fresh meat, you know. This was a real treat to have fresh meat for a week or ten days."

WHALE MEAT   "Whale meat is just no different from any other meat, only there is no fat in it, so you've got to kind of make hamburgers and doctor it up, that's the way we ate it. It's exactly like beef, nice and red. In fact, people in the whaling station would rather have it than beef. But the only thing is, meat has got the fat in it. This is just meat, there is no fat in it or nothing. You see, it's dry, but they doctor it up."

SEAGULL EGGS   "Some of the fellows on the beach would go up hunting seagull eggs. I would never eat seagull eggs, I never really cared for them. Just the looks of them, the colour of the yolk and that, was something that didn't appeal to me at all. But they'd go up on this little trail up towards the lake where the seagulls nested or out on the rock and they'd pick up these seagull eggs and, you know, they didn't cost them anything, just a little shoe leather, that's all. Better than paying fifteen cents a dozen for eggs off the fish tractor or the fish camp.

When we came to shore you'd probably bring a small chunk of salmon or buy something off the packer, a couple of pork chops or something like that, and cook it up with a mess of spuds, and that would be your dinner. And then you'd hit the sack and have a good sleep and you had no alarm clock there to jar you loose in the morning."

BAY BUNS AND RABBITS "We're in this out-of-the-way harbour cutting the wood, and we go over for about three days, so we make up what we call bay buns. Now what's a bay bun? That's a molasses bun with pork in it, raw pork. It will freeze and, gee, they'll last and they won't dry up, your bread will dry up but this will never dry up. You can keep it a month.

You cut them with a big water glass as a cutter, they're made of flour, baking powder, molasses, and hunks of raw pork, and then we bake it, the pork would partly cook, but it would keep moist. You have a flour bag for a week, with your buns, and then we had some bread and tea and pork and beef and potatoes, but you want some fresh, you put some rabbit slips in, you know, a wire for catching rabbits."

A DUTCH MESS "A common dish in Tancook is what we call a Dutch mess, and that is codfish, pork scraps fried out, and onions, and put that over the codfish and then potatoes cooked and that is our common dish here. That's very good, yes."

A MOLASSES MESS "A long-liner will definitely roll in the wind, you know, and if the water is tumbly, she'll roll. And one day, this started a real catastrophe. A friend of ours would come out once in a while with us, to help us haul the trap and get a few fish for himself, and he used to have home-made bread and molasses. So he brought a jar of molasses aboard this day, and molasses, you know what that's like.

When we got around the cape, we got into the wind, and the boat started to roll. I was in the wheelhouse with my husband and we heard the crash down below and when we went down, a pile of dinner plates was smashed up on the floor, and to top it all up was this crock of molasses. Talk about a mess we had! The few forks and knives that was in with the plates we picked out, and the rest we just scraped up, and when we got out in Harbour Grace, I went and put the hose down the hold. There's a board you can take up and I stuffed the hose down and washed it all out. We just took cardboard and scraped up the molasses and glass and throwed it out, all the stuff. It was some mess!"

SMOKE-TENDERS "Smoking fish is an art, there's no doubt about it, and on Grand Manan there's probably half a dozen good smoke-tenders. You have to develop an instinct for it. A good smoke-tender can tell when he walks in the smokehouse what his temperature's like and whether he's got too much heat, too little heat for the type of day it is, and so on, so forth. It's really a rare art.

The fish is strung on a stick which, of course, is known as a herring stick, and they are placed on slats in the smokehouse. A smokehouse probably will take a hundred tons of fish per house, roughly a hundred tons, and salt-water wood, driftwood, is preferable because it has two factors. Number one, it gives more heat than ordinary upland wood, and number two, it gives a better colour to the smoked fish, a more golden colour. But if you have a hot day, very hot at all, well, if it gets too hot you can't smoke. I mean you're gonna build up too much heat in the smokehouse. On a warm day you'll use upland wood because it doesn't give near the heat and you'll get some smoke with usin' sawdust, but if you get a cool day and the wind's in a drying corner and you really want to dry your fish to make 'em up, dry 'em up quick, then what you use is salt-water wood."

CORNCOBS "We smoke all our fish with corncobs in the smokehouse. We get them, the corncobs, from farmers, co-ops, wherever we can get 'em. We've gotta have good dry ones. We have a propane burner which starts the corncobs smoking but you've gotta keep them from flaming, you can't let enough air in to let 'em flame, you just want 'em to smoke. It takes about five hours, according to the weather, four or five hours. On the weekends we smoke two batches a day, thirty to forty pounds, maybe.

For smoking some use sawdust, some use applewood, but I like corncobs. I use about a truckload every month."

STRAWBERRY GOLDEYE "Now a goldeye is a silvery, fairly narrow fish and would run anywhere from eight ounces gutted with the head on, up to approximately twelve, fourteen ounces, fifteen ounces, and this is what they use for smoking. Now, once it's smoked they put it into a brine for appeal and they put it into a strawberry colouring and it makes that goldeye red. That's something that was started years ago in Winnipeg—artificially coloured goldeye, and it's continued. Now, if you smoke it natural, which we did for our own consumption out in the bush, it turns a beautiful golden-yellow type of colour."

RICE AND STOVE OIL "In 1935, my father and I were fishing for cod in the wintertime, out here in January, and the weather was desperately cold, it was down twenty-five, thirty below zero. We run a string of trawl down off Tiner's Point off Split Rock in the Bay of Fundy and we went into Musquash Harbour to make harbour for the night and we planned to come back out the next day, pick up the gear. Well, we got into this little cove there, and that night come a great big north-east snowstorm and snowed and filled the cove right full of slush and ice and it was so cold that night that it froze over. And we couldn't get out of there for three days.

We only had enough grub with us to do overnight, we weren't stocked up, and the second day all we had left was some rice. Father had cooked the rice and we had a lamp, one of the old ship lamps hooked onto the mast. Now our table was fastened onto the mast and underneath that lamp he had the sugar-bowl and the lamp was full of stove oil and the oil leaked down and went into the sugar—and I'll tell you, if you want a tasty dish, cook some rice, nothing but boiled rice, and then put sugar on it with stove oil in it—the tastiest thing you ever seen in your life.

Come the second day, we had run out of wood, we had no wood to keep the fire going, and we had nothing but a wood stove in the boat. So we went down and we took and tore the floorboards out of the engine-room and we sawed the floor up to get enough wood to burn this fire.

I had a pair of them big high boots with leather tops on them and they never thawed out in the cabin. For three days, I put them on, they were froze, I took them off, they were froze, and I think the temperature in the cabin must've been down at sometimes at least twenty-five below, the same as it was outside.

After the third day, the wind had shifted and taken the ice and the slush out of the cove and we got out of there and got back up to the country up home, up to Lorneville, and got in there and whenever we come in alongside the wharf, my father didn't even bother tying a line on the wharf. He jumped out of the boat, up the road to the store, come back with a bunch of groceries, and I'll tell you, I never had a meal that tasted so good in all my life."

SIXTEEN

Rescue

In Johnstone Strait... Just Luck... A Very Foggy Night... Involved in a Search... A Needle in the Pacific... One on the Line... Looking for Survivors... Search-and-Rescue... An Optimist... Marge Standing on a Rock... From the Spanish Civil War... The Resurrection of Jimmy Critchley... Three Men in Georgian Bay... Capsized Dinghies Everywhere... Looking for Me?... A Personal Escort... Everything in Our Power... You've Got Him, You've Found Him!

The bad time is always at dusk. When darkness begins to fall, they start telephoning. Captain D. K. Powick, officer in charge of the Rescue Co-ordination Centre in Halifax, told me: "They call us at night, always at night, if the vessel does not come back, because when the sun sets I suppose you tend to become a little hopeless and they call us. Their main need is to say, 'Is there any hope? Is there any chance of them still being alive out there?' "

Search and Rescue out of Halifax has an eleven-thousand-mile Canadian coastline to patrol, while the Rescue Co-ordination Centre at Esquimalt, British Columbia, has sixteen thousand miles of rugged coastline to look after and there are boats on the water 365 days a year, and planes flying up and down the coast, in and out of inlets, and over mountains.

One of the strangest stories told me by Captain Frank Gavin, deputy officer of the Rescue Co-ordination Centre, happened six years ago. A converted military plane, an old Harvard, left Whitehorse in the Yukon for Vancouver, with the pilot and a woman passenger aboard. They vanished. The weather was terrible: fog and poor visibility, and the rescue aircraft searched and searched for about three weeks and finally the search was called off. They had to assume the Harvard burned or went into heavy trees or went into the water—a lot of the flight was over water.

Two years later, an aircraft pilot spotted what seemed to be a plane in the trees on Roderick Island, a little island about fifty miles south of Prince Rupert. A helicopter was sent in, and there, pretty well intact but upside down, was the Harvard. Captain Gavin said, "They had seat belts on, and when the plane flipped over, they got out of the plane, and left a note saying they had stayed there eight days. Snow had covered the Harvard. The island was very rugged with steep shale cliffs up to five hundred feet right from the ocean. They started walking, and it would take two or three hours to walk a mile. We found bits and pieces of stuff they had left, a pair of socks here, a watch there, a pair of boots here. They blazed a trail where they had gone, they were very smart. The trail finally came to an end at a shale cliff that went down 250 feet into an inaccessible area.

"We figured they must have gone over the cliff, or one of them fell, and the other tried to grab the falling person. Anyway, we never did locate the bodies, nothing has ever been located of these people at all. The aircraft is still sitting there in the spot where it crashed, an intact airplane."

But whether it's a professional rescue team involved or a group of brave and dedicated amateurs, rescues on the water are always a dramatic business, as this chapter shows.

IN JOHNSTONE STRAIT "This particular night there was a distress call. It was an Indian fellow and his wife and little girl about three or four years old, on a gill-net boat. They had come down from Prince Rupert and were fishing in Johnstone Strait and they had no business being out there that night but they were, and it came up real, real bad. Well, they started to sink. Of course, everybody has phones these days, so it's out on the phone there that they need help. Almost everybody's anchored, you know, because it's so stormy, it's blowing about thirty-five, forty miles an hour, and you can't get out. But anyway one seine boat went out and helped them, and so did one real good gill-netter, too, but he couldn't do very much and neither could the seine boat.

Mind you, by this time the boat is sinkin', it's swamped. Now, swamped means that it's gone down to the point where it's gonna hang on for a while, you know, before the last bit of air gets out and it probably plummets, that's it. But it was swamped and they were there on the cabin, the phone still working yet, miraculously. They were still on top of the cabin and they've got the little kid tied to the mast so she won't get washed off—tied to the mast, and the wife she's squealin' away and I guess the husband's trying to do whatever he can.

The seine boat is there and he can't get to him. The seas are so rough that they daren't go alongside this boat because in a big seine boat they'll smash it up and make kindling wood out of it. And they're still on top of the cabin now and, of course, finally their phone is gone, the batteries are dead, it's under water now so they've got no phone, they've got nothing.

But we're getting it from the seine boat now that they're trying to get to them. The only way they can possibly do it is to go ahead, and they put two guys in the seine skiff and let it back with the wind, you know, let the seine skiff back to the boat. And they kept missing, you know what I mean, it's not so easy to do that. The boat would veer off.

Now, in the meantime the little girl washes overboard. That's the end of her. She's washed overboard. So the others still hanging on, you can imagine the desperate plight they're in.

Now this was going on for hours now and everybody's tuned in. What can you do? You can't go out there. You'd never make it. You know, you'd be gone yourself. It's impossible to go out and help them, and the gill-netter, he had to give up and get out of there, but the seine boat, he had to stay with it.

Well, somehow or another they finally got the wife and the man in the skiff, but the wife is in real bad shape. So they're phonin' back and forth, a doctor's talking from Alert Bay, what to do. You know, to try and get the water out and give her mouth-to-mouth resuscitation. Well, they don't understand really. They're not taking in too well what the doctor said. 'Don't you realize there's a storm? It's washing over the top all the time.' Well, you just practically drowned, in a rough sea it's coming over the top. You know, you've gotta hang on and hang on and the thing's rolling—you can't imagine, really. Well, you have to breathe and the wife she died right there, before she got to the hospital she was gone. The little girl, she was picked up in a net the next day. Floated, you know. Picked up in a gill-net, she had drifted into it. So there was two, you see. He come out of it all right, went back to Prince Rupert. The boat, of course, did go down. That was the end of that."

JUST LUCK "In the middle of March, about ten years ago, we started for home from Bamfield. There was me and my brother and a guy named Harada, and Aki Hikida, and Don Narukami, and we headed for Victoria that early morning. The forecast at that time was south-easterly twenty, turning to westerly twenty, so it wasn't too bad. So we headed out from Bamfield and by the time we reached San Juan in mid west coast of Vancouver Island, the wind had already changed to sou'west and then before we got to Sherringham the wind had gone up to a hundred miles per hour.

And, oh, the *Sudbury II* was towing a scow and he was going like this, you know, it was really horrible to watch, and the shrimp boxes weighing about ten to eleven pounds wet were flying just like paper boxes with this wind. And then our table that weighed maybe forty pounds went flying in the air just like a matchbox.

Finally, at Sherringham, Mr. Harada called to say, 'There's something haywire with my boat,' and that was the last call from him. He overturned suddenly, and he crawled out the window and he clung onto the side of the overturned boat. He was still young, a teacher of judo, and he was really hardy.

After many hours of trying, Don Narukami finally detected the boat upside down with a little air pocket on the side, suddenly he found himself on top of Mr. Harada's boat and that's how Mr. Harada was able to jump onto Don's boat.

And a few hours later, to our surprise, the capsized boat had drifted into the entrance to Sooke Harbour. So we took the bow, and it still was blowing and howling gale, and we towed it into

Sooke Harbour and there was Mounties and newspapermen and newspaperwomen. They said, 'How did you ever survive that gale?' I said, 'Well, I don't know, just luck I guess.' "

A VERY FOGGY NIGHT   "One of our search-and-rescue cases happened in the southern half of Newfoundland, on a very foggy, foggy night. Two fishermen on one boat, a Cape Islander, were attempting to get the vessel close to shore, so the man on the bow was saying: 'A little forward, a little forward, turn to the right, turn to the left,' trying to miss the rock that was standing out. Suddenly, he saw a big rock ahead of him so he yelled back to the fellow in the stern of the boat: 'Full astern, full astern or we'll crash.' So the man in the back of the boat pulled the boat full astern, and the man in the front fell off.

The man at the back got the boat turned around and then he walked up forward to see his buddy, and when he walked up he couldn't find him. Fog, you know, when they really get fog out there, it's really thick.

Meanwhile, because of the breakers and the waves the man who was floating in the water thought he heard a fishing vessel hit rock further down and sink. So that man made it to shore and he went to an RCMP station, one of the little outposts, and related the story of what had happened. He was very, very upset that he had lost his best friend and the ship and the whole routine.

In the meantime, the man in the vessel backed out of this cove they were in, and he got back into another cove by himself and he went to another RCMP station and said: 'I've just lost my best buddy; he fell over the front and drowned, and this is the rough position of it.'

The RCMP notified us, so we had a call looking for a man in the water, and in the second case we had a vessel sunk with another guy on board. We must have worked on that case for close to an hour and a half, getting the facts, phoning the RCMP, talking to the bereaved fellow who had lost his buddy overboard, before one of the controllers said: 'Gee, the two cases look like they're both the same. It happened within ten miles. Let's call the RCMP.'

So we called the RCMP and said: 'Look, take this guy,' and we called the other RCMP and we said: 'Take the other guy and have them both meet somewhere and see if these two guys know each other.' And I guess the outcome was just a bunch of laughing, and grinning, and breaking open a bottle of screech and having a good time."

INVOLVED IN A SEARCH   "I don't know what a person who is going to be rescued thinks about when they are out there, but they have no idea what goes in motion. They're out there on a life-raft, the next thing they see the helicopter and they've been found, and that's probably as far as the train of thought goes. They don't realize that there could possibly be five or six thousand people involved in a search, if you count from the person who is in the raft to the airplane to the maintenance to the telephone communications all the way back, pool all this information in one spot, and come out and say we're going to pick that guy out of the water. Involved in any one search, you can have the RCMP, the Coast Guard, the Volunteer Rescue Agency, CAM operators, CB operators, Department of Coastal Defence, Department of Fisheries and Environment. You could have ships in the Soviet Bloc, you could have ships in every country in the world in your area, because if they hear mayday, by the code of the sea they must respond. Hundreds and hundreds of people."

A NEEDLE IN THE PACIFIC   "Oh, in British Columbia we probably have the worst search country in the northern hemisphere, bar none. Our mountains go anywhere from fifteen thousand feet down to sea level. We have coastal conditions that would just utterly amaze people down east, in fact we have more coastline in British Columbia—sixteen thousand miles—than they do in the Atlantic area. And we have three hundred and sixty-five days a year that people can go boating. Last year in the area covered by our group, the Rescue Co-ordination Centre at CFB *Esquimalt*, we had 3,984 'instances'.

For example, late in January 1977, we were alerted in the rescue centre by Bull Harbour Coast Guard radio. A fishing-boat off the coast of the north end at Vancouver Island had told him that they were in company with another forty-five-foot fishing-vessel and this vessel had disappeared. Two vessels fishing together on the buddy-buddy system is quite common out here on the west coast. Although they weren't friends or anything, they were just fishing together, and that's sort of mutual protection—if one goes missing the other one will report him overdue. Well, this guy said, 'I don't know if there's anything behind this or not, but this fella I was fishing with just hasn't been around for a while.'

So, we did what we usually do in the rescue centre in a case like this, when we're not sure whether we have a case. We issued a general marine broadcast to tell all the ships that are around that there's a vessel missing and if anybody sees him they just report in to the nearest coastal radio station. And a lot of times we find vessels this way.

Anyway, in this case nothing turned up and we got back to these people who reported vessel overdue, and asked for some details. There were two people on board a well equipped forty-five-foot powered fishing-vessel, commonly called a troller. Red and white in colour, very easy to find. So we decided, well, if they haven't shown up, then maybe they are in trouble. So we started sending aircraft out searching for them, and we alerted some of our Coast Guard vessels in the area. Well, we searched all of the area for a day and we found nothing and we went back to the original people who reported them overdue and they said, 'Well, you know, the guy probably just went some place else to fish, so we wouldn't be too worried about 'em.' But we decided that maybe somebody *should* start worrying about these people, so we launched a full-scale search. We put two of our Buffalo aircraft up from Comox, we put a Labrador helicopter up from Comox, and the Department of Fisheries sent out their hundred-and-fifty-foot cutter, the *G. B. Reed*, and we just started looking all over the place, any place from northern Vancouver Island all the way to Prince Rupert, because we didn't know where this guy might be missing. We didn't know whether he went some place else fishing, we didn't know whether he'd sunk, or what. We also alerted our maritime squadron, that's the ones that normally go out hunting submarines, and Russian fishing vessels, and so on, out of Comox, we launched them to go out and look.

Nearing the middle of the third day one of the Argus aircraft spotted what appeared to be a life-raft in the water about thirty

miles north of Vancouver Island. They went in and found it was a
life-raft, a covered one, so we couldn't tell whether anybody was
alive or not. So we then alerted our nearest Buffalo aircraft with
search-and-rescue specialists, the people who parachute into the
water. Since we suspected these people had been on the life-raft
at least three days, maybe four, we decided to release our para-
rescue specialists.

While we were preparing to release them, the pilot noticed a lot
of very large fish in the water. Well, these large fish turned out to
be sharks. Maybe you think we're joking, but we really do have
sharks off Vancouver Island. Now the Buffalo aircraft contacted
search-and-rescue in Victoria and we very carefully assured them
that these were only basking sharks and they weren't all that dangerous. But there was no way we could convince one of the rescue
specialists who had just come down, back from down east, that
we didn't have sharks right out of *Jaws*. Anyway, both of them
jumped—and they were armed with knives in their teeth. So into
the midst of the Pacific Ocean in fairly cool water went our two
rescue specialists with their knives in their mouths, of course.
Then they swam over to these guys that were in the life-raft, and
found them both alive and in pretty good shape. They had had
survival equipment, but they weren't really prepared to stay out
there for the three days that they had been in the water.

We found out later that the reason that they were in the water
was that a storm had come up just after these other people had
departed the scene, and a giant wave just swamped the vessel, the
boat sank, and they were left in the life-raft.

I'm telling you, in the large Pacific Ocean twenty, thirty miles
out to sea, a life-raft is just about impossible to see. It's just like a
speck of a needle in a haystack, not even the whole needle. So
they were pretty lucky, actually, to be found. They were certainly
happy to see these rescue specialists swimming towards them, but
they didn't know what to think when they saw knives in their
mouths."

ONE ON THE LINE "Some of the incidents that have happened
in our search-and-rescue are terribly sad, with the loss of lives, and
some of them are extremely humorous, and to give an example of

a humorous one, we had a case where a gentleman left St. Margaret's Bay area in his fishing-vessel heading for Fortune Bay, Newfoundland. Now that's about four hundred miles by sea, and he was leaving on the first of the month and he told his wife he would be in Fortune Bay fishing for five or six days, then he would see his sister in Fortune Bay and phone home on the ninth of the month. Therefore, the woman at home in St. Margaret's Bay, Nova Scotia, didn't worry about her husband up until after the ninth. On the tenth she phoned us and said her husband had not called in and she was terribly afraid that something had happened to him en route or perhaps while fishing.

So we got as much information as we could from the lady in regard to the description of the vessel and where he was going. So, after we had all the information, I scrambled an airplane out of Somerset, and they flew across to Newfoundland and started searching in Fortune Bay, back and forth and back and forth. They spent about two hours searching there.

In the meantime we were running down a description of the vessel, asking if anybody had seen it, and we went through procedures, flying coast air traffic, Halifax traffic, and so on, and we found the vessel approximately six hours after the search initiated. The vessel was in Halifax.

The man had told his wife he was going to Newfoundland—in fact he had a girlfriend in Halifax, and he spent two weeks with her.

We never heard from the parties concerned again. I doubt he's ever got himself in trouble again, though, I imagine he's kept a pretty clean slate."

LOOKING FOR SURVIVORS "As well as being in the rescue centre here, on quite numerous occasions I go up in a search aircraft and actively search for missing people and missing aircraft, survivors from boating accidents. And looking for survivors or looking for downed aircraft or people in the sea is really a hard job. You might not imagine it is, but it's very hard on the eyes. There's very much eye strain and the people in the back of the aircraft that do this are called spotters. They only spot for twenty minutes at a time; they then rest for twenty minutes and new people come on.

You can be deceived by a lot of things in the water. We have objects that look like bodies in the water and on subsequent investigations turn out to be nothing other than tree stumps or logs or pieces of foreign flotation, and it seems like anything that's blown off a ship blows into the water and it'll stay there floating around for ever. So, when we have to check out all this stuff, it's just a monumental task for the spotters, where they have to continue to stare into the water for hours upon hours."

SEARCH-AND-RESCUE "It's not all glory in the search-and-rescue field, although you really get a good feeling when you do find somebody, especially after he's been missing for three or four days or even as long as a month. We've had cases here in the west coast where a boat is reported missing and they just completely vanish, they vanish without any trace. Well, probably what happens is, they could be hit by a giant wave and, as you know, on the west coast of Vancouver Island and the west coast of Canada, where we are, the next point of land when we're looking out in the Pacific sometimes is Japan, and some of these waves you'd swear started building up when they left Japan, and by the time they get here they're built up, and a lot of our vessels suffer as a result of it. A giant wave can come through and completely swamp up to a hundred-foot vessel. If it's a wooden vessel especially, it'll completely smash the boat into so many pieces that even if we do find pieces floating in the water you could never ever find that it came from a specific boat.

The only trace left of a boat that actually has been turned in to us one time was part of the name-board of the vessel, and that's all we ever found of this vessel, just part of the name board. It had three people on board.

Now, the water is cold out here year round. You could not survive in the water for more than a couple of days even if you have your lifejacket on. Once they do perish from the elements, their body will either go to the bottom if it doesn't have a lifejacket on, or it can be eaten up by the sea life that's in the ocean, you know, crabs, and so on. We found skeletal remains of people out of vessels in here still floating in the lifejacket, but not one bit of flesh left on the bodies."

AN OPTIMIST "If they're trying to cross the Atlantic in a balloon and the balloon goes down, our job is to go find it, or if the guy who rows across doesn't make it, then we'll go out looking for him. We have to persuade people not to attempt foolish undertakings. Like, we had a case of one man in a life-raft, who was going to row across the ocean. And he only had one arm, and he was missing one lung, and he had enough food to last him about three days. We persuaded him not to go."

MARGE STANDING ON A ROCK "The light-keeper from Sambro Island and his wife had been into Sambro and they were on their way back to the island in their small outboard motor-boat and they went through what we call the Gut, it's a narrow strip separating what we call Egg Island from the main island. And when they went through, the sea swamped them and they drifted in on this rock and they lost their boat. Now they were stranded on Egg Island, which was no more than ninety feet probably across the top. They had no way of signalling anybody and this was getting up toward dark in the wintertime, in January. The water temperature was thirty degrees and the air temperature was thirty degrees and a storm was brewing, so at about nine-thirty that night, after they'd been on the rock for five hours, he decided that he'd have to do something, or the two of them would end their lives right there. So what he did was, he got right down to the edge of the water to make an attempt to swim across.

It's about thirty yards approximately across there, but you can imagine the sea was rolling right in through this Gut sort of thing. But he got across all right and he hollered back to his wife saying that he was across there, and just after he hollered out the sea struck him and washed him back out again. But he got ahold of some seaweed and he got back up. Now he had a quarter of a mile to walk before he got to his dwelling there on the island, and he was soaking wet and freezing cold. When he got to his house he went in and he turned on the radio and he called here.

If I live to be a hundred and fifty I'll never want to hear anything like that on a radio again. First there was a microphone open and there was nothing, just the heavy breathing, and then when he spoke it was half cry, half pleading; he said, 'We lost the boat, Marge is stranded on the rock, I don't know if she's still there or not,' something like that, you know. Well, after a little bit of difficulty, the man on watch here got the message that his wife was stranded on this rock. Now, I have a radio in my home and I heard the call in my home, you see, and I didn't wait to be called, I came down here and jumped aboard the boat, started the engine, and it only seemed like moments before they told me all was let go, you know, we were on our way.

So we took off out there and it was dark, we had to go three miles and it was dark and a storm brewing, you know, and we got out there and we put the searchlights on and we had to manoeuvre in between two rocks, to get in where she was at.

Once we got the searchlight on to her, we could see her. I put the boat within forty feet of the rock and we put the inflatable boat over and my two men rowed ashore in the inflatable boat. What they did is they rowed in close to the rock, until they got in where the sea was breaking; then they watched their chance and when the sea broke, they went in on it, something like you see a surfer do. By the time the next sea came in they had the boat right up on the rock.

I couldn't get over it, she was standing there as if she was waiting for a bus. She was that calm about it all, you know, and when they came down, I was trying to keep the searchlights on them and trying to keep the boat from going on the reefs and what have you, I had my hands full, and they came down and they brought her down to the rubber dinghy and they watched the sea and when they saw a chance they threw the boat and all three of them jumped for it, and that's the way they got back. They rowed back to the boat.

Now, Marge and I have always been very good friends and, you know, she is from Cape Breton and I'm from Newfoundland, so we're always tormenting each other about, you know, 'you Newfie', 'you Cape Bretoner', that sort of thing, and when she came aboard I noticed she was very quiet. I had seen people like this before in mild shock and this is what I figured she was, in mild shock. So what I was doing was trying to manoeuvre the boat out from where we were now, and in the meantime I was trying to pay attention to her. She wouldn't go down below, she pleaded with me not to put her down below because she gets seasick, and she wanted to stand right in the wheelhouse beside me. So, after a little while I was trying to manoeuvre the boat out and I was thinking, you know, back in my air force days I'd seen people in shock, their faces were cold and clammy. So I put my hands over to feel her face, and when I did she said, 'What the hell are you doing, you bloody Newfoundlander!' 'Well,' I said, 'you're all right,' I said, 'there's nothing wrong with you at all.'

Now, the thing is, the next morning at daybreak, that rock that she was standing on was all awash, was all awash."

FROM THE SPANISH CIVIL WAR "I was on the *Colbourne*, a Canadian ship, registered here in Montreal. We were going down between Trinidad and British Guiana, and we met a Spanish fisherman and he had his basket up on the mast to say, 'I'm fishing, keep clear.' He didn't want anybody to see who was aboard, they were refugees from Spain during that civil war they had. There was fifty-odd men aboard that ship and one woman, the captain's wife, on a small little thing, fifty or sixty people.

They stopped us, and he takes his boat and goes around the stern of the ship and reads the writs and then he comes back and he goes up to the captain's quarters and he said, 'We want some grease and we want a little bit of food to last us to get into Trinidad, we don't want nothing else, just enough oil and grease to get the engine going again.' They were drifting.

So they come alongside of us and took a line from us and some of the boys came aboard and they feasted on jam and things they'd never tasted for years.

So they got their oil and grease and food and wood and we left them, approximately two hundred miles from Trinidad.

The second engineer on the *Colbourne* was a bit of a photographer and he took some beautiful pictures of their ship, and all the men lined the rail with a piece of stick, holding her off so she wouldn't bump our ship. We were steady, but she was rolling around, so much that she put her mast in our rails and broke it off.

She was only about seventy feet long, adrift in the Atlantic. They were all doctors, lawyers, things like that, and they didn't want anyone to see them at that time, because they might take them back to Spain and shoot them."

THE RESURRECTION OF JIMMY CRITCHLEY "Mildred was fine and dandy. Like, when we were first married she was a real good sailor. The biggest, roughest seas there ever was never bothered her a bit.

When our son was four years old he rolled over the back of a boat. This was up at Howe Sound here, he rolled into the chuck. He was used to boats, too, but this boat had a roller right across the back and he was reaching out with a gaff hook and he reached a bit too far and rolled right on her and into the chuck. But he had one of these snowsuits on, you see, which kinda kept him buoyed up. You know, these little snowsuits, fasten at the bottom?

Mildred was screamin' her head off, which woke me up, and I jumped in the water to help to get him, you see. Well, he hung onto me, pretty near drowned me too. He was a little boy but you'd be surprised how strong they are when they're in the water, and of course this was October and the water was icy. He was drifting away, and we were the farthest boat out, no boats beyond us, and the current's going out. Now ahead of us was a fish camp and there was a fellow pulling his net out of the bluestone tank, and he saw Jimmy go over. Well, he threw a rope over the bow so we could grab it but I'm not a very strong swimmer and then Jimmy was hangin' on, making things worse. So, anyway, I finally did grab the rope, but as I grabbed the rope Jimmy fell off.

He'd just about had it by now, you know. He was gurglin' and I suppose kept going under when I did, and taking lots of water too. Well, he was gone, that's it.

These Japanese guys, they heard Mildred screaming and about six or seven of them jumped into the fastest boat they had, and came rushing towards us. Now, by this time Jimmy's let go and I'm looking around really panicky, hanging onto this rope on the bow of this other boat and I can't see Jimmy at all and I'm really worried, now where has he gone? You know, he's gone, that's it.

But the Japanese had seen him sink and they come along with

one fellow hanging over the side, hanging onto the rigging, and scooped Jimmy right out. They just run right alongside him and scooped him out like that and dragged him on deck just drowned, just soaking wet, you know, drowned. He was drowned, he's gone, that's it. So, anyway, they came back and put me on the boat, to take me back to my own boat. I've never been so cold as that in my life, just right frozen to the bone, you know. So they took me on there and they took Jimmy to the hospital about five or six miles away. During the time they took me from this boat to my boat, well, I saw what they were doing. They had him down on his face, flat on the deck with his clothes off, and they were pumpin' the water; there was just blue water coming out of Jimmy like that. He was gone, you know, drowned, definitely drowned.

So away they went to the hospital, and then, of course, I got some dry clothes on and we had to pick the anchor up and away we went after them. There's all these toys and everything all around, we're lookin' at 'em, and I was sure he was dead, but I didn't want to tell Mildred that. Even the Japanese said he was dead. Now, they did a wonderful job. They took him to the hospital at Britannia, and by the time we got there, about two hours after, they were coming out. We seen 'em coming out towards us. Gosh, they're getting closer and closer, a little pile of clothes on the deck, you know, looks pretty grim. But then as they got closer we could see they were sort of smiling. They said, 'He's okay. He wants his mother and dad and he's fine. He's come through.' So away we went to the hospital and the doctor says, 'Boy, you've sure got to thank them Japanese fellows. They sure knew what to do.' He said, 'He was dead but he's fine now.'

Know what the Japanese did? They pumped the water out of him and got him breathin' again, and they emptied every bottle they had and filled it up with hot water. They got the stove goin' and hot water coming along and they emptied all their saki out and their ketchup and all other things, every bottle they could, every available bottle, no matter what it had in it they dumped it and filled it with hot water and packed it around him with blankets and that. They really did a great job. And Jimmy didn't even get a cold.

But Mildred—that's why I'm telling you she's so scared on the water. That started it. From then on, boy, she hasn't that much use for the water and in spite of the fact that I was fishing and on the water, she would go with me all right, but she always wanted to get out of it."

THREE MEN IN GEORGIAN BAY "In Georgian Bay, an eighteen-foot boat with a hundred-and-some-horse outboard on it was cutting along just at dusk, and they ran into a log! Took the bottom right out of the boat, of course, it sank just immediately, and the three guys were thrown in the water. This was out around Hope Island, between Hope Island and the Giant's Tomb, probably not more than a mile from land but it's quite a few miles out from the Midland-Penetang area. But anyway, these guys were sighted and we were called out, and, of course, the OPP vessels in the area. And by this time it was dark and you could miss a person, so it was the next morning before we finally picked up one man clinging to a log, still alive. And all he could say when we hauled him aboard was, 'I thought you wouldn't see me, I thought you wouldn't see me.' Now, that man survived. He had skin gangrene from clinging to this mouldy old log, and he was in shock, but we transferred him and got him ashore.

But his two companions—one we never found, and we picked up the other body an hour or so later with the lifejacket on the wrong way around him, which meant that it could have caused his death because he was being held face down into the water, and as he lost his strength in the cold water and hypothermia, why this helped to cause his death. A very sad thing. But no amount of searching will find an object as small as a head sticking out of the water on a dark, moonless night, where you couldn't see a thing. We could have run him down just as easy as picking him up."

CAPSIZED DINGHIES EVERYWHERE "I think why we have so many rescues in and around Toronto is this, we have the Queen City Yacht Club, the Royal Canadian Yacht Club, Ashbridges Bay Yacht Club, the Toronto Island Yacht Club, the National Yacht Club, the Boulevard Sailing and Canoe Club, and the Toronto Canoe Club. These are all clubs which have sailors who do a lot of sailing and there's a lot of dinghy sailors.

Now, quite often you have close to two hundred dinghies, centreboard boats, out in Humber Bay, and you have another thirty or forty of the centreboard boats, the Olympic type, racing off the Olympic course and a north-west squall will hit. Well, when the sailors see a squall coming from the north-west, they don't head for the harbour, they stay out there.

I've seen one day in particular, this dinghy race is on, and a north-west squall hit when a lot of the dinghies were heading out through the west gap and they were capsizing. But they kept going, some of them righted themselves and kept going out, and they no sooner got the race under way when *another* north-west squall hit, and I would say that at least three-quarters of the dinghy sailboats were capsized. Now, if they're experienced sailors, they know how to right them themselves, it's quite a simple matter in calm water to right a boat if you know how to do it. But when you have a heavy wind blowing and some waves along with it, it's not always possible to get a boat up.

So, what you do in a case like that, you pick the people up, leave the boat, go and run into the closest shore and get rid of the people, and go back out again and pick up more. That day we had every boat in the station out picking people up."

LOOKING FOR ME? "Around 1944 we got a call on the Monday morning when we opened up that a woman had disappeared overnight, and the story there was that she had had a nervous breakdown, and left the house. And her husband called the police and notified them about it, and they in turn called me. Well, I sent two men down first thing that morning and they dragged along the foot of the street that she had lived on, and apparently they had no luck, because after a couple of hours they went down and they started dragging along the outside of the pier and around the mouth and on the other side. And they kept at it for quite a while. And a few kids and persons were standing on the dock and on the top of the storm sewer there—it was about four feet in diameter and had iron railings on it—and there were people standing there, watching them.

Well, next thing I knew, I see three people in the boat, and they're rowing back towards the station. And I couldn't see clearly whether it was a man or a woman or what it was. And I thought, well, maybe they found her, and this is the husband coming up to tell us that they found her and everything's all right. But as they get closer, I notice it's a woman. And she's sittin' up in the back seat of the boat, and the lifeguard had his arm around her, and the head lifeguard keeps rowin'. As they came closer I saw that her hair was wet and her coat was wet— she had a light topcoat on—and we got her to the dock and got her into the station. And all she had on was this topcoat and a nightgown. We got her in under the blankets, and got the coat and the nightgown off her, and phoned the main station, and they got in touch with her husband. And we gave her a cup of tea, and we arranged for an ambulance to come down and take her away.

What had happened—as they were rowing around the end of the pier, after about the third or fourth time, they heard a voice saying, 'Are you looking for me, lifeguards? Are you looking for me, lifeguards?' They thought it was the youngsters on the dock, making fun of them. Well, next time they went around, they looked up the storm sewer, and she's up the sewer! It hadn't been raining for some time, and there was just a thin trickle coming through the sewer at any time other than when there was a rainstorm. And she'd been hiding up in the sewer all night long.

We never questioned her, nor did we question her husband. But he made the arrangements to come down and pick her up, and he came back about a week later and thanked us very much for what we'd done, and I was glad to hear that there were no bad effects—no pneumonia or anything like that."

A PERSONAL ESCORT   "In June of '78, a young lady phoned up, and I was there and by her voice she couldn't be more than in her mid-twenties. She said her boyfriend had just bought a thirty-foot sailing yacht and he was sailing from the Arm Yacht Club around to Mahone Bay, a distance of perhaps forty-five miles out of the Halifax Harbour down the coast to Mahone Bay.

She said, 'Are you people in the rescue business?' And I said, 'Yes, that's our business.' And she said, 'Well, my boyfriend never learned how to swim, so I was wondering if you'd send an airplane up and follow his boat all the way around to Mahone Bay.'

We had to explain very diplomatically that is not our job to follow boats around. If he starts to sink or gets into trouble we'll come to help, but we don't follow people around who can't swim."

EVERYTHING IN OUR POWER   "Imagine searching for a vessel. We search until we as qualified search-masters feel there is no possibility that the vessel is afloat, and there is no possibility of survivors. And you assume that it sank. So you check on the coastline for debris, and there's so much debris on the coastline that it takes an awful lot of time for the helicopter to check everything out, because if we find one lifejacket or one sweater or one boot or something that we can positively identify as belonging to a member or person on that vessel, then we can say: 'Okay, he is presumed drowned.'

But if you don't find a trace of the vessel and you don't find a trace of the people, the next of kin are left with nothing—they've nothing to go on. I think it's better for the next of kin to realize that their loved one is dead at sea or lost at sea, rather than sit there and hope for months that maybe they are floating around in a life-raft.

And they'll phone every day and say: 'Have you found anything?' and obviously we haven't or they would be the first to know. It's very hard to talk to them on the phone; we don't want to turn them off, yet we don't want to give them false hope—yet their main need is to say: 'Is there any hope? Is there any chance of them being alive out there?'

The last thing we'll say any time we talk to them is to say, 'There is no chance, they're gone.' After the end of our extensive search, we'll say: 'We've done everything in our power to locate them and we can't find them.' And we'll have the relatives still calling and saying 'Why don't you do it again?' And they don't understand that we've covered every area; and it gets to the point of tears sometimes on the phone."

YOU'VE GOT HIM, YOU'VE FOUND HIM!   "The only thing I can say about the people who are in the airplane is they are very, very dedicated—to sit there for eight to ten hours, and out of the eight or ten hours, you're working, looking at water, maybe four or five hours of looking at water going by under your wing-tip. You can't say enough for the guys that do that. And I've talked to these guys myself as a pilot, and said: 'It must be boring sitting there.' And they say: 'Yes, it is. But it's very worth while to see that man sitting in his raft waving and you've got him, you've found him. And it's a challenge between all the crews who's going to find him. Well, we're the best, we'll find him."

SEVENTEEN

A Wonderful Way To Travel

*A Wonderful Way To Travel... Turning the Wheel Hard... The Great
Age of the Passenger Steamer... A Great Shudder... Shipboard
Romances... At Home... To Labrador by CN Boat... Old Days on the
Saskatchewan... By Stern-Wheeler to Edmonton... Like the Mississippi*

The years of the pleasure steamers on Canada's lakes and
rivers were joyful, carefree days. On the Great Lakes you
could indeed go from "Niagara to the Sea", and you could travel
in luxury that rivalled that of a trans-Atlantic liner. Alan How-
ard recalls these days delightfully in the first story. Further west,
the Canadian Pacific had five vessels, the Assiniboine, the
Keewatin, the Manitoba, the Alberta, and the Athabasca, steaming out of Owen Sound on Georgian Bay until 1912, when Port
McNicoll became their new home base.

Bertha Shaw, in her book Laughter and Tears, remembers the
Manitoba, and especially remembers being roped in for a recita-
tion one evening in 1902. The hit of the show was a young doctor
who told a story about his father's shirt. Then another passenger,
a young lady, did her party piece by getting up and whistling. "I
was quite surprised when a dear little old lady sitting next to me
said in a not too modulated undertone, 'Listen to that hussy!
She's been making a show of herself chasing that doctor around
all day and now she has to get up and brazenly whistle.' 'But,' I
whispered, 'she's a beautiful whistler.' I had been brought up in a
family of whistlers and knew what good whistling was. But the
old lady persisted testily, 'She's not. She's got a button in her
mouth.' Be that as it may, this young lady's whistling was greatly
enjoyed: so much so that she had to give an encore. In fact it vied
for first place with the doctor's narration of the mishaps to his
father's shirt."

Even further west, from the early 1870s until almost the turn of

239

the century, stern-wheelers churned the muddy and shallow waters of the Saskatchewan the 940 miles from Grand Rapids on
Lake Winnipeg to Fort Edmonton. They also went south to Medicine Hat. It meant solid progress on the Prairies, for one stern-
wheeler could carry the same amount of freight it took two hundred to four hundred lumbering oxcarts to transport. There were
local excursion boats and tugs pulling log rafts on the rivers until
1954, but the luxury boats were beached almost a century ago.
The Marquis, pride of the fleet, was beached at Prince Albert in
1890, and for several years her saloon was used as a dance hall.
That was the end of her. The spread of the railways had killed
off the stern-wheelers.

A WONDERFUL WAY TO TRAVEL   "Up until World War I,
which was quite a turning-point in many ways, you could go
almost everywhere in the Great Lakes system, including visiting
villages and towns on the smallest navigable rivers, by steamboat.
Let me give you an example of the sort of thing that prevailed.

Supposing you were going on an extended excursion from
Detroit, let's say. You could take the Detroit and Cleveland Navigation Company's large, high-speed, side-wheel steamers that
took you to Cleveland and Buffalo. You might leave Detroit at,
let's say, six o'clock in the evening, and when you were cleared of
the Detroit River and out into Lake Erie, have a sumptuous dinner
aboard. In the palmy days, I'm speaking now from perhaps 1880
to 1912, you might be lucky enough to have fillet of lake trout for
dinner, caught within three or four hours and being served on
your plate — and don't ever forget that the meals on the steamers,
large and small, were the highlights of your trip. First-class meals,
well served, great variety, some of them almost equal to the stan-
dards of the great Atlantic liner. So, then, after dinner you'd
repair to the main saloon, where there might be a small trio or
string quartet playing for your edification and for dancing.

There'd be dancing and there'd be deck games and on a fine evening some people would sit out on deck until nightfall.

Eventually you went to your stateroom, which was usually fairly small, because the steamers liked to take care of as many passengers as they could. Then you'd sleep pleasantly aboard the ship, lulled by one of the most delightful sounds afloat and that's the ploom, ploom, ploom, ploom, of the floats of the paddle-wheel striking the water. It lulls you to sleep as does no other sound afloat that I can think of, the beat of the paddle-wheeler, and I've had this experience many times.

Even in the nineties there were usually some deluxe suites that actually had beds, but for the most part there'd be a two-berth cabin, three-berth cabin. The higher-priced ones were at the outside of the ship, and there would be an entire row of cabins on the inside. They had large crews because you cannot deal with a substantial number of passengers without many people to look after them. You have to have kitchen help and pantry help to prepare the food. You have to have stewards to deliver the food to the table. You must have bellboys to provide for night-time sudden emergencies such as refreshments in the small hours of the night. You must have a purser staff to assign the people to their cabins and look after all the needs of the passengers. You have to have safety control, and then, of course, you have to have all the people who actually sail the ship, from probably a captain and three mates and the chief engineer and three or four engineers, down to the wheelsmen, as they're called on the lakes, quartermasters at sea, the men who steer the ship, the lookouts, the watchmen, the oilers, coal-passers, stokers, and so on. So you have a very substantial number of people who look after the passengers and handle the ship. And this, of course, is one of the big factors in the demise of the passenger steamer, the increasing cost of operation.

However, we were aboard, we were on our way. I think we'll go on the through steamer that went directly from Detroit to Buffalo. You arrive in Buffalo seven or a little after in the morning, where you would have breakfast aboard if you chose, and then ashore to the great adventure of overland to Niagara Falls. So you would travel on electric power from Buffalo to Niagara Falls with sufficient time allowed to view the magnificence, then aboard one of the two electric railways that traversed the banks of the Niagara River, the Great Gorge route on the American side, the Niagara Park and River Railroad on the Canadian side. One was a narrow shelf of rock just above the rapids following the contours of the river, the Great Gorge route, and the Niagara Park and River Railway was at the top of the escarpment, so that you were about a hundred and eighty-five feet above the Niagara River, and this, of course, was the time when these were open-sided electric cars such as we once had in Toronto and many North American cities. Therefore, your parents had to make sure you were well buttoned in before you started the route, and you made your way down on the Canadian side to Queenston, Ontario, on the American side to Lewiston, New York, and at either of these ports you could board the steamer of the Niagara Navigation Company, of which there were four in the early years of this century. And then several miles down you stopped down at Niagara-on-the-Lake, Governor Simcoe's one-time capital, then across the thirty-odd miles of Lake Ontario to Toronto. The oldest was the *Chicora*, which was once a blockade-runner in the Civil War, and the next one on the route was the *Cibola* — she operated for only about seven years and was destroyed by fire. She was succeeded by the *Corona*, which was a very handsome steamer inheriting much of the equipment and engines and boilers from the burnt-out *Cibola*. And between those two came the *Chippewa*, the great engine steamer with a vertical walking-beam sunk between the two funnels, and quite one of the most comfortable ships ever to sail the Great Lakes, and then finally, in 1907, the *Cayuga*, a twin-screw steamer. I have a special interest in her, because, of course, I managed the company that operated her in her final days of service.

Then, when you got to Toronto — and it's taken you about two hours and thirty-five minutes from the Niagara River ports of Queenston and Lewiston to come to Toronto — you pull in to the foot of Yonge Street, and within about forty-five or fifty minutes the steamer for the Thousand Islands is ready to sail. This was the next link in your journey, operated by the Richelieu and Ontario Navigation Company, a fine and respected compay that operated services for many years all the way from Lake Ontario to the Sault. Then you made your way across the lake on either the

Kingston or the *Toronto*, big side-wheel steamers similar to the Fall River line, the famous ships that ran from New York to Fall River, Massachusetts. They sailed on alternate days, calling at Charlotte, the port at Rochester, New York. Then, after a call at Rochester, back to Kingston, then calls at Clayton and Alexandria Bay in New York, Brockville, Ontario, and finally Prescott, which was the end of the route for this particular steamer. By the time you left Clayton, you were in the magnificent Thousand Islands region.

One of the most beautiful sights I think in Canada is to ride by steamer through there, because when you were on the upper deck of one of these vessels you're about thirty-five feet above the water, which gives you a great commanding view of all the surrounding islands and their estates, castles, and mansions, which the wealthy built in the late-Victorian era.

You threaded your way through the Islands, in some cases being so close you could almost toss a biscuit from the ship onto the island. Then the steamer would swing around in the river and make for Prescott, Ontario. There greeting you would be the rapids steamer which would take you down the rapids from Prescott to Montreal. There was the *Rapids King*, the *Rapids Queen*, and the *Rapids Prince*. This was a very exciting journey because the steamer's speed might be perhaps sixteen and a half, seventeen miles an hour, but there were times you'd be going twenty-five miles an hour because of the added impulse of the current, dashing you down towards Montreal. Once you boarded the steamer at Prescott you went directly to Montreal down through the most turbulent of the St. Lawrence River rapids, the Soulanges Cascades, Lachine, and so on and so on, at times passing within feet of great boulders as big as a normal house, and going, as I mentioned earlier, up to twenty-five miles an hour. This took you from somewhere around nine-fifteen in the morning until about six in the evening. It was quite turbulent. You could actually feel the ship drop as it headed down the descent of the rapids. I think it was dangerous only in the sense that ships did on several occasions go aground and become stuck on the shoal. But I don't think dangerous to life and limb, because I don't think there was ever a life lost in this way. They always got the people off all right, and usually got the steamer off too. I think on one occasion the *Rapids Prince* was aground for about three weeks before they finally got her off.

So, the *Rapids Prince*, or whichever of the rapids steamers you were travelling in, eventually made fast at Victoria Pier in the Montreal harbour, and this was the departure point of the steamers that took you to Quebec or the Saguenay River. If you were going to Quebec only, you boarded one of the down-river steamers and it took you there overnight; if you were going for the longer cruise up the Saguenay River to Chicoutimi and Bagotville, you boarded the other steamer. You might elect to go down for your vacation to the Tadoussac Hotel, for example, at the mouth of the Saguenay, and there the steamer would arrive at a jetty right in front of the hotel, so you'd have perfect service, right to the door. Or you might go right to the far reaches of the Saguenay, and this gave rise to a very famous slogan which was used for years and years in the steamship literature, and the slogan was, 'Niagara to the Sea', because literally you were going from Niagara Falls to salt water, down to the Gulf of St. Lawrence. You'd leave Detroit on, let's say, Monday evening, you'd be in Buffalo Tuesday morning, Toronto on Tuesday afternoon, Prescott on Wednesday morning, Montreal Wednesday evening, Quebec on Thursday morning, and Tadoussac about another day, say Friday, so it would be Monday to Friday, about ten days return, and it was a magnificent, colourful, picturesque summer holiday afloat. It's some of the very best scenery on the Great Lakes and the St. Lawrence River. That's part of your enjoyment.

What do you do aboard? Well, it's amazing when you travel on a steamer how much time you spend eating. Breakfast, lunch, and dinner. You're just nicely up on the sun deck after one meal, and it's time to go down for the next one. But there would be a tremendous interest in the people on board, too, because in those days you met people from every part of the world. If somebody came from Europe, this is one of the things he did in Canada, so there would be all kinds of interesting people to meet. You're much more likely in those days to be meeting people of your own class and your own position in society, in which case you're more inclined, I think, to chatter with these people than you would talk to the people that sit next to you in the streetcar.

The people of lesser means would take shorter daytime excursions, where you'd go, for example, from Toronto to Niagara Falls for the day, leaving here perhaps eight or nine in the morning and getting back at nine o'clock in the evening, or eleven-forty if you came back on the late boat, and this, of course, was a much less expensive thing and you could take your picnic hampers, all the food if you wished could be taken along, you didn't have to buy it aboard, which reduced the cost. But I think the people were very inclined to visit and talk with each other in those days, and I think that even the day excursion steamers were a much greater mixture of society for the simple reason that there weren't that many things to do, so everybody went on excursions afloat.

Now, we made the trip in memory, let's say, nostalgically, from Detroit to the Saguenay, but you might just as well have gone the other way, and you might have left for instance from Detroit or Sarnia on the steamers of the Northern Navigation Company and made your way up through St. Mary's River to Sault Ste. Marie, and one lock that's just above Sault Ste. Marie takes you up to the level of Lake Superior and you go up to Port Arthur and Fort William, as they were in those days. Some of the services went on as far as Duluth, Minnesota.

Now, this was again in the realm of the luxury steamship. Fine meals, good company, not, I'm afraid, in most cases very lavish personal accommodations, because these ships were of a size that they had to pack in as many passengers as they could. So, you spent most of your time on the deck or in the main saloon or passenger cabin, and then retired to your little personal cabin when you were going to sleep. There were multitudes of such services operating on the upper lakes."

TURNING THE WHEEL HARD "On the Prescott run going to Montreal, to put a bit of fanfare on the thing, the Canada Steamship Lines said that only the Indians could go down the Morrisburg rapid. Now, I've talked many times with Captain Cherry of Kingston and he told me that when you entered the actual current, on the outside of the canal system, you didn't have to steer the ship, you couldn't steer it. You could put the wheel hard over port or starboard, it still wouldn't steer it.

When they came to Prescott, an Indian used to board with all his bonnet, with his feathers flying, he would board the vessel with a fanfare. He didn't receive any pay from Canada Steamship Lines, but he had a concession that he could sell postcards of himself to the tourists who all watched him in the wheelhouse turning the wheel hard to port and starboard, all the time pretending this was a very difficult river. And one day, the business was so good Captain Cherry found no one at the wheel. The wheel was just standing there and the Indian leaning out of the back changing dollar bills for his postcards."

THE GREAT AGE OF THE PASSENGER STEAMER "I guess the great age of the passenger steamer probably began in the 1840s and really lasted through until, well, almost till World War I, I would say till 1914. The war made a great difference in the pattern of people's behaviour, but when you realize that in the great age there were no automobiles, no buses, no motor-boats, no airplanes, your transportation was divided between the steamship and the railway train. Well, the railway trains of those days became very hot in summer, you had to have the windows open and you breathed an atmosphere of smoke and soot, not the most desirable form, whereas once you boarded the steamer, you often left port in a heat wave and in the matter of half an hour were out in beautiful, cool, water-washed air, refreshing and as pure as air can be. The contrast is so marked that people thought in terms of taking their first boat ride, if possible, the weekend that the boats began, when the service began. Like children out of school. You rushed out to take a trip across the lake, and, of course, everybody on the excursion steamers had the strip or book tickets which gave you 'x' number of tickets for a minimum price, and you could use these any time in the season.

The decline of the passenger steamer was brought about by two factors: first and foremost, the automobile, the fact that everybody could go where he wanted to go whenever he chose to go in his own car, rather than have to go down to the pier and stand in a pen waiting to get on board a steamer. And the final coup de grâce was given to the steamships by the rapid inflation of wages and fuel costs, and passenger revenue was declining gradually while this was going on, so that only a few services lasted until 1949. That was the year of the terrible *Noronic* disaster, when the ship burned in Toronto with a loss of one hundred and nineteen lives. This somehow steered people away from passenger travel and very few survived beyond that date. But the last day service, for example, out of Toronto was performed by the *Cayuga* in 1957. I know because I was there on the jetty when she sailed for the very last time, nine forty-five on September 2 of that year."

A GREAT SHUDDER "People would be in the dining-room and suddenly the ship would appear to go aground. There'd be a great shudder, it would actually stop physically, and all the cutlery and things would go across the table. It didn't damage the bottom of the ship at all, it was just it went over this great big flat rock, and this was done deliberately, as part of the thrill of going down the rapids."

SHIPBOARD ROMANCES "I think in the great days — take a ship like the *Cayuga* that operated, with the exception of only two years, continuously from 1907 to 1957 — during that time a couple might have met on a moonlight excursion and fallen in love, and taken considerable numbers of trips during their sparking days, and might live to be quite elderly people and still be going for a nostalgic excursion and re-living the days of old.

There's no question about it that there's something very romantic and appealing about travel by water. It brings out the affectionate instincts of almost everyone, and I'm sure many shipboard romances developed between the crew and the passengers who made frequent trips. It was only natural."

AT HOME "The sea has a mysterious attractiveness about it, that's all I can say now. I've been frightened, obviously, a number of times in bad storms, and I've been scared about what was going on. But I still have a kind of feeling of being at home when I get aboard a ship, much more than any other kind of transport. I know it's probably the most dangerous thing to do, even now, travelling in small boats, but it's almost an instinct — you know, I feel that this is a very comfortable, a very satisfying place to be, and I just like it.

I've travelled by small boat along the north-east coast of New-foundland and part of the north-west coast and along the coast of Labrador in small boats of various kinds, and there's a kind of almost mystical feeling of the rightness of the world out among the islands and along the sea there that I don't get so much on land."

TO LABRADOR BY CN BOAT "Years ago, the people from around Conception Bay would take their families, their boats, and would be transported to Labrador by CN boat. They would take everything with them, their cats, their dogs, sheep, whatever they wanted to take. They'd go down and live for the summer. But this now has fallen off, and this year I think there's only been half a dozen fishermen that left these areas and have gone down to Labrador fishing.

They would settle there for the summer on the Labrador coast. They would build their own shacks, lean-to's and whatever, and the other people with bigger fishing would go down and live in schooners, but these people would go down and live in their own shacks for the summer months."

OLD DAYS ON THE SASKATCHEWAN "At Prince Albert we didn't get our first railway until 1890 and 1891. And then, see, the trend was changing, it didn't pay to ship freight any more. So the old boats that were built up to two hundred feet long, they just disappeared in that era. And then, again, there were three smaller stern-wheelers built in Prince Albert around 1904, 1906, the *Alberta*, the *Saskatchewan*, and the *Deacon*. Mainly, they were used for local freight, when the river was deep enough. But in the early years they did do a lot of part-time services, excursion boats. Evidently around 1906 you could go out in the evening and pay your two bits and have a midnight ride twenty miles down-river as far as LaColle Falls and back. And there were regular Sunday trips in the other direction, down to Colleston, I think, it's about eight or ten miles down the other way. Evidently, both the

North and the Saskatchewan were very undependable. I mean, a storm could silt it up quite badly. A sandbar itself wasn't too much trouble, if there was no rocks, it was rocks that did the damage.

I don't know whether anybody has explained this to you before, but they did have a thing where a steamer could kind of leap-frog over. See, they had a long boom chained to either side of the bow, up front there. So, when you'd get stuck, they'd release the tipped end, it was kind of pointed, and it would fall and stick in the river, you know, and using it they'd actually lift the front three or four feet up, so that was enough with the power to get over it."

BY STERN-WHEELER TO EDMONTON "The *Marquis* was a showboat, she was fixed up for first-class travel, with mahogany fittings and large mirrors, she was really posh. She was the most famous stern-wheeler around Prince Albert.

In 1882 she came to Grand Falls, that's where you can come from the Great Lakes to the river system, Grand Falls connects with the Saskatchewan and is also a direct route from there up to the Churchill and the Nelson. That first season she ran all the way to Edmonton.

When things were going right, she could make up to sixteen miles an hour, and she only needed eighteen inches to two feet when she was active, and four to five feet when she was loaded. See, they had to have them pretty shallow and with an open deck, normally, so they could pull into shore and load cargo directly, you know.

She had a two-hundred-and-four-foot hull, and she went all the way across Saskatchewan and into Alberta. She called at Cumberland House, Prince Albert, Battleford, and all the little places. She usually had trouble at LaColle Falls, there's rapids there, and that's where they quite often got into trouble. Actually, the Saskatchewan wasn't very dependable, except early in the spring on the first run out and then later towards July when you had the excess from the foothills coming into there. The river could change overnight. There's a record of one trip that was made where the water dropped completely, dropped overnight, and

everything had to be unloaded at LaColle Falls, and some of the
cargo for up-river wasn't delivered till next year."

LIKE THE MISSISSIPPI "Back in the thirties and forties there
were four stern-wheelers operating in the Mackenzie River water-
shed. Two of them were on the Athabasca, the *Athabasca River*
and the *Northland Echo*, both owned by the Hudson's Bay Company, and they pretty well looked after all the freight for the Hudson's Bay post, and transferred passengers during the summer
months, mainly the RCMP, the RCCS, and the different missionaries,
when they were transferred out from the North or going back in.
The other two operated out of Fort Smith on the Mackenzie, and
that was the *Mackenzie River* and the *Distributor*, and they made
the connecting trips with the two on the upper end of Athabasca
and took people right through to Tuktoyaktuk on the Arctic coast.

They were similar to the ones that ran on the Mississippi, and
you could hear them. You would always see a big plume of smoke
coming out of them, and every time the wheel turned over, she'd
go 'whuff, whuff', and the puff of smoke would come out, and it
was pretty romantic to see these big ships coming up the river.
They only drew about three feet, but they could come upstream
with a complement of barges at about six to eight knots. They
could really clip along.

Oh, they were very efficient, there was no question about the
efficiency of the stern-wheeler. But the unfortunate part is that
when they went on a sandbar, then they had difficulty moving off.
And these were big things, you know, they took about a hundred
passengers, as well as some cargo on deck. They served the people of the North very well during the period that they were in
operation. But once the airplanes started flying passengers on a
fairly regular basis, why everybody just switched over, because
then you could ship your baggage out by boat and fly out, and
have at least a month's additional time."

EIGHTEEN

A Nice Boat

*A Nice Boat... The Boat Becomes Part of You... My Boat... The
Thumper... In a Twelve-Foot Rowboat... A Steady Boat... Painting 'Em
Up... Down the Social Scale... That Boat Was a Part of Him... The Way
We Built Our Boats... Cape Islanders... Dories... She Laid
Right on Her Side... Not the Boat I Should Be On... Off the Blue Wave...
The Old Bluenose Was the Greatest... Aboard the Bluenose II... On a
Sailing Ship*

I n the course of all my interviews, I came to one very definite
conclusion: boats have personalities. Two boats can be made
from the same design, but they will still be different. Some boats
have very eccentric personalities: the rare adventures and painful peregrinations of the Thumper in this chapter bear witness to
that.

If fishermen have a sort of umbilical link with the sea and
fishing, then, I would say, they have a kind of buddy relationship
with their boats, and they get to know all the large and little
characteristics of them.

Their names roll off the tongue with the smack of the sea about
them. In the Atlantic provinces, for instance, there are Cape Islanders, draggers, gill-netters, purse seiners, long-liners, scallop-
draggers, pair seiners, sealing vessels, side trawlers, stern trawlers, Tancook whalers (which have nothing to do with whaling),
actual whalers, and several more.

In the Pacific region, for example, you'll find gill-netters, halibut long-liners, drum seiners, Pacific trollers, herring seiners and
salmon seiners, trawlers, whalers, and so on and on.

And every single boat has a personality of its own.

A NICE BOAT   "I don't want to be any big name. I just want to
have a comfortable living and a nice boat and nice home, that's all
I want."

THE BOAT BECOMES PART OF YOU   "Every boat I've built,
I've been down in the night when the boat was being built. When
this one, the *Southward Ho*, was being built, I used to go down in
the night with a grinder and grind the steel, and smooth, and
different things. And every part of the boat, of every boat I've
built, has been part of me.

And when I sold the one I had to get all the logs for, I felt very,
very bad. I thought it was a huge boat at the time, and a few years
later I was in there looking in the wheelhouse and it's so small,
you know, everything was so tiny.

I think a person who builds a boat and works with the boat like
I have, there in the evening and early in the morning, trying to
make sure that you get everything just as right as you can, the
boat becomes part of you. Every time you sell that boat, every
boat I've ever sold, it always leaves me with a kind of a lost feeling, like getting rid of a farm. I think a boat is like having a farm; I
mean, say a farmer is laying in his bed and all of a sudden he
jumps up because somethin' bothers him, he goes out and here the
cow's having a calf. Well, he's got to be there, and it's the same
thing with a boat, you might all of a sudden, something comes,
and you go down, here's something just about ready to fall off the
engine or the boat's leakin' like a basket, some valve's been left
open and you just caught it in time.

I know a chap who had a very fancy yacht, and he put it up on
the ways and he had put the fresh-water hose in to fill up the tank.
He was home in bed and at one o'clock in the morning he woke
up and thought about the hose, went down, and here the engine
was under water, the boat was half full of water, was sittin' on the
ways and filling up with water from a fresh-water hose."

MY BOAT   "Well, my boat she's sixty feet long, sixteen feet
wide, drawin' about five and a half feet of water. Now, by today's
standard she's about a third as big as a normal sixty-foot boat. My
boat is thirty years old. A new sixty-foot boat would draw twice

as much water, it would be half as wide again, it would be three times as big really, tonnage-wise and displacement. But I go further than any of the rest in that size boat, I know what my boat is, I know what the boat'll stand, and I feel I know what I'm capable of, and if we get caught in a bad breeze we don't push the boat tryin' to come home, we just lay her to. And if you lay 'em to they'll take an awful lot of weather without hurtin' you any."

THE _THUMPER_ "A lot of things has happened to my boat, _Thumper_, which I built myself. I've had her twenty years and I guess she's like the old woman, I think I'll keep her to the end now. I wouldn't trade her in.

One time she went adrift from her home and she had been gone for about six or seven hours and there was a boat that used to tow a big oil balloon to Grand Manan. He was coming up in the fog, picked her up on the radar, and he thought it was a boat vision. On the way back about an hour or two later, he run across the same thing practically in the same place, so he investigated to see what it was, and here it was my boat that went adrift. So he turned and he towed her in the crick. And it was a year later before ever I knew that the boat had been gone adrift and was brought back.

The _Thumper_, she was a boat that was very much like a woman, you know. She was very unpredictable, but she was a good sea boat and a good producer. But if she took a notion that she wanted to do somethin', I guess she just about done it."

IN A TWELVE-FOOT ROWBOAT "When I first started fishing I was twelve years old. I originally was alone with a twelve-foot rowboat which I had purchased from a native from Metlakatla, B.C. I paid twelve dollars for this beautiful double-ended cedar rowboat. It was the most easy-pulling boat that I'd ever set oars in, it was just a beautiful thing, and twelve bucks was an exceptionally good buy for a rowboat of this size. The workmanship in it was just excellent, it was just fantastic.

I recall one time there was two Scandinavian men out at Thetis Island, and of course I was pretty husky in those days and we decided to have a little race. These two pretty fair-sized Norwegians started to haul against me and I pulled ahead of 'em, and this was particularly the design of this boat. They had a much heavier boat, they had two sets of oars, but I with my one set of oars and this very light boat—well, they took a back seat to me that day.

We used to hand-troll out there from daylight, which was one-thirty in the morning, and pull until maybe twelve, one o'clock in the afternoon and then rest, tie up to a kelp bed and rest for an hour and a half, and then go on until ten, eleven o'clock at night. And you might be fortunate in getting a dozen fish—coho, spring salmon—for the day, but you were well satisfied if you did that.

We used to hand-troll along the edge of the kelp in most of these areas, and you'd go up into the kelp and you'd take the kelp head and just jam it in your oarlock, and that's all you had to do. It was just like anchoring yourself to the beach, because the end of it is fastened to the bottom. I'd snooze for an hour and a half to two hours and then go on fishing again. I would row all around Thetis Island and it would take the whole day to row around. Depending on how fishing was, if fishing was good in one location, then you would stay there for the whole day. I would put in sixteen hours a day fishing—at twelve, thirteen years of age.

When you got into your tent at night on the beach you were ready to go to sleep. I had sandwiches made up the night before, and you'd take hot tea with you in a thermos, and oranges, apples, anything that would, you know, keep your energy up.

The fellow that I sold my fish to was an old captain, Thomas, who lived at our home in Prince Rupert, and he used to bring the fresh supplies out, the meat and vegetables, and we would buy all that stuff off him and sometimes dig a hole in the ground to keep whatever we needed to keep cool. We just got enough to eat, that's all, there was nothing extra, you never took very much home in the fall. If you took fifteen dollars or twenty dollars home after your summer's work you had really worked."

A STEADY BOAT "I never looked at the sea in a romantic way, but I have great respect for it. I mean, it's like everything else in nature, if you don't respect it, well, it may lose respect for you. You have to be very careful because it can always be waiting there.

I have a very good friend that was with me for nine years on a boat. He wanted a boat he didn't have to paint on and everything, so he built this aluminum boat, and the boat was a nice steady boat, and one day that thing just flipped over upside down and drowned the whole works of them. You see, it just fooled them. It was a steady boat but it was just waiting there.

I've had some close calls. I don't think there's anybody fishing that hasn't had a close call one time or the other, and it's through grace of God and good luck, you might say, that you survive."

PAINTING 'EM UP "Every spring before you'd start fishing you'd always clean your boat up on the bottom and paint her with copper paint, and then whatever colour you had on the topside, you'd paint 'em up. You'd paint 'em all through in spring before you'd start, and in the fall again when you knocked off fishing. If there was a slack time in fishing you'd paint her up again.

Wouldn't have to necessarily be put in drydock. We used to put our boats ashore in a cove, we'd have them standin' on rows so we could work at the bottom of the keel at low tide. When the tide fell off we'd clean 'em up and paint 'em on the bottom. The copper paint is a special paint for to keep worms out of boats. Just little worms. They go inside and eat the keel and when you take the keel out it's just like a jelly. They fill right full, clean the keel right out of them."

DOWN THE SOCIAL SCALE "When the halibut-fishing was over, the boat was so dirty. We used herring for bait, and scales, they were everywhere, all over the woodwork, you just couldn't get rid of them, the herring scales really stuck.

I remember when we went into Rivers Inlet after the halibut and our friends were there, a few fisherman friends that had their wives up, they were ashamed of us, our boat looked so terrible. You know, it was dirty."

THAT BOAT WAS A PART OF HIM "You built the boat, it was part of you.

I've gone out with my dad to cut the frame of a boat, he had a vision of a boat in his mind. A sea boat was not too flat, not too much rise, it had to be thin aft, so it would ride the waves, and he knew the kind he wanted. He'd been all his life at this, you know. Different bays had different types of timber, and the waves, the tide is different, every bay is different. Our boat had to be tough, a sea boat.

He went in the woods with a hatchet; he'd look at a tree there, a big crooked tree, and he'd take his hatchet and hold it up and you'd say: 'Look, would that make it?' 'No, don't touch it—let it grow on—it's okay—let it grow. Yes, that one, cut that one.' But he'd just hold the hatchet up and he could look at it the way he wanted the lines, by the shape of the timber, you know. 'That will make it and that won't make it. Don't cut wood just to cut it down, cut the one we want.'

We cut that down; we bring it out; he'd shape it; he'd build the boat and then he nailed the nails, every nail. He knew the frame of that boat, and when he struck a storm he'd say: 'She'll take it, she'll take it. I built this boat; I didn't build her for a calm day. I built it for the next storm that was going to come up, the forty-mile wind, and she's heading away home and that's where she's going.' And the boat took him home and an everyday hitch. That boat was a part of him as I was his son, a part of him."

THE WAY WE BUILT OUR BOATS "I was buildin' ships in the winter months, from the forties up until around '65. I'd say it would be about five or six around Lunenburg that used to build their own boats, and build boats for outside people if they came in.

Well, it was all local wood from around here. We used to use oak for the timbers, we'd use different kinds of hardwood for the keel, and most generally we planked 'em with pine. We had around a hundred and fifty or a hundred and sixty boats built, so they'd come in and just say to us, 'I'd like to have one like so-and-so has. Could you build me a boat like that?' And we'd say, 'Yes.'

We had the model here, we'd show him the model. There was no blueprints like today you work off of. We'd make our own model and then we'd draw our own draft offa that model, and that's the way we built our boats. We could build a boat, like a twenty-eight-, twenty-nine-foot boat, in about two months. There was two of us working, and we could have the boat ready to go in two months."

CAPE ISLANDERS "One of the vessels used in the fishery of Nova Scotia, and in Newfoundland also, is the famous Nova Scotia Cape Island boat. This was a vessel that was developed from the schooner hull about 1907, adapting a sailing-ship hull to motor usage. The Cape Island boat comes in sizes from about twenty to forty-five feet, and it has been used ever since that time basically for inshore fishing, lobstering, dragging for ground-fish, and for sailing and numerous other fishery usages. It's the workhorse of the inshore fleet.

There are adaptations of this and variations of it used on the Northumberland shore of Nova Scotia, and similar boats are used in Newfoundland. Often the Cape Islanders that are used in the fairly wealthy south-western shore of Nova Scotia—where it's the principal boat used in the lobster fishery—are later sold or traded in Cape Breton, and then they're traded to Newfoundland."

DORIES "The dory is a fascinating boat and has a fascinating history. They come in various sizes, I suppose anything from twelve to twenty-four feet, and even larger if someone wants to build them that large. I've talked with dory-builders down in Lunenberg who've been building them for years there. They are a peculiar small boat, they're almost double-ended, but not quite. They're very seaworthy and just where they come from no one is quite sure. Some people try to attribute them to the Portuguese, but essentially the dory appears to have been an American invention, probably developed in the Gloucester area, and it was one of the first mass-produced boats. It's built the way it is so that they could be nested, that is, one could be put on top of the other, for the decks of the schooners. Initially these particular fishermen's dories were built in two varieties, a two-man dory and a one-man dory, and they were nested on the old offshore fishing schooners, or salt-bankers, as they were called. As you know, they were lifted off and crewed, and they would use what you call trawls, which in this case were long lines with a series of short lines attached to it, with numerous hooks on each of those lines. And the two-man dory would carry about two thousand pounds of fish, so they were fairly hefty boats. And the fishermen occasionally would get astray from the schooner, especially in the fog in the Banks or in the seas, and would become lost. And the trials and tribulations of the lost dorymen are legion and very romantic history hereabouts and in Newfoundland."

SHE LAID RIGHT ON HER SIDE   "This one trip, we were going across in the straits, there was going to be a little storm but the weather prediction wasn't too much, around forty-mile, you know, that wasn't too bad, and we started across. We got a little over halfway over and the wind was up over a hundred miles an hour and we took a sea over the side of the boat. It smashed into the side of her and laid her right over till she laid right on her side, laying just as flat as a boat could be. Nobody was on deck, everybody was inside, but she laid right over like that and laid there. Of course, she smashed the windows in on one side.

I said, 'Jesus Christ, we're in real trouble now,' that's the word I used right there. And all of a sudden she started to shake herself a little and she started to straighten up—and it was a really nice feeling to feel her coming back up."

NOT THE BOAT I SHOULD BE ON   "I've had lots of experiences where you get into a real nasty blow and fairly steep seas, and the boat'll heel over and you'll think, 'My God, is it ever going to come back?' and then all of a sudden it comes back.

But, believe me, I've never felt on any fish-boat I've been on that she'd never come back, although there have been fishing-vessels here on this coast that have turned completely over and lost with all hands. I've never had the feeling, never had it on any of the boats I've ever been on. I always figured, well, if you know how to handle a boat, it'll go over, sure, but I always felt that it would come back. You had to have confidence in it.

See, you'd almost sense it. You'd heel over and it'd stay there for a while and it's just borderline, well, then you think, my God, maybe this is not the boat I should be on—then you get off of it.

But practically all the ones I've been on, they've gone over but they right themselves pretty quickly. All the vessels I've been on have been built solidly, they've been ballasted properly, and they'll right themselves without any problem."

OFF THE *BLUE WAVE* "One time I was master of the ill-fated *Blue Wave* operating out of Job Brothers. I was master for sixteen trips. She was a very dangerous boat, and when you were fishing in bad weather she would get filled up with water. And to tell you the truth now, I could almost see my coffin on board that boat if I stayed on her. I just didn't like that boat. About a year or two after I left her, she was coming off the Grand Banks, she had sixteen men in crew, and about sixty or seventy miles off Cape St. Mary she rolled over and was lost and all hands; we got her S.O.S. mayday call saying she was in a bad shape."

THE OLD *BLUENOSE* WAS THE GREATEST "I went to England in 1935 on the *Bluenose*. We left Halifax around the first of May and in twenty days' passage landed in Portsmouth, England. We were taken in the King George V review, when all his boats from the Commonwealth countries were called back to be reviewed and we were in the line-up. When we started back for Canada we ran into this gale four hours out of port, it was one of the worst gales that was ever known of around the coast. The storm came up on a Wednesday and it lasted till late on the Sunday night. We had some old seamen, fellas that sailed as captains was there as sailors, and they said, 'Boys, you'll never see anything like this again.' The cook who sailed the sea for many years said it was his first experience of a gale like this, that it was the first time he couldn't set the table. He had to put the cloth in buckets of water and throw it back on the table, to try to hold the dishes, but no way. It was well over a hundred miles an hour. We had no sail on, men were standing on the pumps with a lifeline at the mainmast pumping.

She went over so far that she took the stove right off of the forelegs and threw it into the shack locker. I think probably that all hands thought it was gone, 'cause she went over so far that there was one man who was on deck with the lifeline, six feet of rope on the mast, said he had no deck under him and the light box was under. Our passengers asked the mate if he thought it would soon

be over and he said yes—but he meant over for all hands. He
didn't think she could come back. She just lay and trembled, and
finally she uprighted herself after a while. She was over, I
wouldn't like to say the angle but she was over the light box. Well,
you don't get the deck in, nobody standing on deck, nothing
underneath them, unless she was well over, I'd say, a hundred
degrees. She had to be over that much. And it shifted the chain
locker—that's a box standing about six feet long and about three
feet wide and two feet deep full of heavy chain—it takes quite a
sea to move that back a number of feet, six feet back on the deck.

We had two men at the pumps at all times pumping, trying to
keep her afloat. She was leaking bad and it was only hand-pumps
that you had to use and that's why they had to keep a lifeline on
'em at the mast. They put the wheel in the becket, the becket is
two ropes that fasten to the spokes to keep her steady when they
can't have a man there steering. The two men that were pumping
took shifts, they had a watch, and every two hours they'd change.
They couldn't move very far with a six-foot rope on them, but at
times they said they were in the ocean hanging on to the pump-
brake. She was well built, she was sturdy, and the pounding she
took, I don't know how she ever survived it.

During the time of the storm I was down below in the fo'c's'le
most of the time, wasn't fit to be up on deck. We ate anything
we'd get our hands on. There was no way we could cook anything
as the stove was smashed, so we had water or cold tea or bread
and cold meats that were left, and I think that most of the people,
including myself, if we ever prayed, we prayed that time. We got
some sleep after a while, you had to after two or three days, but it
was pretty rough, 'cause you didn't know if you were going to be
thrown out of your bunk into another one or not. You just tossed
around, you just hung on and prayed to God you were going to
stay there. There was a hole in the stern. You could go down into
the paint locker and look out through the stern, but Sunday night
the wind diminished very much and we were back in Portsmouth
on Tuesday, I think it was, just about a week. Well, we were
happy to see land again for a while, and we were almost a month
in drydock while they put a false stern on her to get us back
home.

Well, I was thinking one time that probably if I'd have found another ship I might have come home, but they said, well, we came over with it and we'll go back with it. She was leaking pretty badly going home. We always kept watch with the four of us, you always kept two at the pumps, you didn't have to pump steady but you had to keep pumping.

And she wasn't really permanently damaged by the gale. She went back to fresh fishing until 1938, when the challenge was issued again for racing. That's when I joined her in the crew to go to Boston and race. We won three out of five in the race off of Boston. When the *Bluenose* was sailing and there was a nice breeze of wind I think it was probably one of the happiest feelings to anyone to see her, while she lay down and her scuppers were underwater and really moving. I was on her when she was doing sixteen to seventeen knots, so that cutters could not keep up with us in the race. So, you do feel very proud and happy. To my mind the *Bluenose* was the greatest, not one of, *the greatest*. That's what I think of her. To my mind the *Bluenose* was the greatest schooner ever built.

There aren't too many of the crew left. In the trip to England there's only about five left from that out of eleven. In the racing days in '38 I'd say probably there's half the crew, fifteen maybe left still living yet."

ABOARD THE *BLUENOSE II* "The feeling of riding aboard the *Bluenose II* here is actually different than a yacht. A yacht is small and just seems to skim over the water. When you're under sail on something this large — and we're the largest of this type in the world—when all the sails are on, you can almost feel the power of it, because there are 285 tons being driven through the water at sixteen knots, and the water is rolling out under the bow and a huge wake is at the stern, and the ship is creaking, you can hear it creaking all the time, and when she hits a big sea, she's shuddering and drives into it. When we were sailing off on a two- or three-months trip, if the winds are light, and we're just motoring along in a calm water, it feels different, everybody in the crew is either down below sleeping or just sitting around. But when there's a strong breeze and we're sailing fast, everybody's up on

deck and they're watching the wake and they're watching the
sails, it feels different on a day when there's a lot of wind, everybody gets excited, you get the adrenalin going. As far as the handling, it's quicker as the speed increases. So if we were sailing in
thirty knots of wind so that she was making more than twelve
knots through the water, she would come about in two boat-
lengths. The manoeuvrability at those speeds are as great as a
powered boat. It would take eight men to put the sails up, the
foresails are run up in about ten or twelve minutes and the topsails are set from aloft, four guys would go aloft and set the topsails, and that would take another twenty minutes.

I've been aboard her on different occasions when the winds
have gusted up very quickly and so strong that you can't get the
mainsail down. The pressure of the wind will hold the sail up
there and you can't get it down, and if you bring her into the
winds to get it down, she's luffing so badly you're liable to damage
the railings. The sails are just swishing back and forth, and the
mainsail here is 4100 square feet, and with a sail that big shaking
like this, you're going to break something. In those conditions
you've just got to hold on and hope that the wind will die off, or
the sail will carry it away.

Two summers ago we were in Northumberland Strait under
similar conditions with more sail up. We had topsails up and the
wind gusted up to fifty, fifty-five, and that's bad news. We were
just carrying too much sail and the pressure on the sails snapped
the bowsprit off. On this particular ship that bowsprit is eight-
een-inch diameter, seventeen feet long—a big piece of wood—and
when that come off, it went clean over top of the mast and lit
about four boat-lengths astern of us—that's a lot of pressure driving this big log a long way. I heard a couple of guys yelling and
that's when I saw the bowsprit going by. I didn't actually see it
come off, it had already gone past the stern of the ship when I saw
it. Now, the main cables that hold the mast up are attached to the
bowsprit. So, with the bowsprit gone, under those conditions
these masts looked like they were made out of rubber, in the middle of that main they could be flexing back and forth six feet
either side of the centre, like a big piece of rubber.

The first thing we did when that bowsprit got carried away was to get the topsails in, and then the rest of the sail down before it carried the mast away. We were lucky that we went out of it that time with just a broken bowsprit—a lot of ships would have been dismasted in those conditions."

ON A SAILING SHIP   "I've always been on sailing-type ships. I don't think I would want to go on a big closed-in ship. I couldn't think of doing any other sort of job except going to sea, I live on the sea. I've a little boat at home that I sail when I get my day off, and when I'm doing nothing aboard here, I sit and make models of ships.

On a sailing ship you become more conscious of the wind; in fact, the seamen who have only been aboard here a couple of years can steer the ship in a straight line in a good wind, not by watching the compass, but just by feeling the wind, the way the wind gusts. You know how she's going to act when the wind gusts up and they can alter for it, and I don't think it is difficult to do this, sail the ship in a straight line just by the feel of the wind. The steering on a sailing ship was outside, so the guy could feel the wind and keep it straight by the feel of the wind. And even in Halifax Harbour we can do it by looking at the condition of the water, by the strength of the wind, and anyone knows when you look at the water you can see the puffs of the wind coming across the little ripples on the water, and as the puffs get stronger, that little patch gets darker. And if you're ashore and see the patches, you can tell after a while the strength of the gust that is going to hit you by looking at that.

And it always has seemed to me, I don't know why, that nice-looking ships always sail well; the ships that aren't nice-looking don't seem to sail well—and you'd think they have an inferiority complex."

NINETEEN

Guiding

*A Big Fish... Nine Days a Week... Propeller Fishing... Guiding...
Kentucky-Fried Shore Dinner... Duck-Hunters... Teaching People...
Looking Down at a Mirror... Kazba Lake Trout... Camp Fires from the
River... Trout in the North... White Water on the Ottawa...
Niagara—the Dream River... The Yukon River Fan-belt... She's Come
Awful Close... The Travelling Restaurant... The Back of the Boat...
Gib's Gotcha... You've Got a Fish!*

G uides are colourful fellows. They are either "characters"
by nature or turn themselves into "characters" because
men and women who hire guides want to be entertained by droll
stories when the fish aren't biting. A guide's life is an arduous
one—sometimes from the wee small hours of the morning until
late at night. Fortunately, the men who take up guiding as a profession have a genuine liking for the water, and they enjoy seeing
their clients catch fish.

Bob Brown, a resort owner at Lake Temagami, Ontario, who
happens to be one of the few owners who guides as well, makes
it clear what the open-air life means to him: "About four-thirty in
the morning in June is awfully nice. It's a little cool and misty on
the water, and, if you can pick a really nice morning with the sun
coming up, and the water like glass, and the fish rising to the fly,
well that's great."

The stories in this chapter range from Ontario to the northern
Prairie provinces to the Northwest Territories and into the Yukon. There's fast-water rafting on the Ottawa, which is becoming
increasingly popular and is for those who don't scare easily, and
there's pleasure cruising on the Yukon River, exploring old cabins and settlements.

It's a big country, as we all know. It often seems Canadians
want to go to Spain or Greece or Nepal, or even just south to
Mexico. I think that many of us could get greater satisfaction

from roaming around our own marvellous country. I hope this armchair trip may tempt you.

A BIG FISH "I was guiding for a party, a man and his wife, they come to the lodge every year, and they would have been in their early fifties at the time, business people from the United States, and the lady was quite excitable. We were fishing for lake trout with wire line and in about eighty feet of water, and we were trolling along, and just chit-chatting about little things, I think he had a beer in his hand, and all of a sudden a big lake trout hit the lady's line, and she hung on—didn't know what the hell to do with it. I couldn't reach over and grab it, she was on the wrong side of the boat, so I just speeded the motor up and gave it a little shot. The fellow fell off the seat, dropped the beer, hung on to his fishing-rod, but it set the hooks in the fish.

Well, then, she really wasn't strong enough to hold on to that trout, I knew she'd never bring it in. She'd be at least an hour, and she'd get all tired out. She was yellin' and screamin' and he'd got up off the seat to open another beer, and he was goin' crazy, he knew it was a big trout. He'd been out many times with me before, and he knew this one was in excess of twenty pounds, but he didn't make any move to take the rod from her, and I didn't either, and I told her to hang on to it. I think he held her wrists so that her arms wouldn't fail her completely, and I kept the motor goin' and in gear, and kept the fish headin' the right way, and when I felt it was right, I opened the motor up a little bit, and with the drag on the line we eventually had that fish within two or three minutes right on top of the water from eighty feet. But mind you, he was three hundred feet behind the boat, and he was just flashing along like crazy, sort of like a water-skier. So she brought him in that way, and it made it a hell of a lot easier, because he couldn't fight so hard. When we did get it in it was twenty-four pounds. It was kind of a big fish. And she was pooped right out."

NINE DAYS A WEEK   "It's not everybody that can be a guide. There's no hours for fishing, as a guide there's no hours. It's seven days a week—I always say, nine days a week, five weeks a month, and four hundred and ninety days a year."

PROPELLER FISHING   "Once I lost a propeller off a big engine with no secondary engine, and we were fortunate in that it fell off the boat as I put the boat in reverse coming in to the shore. We were moose-hunting that time, and we were about eighteen miles away from the camp, and we were lucky enough that the propeller landed in about twenty feet of water, and being white, we could see it. So we put a spruce pole on a fish-net, tied it together, and pushed it into the mud and fished the propeller out. Then I had to walk about a mile into the bush where I knew there was an old lumber camp and dig a nail out of one of the old buildings there and take back to use for a shear pin to get us home."

GUIDING   "Guiding, I suppose, is a little different than any other chore, in that you're in direct contact with your people for an eight or ten-hour day, sitting three to four feet away from them. You have to approach life with a very cheerful attitude, regardless of the weather or the people that you're with. Some of them, of course, can be very, very hard to deal with. But you have to really entertain them. They like to hear stories of the weather, of the winds, of the fish. They always, of course, look forward to the shore lunch—fresh-caught fish on shore."

KENTUCKY-FRIED SHORE DINNER   "Years ago people were quite pleased to jig a wire, a copper line, all day to get their fish. But with technology, with magazines that we have around, the younger generation are coming up and they're reading these things. And they phone me for a booking, for a day outing on Lake Simcoe, and they'll say, 'Oh, have you got a sonar on your boat? Have you got a down-rigger on your boat? What kind of rods do you use? What kind of boat have you got?' They just want lots of fish.

And they don't believe in shore dinners any more, they'd rather stop—and you know these chicken places that they have, you buy buckets there, they'll bring that aboard. In the old days, you know, we'd stop, rest our legs, fillet a nice bunch of lake trout, put them in the pan, just relax, have a nice feast, have an hour's snooze or so, and then go back in the boat, do a bit more fishing, and go home.

Today it's not like that. It's go, go, go, go, go. I've been at it a long time and I've had to change. If I want to stay in business I have to go that way, they just want lots of fish."

DUCK-HUNTERS "Most of them, I guess, are excited the first time they come out shooting the ducks, you know, they get excited. But you slow 'em down, you teach 'em how to do things, and then they get on to it. I've had guys that I take out, they get on to it, and after firing maybe ten shells or something they get on to it, they start hitting. You tell 'em where to shoot 'em and when to shoot 'em, when they're in range."

TEACHING PEOPLE "The satisfaction you get out of guiding is teaching people. There's lots of guides I've known, they take people out fishing and that's it. But in my case, I like to teach people how to go about it, what to use, what time of the year to go for certain species, you know, because I was taught by my father one time. And I feel it's only right that I relay it on."

LOOKING DOWN AT A MIRROR "If you're landing on water and it's a bad blow and big waves, if you get in waves that are beyond the capability of the aircraft, or beyond the capability of the pilot, or beyond the stress on structure of the aircraft, water can be pretty tricky. Pretty cruel also, because water, really and truly, is solid just as much as rock is.

If you're coming in late in the evening and there's no wind blowing you have a lot of trouble with depth perception. You're looking down at a mirror. I've had bets with Americans that they tell me when I touched down, how far I was off the water. In one particular instance while I was flying for Morberg's Camps up at Stony Rapids on Lake Athabasca, I had a man pooh-pooh the idea that you couldn't tell your height above the water. It was very, very glassy and I was coming in on a long glide with power on and he said: 'Well, I'll just put a five-dollar bill here on the dash,' he said, 'I can tell you when you're gonna touch.' I said, 'Okay, you look out at the water and I'll do the landing.' He didn't say anything and all of a sudden he saw the bill wave where I had touched down smooth enough with power on—so he sure as hell couldn't tell how high he was."

KAZBA LAKE TROUT   "I come from Kazba Lake, Northwest Territories, Keewatin District. Perhaps the most interesting fishing story from Kazba Lake in 1978 would be one concerning my son who was fishing with a guest of his on the Kazan River which flows easterly toward Hudson Bay out of the Kazba Lake. The guest caught a grayling between two and a half and three pounds and was getting it pretty close to the boat ready to be landed. He was standing there with a small landing-net suitable for landing a grayling in and a trout, a large trout about fifteen pounds, came up and grabbed the grayling and took off. The guest managed to finally fight the trout back to the boat. My son was standing there wondering how he was going to land this fifteen-pound trout with his little net suitable for a two- or three-pound trout, and while he was trying to make up his mind how he was going to do that, another trout between thirty or thirty-five pounds came up and grabbed the fifteen-pounder—and that was the end of the fishing story!"

CAMP FIRES FROM THE RIVER   "In the Northwest Territories wood is available, but then there's a law, too, that you're not supposed to pull anything out of the ground, any vegetation or anything. It's against the law, you know that, so for camp fires you've got to go around and look for driftwood, and if you're going to be set up in a certain place, you're going to do some fishing there for a month, you go around and pick up all the driftwood you can get and you pile it. You make a stack, because basically it's wet, but in a matter of a few days it will be nice and dry. You take anything that's been drifting, and that's where you have your shore dinner every day. And in any emergency, if you have to come in, you come in that spot and you know you've got wood."

TROUT IN THE NORTH "I held the record there for a little while, the biggest trout I got on Slave Lake was sixty-five pounds, then a guy topped me, he got one at seventy-eight pounds on Great Slave Lake. That held the record, but then a man from Hudson got on Great Slave Lake, his picture was in the paper, a hundred-and-eight-pound trout, so he holds the record, I guess, for an inland lake."

WHITE WATER ON THE OTTAWA "We do white-water trips in big rubber rafts, twenty foot long and eight foot wide, with twenty-four-inch-diameter tubes. They're real tough, they're very well made. A twenty-foot raft like what we use costs four thousand dollars. These aren't toys, they're very sophisticated boats, made only to run wild rivers, and they hold ten to twelve people.

The Ottawa has some of the biggest rapids in Eastern Canada, every bit as big as the Colorado, or as the Fraser. As far as the size and the scale and the intensity of the rapids go on the Ottawa, it's some of the biggest you'll find anywhere. We're talking about fifteen- and sixteen-foot waves.

We do both one-day and two-day trips. Each section is about six to seven miles long and our trips take about six hours each, for each section they take about six hours, only because we don't run straight through. We start off with an instruction period. Because we are running very, very big rapids we have to stop at certain places to set up guides with a throw-line. We accompany the trip with kayak guides and they have to get set up so that when we run through the big rapids, one raft at a time, if the raft gets into any problem the guide with the rope or the kayak guide can rescue them, and when we continue on, the next raft comes through.

At another spot there is about a hundred yards of seven- and eight-foot standing waves that everybody jumps in and floats through with their lifejacket on, and then we stop for lunch. We cook hamburgers and hotdogs for lunch. There's one place on one of the islands that we go by that we've discovered a rookery of great blue heron, and we stop and look at that. So that's the reason the trip takes about six hours. Plus, there's a lot of water battles in between in the calm spots.

The raft wouldn't make it without a professional guide in the back of the raft steering, shouting out paddling instructions. So it is a guided trip. It does take a lot of skill, and if you don't have everyone in your raft working as a team the raft won't make it through safely. On our paddle trips, which we do in the second half of the summer when the water volume is down, everybody gets a paddle and the guide sits in the back and uses his paddle as a rudder, and that's how they are steered and controlled through the rapids.

The only way to manoeuvre a raft in fast water is to either be going faster than the current or slower than the current. If you go the same speed as the current you have no control, so to go faster or slower requires a lot of forward paddling or backward paddling, and once you get into the rapids proper you're pretty much at the mercy of the river. The most important thing is to get the raft lined up at the top of the rapids where you want to be, so that the rapids do the work.

Sometimes, of course, we don't hit the right spot. When that happens the raft sometimes goes up on its side, people fall out, and we rescue them. We've been doing this for five years and have never had an accident. Usually the most that can happen to a person when they fall out is that they have a big lifejacket on and we're there with either ropes to toss to them or with a kayak guide to rescue them, and these kayakers that I have as guides are expert paddlers. They can go anywhere on that river in seconds. They can do things with a kayak that are just phenomenal—in an expert's hands a kayak can do anything—and so no one can get away from them.

When people fall out it happens so quickly, most of the time they don't have time to think. Like, they're out of the raft and rescued in seconds. Before their minds can even comprehend what has happened to them, they've been knocked out of the raft and they're at the end of a rope being pulled in to shore before they know what's happened. Sometimes people do get a little upset and we just calm them down, but they are there for the excitement. They know what they're getting into. People only go on these trips because they know it's a wild river.

We limit the age of the people that we take on our trips to about fifteen years old now. We don't check identification cards. We've had people show up with ten- or eleven-year-olds—well, they are there from Detroit, they have nothing to do, they are children, we take them with us. At certain spots we make them sit in the floor of the raft and just hang on rather than paddling, sometimes we make them walk around the big rapids. As far as the other end of the spectrum, we've taken people, the oldest I think that we've taken was eighty-two.

The people that go on this trip, they shout, scream, yell, clap, applaud. We take them because for most of them it's the most excitement they've ever experienced in their life. It's just like going on a wild roller-coaster, but this one is for real. And there's just enough risk in rafting to make it, you know, even though it's about ninety-nine and nine-tenths per cent safe, about as safe as you could make anything, it's that tiny bit of risk knowing in the back of your mind that the raft can flip, that is what makes it interesting, and why people do it. If it were a hundred per cent safe I couldn't get anyone to go down this river."

NIAGARA—THE DREAM RIVER "I'm obsessed by the Ottawa River but by also other rivers. Rivers among river guides, it's like a cult religion. When river people are together, when they're not paddling on the river either in raft or kayak or canoe, they're talking about rivers. You're either into rivers or you're not. It's almost like an obsession. When I spend all summer running rivers, I spend all winter thinking about rivers and talking about rivers. Whenever my friends get together we talk nothing but rivers, about rivers that we haven't paddled, or just about rivers in general. I can't cross a bridge without looking at the river. Any bridge.

I can't drive through Buffalo without going to the Niagara River below the falls. My idea of a perfect afternoon is to go down into Niagara Gorge and sit and watch the rapids all day, it's almost hypnotic.

The only river that I'm aware of that hasn't been tamed yet is the Niagara River, through the gorge below the falls, so that's my dream river, to do that. No one has been able to conquer it successfully. They tried in 1972 and they didn't make it. They dumped a lot of very important people in the river and they closed down. And then in 1975 they tried again and they had three fatalities, and so it hasn't been conquered. Nobody's been on the river since 1975—and I'd like to be the next to try it."

THE YUKON RIVER FAN-BELT "I'm from Whitehorse, Yukon, and I operate Goldrush River Tours. We call it that because it follows the old gold-rush route of 1898 down the Yukon River. The tour that we run from Whitehorse to Dawson City is five hundred miles through pretty well no-man's-land wilderness. You may be coming around a corner about two hundred miles from Whitehorse and suddenly see a big old steamer sitting up on the mud bank. It's been there, say, since 1930. You know, at the peak of the gold rush there were about 275 large steamers operating on the Yukon River, most of them built in places like Seattle, San Francisco, and Portland, and brought in up the Yukon from St. Michael's at the Bering Sea. Nowadays we run the largest boat between Whitehorse and Dawson City, it'll carry twelve people. It's a thirty-six-foot river boat. We have an inboard-outboard motor in it and we carry two weeks' supplies with us. All the traffic on the river nowadays is recreation.

Basically what we do is we retrace the route between Whitehorse and Dawson and we stop at all the abandoned villages, mines, and old post offices, and generally, you know, visit all the buildings and remains still intact along the route. We only get anywhere near civilization one night, the rest of the time we're on our own. The boat has a galley on it and pretty well all the comforts of home, except the sleeping-quarters. We use tents for that at night, and on several of the days we put the people up in log cabins along the river. Mosquitoes, particularly along the water, are never as bad as everybody makes them out to be. They bother us very little. As far as the wildlife goes, things like moose and bear and a lot of wildfowl are always in evidence along the river.

On one of the short trips out of Whitehorse one time I broke the fan-belt in the boat, and unbeknownst to me we hadn't put a spare fan-belt in. So the only thing that I could think of works in place of a fan-belt is a woman's pair of pantyhose. It was a particularly hot day and there was only one woman on board that had a pair of nylons. She was a lady in her fifties from Idaho somewhere. She had to stand up in the middle of the boat and take off her nylons, which I used to get back to Whitehorse!"

SHE'S COME AWFUL CLOSE   "We designed and built the boat ourselves and it's very stable, but it's not a lake boat, and we do have to cross Lake Laberge, which sometimes gives us a problem. That's the old Lake Laberge that they cremated Sam McGee at, in Robert Service's poem—it's about thirty miles out of Whitehorse, in the first day of the trip. But elsewhere, too, Irene and I have been in some tight spots where we've had an engine failure, you know, you have it at the oddest times, so if you're in a fast current and the engine cuts out on you, you're drifting and you have to make the best of it. You try and drift as close to shore as possible and Irene jumps off and snubs the rope up against a tree and stops the boat. Then, when we take off she'll untie the rope, and she only has so much time to jump on the boat before the current takes it off.

She's never actually missed it, but she's come awful close to it."

THE TRAVELLING RESTAURANT   "We're about the only commercial boat that runs along the Yukon and there is an old couple that lives at Fort Selkirk, one of the old gold-rush towns. Every time we roll into Fort Selkirk he brings his wife on board, and we cook 'em a steak and open a bottle of wine for 'em, and his story is that that's the only time he can take his wife out for dinner because that's the only time the restaurant rolls by."

THE BACK OF THE BOAT   "As a tour guide on the Yukon I make sure everybody's happy. I fix meals, set up tents, answer questions along the way, try and entertain a little bit, and when I'm not doing that, for the past few years I've been driving a jet boat on a local tour. It's a two-hour tour down Lake Laberge.

I had a group of people from Ontario on the jet boat one time who had a little bit to drink, and they all wanted to use the head and there's no head on a jet boat. And then they wanted me to beach the boat so they could all climb off and use the beaches. So I told them that they'd just have to use the back of the boat as easy as they could. I didn't think any of them would, I thought they'd all hang on until we got back to Whitehorse—and then the boat started swaying back and forth and I looked back and one of the fellas that was sitting beside me, he said, 'No, no, don't look back.' And here were all these guys just using the back window for a biffy. I thought that was pretty funny. They all did, you know, they didn't seem to mind."

GIB'S GOTCHA "I invented my own lure, you know, maybe you've read about it in the *Toronto Star*. It's not on the market, it never will be on the market. It's known as the 'Gib's gotcha'. Different colours. It works for me. I could put it on the market. There's guys like John Power, *Toronto Star*, used it. Up in the Northwest Territories it was above all the other lures, the 'Gib's gotcha'. It's not on the market and it won't be on the market because if you come fishing with me I've got to get you fish or you won't come back, because I make a living at that, you know.

And when you do hit a lure you use for five years, and you have people fishing around you, five charter boats around you, and nobody's got fish and you pick your limit right in front of them, then one guy comes up and says, 'What are you using?' 'The "Gib's gotcha".' 'Can I have one?' 'No.'

You know what I really get enjoyment out of? I can be fishing, let's say all day, on Lake Simcoe, nine hours, trying to please people, trying to get them fish, cleaning their fish, and all that. My enjoyment of life that day is to come home, have a nice dinner with my wife and my kids, take my fly rod, and just drive out maybe six miles to a little stream, barbless flies, and get a little pickerel about that long, put an hour in. I can fish all day and go fishing at night and enjoy it. A guide is a person who is not out there for the dollar—mind you, he's got equipment to pay for, and gas, and all that. I'll never be a rich man, never, but the memories I have and the people I meet, money cannot buy."

YOU'VE GOT A FISH! "Most days people will ask me when we leave the marina, 'Well, what kind of a day are we going to have, Gib?' And I always say, 'Oh, today's going to be bad. No fish.' But if they manage to get one, two, three, four, or five lake trout, whatever, then they're all happy.

But I had an episode one time, a lady and her husband used to own a little sporting-goods store in my home town. They come fishing maybe twice a year. This day they came and it was really rough and they got real seasick. Oh, every one of them—her and her husband, her father and her mother, they were all sick—and I was trying to get back to the north shore to go home, and the waves were about four feet, a bad sea. We were fishing away there and all of a sudden she says, 'I've lost the lure, Gib.' I picked up the rod and I started reeling it and I felt it and I said, 'No, you've got a fish.' I gave it back to her and she was sick and she never gave up. She reeled it in and she shook like a leaf but she kept reeling and I saw her fish come over the swell and I just put the gaff to it, brought it in. And she yelled, you know, like a lady yells, 'Ohhhhh,' and started crying and shaking. She couldn't believe it, and there's that fish laying right across the boat in the back, and it was so rough I didn't have time to put him in the cooler because I had to get back to the wheel and keep that boat in the waves, to get back home.

Thirty-two pounds, which was the record for Lake Simcoe at that time. I couldn't believe it."

TWENTY

Great Seaplane Country

Great Seaplane Country... Fishing from a Plane... The Face of a Mountain... Vancouver to Victoria... Amazing Aircraft... Mercy Flights ... Searching... Skis on the Lakes... Bringing Home the Bacon... Just Testing... What the Hell's the Matter with the Water?

I n the Canadian North the rivers and lakes have always been the local airports—in summer for seaplanes on floats, in winter for planes with skis attached.

The bush pilots who flew these planes and opened up the North had a host of worries. The autumn freeze-up and the spring break-up stopped all flying for the time being. Pilots pushed their luck and float planes were frozen in or ski planes went through the ice. Floats were dented by logs and rocks. Glassy-water conditions meant a pilot could fly into a lake or try to land in the air above the lake and then drop or spin into it. Float planes could bounce on a heavy swell, and, as the bouncing increased, so did the pounding the undercarriage took. Bush flying wasn't a profession for sissies and none of the pilots were.

The men who fly in the North or over our coastal waters today are brave men who live with danger every day. I had tragic proof of this when I gathered the three stories "The Face of a Mountain", "Vancouver to Victoria", and "Amazing Aircraft" for this chapter.

I interviewed Mark Goostrey, 27, jovial Air West Twin Otter pilot, and his equally friendly co-pilot, Douglas Johnston, 23, at 10:30 a.m., Saturday, September 2, 1978, in the pilots' room at the tiny Air West terminal at Coal Harbour in Vancouver's harbour. They chatted with me cheerfully about the Vancouver-Victoria air shuttle they worked on, about weather and water conditions and the problem of small craft in the harbours, and Mark Goostrey told me two stories of lucky escapes he'd had with forced *landings of float planes. They stayed with me really longer than they should have, and finally had to rush off for a Victoria flight after an urgent call on the intercom. At noon that day I met Mark Goostrey running along the dock to the Twin Otter for another flight. I said, "Gee, they don't give you much time to smoke cigars, do they?" and he made some joking reply and climbed into the Twin Otter.*

The next morning, Sunday, in my hotel room I listened to the news on a transistor radio: late Saturday afternoon, Goostrey and Johnston were coming in low over Stanley Park for the last landing of the day in Coal Harbour. They had eleven Japanese tourists aboard. Just as it reached Coal Harbour, the Twin Otter suddenly dipped sideways and plunged into the water. Of the thirteen people aboard, eleven died, including Mark Goostrey and Douglas Johnston.

GREAT SEAPLANE COUNTRY "Fort Smith to the east, Yellowknife to the north and east, that's great seaplane country. There's a landing, an airport, every mile almost. I just love flying up there on floats in the summertime because the lakes are clear. Most of them, if you land on them, if you're thirsty you can scoop up the water and drink it and it's great. Oh, I love flying up there in the summertime.

Wintertime is a different kettle of fish. It's treacherous and it's cold and you get out beyond the tree line in the barren lands and, you know, if it's overcast it's a mean thing to fly in. One pilot, I remember, used to go out in the barren lands to service a trapper and the only way he'd ever find that trapper's cabin was if the guy had the door open—there was a little black rectangle and all the rest was snow-covered."

FISHING FROM A PLANE "For a very brief time, I was involved both with the fishing and flying, commercial fishing. In this part of the country there is a tremendous amount of fishing, I think, which might surprise people, Saskatchewan being known as a wheat province, but in the northern area there is a tremendous amount of fresh fish. Our prime catch in this country is trout, whitefish, and what we call pickerel or walleye, walleyed pike, and jackfish or northern pike. We had taken a couple of men in with us to do most of the fishing, and the fishermen in the north are among the better class of individual, quite industrious. It was an early-morning, late-evening operation. In fact, it was an all-day operation from daylight till dark, you might say, by the time you went out and lifted the nets.

We'd even lifted some of the nets with the aircraft. We would put a box on the float and once you picked up the net you can pull yourself along with the net itself. You'd just take the fish out and you'd drop the net back in again. It's anchored at both ends to the bottom. The standard nets in this area are a hundred yards long and you could put three or four nets together. You'd just pick up the float line of the net and just pull yourself along with the actual line of the net, in fact using the net to pull yourself along as you pulled the fish out, working the whole length of the net on the aircraft."

THE FACE OF A MOUNTAIN "I was flying in northern B.C., out of Watson Lake, Yukon, which is just in the Yukon, and I was a couple hundred miles from base. I had been working very hard, very long days, twenty-hour-duty days and this sort of thing, and I was flying a small Piper aircraft on floats and it got caught in a very bad downdraft, and I ended up landing a float plane on the land on the side of a mountain. As it was, I was within about a mile of a mineral exploration camp, and so I just hiked in there and asked them if I could borrow their radio telphone, because I just smashed the airplane up.

The aircraft initially was not in that bad a condition. The floats were banged up pretty bad and it had just sort of rolled over on its back, but it was still all intact. And because it was a float aircraft and it was sort of on the face of this mountain, it was about fifty-five-hundred-feet elevation, the helicopter pilot came in to pick it up and he didn't take the wings off or anything. He just hooked onto it and picked it up.

And, of course, as soon as they picked it up, the aircraft started to fly and he started losing control of the helicopter, so he had to let go of the aircraft and it just smashed into the mountain. So it was actually in pretty darn good shape when he started and after it had been dropped it was pretty bad."

VANCOUVER TO VICTORIA "If you're flying on water you don't have somebody telling you what the wind's doing, or where it's coming from, or which way to land. It's all at your own discretion more or less, and it's your judgment that counts. Like right now. We get some pretty strong winds sometimes in the Twin Otter aircraft. It's a STOL aircraft. In other words, it's good for short take-off and landing. And I've been into Victoria in it blowing, I guess, fifty knots, which is about as good a clip as you want to be landing in because the aircraft starts flying at about sixty knots.

Landing in gusts, well, it's all in how you read the water. You get indication on the water of which way the wind is coming from and what kind of speed it's going, you can see the cat's paws in the water giving an indication of gusts. If it's a big gust you land in it. But if there's a whole bunch of little gusts the aircraft wants to fly and then it doesn't want to fly. So, if you can find an area of calm water where the wind is constant you can try to land in that. That's preferable. If not, look for a big area of wind, a big gust, and set it down right in there.

If you're getting whitecaps in this area, that's just about time to shut it off. We've had occasions in Vancouver Harbour and in Victoria Harbour when it's been just too rough to take off. The wind isn't too strong, but the water conditions will be just too rough on the aircraft with a big load. You could end up breaking fittings and struts and things like that. So I would say about two- or three-foot waves that's breaking is about time to shut it down all right."

AMAZING AIRCRAFT "We've had a couple of close calls with people pulling right out in front of us when we're just about ready to touch the water. Somebody decides to scoot across with a boat, you've got to do some fancy footwork. But they're still a light enough aircraft and they're very manoeuvrable at slow speeds, so you don't have that total commitment that, say, a great big heavy jet has on final going into a runway, once they get close to that ground they're committed to land.

Till we touch the water, and even if I've touched the water and all of a sudden there's a big log there. I can just pick one float up and go over the log or just pick it back in the air and then land it on the other side of it. So, they're really quite amazing that way. They're still small enough to be very manoeuvrable."

MERCY FLIGHTS "You can get into lakes, small lakes, but you're not that awful sure you're going to get out again. It would depend on what you're taking, if you're loaded or you're light. Some of the airplanes, a Beaver or an Otter for instance, will go into the most amazing itty-bitty potholes and come out again, if you're not too heavily loaded and if the trees are not too high around. And there's times when you've got to get into small lakes, mercy flights, emergencies. Oh, you never knew, somebody cut himself with an axe. One time old Palsen, a heckuva fella, he brought out a guy with a bandaged foot, an axe bounced off a knot or something and hit his foot. He filled out the form and it says on it, 'What action has been taken to prevent the recurrence of such an accident?'—'I took away his axe.' "

SEARCHING "I know of one painful incident where I searched and finally found the body of a young Hudson's Bay man who tried to cross from a place called Dillon, across Peter Pond Lake, to Buffalo Narrows. He had a cedar boat and the ice was about half an inch thick and he was breaking ice. He was inexperienced, he didn't have any logs hung over the side to prevent the boat from being torn with the rough, sharp ice it was breaking. Two or three days later he hadn't arrived and the Moccasin Telegraph, in those days they didn't have the radios, and men came with a dog-team to see if we had seen him and we hadn't, so we started to search and we didn't find him. There were two or three pilots that were flying out of there, and we all searched along the new ice line. I'm not just sure who spotted it first from the air, but here was the boat floating against the ice from underneath because it still had buoyancy, and the man's body was underneath the ice, which had frozen over. He'd cut the sides out of the boat and sank in the boat, drowned in the boat. When the water is within two or three degrees of freezing, it's just paralysing."

SKIS ON THE LAKES "Landing with skis on lakes in the wintertime does present a problem, but it is primarily a question of experience and getting to know what to expect. The main problems are in the dull, overcast days where there is no shadow. This makes it extremely hard to pick out drifts and also to judge your height. If you don't have a runway marked out for you, then you land as close to a shoreline or some object that you can definitely define, to give you some depth perception. On sunny days it doesn't really present too much of a problem. You have, you might say, unlimited landing areas.

The thickness of the ice is not so much a problem in the spring as in the early fall when you're deciding whether you can or cannot land on a lake. Today it doesn't present too much problem because there are usually people that you can contact by radio. In the old days, you used to have to use your own judgment and decide. Some lakes freeze earlier than others and, naturally, shallow bays with no rivers freeze early, you have good ice there. In the spring, you have the opposite problem, where you have all kinds of ice—the ice may be deep but it's unsafe, it's rotten, it's candled ice, honeycombed ice, there's various phrases that's used to described it and you can drop right through two feet of ice with a very, very small load, even with a footprint through that ice. In spring the ice changes colour during the thawing process. When the snow goes you'll have immediately a kind of a white ice. Then as the snow is completely taken off, it will turn dark blue, depending on how much slush has been on it from the wintertime. These are all things that have got to be taken into consideration. Well, then it turns white as the water starts to go through the ice, which creates a porousness or honeycomb, as it's called. And then when that is completed it will turn black, and that's when you stay off the ice, because after that you could drop right through.

I myself have not gone through the ice to the extent of damaging an airplane. I have broke through with the skis where you might see you were planing on the water, and managed to get out of it. But there's numerous cases of aircraft going through the ice, both in the spring and the fall, and in some cases there have been even fatalities. But usually when an airplane goes through the ice, it goes down just to the wings, and there is time for the passengers and crew to get out."

BRINGING HOME THE BACON   "In the barrens, two hundred and fifty miles north of Churchill, I holed a float, put a rip in it from a rock about ten or twelve inches long. Now, this story is very hard to credit but I did have witnesses. I had no patching material and I got a slab of bacon rind off a piece of side bacon, about eight inches wide, ten, twelve inches long, and we had a hand drill and lots of stove bolts, and I put those stove bolts with washers through this rind and got a passable fix. It leaked, but by warming the airplane, getting everything ready, pumping it out—there's a pump place, each float has seven or eight compartments so that you could hole a compartment, maybe six or seven or eight compartments to each float—I made this fix with this bacon rind and got back to our camp with it. It was hard and dry as bacon hanging in a warehouse in the north is, the slab bacon, but soaking in the water it was gradually softening up, but it held."

JUST TESTING   "When we first decided to get into the water-bombing business, myself and another engineer from La Ronge had fitted the tanks on the Otter and decided to do some test dropping. When I passed him after doing several drops, one of our pilots passed a remark that I couldn't hit anything with water—not in those terms, there was a little profane language used, he said I couldn't hit a god-damned thing with the water.

As I went over the base, I happened to see him standing on the wing of the aircraft with his uniform on, putting some gas in, so I thought I might as well see whether I *could* hit a god-damned thing, and we managed to dump the whole load on him.

He got off the airplane and went back over to our crew quarters to put on another uniform. In the meantime, when I landed, one of the pilots said he would get his wife outside of the office and see if I could drop the load on her—he was gonna step back in the office.

As I came over the base, I saw this second pilot's wife standing outside and the pilots themselves stepping back inside, but what I didn't see was the first pilot coming around the corner of the building, and he come around in his nice dry uniform on, in time to get the second load along with her."

WHAT THE HELL'S THE MATTER WITH THE WATER?   "Big River's about ninety miles north-west of Prince Albert and I was flying a Waco, with three passengers, returning there one day. I was checking the water and circling to land and I was pulling away from the lake to make my circle, and there was a couple of splutters and my engine quit. I could see where I wasn't going to make the lake, yet I was equipped with floats. There were a lot of young green poplar trees and I had to go down somewhere, so I elected to land in those trees. One man started to yell something about 'We'll all be killed' and the other fellow—they were all fishermen—told him to shut up and let the man do his job.

We managed to put it down in these trees, and it didn't even bend the propeller. I touched the trees about ten feet off the ground and it slid down the trunks of these young white poplar trees, three, four inches in diameter, and we never even got a jar or a nosebleed or cut or anything. It was very lucky. It came to a stop one or two feet off the ground, resting on the bent-over trees that we'd bent in the descent. There was some damage to the floats, some damage to the leading edge of the wings, but no one was hurt. Well, we had safety belts on, and as soon as the plane stopped, it was rather a race to see who would get out first. I'd say we were all out of the plane in a matter of three or four seconds. Well, we just looked at the wreckage for a minute, not knowing that Jimmy Barber was coming, and one man said, 'Well, we might as well start down here to the shore of the lake and maybe we can holler across.'

The rest of the story was that Jim Barber, a well-known bush pilot, was shaving and his wife looked out the window of the suite where he lived on the lake at Big River and she said, 'That's the Waco, that's George.' He said, 'Okay, that's fine. I'll be ready to go pretty quick.' He was going out in the plane. And all of a sudden she said, 'Jim, is there a lake just beyond this one?' And Jim said, 'No, why?' 'Well,' she said, 'that's where George went down,' and he said, 'Oh, did he? *What?*' And he rushed out with his shaving-cream on his face and got in this truck, drove down to the end of the lake, a matter of a mile, crossed over onto this little trail, and there's an Indian boy there was picking berries and he said, 'Did you see the plane? Did you see the plane?' and the Indian boy said, 'Yeah,' and Jimmy said, 'Where? Where?' He said, 'He landed over there in the bush.' So that's kind of a silly story but that's the truth, that's what happened. So, Jim came over to us still with shaving cream on his face and all he said was, 'Oh hell, oh no, Greening, oh no,' and then he added, 'What the hell's the matter with the water?' and, of course, we all sort of got a laugh out of that."

TWENTY-ONE

In and Out of the Harbour

A Pilot's Life... To Take That Ship Out... Forty Minutes To Get To Know a Ship... Even the Best Pilots... An Apartment House Coming Straight at You... The Queen's Escort... No Steering... A St. Lawrence Pilot... Fire in Toronto Harbour... Who Stole My Ship?... Christmas Icing... A Narrow Escape for Saint John... A Whale of an Explosion... Tragedy in the Vancouver Harbour

Harbours have an active, at times almost a frenetic, life. Water traffic doesn't have to follow the rigid geometry of streets, although there are more rules and regulations than may seem the case. I talked to pilots who took ships from Halifax harbour out to sea and to pilots who worked on the St. Lawrence, west and east of Montreal. Either they were the sons of pilots, or they had yearned from boyhood to be a pilot. When ship movements were heavy, it was common for them to work long hours. They took pride in their profession because at certain times, such as docking, or passing other craft in narrow channels, they had to make precise judgments and immediate decisions.

Fires in harbours can be not only sensational but terrifyingly dangerous. I think one of the most dramatic stories in this book is that of the oil barge that blew up in Coal Harbour at Vancouver (there's a picture of that accident too). And in this chapter you'll learn about the suicides that often take place in harbours, as people head for the water to end it all.

Harbours, in short, are one of the most fascinating arenas where life goes on. There's excitement and fun there, but, also, tragedy and death.

A PILOT'S LIFE   "I set out to be a pilot, like my father. When I started going to sea in 1959-60, I decided I was going to be a pilot, and everything I did all the time that I went to sea was working towards it, and it took me from 1959-60 up until 1973 to get the job. In the Port of Halifax our pilotage district starts at Chebucto Head, the line is drawn from there across the mouth of the harbour. We board the ships just about on that line or close to it, and from there on in, the ship is under the control of the pilot.

We go out to the ships in a pilot boat; we have one here in the Port of Halifax now—it's a sixty-five-foot boat, fairly fast, probably around sixteen knots, it's an all-aluminum boat, specifically designed for this job. Sometimes we go up a rope ladder, though now on the particularly high ships we have what they call a pilot hoist, which is a section of ladder about ten feet long; it is lowered over the side down to the level of the pilot boat, I get on it, and they've got the winch and they hoist it up to the deck level. Other ships have a door on the side, and they open the door much the same as the old passenger ships used to, and it's only a step in from the pilot boat in to the chamber store and you go up inside.

You don't actually become master of the ship, the pilot is there to advise the master. If the master decides that the pilot is doing something that is not quite right, he has the prerogative of taking over control of the ship. However, if he does that, then he must within three days give a report in writing to the pilotage authority explaining his reasons for doing so. If he doesn't do this, or the reasons aren't true, then he is subject to fine, so it's a grey area.

Some communications between the pilots and masters and officers on the ships are essential. Sometimes you end up drawing pictures on a piece of paper or pointing to what you want, but ninety-nine per cent of the time—with ships other than Russian ships—you can get by with English. On Russian ships, especially small Russian ships, trawlers, sometimes it is very difficult to get by in English. So, as a result of that, myself and the other thirteen pilots here in the Port of Halifax all speak a little bit of Russian, which we pick up here and there. I can also understand French, English, German, Norwegian, Swedish, and how many more, some Polish and so on ... not many words, but enough ... important words to me, like the commands I would give on the ships. I know what they are, and I know when I tell the captain one thing, and he says something else, it registers in a way. I know what to say to him, usually ... it doesn't mean that it always happens, but usually it does.

The weather does affect the performance of everybody. It becomes more difficult to board the ship and it becomes more difficult to get off the ship. I myself several years ago got carried away to New York on a ship that I couldn't get off. It was a container ship and I slept and I ate till I got to New York, which was only thirty hours. It wasn't a bad trip.

You have to keep your wits about you, particularly in ice. We have a lot of ice on the coast, and you might be jumping for a ladder that's covered with ice, and I remember a container ship from Montreal with a ladder that was covered with ice—and those are things you think about a little bit, ice and the condition of the ladder. We had a case a couple of years ago, this fellow was going aboard of the ship and he stepped on the ladder and went up about three rungs—and the ladder came down on his head. It wasn't tied on the ship.

Fortunately he was able to hang on to the ladder, which had a lot of wooden rungs and that, and he had enough clothing that the pilot boat was able to pick him up. He borrowed a pair of coveralls and went aboard the ship and brought it in."

TO TAKE THAT SHIP OUT "Nowadays you don't have one tug. They have maybe a dozen, eight, ten, twelve tugs pushing. Well, these big ships over there now are drawin' fifty and sixty feet of water when they leave the dock, and with the tides running the way they do, it's quite a job. There's several pilots and they take charge of the ship and they give all the signals, they call the boats where they want them to push, and they all do this. This is their responsibility, to take that ship out from the dock. You do what they tell you.

So the pilot talks to eight or ten tugs, depending on how many are assisting the ship. He knows where he wants the most power, so he knows that's the boat he's gonna put where he wants the most power. He calls what boat he wants pushing maybe full speed, or if he wants you to just idle alongside the ship, or to stand by to get the ship out of there. He calls the name of the boat and he says, full speed, half speed, or stop, you know, whatever he wants, and if he wants them to move, to go around to the port bow and push, he tells them to. They don't stay in the same place all the time. He has them moving around.

You have to watch your own safety as far as the tug goes. You get in between the dock and the ship and anything happens, you have to make sure you're not gonna be there. If that thing's coming in, you get out of there, because the pilot can't see half the time down to where you are and, of course, he's got enough with handling the ship. Some tugs, they get caught under the bow or the anchor hanging over the side, their housework catches, they can't get out to clear in time, and it tears part of the housework or tears the radar scanner or something off.

If you're squeezed between the dock and the ship there's no way you would get out of there, you know, unless you get other boats pushing, because when you get a ship that's drawin' about fifty feet of water squashing you, that's it.

But when a big ship's moving it has a tendency to suck the tug into it, you see, and it's hard to get away from it at times. Like when he's backing out and you're alongside and he tells you just to push slow, once you start pushin' slow and the ship's moving, you haven't got the rudder power then when you're only going slow, so you drop back alongside of it and you slide along with the thing—and it's hard to get away because your steering won't come away when you try to turn, you see, it just sucks in and holds you to that ship. Then you just have to go with the ship as much as you can. If you're sliding you just go astern and try and hold where you are till he stops and then comes ahead again, till he's finished manoeuvring."

FORTY MINUTES TO GET TO KNOW A SHIP   "Bringing a ship into the harbour is a considerable operation, and it's not really a matter of whether it's a small ship or a large ship. There's a set channel that we use, there are places you can go in smaller ships that you can't go in larger ships, and there are accommodations you can make for other ships moving you can make in small ships that you can't make in larger ships, so it's a matter of priority. We here in the Port of Halifax have fourteen pilots; we know each other; we've worked together for a long time and we know how we feel and react in a given situation and we are going to avoid certain situations where you are moving two ships in a bad area. We have inward and outward traffic continuously and if you had two large tankers moving at the same time, there are a couple of spots where one pilot might hold back a little bit to let the other fellow pass that point before he approaches it. And usually this is at the turn, because when you turn a ship it takes quite a bit of judgment to be sure you're turning in the right spot and you're going to be in the right spot when the turn is completed.

You must remember that when you turn a ship it's not like turning a car. You may turn the front or the bow of the ship, but the body of the ship moves crabwise for a considerable distance, it will slide around the turn for a considerable distance before it loses that momentum that it had built up on the previous course. Well, these are things you have to keep in your mind and you allow for it. So coming into the Port in a ship can be a very routine thing in a small ship most of the time. But occasionally it can be very exciting, because anything can go wrong on a ship. Machinery is only machinery, and it will only work as long as it is maintained. If it doesn't work, you're going to have problems, and you can have any number of problems. You can take the same ship in the same condition of lading and move it to the same place twice in a row under presumably the same conditions and do the same manoeuvres—and the same thing won't happen. It will be different each time. You never see two ships built identical that act just the same. They're all different; every one is different.

The pilot that goes aboard any ship is at a bit of a disadvantage in that from the time we board the ship until we get to the dock we have approximately forty minutes, on the average. And if it's a strange ship it takes me forty minutes to figure out how that ship is going to react to certain movements and conditions. In that forty minutes we have to discover how fast she turns, how she manoeuvres, whether she's got a lot of stern power, no stern power, whether she follows a certain rule, is she going to swing one way or the other, how the wind is going to affect her, how much you're going to have to allow for that, and all sorts of things like that.

The primary purpose of a pilot is to move the ship through a congested or narrow waterway or into a harbour in as safe and efficient a way as possible, and to do it as quickly as possible so there is no time lost to the ship, to the stevedores on the dock, or to anybody.

When you get aboard of the ship and start into the harbour, well, you find out everything else, visibility, how the traffic is moving, all those things enter into which way and how you're going to go about these things. But the final berth of the ship at the dock is one of the main parts of the thing, and one of the most satisfying parts of the job is putting a ship into a difficult berth with a minimum of movement and fuss. That certainly inflates your ego a little bit."

EVEN THE BEST PILOTS   "I remember in 1965 a laker, 730 feet long, was hit by a freighter going down the river for Seven Islands just below Isle aux Coudres, sixty miles below Quebec. And the laker sank five or six minutes after it was hit in dense fog, and no life was lost but the ship was a total loss, a brand-new ship, two years old.

It was hit right in the middle of the ship, around number three hold. Both ships had pilots on board, and I know the pilots very well. And the pilot told the captain, 'The ship coming is very close but we'll make it.' Two minutes after, the accident happened.

The ship's still there. You can still see the mast. At low water you can see the wheelhouse."

AN APARTMENT HOUSE COMING STRAIGHT AT YOU
"There are some small craft that will persist in crossing the bow of a large ship. Now, fortunately I haven't hit any yet, and I hope I never do, but I would say there has been some very close calls, and it's stupidity on some people's part. Mostly what happens is a sailboat will attempt to cross the bow of a ship, but a large ship that is high out of the water will change the direction of the wind for a considerable area around that ship, or will blanket the wind,

and all of a sudden the fellow finds his wind is gone, and there he sits.

And to try to stop a large ship like that is virtually impossible on that short a notice. The easiest way to avoid it is to change the direction of the ship—it's much easier to alter the course rather than reverse the engines. If you reverse the engines, you know, you just sail along for another three miles before you get stopped. So you alter the course and hope you get around.

Container ships are quite fast, quite powerful things, really high-powered, and they are quite manoeuvrable and move like a motor-ship. A lot of people who are used to small boats will look at a ship and will say, 'Oh that's a long ways off.' They don't seem to realize that me or anybody else standing on the bridge of that ship looking at a sailboat a half a mile ahead or a quarter of a mile ahead—I can just see them disappearing under the bow of the ship. We may have a quarter of a mile, but a quarter of a mile to me is nothing.

Well, there is no question about it, we do worry about these people for their own sakes. Because you would think if you saw something of the size of a large apartment house coming straight at you, you'd certainly get the hell out of its way, but they don't consider the distances. Because if I'm looking at the bow of a ship from the stern, and I'm probably six hundred feet from the bow, then the shadow area that the bow creates in my vision extends to every ship for, oh, a couple of thousand feet."

THE QUEEN'S ESCORT "I think the top wind that we've been out in is fifty mile an hour and that time was when the Queen was here in Halifax. She came by the *Britannia* from the States and the ship that was escorting her was the H.M.S. *Eskimo*, an English destroyer. They had a chap aboard that had some kind of a kidney ailment, and we had a call to go take him off.

The wind was south-east running about forty-five, fifty knots. That was a real miserable night, thunder, lightning, the whole works, and the interesting thing to me was that they sent out two medics, medical people from Stadacona Hospital, to go with us. You see, this was a very important thing, eh, it was the Queen's escort, you know, they didn't want to take any chances. But I'll guarantee you by the time we got the chap off the destroyer, at least one of those fellas that we took with us was much sicker than the fella that we took off. He was as white as the snow.

These were the most efficient people that I've ever been involved with in an evacuation; of course, escorting the Queen they probably would have to be. The destroyer itself was spotless, it was just beautiful, and as soon as we touched alongside of 'em they had a derrick and they had the injured man slung in a bosun's chair and they put one of the ship's officers on the cable with him, with his leg wrapped around the patient, and the whole thing was done in just a matter of split seconds. We went alongside and down comes the bosun's chair, just as quick as that, and they had him unhooked and out of the chair and the ship's officer was gone off again just as quick, well I couldn't believe it, and that destroyer turned on her heels so quick there, and she was a big destroyer too. When I turned around to look back all I could see was foam coming out from the stern of the destroyer."

NO STEERING   "In 1961 I had been sick for a year and a half, and on my first trip back, I boarded the Norwegian ship *Divine* in Kingston as pilot. And going down the river around midnight, I was steering on the north pier of the bridge that was built in the centre of the river, the International Bridge from Prescott to Ogdensburg. My ship's course before going to the Iroquois Canal was on that north pier of the bridge. I was at the point where I wanted to change course, and I asked the wheelsman to go to the starboard side, the right side, to pass between the two piers, and then I found out that the steering-gear wasn't working, the power was off. We were about fifteen hundred feet from the two bridge supports, going full speed, so I put my engines all full astern and I told the first mate to go and get ready to drop the anchor. When I realized the first mate wouldn't have time to go to the front of the ship before the impact, I hollered, 'Come right back, you will get killed!'

It takes a long time to slow a ship down—we had five or six knots of current going with us and the ship's speed was about thirteen, fourteen knots. The engine didn't have time to slow down the ship engine, and we hit the pier head on.

There's a bar in front of the wheelhouse to hold on to in case you have heavy seas, and when I saw that coming, I just held on. The bridge support held good, though it made a lot of noise. We hit nose on, and then the ship swung sideways and we hit on the back too, and got another hole in there, not as big as the front, where the hole was so big you could run a bus in it, but about twenty feet diameter.

Nobody was hurt, but she started to take water very fast. It was sixty-five feet deep where we were, and she was taking water fast, and I realized she could sink right in the middle of the channel and it would block the traffic for other ships. We had word from the engine-room that the power was back on the steering-gear, so then I decided to head for the beach—the St. Lawrence at that point is about half a mile wide.

I gave the order to swing the ship to starboard as fast as possible and head for the beach, full speed. I let her go until she landed on the sandy bottom. The water was coming in fast in the cargo hold. But I saved the ship and probably some lives too. The superintendent of pilotage came aboard from Montreal. I stayed there all day. The captain told him after the investigation what happened, that I was not in fault. So I got off and took another ship the next day."

ST. LAWRENCE PILOT "Pilotage is different than it was because the river wasn't marked the way it is today. There's no more old canals to train men like there was in those days. You find quite a difference between the men that are piloting today and the old-timers. The old pilot had to know the river, had to know the land. Today what they do, like I did myself in the last few years, is look for gas buoys. They had a gas buoy planted every place. The only thing confusing was that if it was a nice clear night you'd see so many buoys you wouldn't know which one was which."

FIRE IN TORONTO HARBOUR "Well, back in about '65 or '66 we had a Greek freighter that caught fire in Toronto Harbour and she was berthed right alongside the dock. She had a cargo of crude rubber on board and that rubber started to burn, and rubber is very hard cargo to extinguish when it gets burning. It's very acrid black, dense black, sooty smoke and so it was very hard to extinguish and the fire tug for Toronto Harbour, the *William Lyon Mackenzie*, came out to fight this fire and so did our Coast Guard cutter, *Spray*, because we had a turbine fire-pump on board with fire monitors too. Because they thought that the freight sheds were in danger, why, the freighter was cast loose and towed out into the middle of the harbour and put aground. This started around noon and we subsequently worked on that fire right through until the next day. It was about forty hours that the *William Lyon Mackenzie* was actually fighting the fire. Both of us were right alongside, and going on four o'clock or so in the after-noon, the hull plates around the ship were glowing red and we were moored right alongside it, so we had to play one hose on the hull plate to keep it cooled down and try to fight the fire with the others, and the *William Lyon Mackenzie* was doing much the same thing on the other side. Of course, she had much greater potential for firefighting than we did, but what they did was they came alongside the freighter with a cutting torch and cut a hole in the plates in the hold so that we were able to hold the *Spray* right alongside the freighter and pour our fire-monitor water jet right into the hold through the hole. And while we were doing this on one side of the vessel, the fire tug was on the other side, so that occasionally in playing the water across, why, they were dousing us with water just as much as I suppose we started shooting water across the deck at them. We were getting each other down pretty good.

All the smoke was billowing across, but fortunately, being as low as we were, we were underneath the worst of the smoke. We were so close in that the smoke hadn't got a chance to get down to the water level, and we actually did blister a little paint on the side from the heat of the hull. But eventually our turbine pump gave up and we could no longer pump water. Just about that time the *William Lyon Mackenzie* started to run out of the smothering foam that they were using on the other side, pumping into the hold to try and extinguish the fire, so we came around and started ferrying out canisters of the foam mixed with the water to make this smothering foam for the fire.

The *William Lyon Mackenzie* fought this fire for a total of about thirty-eight hours, I believe it was, and we were used, as I say, as a ferry for bringing out extra manpower and changing the watch, so to speak, on the fire tug, so we weren't up for the entire time. We managed to get a few hours' sleep while they were in.

The freighter was subsequently towed out as completely unfit for use, and scrapped, because all the steel in the structure of the vessel was all buckled and twisted and generally half melted in spots from the intensity. So that it was a complete loss.

The poor old *Spray* was very smoked up and took quite a bit of washing down to get it back to its normal looks. The smoke just got imbedded right in the white paint. We eventually turned around, washed it off, and then repainted it because it was just smoke-scarred all through."

WHO STOLE MY SHIP? "A local sea captain has a great tale, and a true one at that, to tell on the loss of his small coastal vessel in May 1960 in the Port of Montreal. His ship was snugly berthed and loading cargo for the Arctic and he left the ship in mid-morning to visit the local ship agent downtown to discuss business and give orders for stores and equipment and crew changes.

Five hours later he returned to the shed where he had left his ship loading cargo, to find that it had disappeared completely! You can imagine the anxiety and indignation on the man's face, not seeing any of the crew or the ship tied up at the berth. He could hardly believe his eyes. It's bad enough to park a car and find it gone, but when a ship disappears, it's even worse. It was only after making numerous alarmed inquiries that he was informed that his ship was at the bottom of the St. Lawrence some miles downstream.

What happened was that while he was away, another ship had left her berth upstream of his, and while descending with the strong St. Mary's current, had a malfunction in her stearing-gear which drove the ship into the captain's berthed vessel, tearing her from her moorings and doing sufficient damage that while drifting downstream she foundered and sank in the ship channel.

A happy side to the story—there was no loss of life. But a difficult wreck-removing job lay ahead, as the ship had sunk in

the main ship channel near the entrance to the St. Lawrence Seaway, in an area with a very strong current. I believe that a coffer
dam was later built round the vessel and she was eventually
raised, but to my knowledge she didn't sail again. The captain of
that ship is master of an icebreaker today in the Maritimes—in
Prince Edward Island."

CHRISTMAS ICING   "During the winter months in Lake Ontario, Captain Hodge used to take the *Porte Dauphine* out just before
Christmas, and for the last cruise before Christmas we'd always
be looking for a little bit of weather to try and develop some ice
on board. And sometimes we'd get ice that would make the
shrouds on the mast change from one inch in diameter to about
eight inches in diameter, and we'd have big thick icicles hanging
all over all the superstructure and all the mast fittings. And maybe
as much as six or seven inches of ice formed on the decks, so that
just to get from the fo'c's'le back aft, why, you had to turn around
and break out a patch with sledge-hammers on the steel deck.

But then we'd get the Christmas icing, and phone up the local
newspaper, usually the *Globe and Mail* and the *Star* in Toronto,
and they'd come down and would publish these pictures of this
ice-encrusted thing that resembled a ship.

By the time we collected that much ice, she was gettin' very
lazy in her ways. She'd roll, take slow rolls."

A NARROW ESCAPE FOR SAINT JOHN   "I was doing a survey
job there for a drilling outfit, and we come down one morning and
looked for to go to work, and the boat was gone. And so we got
looking around and couldn't see no boat, so we took a walk
around the shore. Here the *Thumper* was sitting up on top of the
rocks about right at the tip-top of high tide about a mile away
from where I tied her to the wharf. So I called the harbour police
and we asked him if he knew anything about it and he said, 'No.'

Well, in the meantime, the city police had picked up three
young kids up on the street and they had two big shoppin'-bags
full of stuff. They had my sleeping-bags and my blankets and
everything out of my boat. They had stolen the boat at one or two

o'clock in the morning. One was nine, the other was twelve, and the other was thirteen, three kids.

They got aboard the boat and got her untied and tried to get the motor to go but the motor wouldn't go. So they drifted out there and they drifted up on top of the rocks, so she just naturally went up there and grounded out with the tide, but if they hadda got out to sea, hadda got out in the harbour, I presume that probably the three kids would've probably been lost and the boat lost too. But, anyway, we had to get jacks and planks and everything and jack the boat up and get her launched back to the water again for the next tide. We lost a twelve-hundred-dollar day's work, and I figure it probably cost me three hundred and fifty dollars for the damage they done to the boat.

So in the afternoon the city police come down and they said, 'We've got your stuff that the young fellows stole out of your boat, your binoculars and everything,' and I said, 'Yeah, but there's one thing missin' here,' I says, 'I want you to check on it because they're dangerous. I've got six flares aboard this boat,' which you carry for distress signals, you know, there's six red and six blue, six green—you just stick them in like that and you light them and they burn, like the phosphorus, and then they shoot a big flame up in the air—and I said, 'If they've got them and they light them off they'll set something afire or they'll burn themselves up.'

Now, where she went ashore she was about a hundred and fifty feet away from one of the big oil tanks, storage tanks down here in the harbour, and one of the policemen said, 'You know, I seen them things going up last night and I didn't know what they were,' he says. And I said, 'If one of them hadda gone up and lit on top of one of these tanks you'd knew what they were. The whole south end of Saint John would have been burnt up.'

So we got questionin' the kids, and the kids told us they put the whole six of them off a hundred and fifty feet away from a big oil tank and nobody in Saint John seen it."

A WHALE OF AN EXPLOSION   "One day in 1957 at Stanhope, Prince Edward Island, it was reported a dead whale had come ashore. Being a major tourist area every effort was made to get rid of the whale or discover how they could dispose of the body, which was huge, about forty foot in length. Varied experts had come and had looked at it and decided, well, we could dig holes, we could drag it and bury it, but then an expert from away, meaning off the island, came down and said it was no problem at all, a few sticks of dynamite would do the job.

So people were hired down, dug a hole partially underneath the whale, and put four or five sticks of dynamite in. Everything was set, the trigger was fired.

Lo and behold! They got rid of half the whale, but it was now hanging from the tree branches and from every piece of driftwood it could be found to hang from, and half of it was still there to be buried. The aroma the following day, when the sun was quite warm, was almost unbearable for a mile away. Eventually they had to hire a road construction crew to dig a huge hole in the beach and push it down in and cover it, and eventually natural decomposition while it was buried got rid of it. That was the last time anyone used dynamite to try and dispose of a whale."

TRAGEDY IN THE VANCOUVER HARBOUR   "The Home Oil barge, three years ago last January, it blew up in the Vancouver harbour here. There was no survivors. There was a small pleasure craft came alongside and there was one gentleman and a seventeen-year-old youth on it, and they perished along with the attendant.

I was fuelling up one of the Seaspan tugs, the *Seaspan Prince*, at the Shell Oil barge here and I heard this bang. I thought it was the nine o'clock gun going off, which it occasionally does for some special occasion, but when I looked up there was the Home Oil barge engulfed in flames from one end to the other, the flames I guess would be sixty, seventy feet high, clear orange and reddish flames, immense flames—from one end of the barge to the other, there wasn't a spot on her that wasn't burning.

When I first saw it I was really startled, I didn't know what to do, so I had a young lad on with me called Scotty, and I asked Scotty to bring our little tender around to the west side of the barge, which was the opposite side to what the fire was, and we were there with the engine running just in case we had to evacuate. Well, I don't mind admitting I was pretty worried. I was glad the *Lawrence L.* went in and they put a line onto the barge. How they did it, I don't know, but it was a rope line and it burned. So, they went back in again—I heard that they sprayed a water mist over the chap as he went in with the wire—and they got a wire line on it and they start pulling on it and then the *Seaspan Venture* rammed the barge on the opposite end to break loose the cable and then they towed it over to the north shore, where they beached her, and she burnt for over twenty-four hours. You don't know in a case like that whether there's going to be another explosion when they're just getting in there, you know, there could have been another explosion and then it could have damaged the ship or killed somebody. It was a really dangerous job and all these gentlemen off the *Lawrence L.* were awarded with a citation for bravery.

The *Lawrence L.* was towing the burning barge to the north shore and she was burning all the time and the fire-boat was alongside her, played her monitors on to it, trying to put it out, but you can't put oil out with water. And it would amaze you the number of boats that seemed to pop out of nowhere when this happened. Tugs were coming from all points of the harbour there, all homing in on the Home Oil, but it was just the *Lawrence L.* and this *Venture* here were the two that did all the work. It took them about an hour to go across, and they beached her over on the north shore. She burned all the rest of that day and all night."

TWENTY-TWO

Booze

Away You'd Go for the American Coast... To Cuba and Back in Eight Hours... Big Money... Up Goes a Rocket... Gone Fishin'... Good Old Rum... Out of Their System... No Booze on the Boat... Drowned Over Drunkenness... And Some Vanilla... No Whisky... Eleven Quarts of Whisky... Drinking and Driving... No Time for a Drunk... Irish Moss... We Stand on Guard for Thee

In prohibition days, as much money went into Lunenburg pockets from rum-running as from fishing. The Niagara frontier didn't complain, either. There were searchlights in the night, guns going off, men killed, but it was such a lucrative racket, and there was such big money behind it, that it was impossible, utterly impossible, to stem the tide of booze that washed up creeks and inlets and every likely place along the American north-east seaboard. If you got caught rather than shot and were hauled into court, the bail money was there at the same time you were. Strangely, even after all these years, I found people reluctant to talk about rum-running. The excuse was always the same: "The families are still around here."

Many's the time, of course, fishermen went to sea with whacking hangovers, but very few indeed drank while fishing. The hard work was too demanding. There is, I think, one exception. Fishermen of Icelandic descent, living in Gimli and other places along the west shore of Lake Winnipeg, drank and drank hard, and some of them were still draining bottles while fishing. One of them told me a hairy story about being well sloshed on one occasion, and, while the boats tossed about on the rough lake, he jumped fifteen feet or more from a big boat to a smaller boat because they were running out of booze on the big boat and the little boat was well supplied. He was quite athletic, but, nevertheless, he just made it.

"A good grip round the tail."

Another halibut gets "a good club in the right place".

Aboard the west-coast troller the Doreen C., Ed Zifko brings a spring salmon alongside, gaffs it, and lands it. (Photos courtesy of Josef G. Bauer)

Edging cautiously through the ice.

Teams of horse-drawn sleighs haul loads of fish from the winter fishery. Photographed at Riverton, Manitoba, 1916. (Photo courtesy of Foote Collection, Manitoba Archives)

Ice-fishing at Gimli and at Riverton. (Photos courtesy of Foote Collection, Manitoba Archives)

On the Athabasca River, the s.s. Northland Echo pushes its barge along, northern style. (Courtesy of Hill Photo, Fort McMurray)

It's May 1946, and the motor vessel Slave, out of Vancouver, is trapped by ice on the Mackenzie.

Pushing down the Mackenzie, out of Mills Lake.

Going down the Slave River, pushing the load ahead. (All photos courtesy of S. Mortensen)

Mackenzie River tugs lie in Vancouver Harbour waiting for the annual convoy to set off for the North.

Vancouver Harbour fireboats let off steam.

There was not time for high spirits when an oil barge moored in Coal Harbour caught fire and threatened to destroy everything within range, as described by Fred Clegg in the text. (All photos courtesy of Fred Clegg)

For some, a northern river means a fishing holiday with a guide in the Northwest Territories.

For some, it means a slow trip down the Yukon, stopping in at abandoned pioneer cabins along the way. (Photo courtesy of Goldrush River Tours)

For others, it means crewing a rubber raft down the wildest white-water sections of the Ottawa. (Photo courtesy of Wilderness Tours, Pembroke)

"Great seaplane country" is how one pilot describes our northern lakes. Here pilot Ray Bernard looks after a fishing party in Northern Alberta.

For those who work on the water, planes play a life-and-death role; this 1976 photograph shows two survivors from the fishing-vessel Marble Isle, finally discovered from the air. (Photo courtesy of Rescue Co-ordination Centre, Victoria, B.C.)

Janette Barber examines the hull of H.M.S. Sapphire, a Royal Navy frigate sunk off Newfoundland in 1696.

Beecher Court, born in 1888, mending nets on the wharf at Rustico, P.E.I. "Why should I stop fishing?"

Keeping up the family tradition, Quentin (foreground) and Vance Court haul in the nets. As one fisherman said, "The sea gets in your blood." (Photos courtesy of the Court family)

AWAY YOU'D GO FOR THE AMERICAN COAST "In those times, in the twenties, fishermen wasn't making too much money and the Americans would come down here and charter one like this with no engines, all sails, and get a crew and away you'd go. A lot of times you'd go over into the American coast and go up inside of a steamer and get a load out. We loaded out of a steamer over on the American coast offa New England, practically down off Nantucket Lightship, mostly whisky, rye and scotch, and wines, champagne, and stuff like that, but very little rum. We'd pick up five or six thousand cases.

Then we'd leave the steamer and the steamer'd leave us and we'd go to a certain position pre-arranged. You had a wireless operator aboard, key, and they had a special code book ashore and one aboard the boat, and when they wanted to contact the boat to come out to us, why, you'd have to give them a certain position for this boat to come out and meet you, and then he would take maybe five or six hundred cases and away he'd go.

Always had to be in the night. Nothing happened in the daytime.

We were okay outside the twelve-mile limit, but if they caught us with a boat alongside, that wouldn't be so good. If they caught the small American boat right alongside of you, the Coast Guard could tow the both of you in, even though you're outside the limit. Booze from England, Scotland, and France, all those places, wherever they make the different kinds of liquor, came over here on steamers. In later years, when they wanted their liquor the year round, they built boats like the *Rio* here, boats like that of their own, and they'd go to St. Pierre. These big ships would bring it over to St. Pierre and Miquelon and land it there, and then you'd go down from Lunenburg or Yarmouth or Liverpool or Halifax, you'd go down there and load up a load and away you'd go for the American coast.

A rum-runner was built like the *Rio* here — no mast, just a little thing up for an aerial, for a wireless, and when she was loaded you had a hard job to see her in the water. She was right down, just the wheelhouse stickin' out. And painted grey, dark grey like the water."

TO CUBA AND BACK IN EIGHT HOURS "The rum-running days were really exciting days. Boats would leave Niagara here for Cuba and they wouldn't take long, about eight hours they'd be back from Cuba and they'd have you unloaded and everything. It was illegal to ship liquor to the States, so they had to make all their papers out for Cuba. So when they pulled out of the slip here with their boatload of liquor, according to their papers they were headed for Cuba, but the destination was the American shore, and they'd be back in the morning with their empty boats again."

BIG MONEY "Rum-running, you made good money. See, even as a sailor, I got eighty, ninety dollars a month. Christ, I went to mate and I got a hundred and twenty-five dollars a month. In the twenties, or in the early thirties, that was big money. That was big money then."

UP GOES A ROCKET "We was gonna go right in to this dock in Buzzards Bay. We got in, got the anchor down, and a boatload of men from ashore came off, and we just had the hatches off and up goes a rocket, lights us all up. Two of our men got ashore and the rest of us didn't go. So these fellows on the Coast Guard came along with machine-guns, stickin' them in your ribs, 'Get the hell below.'

So we all went on the fo'c's'le and sat there in a small place, eight of us, I think, yeah, four fellows from ashore and the rest of us, our crew, and we had to wait till daylight. Then a cutter came along and towed us up to Providence, Rhode Island. We got up there, they came aboard and started questioning us; a Black Maria stood right on the dock and after they handed us all the questions, we wouldn't answer any questions, we hopped in the Black Maria and went up to the police station. We was there about fifteen or twenty minutes and a lawyer was there and we went in and signed our bail slips and he took us across the street to a hotel.

Two days after that we came home. Eleven days after that we went over and got the boat and started out, left Providence in the morning, that night we had another load aboard."

GONE FISHIN' "I was only a young fellow sixteen years old when I came to Lunenburg. I was fishing, see, before, started out when I was twelve, so I came to Lunenburg and somebody said, 'This man's goin' rum-running. Do you want to go?' 'Yes,' I said, so I went and saw the captain, yes, he wants some men, so I went up in the shippin' office and signed on at eighty dollars a month. Well, I went rum-running for three or four months.

See, we didn't know enough to keep at it. When the spring come we went back at fishing."

GOOD OLD RUM "There was always rum in this area at the time. Good old rum. In the rum-running days the boats came in here but they were always empty. But that time when they were going they made two hundred dollars a month and that was big money when the rest of us were working ashore for fifty dollars a month. Well, it was a very good life. I tried to make it, to get on one of the rum-runners. Another chap and I were working in the fish plant, my friend's brother was captain and he said, 'No, I'll take one of you, but I can't take two greenhorns.' So, we never got rum-running.

Most of the booze was picked up in St. Pierre, and they went off outside the twelve-mile limit and waited for someone to come in from the Canadian shore, or if they went off the American coast they waited for these small boats to come in. These fellas were just more or less the mother ship to the smaller boats with outboard motors that could do thirty, thirty-five miles an hour, and they took them in New York, and Boston, and they would pack the cargo on and run it in different places, always at night.

You'd get towed in occasionally in New York. My father-in-law told me that his boss told him that he should come in one night, and he took the cargo in and he got caught, and the next day he was in court and he said, 'Well, I'll be, the judge is my boss.' So he paid a small fine and lost the boat for a while, and he stayed in a hotel for a couple of weeks and then they cleared him back to Canada. There was always plenty of rum around in this area, but I don't know where it was landed. I know there was cases of it they used to find buried in the woods, but nobody could claim it. They couldn't say whose it was.

Well, the Coast Guard was out and they were on the move all

the time, but there were so many rum-runners that there weren't enough coast guards. I remember one man from here on a rum-runner, Captain Cluett from Lunenburg, was killed at the wheel, shot through the hip by the Coast Guard. They fired at him, a warning shot, he wouldn't stop, and they put one right through the wheelhouse, and he was killed instantly. One fella in Blue Rock was lost. He was shot while transferring across from Blue Rock to Eastern Points, which is only a small narrow passage, and I understand he didn't stop when they got him and they claim that Kelly was the man who shot him, he was the customs officer and also I believe he was a Mounted Police. Yes, he was killed too. The Coast Guard didn't fool with you. They gave you a warning shot, the next one if you didn't stop.

Another time the coast guards took ahold of another boat, put a line aboard and were towing her in, and the captain cut the rope with an axe that night and skipped him. But they went after him again and got him and he ended up doing three years in Dorchester."

OUT OF THEIR SYSTEM "As far as fishermen and booze are concerned, I think the general pattern is that most fishermen, after they've been out for a trip, they come in and they wanna let their hair down. So they go out on a night on the town and they just raise hell and get it out of their system. And sure, the night you sail or the day you sail you tell them to be there at a certain time, they'll come down, maybe they're loaded. Well, that's fine, but you only have to be out twenty-four hours and they're back on their feet and they can, you know, cut the mustard.

And if they can't, well, it's time to dump 'em. You can't have three or four other fellas keeping up the other guy's end for 'im. It'll only last so long and then they'll revolt, they'll just say to hell with this, how long are you gonna keep this goin' on."

NO BOOZE ON THE BOAT "I know a lot of fishermen who drink. I know a lot that don't touch it. Needless to say the excess drinker at anything will not be a success. I think if you look at every successful fisherman, he will drink, yeah, like we all do, but the man who has a drinking problem will not be a success at anything, marriage, fishing, or working for General Motors at Oshawa. Drinking is a problem like it is everywhere else.

When they're out there you'll never see any booze on any boat. There's no way. That's an unwritten rule. When they go into international water actually they can buy it by the case, duty free. They don't, no way. Why? What are you going to catch with five drunks aboard? If a man has a drinking problem and it starts to affect his work on the boat, he's not there on the second trip, pure and simple.

When they come in, of course, they make up for it. I've seen guys, scallop-draggers, come in here and blow three or four hundred dollars in five days, you know, not knowing where in hell it went. That happens."

DROWNED OVER DRUNKENNESS "Well, it's nice at Great Slave Lake in the summer, but towards fall it gets pretty rough. Last year I was up there, there was nine men drowned, and when you drown on Great Slave Lake your body never floats, the water's so cold and so deep the year round. Well, some of them drowned over drunkenness, mostly. There was one boat come out of Yellowknife, ten miles out of Yellowknife, with three men, must have got in a fight or something or grabbed ahold of each other, and the boat was found with the motor still running, with no men on it. I don't think they ever found the men."

AND SOME VANILLA "In 1968 we started out about the 28th of May for the whitefish season, heading for Warren's Landing. We only got half way and we were ice-bound south of Poplar Point for nine days, till the 7th of June; the season had been open then for seven days. We had a habit of taking liquor with us when we left, and this year I was not drinking and I heard, they had told us later, that Albert Holm wouldn't even get a pound of fish this summer, he was going out there sober! So when we got through the ice, after being there for nine days, my first lift was eight thousand pounds, and that was more than some of them caught all summer. I had three men working with me, and they were drinking, I mean they were drinking on the way out. The whisky pet-ered out. They finished a case of twenty-six-ounce bottles, and some vanilla. Between the three of them. Good workers."

NO WHISKY "When you hire me for a party of four, I will allow one box of beer on the boat, which is six beers per person, and that is all. I've had them at the dock with twelve cases of beer and I said, 'Where are you going?' I says, 'Leave all that stuff behind.' 'We hired you.' I says, 'No, you didn't. You just take all that stuff back and take one box.' 'Oh, we hired you.' I says, 'Sorry, friend, I need a day off anyway.'

No, I don't operate with such men. My fee is two hundred dollars a day. I figure I'm the best, and I don't deal with that."

ELEVEN QUARTS OF WHISKY "My brother was down on the Grand Banks harpoonin' swordfish and they were having a fairly good trip, and through the night, well, something happened to their boat. They didn't realize until it was too late, but she was fillin' full of water. So they got up in the night and there was two or three foot of water in the fo'c's'le, and they went down in the engine-room and she was full down in the engine-room. So they started their pumps and the pumps couldn't keep up with the water that was comin' in, till the engine got under, you know, and stopped. So in the middle of the night their lights went out and everything, and they had to abandon the ship.

So they put their dories over and the first dory they put out, they put their food into it. It was blowin' quite hard, and the dory got in under the stern of the boat, and her stern come down on it, smashed the dory, and they lost all their food.

So then he got down in the fo'c's'le trying to get some food out of the locker, which was by now three or four feet under water, you know, and he was reaching down in the water gittin' food, he got a little bit, but the fellow with him lost the flashlight in the water, so then they were in the dark in a boatful of water.

So they ended up with fifteen cans of mixed soup and a couple of cans of fruit, seventeen cans in all. He had eleven quarts of whisky up in the wheelhouse, he saved that, and I think he figures the whisky saved their lives, they'd just take a sip of whisky, you know. But they were in dories rowin' for Newfoundland for seven and a half days before they got ashore."

DRINKING AND DRIVING   "Drinking on board ship is much the same as drinking in your car. Let's face it, you've got a high-powered vessel that doesn't manoeuvre as easily as your car does, it's got a lot more weight to it so it doesn't stop as easily as your car does, it doesn't have brakes, and it's proven that alcohol dulls the senses and your reactions, therefore, it has to be a big factor in the collisions between small boats and whatnot. This is why the general rule is, you don't drink and drive — and it applies to boats as well as to cars.

We have incidents where drinking has been a direct problem, where the parties on board were virtually incapacitated and actually missed the harbour entrance and ran up on the shore, right up. Just fortunately there was no one swimming there right at that time. But they came out to a point where people from the shore waded out and helped push the boat back into deep enough water that the guy could get off the shore. He'd missed the entire harbour approach."

NO TIME FOR A DRUNK   "That was the trouble with trawling. When you come in, you had that forty or fifty tubs of trawl to bait. Christ, you couldn't have no drunk, if you had forty or fifty tubs to bait it takes a long while. We had to bait all that to get ready to go again. If you was in, say, four or five days you were two or three days baiting that trawl, so there wasn't too much time for any drunk."

IRISH MOSS   "Irish moss is a weed that grows on the rock on the bottom, and you have a rake called a moss rake that's made perfect for draggin' for moss. You dragged them on your boat and she'd pull the moss off the rock, you see. Made like a rake but the teeth are right close together, and there's where the moss sticks in there, and then you'll hoist your rake up and you'll take your moss off, and then you'll drop her out again.

Irish moss is sold for plants here that's on the islands, and it's put up in different ways. Some of it's put in a chowder and more is put up for Jell-O or ice cream or even goes in beer. When you're drinking beer, you're drinking Irish moss."

WE STAND ON GUARD FOR THEE   "In 1942 or '43, I was away in the Navy at the time, our Navy patrol-boat run him down and sunk his boat in the middle of the afternoon. And at the same time, the Navy patrol-boat run down the second boat, Captain Andrew Wilson's fishin'-boat that was alongside of him, run him down. And he was in the water I guess for half an hour before they picked him up, and they brought them back in and repaired them up. Well, they got paid for that one.

In the middle of the afternoon, sun shinin' bright. They were all drunk on the patrol-boat."

TWENTY-THREE

The Elements

Respect for the Sea... The Sea Is Beautiful... The Smell Off the Beach...
A Close Shave in the Fog... Like a Bird... A Storm for Sure... Encounter
with a Hurricane... Right on the Shore... Dipsy Lead... Hitting the
Weather... A Variable Wind... A Close Call on Superior... All Roads
Lead to Nova Scotia... Too Scared To Be Seasick... It's Goin' Blow...
Ready with a Butcher Knife... A Big Storm, a South-easter... Caught in a
Gale... In Hurricane Hazel

W hen you're working on the water, the waves, the clouds, the sun, the rain, and the wind all form an important part of your daily life. On occasion complete familiarity with these elements can be literally a matter of life and death.

Men at sea endure the elements. Patience, endurance, the sheer guts to see it through, and an ancestral pride handed down through the generations, make them able to battle the sea, not on their terms, but always on its terms.

The importance of the elements to a seafaring people is clear when you consider the number of fascinating sea words that enliven Newfoundland speech: barber (a vapour off the water on a cold night), ballycatters (ice formed on the seashore), dally (a lull in the wind during a snowstorm), rote (the roar of the sea), send (a swell during a calm), glitter (a severe "silver thaw"), and swatch (patch of open water in an ice field). Dr. G. M. Story of Memorial University in St. John's, and others, are working on a comprehensive dictionary of Newfoundland English, and it should be a treasure.

Then there are Newfoundland phrases and proverbs that sparkle with imagination: the heel of the day (meaning the sunset); when the snipe bawls, the lobster crawls; the more the fog, the more fish; as busy as a one-armed nailer in a gale of wind.

The elements dictate the condition of a fisherman's working life. They also enrich it.

RESPECT FOR THE SEA   "I would say a fisherman has a respect for the sea. Now, whether he sees it with the eyes of the pain-
ter or a photographer, I don't think he even thinks of that. But if
he does at times, it's very hard for him to express what a sunset is
through a foggy haze and this sort of thing. What he's looking at
basically is calm water. He wants calmer water. Why? Because
then he can go about his trade. When there's a storm it's trouble.
Why trouble? He can't go out. If he can't go out he don't get paid.
Pure and simple.

I think it's more respect. It always changes, unlike the land,
where, okay, fine, you can plough it and in the fall the leaves are
there, but it's still your basic sixty acres of whatnot out there. You
have sixty acres of water out there forever changing, and it's full
of surprises. The best accidents happen usually to the most sea-
soned mariner, you know. I think it's sort of a gradual respect —
you know, it gives and it takes, and he gives and he takes."

THE SEA IS BEAUTIFUL   "I do like the sea because the sea is
beautiful. You go out on a nice calm day and there's a nice breeze
on the water and you leave the hot land behind, so hot and stuffy,
and you go out there and get a nice cool breeze on the water;
skimmin' around on top of the water, it's beautiful.

On a night if you're at sea, a beautiful night and you're steamin'
down through the bay, you can look out and see all the little settlements with their lights on, and just like jewels they are, sprin-
kled along the coast. It's really beautiful on water if you get a nice
night out.

And the best thing I like is watchin' the dawn comin', watchin'
the sky breaking', watchin' the colours in the sky. If anybody
hadn't been up at dawn on the water to watch the sky breakin' —
when it breaks on land it don't look the same. You see it with
nothing but the clear blue sky. Breaking and sunset, oh, it's beautiful, all the vivid colours, the purples and oranges and the pinks
and different shades of blue, really lovely."

THE SMELL OFF THE BEACH   "Boy, one of the nicest experiences ever is to be in a beautiful place, you know, with the sun
shining and the seas rippling and the smell off the beach, some lit-

tle animal runnin' around, even a big grizzly bear or something, a whale blowing. It's all part of the sea, you know what I mean. So I think the sea has got a lot to do with it and the sea it is that draws you."

A CLOSE SHAVE IN THE FOG   "I've fished in fog all me life, I've never had a radar on my fishing-boat, and I seen one summer here we fished, we had thirty-eight days' continuous fog. The visibility was no more than two hundred feet for thirty-eight nights, and we fished in every bit of it. We had a compass course and I had a depth-recorder about the boat, and I've covered the bottom so much in the Bay of Fundy that I could take my depth-recorder and I could take you out ten miles out to sea and put you on top of a rock there ten feet high, because I've gone over it so many times by watchin' the bottom with a depth-recorder I could tell where it was in the Bay of Fundy without ever havin' a radar.

Yes, it's dangerous and it's dicey. I depend on a compass, using a compass and a depth-recorder, and I've had some close shaves. I had an oil tanker one time that come so close to the boat — I was tied onto the end of the net and I didn't have time to untie the net or get clear of it — I seen it comin' through the fog, comin' right at me. I just hit the starters and hauled the throttle on her and parted the net off and when the net parted off from the boat it hit the bow of the tanker. That's how close I was to a big oil tanker, and the fog was so thick that the visibility wasn't any more than two hundred feet and he never even blew a blast of his horn."

LIKE A BIRD   "When we were getting close to land in a fog we'd listen for the rote. A rote means you hear the sea washing by the land . . . you listen and you keep a sharp lookout and you are so intelligent then, a man is almost like a bird, he knows land as soon as he see it. Yes, in fog, you know Shag Rock or you know Pine Island or Green's Pond Island or you know Shugal Point, you're almost like a bird — you have to be."

A STORM FOR SURE   "I have a healthy respect for Lake Winnipeg and its storms. Yeah, we have an instinct, I think, and also we look at the clouds, the threatening clouds. I can tell not only from

the clouds, but when the seagulls are flying high, then you're
going to get a storm for sure. That's a proven fact."

ENCOUNTER WITH A HURRICANE   "We've been out in several of those hurricanes. I remember one time in particular, we
were comin' from the North Carolina area and my brother was
coming along with us in his boat and we were somewhere off
New York, we were on our way home, and we got caught in one
of those hurricanes. When I went down to get my dinner it was
blowing about twenty-mile winds, and by the time it came up it
was blowing about seventy-five, just within about half an hour.
That quick, and the pressure was so low it was just pushing right
in your head. I just come up from getting my dinner from the galley and I looked over at my brother's boat and we just could see
him, you know, once in a while his spars would go right down out
of sight. The big sea hit us and I could see his dory go, he had his
dory on top of his cabin and it just went right in the air. The wind
was supposed to be blowing a hundred miles an hour, and in that
type of boat that's quite a storm.

We couldn't even get a man on deck, the deck of the boat was
just awash, you know, so we just stopped the engine and more or
less just let her drift. It was quite bad, but it only lasted six or
seven hours. The deck all awash all the time, you know. It didn't
hurt our boat, but my brother's boat was smashed a bit, he
smashed his wheelhouse and the windows went out and everything, but we had a little larger boat and it didn't hurt our wheelhouse.

It depends on how you use your boat, too, you know. If you
keep riding the thing into the sea, you know, you're going to
smash it all to pieces. Just take it easy, relax, and let it take its
course. When you're out there you don't mind, but if you're on
shore you'd say, 'Boy, I wouldn't want to be out there today.'
When you're out there you don't mind all that much. Not when
you know you've got a good boat."

RIGHT ON THE SHORE   "When we first started fishin' in the
wintertime you had to be very careful of the weather. When you
went out in the morning you watched the weather quite close, and

as most of the fishermen said then, you had to keep a good weather eye because when it got dark or if it shut down thick snow, all you had was a compass. As a rule if it shut down thick snow you had nor'eastern northerly winds, which is right on the shore.

I remember one night that it breezed up nor'east and started to snow, and it had been a lovely evenin' and nobody expected anything like this. And that night there was three boats lost that didn't make it back in because if they got in too close on the rocks and got shored, they couldn't get off because they had no way of knowin' where the gut was. They had no other than their compass, and it might sound as though they didn't know where they were goin'; but at the same time they only had to miss the gut by a hundred yards. If they were a hundred yards down from the point in a rock-pile, well, that was just as good as if they'd been twenty miles."

DIPSY LEAD   "Most of these boats today are equipped with direction-finders and depth-finders on them that they can practically see the fish, where they're schooling, and they do have a pretty good idea where to go. Well, in the old days the fishermen, especially salt fishermen, all they had was a dipsy lead, a chunk of lead with line onto it, and they put some fat or butter on it and they dropped that over till they got ground and hauled up and saw what kind of ground they were on. If it was gravel they fished on it. This was the only way they knew the bottom, what kind they were fishing on.

With a big dipsy lead, you threw that overboard and it would tell you how many fathoms of water it was, haul it back, and the captain would look at it and, 'Oh yes, we're down to such-and-such bank. We'll fish here then. Drop anchor."

HITTING THE WEATHER   "In them days they just had a compass and an almanac and a calendar, but this old captain that I went with first, Charlie Staley, he'd come out on deck about a half an hour before sundown and nobody'd dare speak to him. He'd walk up and down the deck and the blue smoke'd be flying out of that pipe and he'd be watchin' it, see, and he said, 'Go on.'

Nobody would say a word to him and after he'd get done walking he'd say to me, 'Well, I guess you can leave them light sails on tonight.'

Maybe the next night, he'd come out: 'You'd better take in a couple of them light sails.' He could hit the weather, mind you, he never missed. It was wonderful.

But I can hit the weather pretty good myself. I don't smoke but I go a lot by the clouds and things. If you see a fuzzy cloud comin', you can look out that there's wind breakin' that cloud up, that's what's doin' it, see. If you see a real red sunset, you can figure on a nice day tomorrow. I never give that up. But if you see a hazy kind of dusty-looking sunset, don't gamble too much on the next day."

A VARIABLE WIND   "If the gulls perch onto roofs and that, there will be a fair weather tomorrow, and if the gulls fly high, you know, with the wind, then there is gonna be a storm. And if the wind is variable, starts blowing from the east and then turns to the south-east and then all of a sudden it starts blowing from the west, then you have to watch out. It's not a steady wind, they call it a variable wind, but once in a while that variable wind would be just like Hurricane Nora or Hazel or whatever, you know."

A CLOSE CALL ON SUPERIOR   "I was goin' up Lake Superior with a four-hundred-foot boat loaded with coal, called the *W. K. Bixby*, out of Buffalo. I was wheelin' in her that summer, and out in Lake Superior it was blowin' a good smart breeze of wind and rainin' and foggy.

Well, we could hear this boat comin'. With the wind, we could hear his whistle but he couldn't hear our'n, you see. I was on watch till twelve o'clock and I could hear it plain when I went offa watch, and so it kept gettin' plainer and plainer, and I went off watch but I didn't go to bed. Our captain was blowin' his whistle, but it was blowin' a hard and nasty night. Everybody was out with their lifebelts on and everything.

Well, he went by us on the port side — you know what it is in the fog, you think a thing is closer, but I thought he was as close as from here out to the street or closer, and that was a close call. If he'd ever hit us we'd have been all gone, because it was blowin' hard, we were going headwind, and we were loaded with coal. He was loaded with iron ore. Probably both boats would've sunk right there."

ALL ROADS LEAD TO NOVA SCOTIA "In Nova Scotia we never believe weather reports. The weather can change so fast in a matter of hours. We are located in an area where the weather system tracks across the west, from west to east and on, so if there is a low-pressure area comes in off the Pacific from Prince Rupert across the mountains, it will go south, it will come down across the southern part of Alberta across the country, over the Great Lakes, across northern Maine, and right over Nova Scotia. If one comes in off Los Angeles, it comes across to the Atlantic coast and it comes north and it comes across Nova Scotia. If one starts in Texas, it makes the same trip and comes across Nova Scotia. All the weather systems that comes across this continent come either north of us or south of us."

TOO SCARED TO BE SEASICK "When we hauled the trap we had about forty thousand pounds of mackerel. And when some of these small boats that was out fishing saw us hauling the trap and saw the whole area of mackerel — they couldn't believe it, so they came up broadsides just to watch. When we got all the mackerel hauled up, they had an eighteen-foot paddle, and you couldn't reach the bottom of the mackerel with the paddle, the mackerel was that deep. So we filled the boat, piled up our deck and everything.

When we hauled the traps we left to go to Harbour Grace with the fish, so we went across the foot end of Bell Island down there and she was going along beautiful, the water was just like silk. But when we got over the other side of Bell Island, there was a gale come down the bight, rough water hitting us side on, and the old boat started to roll. The water was comin' in over one side of the deck and going out over the other side. So the mackerel on the deck was startin' up the waterways, so we had to take them and throw all them overboard, the mackerel we had on deck.

Partways across my stepson stopped the boat and went down to get the pump going to drain some of the water out of 'er, but when he went down, the pump wouldn't work. Not a jerk in the pump. So we started up again and started steaming on a bit further.

In the meantime, a boat from Corner Brook saw us and knew that we were slowly going down deeper all the time, knew we were takin' water or something, so this boat came up beside us and he said: 'Are you having trouble?' And we told him and he sang out and told my stepson to do something with the pump, so he took the big old wrench and climbed down the hold, there was water up to his knees down there, halfway up to the engine by this time. So whatever he did with the old wrench, he went right bottom up, got a good dunking out of it, but the old pump cut in and started pumping water. Before this happened, two young fellows was down with five-gallon buckets dipping water out, and they were dippin' water up with the five-gallon buckets and throwin' it back up on the deck, and it was slappin' in there when the water was going over the deck. And my little boy was with me, and I said: 'If it gets any rougher and they got to come out of that hold, me and you is goin' out on the deck and gettin' in the fleck and takin' the fire-axe, to cut the boat loose.' If the boat started to sink, you know, we could always cut the fleck loose. And it was rough, but I was too scared to be seasick.

By the time we got up to the wharf, half Harbour Grace was watchin' us, they was watchin' us come in, just waitin' for us to go under. All they could see, they said, was the wheelhouse comin' along on the water, because the main body of our boat is blue and the top part is white, and she was down to the white. The engine was still running — it wasn't down far enough that the water had got into the engine — but it was only a matter of three or four more inches and she probably would have shut off, and then we would have to abandon it."

IT'S GOIN' BLOW "You'd get up in the morning and look at the sky and you'd see these thin, high, wispy clouds and you'd pretty well know that there's something goin' happen, that it's goin' blow from one direction or another, generally north-wester but it could be the other direction.

Like when I was sailing up the west coast of Vancouver Island for a number of years, I'd leave Kyuquot heading for winter harbour. And all you had to do was look up at Cape Cook, and if you saw little clouds, if you saw that cap on the top of Cape Cook there, you knew damn well there was goin' blow a nor'west. It would just tell you right now and as sure as lightning it would blow nor'west that day."

READY WITH A BUTCHER KNIFE   "We would go out to the west coast of Vancouver Island, and that is all-night fishing for gill-netters. And, of course, at times it was so foggy you couldn't see a thing and all these big traders would be blowing coming through the Straits of Juan de Fuca and we only hoped they were going to miss us.

At times it was quite scary. The odd time they came so close you could see them coming, but if it was foggy they would just glide by quite close. It gave you a funny feeling. My husband was always ready with a butcher knife, all set to chop that net off if we had to get out of the way in a hurry."

A BIG STORM, A SOUTH-EASTER   "I used to run out into the Gulf of Georgia, too, right here out in the Gulf. You know, it was a pretty dangerous business with that little bit of a boat, a five-horsepower engine, in the late fall fishing dog salmon. You know, storms would come up. So, anyhow, I had a pretty good catch this night and had quite a few fish and up comes a big storm, a south-easter, so I thought, gosh, this is pretty bad. And this boat was square stern, and the seas kept pounding the stern like it was threatening to pound the caulking out. It was a wooden boat, you see, and if you keep getting pounded like that the caulking will come out and you'll start to sink, and that's all there is to it. And I had quite a load, for this small boat. I was taking water and bailing out. No pumps, just bailing, you know, and oil and stuff swishing all over the place — and the trouble is, I couldn't get any place because this hot-shot battery had died on me and there I am, I've got nothing. I've got no engine, I've got no oars, I've got nothing —

only troubles. There are the nets out, it's gettin' dark. I can't even go and put the lantern on the end, to mark the net, you know, because I can't move. You know, I'm beat.

But then it got so bad during the night, I had to try something. I had to turn the boat around. I didn't have a long enough line on the net, I didn't have any extra line, so I took a chance. I thought I might be able to rush it around quick and tie it to the bow. If I could tie it bow on, it'd be a lot better because the bow will cut into the water better than the stern, and the stern was flapping, and the seas were coming over the top all the time, you see. Pretty big seas.

Well, gosh, I get halfway with this rope along the cabin, creepin', around the side, and it's gettin' away on me, oh boy, there she is, there goes the — and I'm hangin' on, you know, and the boat's listing over and that. Well, I'm beat, that's all. There's no way I'll ever get to that bow. So, what happened? I just had to let my net go. There she goes.

And there I am out there. Now I've got nothing to hang onto, one way or another. My net's gone, yeah, and it's a new net too. Expensive net. It's gone, fish and all.

So here I am, and the wind's blowing me. Well, I'll tell you what I did. I had an anchor, of course, so all I could do was put the anchor right down, as far as it would go, and I know I'm gonna blow someplace and it'll catch somewhere.

Well, it did. It caught right by Bowen Island here and just enough offshore to keep me from smashing against the rocks. And there I am all night, got no food, not a bit of food, because I was running in and out of Steveston, you see. I was supposed to go back and meet the packet and then he'd bring some food, you see. I didn't have a darned thing. And there I am really miserable and getting so weak and weary and the boat filling up. Gotta keep bailing, you know. That's the trouble, it's hard, hard work and she's rolling around, you know, all the time, a little twenty-two-foot boat and out in a storm, and there you are in front and you can hear the waves smashing against Bowen Island and I'm right there, about ten feet away. This is where I stopped, you know. It was that close, about ten feet away. It caught just in time and hung on. I had a pretty good anchor. I was lucky that way."

CAUGHT IN A GALE "In 1937 we were coming off the Labrador in September — it was on my birthday, the 23rd of September. Now, usually in September, from the 18th to the 21st, the sun crosses the equator and you have the bad storm either before the 18th or after. And I got caught out in a gale of wind, and I had a crew of five men and I had twenty-five stationers, that is, fishermen that go on the Labrador, stationed on the Labrador, and I was bringing them home on the vessel, and we got caught in a gale of south-east wind off St. Anthony. I could have went into St. Anthony, but somehow I was young and wanted to get home; and I had this crowd aboard and I wanted to get on as quickly as I could, so I took chances on it, and I got caught in a real bad storm off the Horse Islands and we lost all our deck cargo; we had seventy-five barrels of herring and some cod-oil on the deck. And we lost our mainsail. We had two engines in the vessel and the two exhaust pipes got broken off and both of the engines got filled with salt water.

And the next morning the wind chopped from the south-east to the nor'west, a gale of wind, and we were forced on top of the Gray Islands, and I wouldn't give five cents for my life. I had no engines and no canvas, nothing, and I thought we were going to be lost on the Gray Islands. But she happened to go around the point and we got clear of the island and we went adrift at sea. The next day the weather calmed down a bit and we got the two engines cleaned out, the water out of them, and we got one engine going and got into Seldon. And we were there a week, got our canvas fixed up and the two engines cleaned up, and we got some gas and got back to Carbonear. That is the most dangerous time I saw ... to tell you the truth now, I wouldn't give five cents for my life that time, but I made it anyway."

IN HURRICANE HAZEL "In 1954 there were three fellas from Nanticoke out on the the point and they were caught in that north-east wind, Hurricane Hazel, and they swamped just off the end of Long Point. And the one fella was never found, not any part of him was found. The only thing I can see is, when that little boat went down there was three big tugs rushed in to pick the guys up and they got to 'em, but everything was floating up and popping up to the top of the water, and they got two of them off, but there were three on it. And the other fella, the only thing that I could see would be that he might have got cut open, you know, with the wheel of one of them boats; maybe when he come up, he come up under one of the other boats that were there to try and save them. As I understand, if you get cut you don't float up, you just stay there. And I think he went into the mud and stayed there."

TWENTY-FOUR

Down North

Steamboat! Steamboat!... Waiting for the Barges... Stopping at Every Trapper... Loading Cordwood, and Other Bullwork... Okay, If You Insist... Hard Cussing... Make Your Own Dock... Reindeer Hides and Mosquitoes... On Lake Athabasca... He Didn't Have a Chance... A Matter of Life and Death... Holding On for Dear Life... Passengers Going North... The Beaver Mackenzie and Flying Bears... Sixty Men on a Beaufort Barge... On Your Own... Plus Meals... Runs Like a Bird ... Looking After the Eskimos

N o more than a few decades ago, it was a pioneer country, where men were on their own, and tugboat captains had to cope with emergencies as best they could, using only what materials they had on board. The Mackenzie River was a long, lonely country of Indians, trappers and traders, missionaries, and oilmen at Norman Wells.

Before the tugboats there were stern-wheelers on the Athabasca River and the Mackenzie River. The Hudson's Bay Company had the Athabasca River and the Northland Echo on Lake Athabasca, and the s.s. Mackenzie River and the Distributor on the Mackenzie. The Distributor was the most famous of them all. They were called steamers as well as stern-wheelers because they had boilers and steam to work the paddle-wheels. They were patterned after the Mississippi River stern-wheelers, except that they didn't have gamblers and fancy women aboard. Clark Gable never showed up.

What they did have were sweating Indians loading cordwood, and hordes of ravenous insects. The "moccasin telegraph" alerted people well ahead of time of the coming of the stern-wheeler and there was unconcealed excitement and expectation. Finally, the anxious settlers would hear the "whsh WHSH whsh WHSH" that accompanied the white puff of smoke from the boilers, and the slap, slap, slap, slap, of the big paddle-wheels.

*Even today, in the era of the airplane, the waterways of the
North still play a major role in the life of the hardy people who
live there.*

STEAMBOAT! STEAMBOAT!   "In those days, the main mode of
transportation on the river was the stern-wheeler, and everyone
along the river looked forward to the steamboat coming. The first
trip in the spring, that's what everyone looked forward to, 'cause
they was bringin' fresh fruit and vegetables, and everything that
they had ordered, and, of course, bringing people into the North.

And it's a funny thing, there, in the North we have what is
known as the 'moccasin telegraph'. People seemed to know ahead
what was happening. For instance, we would leave, say, Fort
Good Hope in the north, and head for Arctic Red River, which
was two hundred miles away, and before we got to Arctic Red
River, there'd be canoes coming up-river to meet us. They knew
we were coming. How they knew, I don't know, but they'd know.

And when you were coming into a port, they'd all be watching
for this first white plume of smoke comin' puffin' out of the stack,
and the cry would go up 'Steamboat! Steamboat!' You know.
'Steamboat!' First thing you know, everybody would stop. They'd
shut the school down for the day. All business closed up, and
everyone came down to the waterfront."

WAITING FOR THE BARGES   "On the Mackenzie, the season
would start on the first week of June and it would end in, oh, the
10th of October. Some years you're in heavy ice. Some years, you
have to come out in the end of September. It depends on the season, but normally it is the middle of October.

Unfortunately, I have been in the ice a couple of times up there,
and you try not to be in the ice, it's not an easy chore. I mean, the
idea is to get everything home if you can, back to head base. Most
of the time you don't succeed. You just put barges in a place like

Horn River then, and winter in there, or into Tuk Harbour and winter there, or into Inuvik and winter there, but that's all you can do if you can't make it. Once the ice forms in the river, there's no way you can get back up-river.

There's supplies for an extra year aboard all the vessels at all times, up there. There was so much traffic, you could never catch up. That's how much there was. Even at the end of the year there was always freight that never got down. Even in the fifties there was freight that never got down till the next year. You'd try to get it all down, but then you've gotta watch the season and then call it quits. When the season opened they were waiting for the barges. They were waiting mostly for their fresh stores. They'd been all winter up there, six months, without the perishables like milk and oranges and apples which they don't get in the winter unless somebody flew it in to them or something. But that was the main thing, the perishable foods. But then generally when we got down there, that was the first thing they were after was the booze, I guess, in a lot of the places."

STOPPING AT EVERY TRAPPER   "We would generally be the first boat down the Mackenzie, and the first boat down would have every stop in the river. We'd stop for whoever ordered freight. It would be Fort Providence and a few of the trappers in between. Like at the Rabbitskin River we'd stop at a trapper there and throw off a few parcels and a few kegs of oil and some groceries. Then it'd be Fort Simpson. Then there'd be two or three more trappers on the way down and, well, just about every trapper, you'd have to stop at every one all the way down. You'd be stopping as many as six, eight, ten times a day. The loading was done very systematically. The last stop you went to was loaded on the barge first, so that the first stop you went to was handy, and it had to be loaded on the barge at the side of the barge that it went off on on the river. Like, say you went to a trapper at Rabbitskin River at Green Island Rapids there. Well, that would be a port landing. Well, they had to make sure that freight was on the port side of the barge, of your two. If you had six barges it had to be on barge number one on the port side. It couldn't be on barge number six on the starboard side.

It wasn't just a matter of loading one barge. It was a matter of loading six barges the right way so you could unload them all at all the stops."

LOADING CORDWOOD, AND OTHER BULLWORK "Cordwood was our fuel, and most of the time you would have between fifteen and twenty cords of wood stacked on the main deck. This took up most of the main deck, and we carried some freight on the main deck, but most of the freight in those days was carried in a barge ahead of the steamboat. They started out with one barge, and then gradually, as business increased, they worked the two barges, and finally, by the time the steamboat era had ended, they were moving three and four barges at a time.

The Hudson's Bay arranged for woodcutters to go into the bush during the winter months and cut all this cordwood, jackpine mostly. The first trip in the spring, the steamboat would bring down a man with a team of horses, and we would put him off ashore at the first location where there would be a woodpile, and he would get off, and while we continued on river, he would move all the cordwood out to the river bank, and pile it up there. And then, next time we stopped, we'd pick him up again, move him to another location, and so on, until all the wood cut during the winter was moved out to the bank during the summer. In the meantime, there was always a supply from the year before. On the Athabasca we stopped every day at a woodpile. On the Mackenzie, you had to carry a little larger supply. It could be every second day that you'd hit a woodpile. To load the wood, we would tie up the barges ahead to a tree. Then we'd come in to the woodpile, run a cable ashore from the bow and winch the bow in as tight as possible, put your cargo planks ashore, the planks that you carried for loading everything, two of them about fifteen feet long. We'd put those planks ashore and get your deck-hands to work, and in those days on the steamboats we carried ten native deck-hands. We had to have a lot of men to be able to load wood. We would load this into special little wood-trucks, hand-trucks that we had, to wheel the wood down the gangplanks, down onto the main deck. And they would pile up in rows alongside the boiler. You could put a lot of wood on one of those trucks. In fact, the

Indian deck-hands used to compete with each other, see who could put the biggest load on.

Then once you got going, you had to turn the deck-hands into wood-passers. Someone had to pass the wood to the firemen. There were two firemen, and they worked in six-hour watches, while the deck-hands worked in two-hour watches. Every two hours they would change, so they were continuously passing wood to the firemen, keeping them supplied.

And then, of course, besides that they had to keep the vessel clean and hook up the barges, and at the ports of call we'd unload freight, and this was done in the same manner. It was unloaded with these little hand-wheeled trucks, those days. A lot of bull-work."

OKAY, IF YOU INSIST "A story they tell on one of the skippers on the *Northland Echo* was that they were coming in to tie up to a barge or something, and he wanted to drop the anchor, to winch this off. And so he told the deck-hand, he said, 'Now, when I tell you "drop the anchor" you drop the anchor,' so the appropriate moment came, and he said, 'Throw the anchor overboard,' and the guy said, 'But Captain.' And he said, 'Throw the anchor overboard.' And he said, 'But Captain.' And he said, 'I told you, throw the God-damn anchor overboard,' so plop goes the anchor — no rope on it — and this's what he was trying to tell him, there was no line on the anchor."

HARD CUSSING "You could do almost anything with a good stern-wheeler and a couple of barges ahead of you. Well, once in a while, you know, with human errors, you'd go into a sandbar, and you spend a little time getting it off again. I've seen us be on a sandbar for a good twenty-four hours, and run cables ashore to a tree on the bank, and hook it to a steam winch, and work back and forth until you finally got them off. You'd always get off one way or another, sometimes with a lot of cussing and swearing, in Icelandic and English."

MAKE YOUR OWN DOCK "At some places on the Mackenzie the water was deep enough to let you get in to the shore to unload.

Other places, it's not. You might get within a hundred feet of the beach only, and then if that's the case, there is no docks in these places. You just beach and you make your own dock as you go along.

You have steel gangplanks or wooden gangplanks aboard and you run them out from the barges to the beach. Then you brace them up with pallet boards, empty boards underneath 'em, and bridge out to the beach, and then we would unload over the bridge to the beach with every barge. The barges would be tied up probably to trees, to start with."

REINDEER HIDES AND MOSQUITOES "Up there you can't see for the mosquitoes, there's swarms of them, and, of course, there's nothing you can do with mosquitoes except grin and bear it. Well, the first five or six years I was there the mosquitoes didn't even know I was there, and I'll tell you, when they discovered I was there they knew it, I knew it. Maybe before then I stayed indoors more than I should have, I don't know. But all the boats are well screened. There's no mosquitoes can get in the boats, but I was not out in the mosquitoes as much as the crew was. I would make sure I stayed inside in the pilot-house or something, and get on the loudspeakers and blare away at 'em.

But at Reindeer Station, with all them pelts and hides, reindeer hides, that we had to pick up there, it was just like a big cloud comin' at you. You know, the pelts would be layin' out there in that sweltering heat for weeks waiting for you to pick them up, and then you'd get in there and the stink and all the bugs, you knew you were in mosquitoes."

ON LAKE ATHABASCA "Oh, Lake Athabasca was shallow in the Athabasca River out for ten miles. In fact, coming out we used to put willow branches to navigate by. In the spring, the first trip out you'd be sounding all the way and then you'd put willow bushes, dead willow trees, in the mud and just follow them out till you got out in blue water, and then, of course, you'd head across to Uranium City, which I believe must be a hundred and sixty miles to a hundred and eighty miles.

Lots of wind out there. Heavy seas worse than you get on the coast here, but they're short and choppy. They're not long rollers like you get here, they're short and choppy.

On the south side of Lake Athabasca there's a desert. I've got no idea of the acreage of that in square miles but you can see it from the water. On a clear day it's just like a beautiful big desert, just like in the Sahara."

HE DIDN'T HAVE A CHANCE   "While we were patrolling on the north shore of Lesser Slave Lake we came upon a boat that was tied to a gill-net, and when we lifted up the gill-net we could see a body floating. We picked the body up, well, we picked the gill-nets and the body up, and took them into shore.

He'd been a fisherman who'd been fishing nine years at that time and apparently he had been setting his nets and the gill-net caught onto his shirt buttons. He had what they call a bush shirt on, with big heavy buttons, and the gill-net snagged on one of his buttons and pulled him overboard and, of course, he didn't have a chance to get loose. You can't fight a gill-net in the water, and he just drowned there.

The gill-net was still attached to his shirt, and we had to cut him loose."

A MATTER OF LIFE AND DEATH   "I was careful. On Great Slave Lake I trained my men, every time I took them out, like lots of guys never done. I'd be travelling my ten miles an hour and I'd throw a buoy over, a lifejacket, and I'd tell them what to do if I fell over — just keep going that same speed, and make a circle and come back.

There was a mistake at Elk Island here when Albert Holm run. One of his men fell overboard and they stopped in order to back up and they couldn't get the motor started and the man drowned. If they didn't stop that motor and try and reverse, if they kept going the way I learned my men and turned around and made the circle and come back, they would have picked him up and saved his life."

HOLDING ON FOR DEAR LIFE   "Bill Zarwin was a Ukrainian boy and he was fishing with me and we were bringing a load of fish down into Lac du Bonnet. There was a little rapid you had to run through and the procedure there was, he would stand on the rock holding the rope, then he would let it through and I would have another rope on the back end and pull it through. We'd line it through.

It was just like a spillway going through there, and by gosh if the boat didn't turn over and knock him off his feet, turn right over, knocked him down under, and he was in the spillway.

Luckily he had the rope and I'm on the shore with the rope. I sat down just holding for dear life, just holding for dear life, and he crawled all the way back up the rope and held onto the keel of that boat. And I was saying, 'For God's sake, Bill, don't let go, hang on. Get on it. Get on it.' And he was in there about ten or fifteen minutes, but you know it's like an hour, and he came right back and grabbed ahold of the rope I was holding at the back, and that's the way he got out. That was a real close one because that spillway could have just taken him and he would never have got out because just below there's some pretty rough rapids. That would have been the end."

PASSENGERS GOING NORTH   "The passengers were a mixed crowd. Let's see, we would get Roman Catholic priests and nuns going down to the missions in the North. We would also get the Anglican mission people that were going to Aklavik and Fort McPherson, Fort Good Hope, and various other communities in the North. And then we carried the mounted policemen that were going in and out of the Northwest Territories. They travelled by steamboat. Also, the Royal Canadian Corps of Signals, who looked after the radio communications in the North in those days.

Not too many prospectors and trappers. The trappers mostly travelled on their own, in their outboard motor-boats and canoes and whatnot. We'd have the odd one, but not too many."

THE *BEAVER MACKENZIE* AND FLYING BEARS   "The *Beaver Mackenzie*, our dredge ship, was renovated in Liverpool in spring of 1975 and sailed through the Panama Canal and up through to Dutch Harbour and the Aleutian Islands and then through the Bering Sea and back into the Beaufort Sea that year, and it was one of the bad ice years, 1975. It was the year they had all the difficulty getting all the shipments into Prudhoe Bay, and the *Beaver Mackenzie* made it in but it was caught in ice floes. There were polar bears on the ice floes and the men who were the crew that brought it in were English and they called them ice bears and they probably enticed them with a little bit of food. So the bears started to come up on the ice floes and wanted to get up on the decks of the ship. I don't know whether they really got on the ships but at times they were getting right up there, but the ice floes opened up and the *Beaver* made it in into the Beaufort.

In talking about polar bears, of course, in the wintertime when the ice freezes over, the hunting gets rather sparse and they go looking for food, and it's probable that the camps and these sewage units smell pretty good to a hungry polar bear. In the wintertime, on every camp along the shore or offshore, we have a polar bear monitor who's a local inhabitant and he brings dogs which serve to alert the camp. They're the early-warning system, and the monitor makes regular excursions around the ice every day it's feasible to do it, to watch for polar-bear tracks, so that we don't have a polar bear catch us by surprise. The polar bears fortunately tend to disappear like they came, back over the ice again, but it was set up that if they did bother us consistently, the environmental people would come out and shoot them with tranquillizers and then we could sling them under a helicopter and take off, away up far off.

Actually, on any of the offshore islands we've never had to use this, though we did once on a rig that was on land on the nearby shore and a bear got a free ride."

SIXTY MEN ON A BEAUFORT BARGE   "The islands are built to drill an exploratory oil or gas well, and they're only made to last as long as you can perform that operation, which is about nine months.

If we make discoveries in the Beaufort Sea and they were exploited, then we would have to build permanent islands. The wells that are drilled are drilled, tested, and then abandoned. Usually it takes about four months to drill a well, and during the drilling of the well their drilling-rig is on the island along with their camp, and the men live right there, about sixty in all. Some of the islands deliberately weren't made big enough to contain a camp, and we had a barge with a camp on it located right next to the island."

ON YOUR OWN   "The earlier days on the Mackenzie River, it was a long trip from Fort Smith down to Aklavik, about fourteen hundred miles, and when you left with a stern-wheeler or a tug in those days for that voyage, the skipper of that boat was in complete charge of that vessel for the trip. It was his own little world. He was strictly on his own and there was no communication, so when you left Fort Smith the chances are the office in Fort Smith or Edmonton wouldn't hear anything about you or know anything about you until you returned, and came around the bend just north of Fort Smith.

So you had to look after everything. You made sure that the crew was okay and your freight was unloaded, you loaded your return freight, and your repairs had to be taken care of, and you had to make the best time possible.

Oh, things would happen. Sure. You could have engine trouble and you could be delayed. You could run onto a gravel bar and lose a day and a half, that could easily happen."

PLUS MEALS   "We've never had any problems with the Eskimos and Indians, good, honest people. The only problem was that when we had to hire 'em to work, they would work long enough to get a few dollars and away they'd go, and we relied strictly on them for all our discharging of cargo. We made it a point to hire them, and as we hired them we had to feed them. That was the law up there. When you hired an Indian or an Eskimo, you fed him, and if you didn't feed him he didn't work."

RUNS LIKE A BIRD   "The native fishermen were very innovative. I recall, I used to order a lot of outboard motor parts in the late forties and fifties, and these motors were old, I don't know how old they were but I used to go into Kaddies Hardware in Flin Flon and order outboard parts for Johnson motors. And I can recall that one fellow had made a gear out of a piece of bird bone and made it work. That was at Deschambeault Lake or Pelican Narrows, one of those points."

LOOKING AFTER THE ESKIMOS   "We carried the people that were supposed to look after the Eskimos, Northern Affairs people, and we had the medical party, Health and Welfare, with us. So when we got into port we took all the Eskimos on board the vessel, some of them came in their own boat, and to them that was their Christmas treat, because that was the big event of the year, the supplies coming in, everything was pretty well dry on the shelf of the Bay by that time, you see. And the Eskimos were looking for tobacco and cigarettes and pop, and you know, to have a little party. So they all came on board the ship and we fed them lunch at meal-time and they were all over the ship, about a hundred roaming around the bathrooms and on deck, and waiting for their turn to be X-rayed, you know, and examined.

Well in 1951-'52-'53, we took back to Churchill around sixty Eskimos, because at the time, you see, they hadn't been looked after for quite a long time and there was a lot of bad flu, and some TB. So the first four years we were loading the boat with them and taking them to hospital. When we took them off from the hospital, the organization bought some soapstone for them in Montreal somewhere and put them aboard the ship and they carved on the way up. But you know, as a consequence of travelling with the crew, they'd sell it to the crew and the crew would buy them — and when they saw there was such a market, you know, they carved faster."

TWENTY-FIVE

Poachers, Bureaucrats, and Other Troublemakers

Oyster Poachers... Poached Oysters and Potted Lobster... A Stake-out ... Poached Eggs... Cinders and Other Refuse... Mostly Sharks... A Rustler in the Sturgeon Corral... The End of the Herring... A Licence for Everything... Haywire Bureaucracy... Wherever You Look... Seventy-two Consecutive Years... A Frustrated Salmon Fisherman... Joe Blow, the Fishery Officer... A Fact of Life

How can an older fishermen, who went to sea at the age of nine, and whose formal education was nominal, to say the least, understand the endless flow of words from Ottawa regulating the fisheries? The answer, of course, is that he can't, and fisheries officers are forever running around trying to explain the latest ruling to fishermen. Fishermen hate being told what to do. Fisheries officers, who drove me around to interview fishermen, warned me I'd get a big blast about the government interfering with the fisheries, and once in a while I did. Oddly enough, while fishermen moaned about unending paperwork, about the government issuing one regulation and then countermanding it two weeks later, and about certain unfairnesses, there was a kind of an understanding that the government was trying to conserve fish stocks, although doing so uncertainly and sometimes in a partisan fashion. They might yell at fisheries officers, but they knew the fisheries officers were doing their duty, and that was it. Not all fishermen are so charitable, however; they're mad as hell about the whole business.

Poachers are everywhere, and it would take an army of wardens really to cope with them. Poachers sneak in by night in the bays off Prince Edward Island where oyster "farmers" have their oysters, though sometimes the oyster farmers will wait up through the dreary night for them. In northern New Brunswick

poachers are estimated to be snatching $3,000,000 worth of lob-
sters each year. Salmon poachers are busy in Nova Scotia and
Newfoundland. Smuggling swordfish out of the Shelburne, Nova
Scotia, area was big business. A good trip to the United States
could bring a captain and five or six crew-members $32,000. I
read just the other day that the ban on swordfishing has been
lifted. There'll be some long faces around Shelburne.

As for the other troublemakers — well, they gave me some bi-
zarre stories, as you will see.

OYSTER POACHERS "We don't buoy our oyster beds off
because it makes it easier for people to steal our oysters. So we
leave them unmarked and we know where they are just by taking
landmarks. Poachers are quite common and they are one of our
biggest drawbacks lately. Poachers come in different ways. Some
poachers will disguise themselves as eel fishermen. They'll go out
at night with an eel spear and spear eels, and when they come
across our oyster beds they always seem to have a pair of oyster
tongs or something similar, and they help themselves to some of
our oysters. Or they could come with a drag aboard their boat,
and they would just drop the drag, drag it across our lease, and
take up approximately a hundred dollars an hour on us if they
had a good drag and a decent-sized boat.

We may suffer ten per cent loss with poachers, yes. The natural
mortality on oysters would roughly be about five to ten per cent
of our volume, just natural deaths. We haven't caught any poachers, but we've scared quite a few away. We have a strong searchlight and you just put the light on them and they move on. They
usually have a fast boat."

POACHED OYSTERS AND POTTED LOBSTER "Well, the
oyster-poaching is pretty bad, but it is mild compared to the lobster. The lobster-poaching in P.E.I. was really something else. But

poaching has always been bad. When they come in at night, they
don't mark the corners of their leases; they know exactly where
they are, and they don't mark them so that the poachers won't
know, because they've seen them out planting oysters and whatnot and they've taken some bearings too, so they go out. So
they've pretty well got to have a watchman on patrol. And this is
the way they do it all down the American Atlantic coast where
oysters are grown in great quantity.

There's various ways of catching poachers. Some of them just
row up with dories from the shore. They are pretty easy to catch.
Some of them have fast boats, but the thing was, I had a faster
boat. This is what you had to do, have a good, fast boat. Other
things was that you knew when they were going to come ashore
with a catch, so you just waited for them. Many a night I laid out
in the swamp just waiting for them.

And when you're thinking of law enforcement, for the protection of a resource, prevention is much more important than prose-
cution. You could take them into court and they were fined
twenty-five dollars, and the oysters were taken away from them,
that time, but it didn't take them very long to make up that
twenty-five dollars.

The thing was that in P.E.I. there's two seasons, one on the
north shore and one on the south and strait shore. There's small
canneries just work during the season. So, all right, here is a cannery working on the north shore when the season is closed on the
south shore. So the fellows who are poaching on the south shore
are sneaking across to the cannery that is operating on the north
shore, and vice versa, as the seasons change. So it's just a poacher's paradise.

Another thing they would do, they would poach the lobsters
and then they would can them themselves, and then they would
sell the cans to the cannery. And the cannery would just put their
label on them, and away they'd go. So the thing was that they
were canning them illegally, and sometimes they would do it in
their own kitchens.

And there's one incident near Albert, where a raid was made.
We went into the kitchen, we could smell them and knew they
were there. The woman was boiling clothes on the stove and every-

body was sitting around talking, you know... 'What do you guys want?' And she was quietly putting the clothes in the boiler — and that's where all the cans were cooking.

Another incident. The family was sitting around and a child was on the potty, that kind of chair, you know, and we could smell the lobsters that were cooking. The kid got up and said: 'I can't stand this any more.' They saw us coming and they planked the lobsters under the kid and they planked the kid on the chair."

A STAKE-OUT "I don't believe we have too much poaching in this day and age, but in the earlier years it was a way of life. Some fishermen had to get out and do a little poaching to feed their families.

There was quite a bit of poaching went on all right, and it wasn't any problem to sell the fish to the fish-buyers. They were always in a position where they could cover up the catches with legal catches, you know, to get rid of the fish without any problem. And there was a number of mink-ranchers in a lot of these fishing communities that required fish year-round, and they weren't past buying fish from the poachers whenever they got a chance. They could always buy it a few cents cheaper. So there was always a market for poached fish.

In those years there weren't too many fishery officers, so they had to use what methods they could, and one method was staking out at night and listening for boats on the lakes, and during the day you would patrol the lakes and find out where their landings are, where they would be coming in with their catch. So they'd stake out and wait till the boats come in, and nab these fellows.

We had the authority to seize the gear, seize the fish, seize the boat if need be, and take them before the courts and deal with the matter. The poacher would get a citation. We would have to issue a receipt to the poacher for his nets and his boat or whatever we seized, and he would be issued a summons to appear in court on a certain day.

We had real good magistrates. They understood the situation and some of them were pretty good. They would hit them anywhere from fifty dollars to a two-hundred-dollar fine, plus their gear would be confiscated. We certainly didn't get them all, but we got a good many of them and slowed down the poaching."

POACHED EGGS   "There is a lot of salmon-poaching, yeah, on the Fraser River especially, and mostly by Indians, because they figure that it is their right to fish on the river, you see? But the trouble is, they are allowed to fish a certain amount. I'm talking about up-river, you know. Right now, I'm particularly thinking of the Lillooet area and I'm not talking about only Indians — a lot of white men, too.

You see, the salmon industry, it's changed a lot in the last two or three years especially, because the eggs have become very valuable. Now, what a lot of miserable poachers do, they'll go and scrape all the eggs out of the salmon, throw the carcass on the bank, and that's it. The poachers sell the eggs, and there's a tremendous price for fish eggs right now, Salmon eggs bring about two or three dollars a pound to the fishermen. They sell in Japan mostly; Japan's a big market. They pay fifteen, twenty dollars a pound for them there.

They figure there was at least a hundred trucks — mostly pick-ups — from Alberta, too, over in the Fraser River poaching; taking the salmon and the eggs and selling them. They caught the odd one. But they do a lot of it at night, and it's pretty dangerous for one or two fishery officers to go in amongst a bunch of poachers. You know last year it was pretty bad up there — there was darned near shootin' goin' on."

CINDERS AND OTHER REFUSE   "Well, the lake freighters in those days used to run on coal, steamboats, and they threw their cinders overboard. And I've seen cinders as big as that thing right there — three feet across — all tangled up in the gill-nets. This type net you're lookin' at right here. And it was a mess, let me tell you. Roy Jacks come and got me at eight o'clock at night once and I worked till four in the morning, and they'd been out there all day after herring and worked all day and all night, and there must've been, oh, over fifteen people on the boat that night, takin' cinders out of the nets. The cinders, you see, were setting on bottom, out on the steamboat course, out there on the point. Then they got a blow, and they'd get a current in the lake, and them damn cinders just roll around just like balls on the bottom of the lake. A few years after that they made 'em grind 'em before they put 'em overboard, the fishermen got squealin' so much that they made 'em grind 'em.

But for years we had 'em getting caught in our nets up until the last fifteen years. There were other things, too. I think everybody in Cleveland and up there, they flushed all their French safes down the God-darned drain, and never even tied a knot in 'em."

MOSTLY SHARKS   "In the wintertime we'd go down the Gulf Stream, you know, down off North Carolina, and fish down there, and in the Gulf Stream there's a four- or five-knot current, you know, and we'd always fish swordfish right on the borderline of the warm water and cold water. You'd fish on the warm side, of course.

Some days, you know, you'd get in a lot of trouble with sharks. Some days you'll get four or five hundred sharks. Your gear might be bit off maybe fifteen or twenty times, and you'd be all day just more or less searching for the pieces. When we set out our long-line gear for swordfish, you set for swordfish, of course, but you didn't always get swordfish. Lots of times you got mostly sharks."

A RUSTLER IN THE STURGEON CORRAL   "Sturgeon is a fish that you can take and put in a corral and keep them. You'd get a bay — a quiet bay — on the river or the lake, and you'd get rocks and you'd build a corral around it with rocks, and then when you caught your sturgeon, you kept them in the water. The corral would be, say, twenty feet around, and in the corral they would be loose and they'd just keep swimming in there. And then when you wanted to, you could take the fish out by canoe, portaging, taking it to Point du Bois, taking it on the train, and taking it to Lac du Bonnet and bringing it to Winnipeg. Instead of that, we used to have the airplanes come out of Lac du Bonnet, pick up the fish, and fly them in, and we had a truck at Lac du Bonnet to take them to Winnipeg for you.

Well, we had these fish in a corral and by God we were losing the odd fish, and we couldn't see where the corral was broken, how the fish would get away. So we watched, and here it was a bear. This one bear was a pretty crafty bear, and he just came and got what he wanted and away he'd go. Also, if you were out fishing he thought nothing of getting into your tent and racking it up. He was a real terror. They could never get close to him, he was on the move.

So a bunch of fishermen got together and they got some bait-hooks with a twelve-inch hook and they tied 'em three into a bundle and they tied it around a tree, The bear went up the tree after this jam that was up above the hooks, and going up, the hooks wouldn't bother him. But when he started to come down, the hooks got under his skin. Then he started really hollering and the fellas at the camp heard it and ran over there with a rifle and shot him. That was it. After that there was no more problem as far as the sturgeons were concerned."

THE END OF THE HERRING "The late forties were the best days of fishin' in the Lakes. They were the best days for the blue pickerel. They were the best days for the herring and the white-fish. In those days, you know, in the fall of the year, the whitefish'd come in on the bait. And you had pound nets on stakes, and they'd catch boatloads of these whitefish in the fall of the year, and they used to milk the female. Yeah, take the spawn out of 'em, and then they'd milk the males in with it, in a certain amount of water, and then they'd take them to the hatchery and they'd re-hatch 'em and put 'em back in the lake.

They used to do that with the herring in the fall, too. They used to have two big milk-cans, full of spawn, every boat took a couple of milk-cans, they may be 'bout eight or ten gallons, and when the herring were spawning, they would take and squeeze the eggs out of the female, and then they'd milk the male, and they milked it, and that fertilized the eggs, and then the Department'd take 'em away and hatch 'em, and then, when they were small, they'd put 'em back into the lake.

Well, all of a sudden the government got stingier'n hell, says it wasn't worth it, and they didn't do it any more — and that was the end of the whitefish, and that was the end of the herring."

A LICENCE FOR EVERYTHING   "It's hell with the government these late years, they're into it, Christ, head over heels, like you can't do this and you can't do that and you can't do something else. You know, fifteen or twenty years ago that was never heard of. Christ, you just got aboard of a boat and went fishing.

You've got to have a licence for everything now. You have to have a licence to go home and see your wife. The fellas working in the fishery department, they don't know, Christ, you gotta keep books just the same as you're keeping if you were running a business. Now you've got to save every goddam slip.

Years ago we used to go fishing, you know, and come in, some of the buyers would figure your trip up on a shingle. You'd go down aboard the boat and settle up with the men and file the shingle away, that was it."

HAYWIRE BUREAUCRACY   "Bureaucracy in our fishery is something that has been going haywire for this last ten or fifteen years because they come up with regulations that don't even make any sense. They may look good on a piece of paper behind a desk up in Ottawa, but take the same regulation and put it in a boat out in the fishery, they don't go together at all.

It seems we've got a regulation on haddock catches. Well, you go out and you're allowed so many thousand pounds of haddock a week. You may get that in one day. What're you going to do the rest of the week? You either throw your haddock overboard, they're dead, or you turn around and tie your boat up for the week. You've got a crew working, they want to make some money. You're tied up. 'We can't go fishin' because I've got my quota for the week.' And if they keep fishin', which they do, for other fish, what haddock they get they're throwin' away, maybe fifteen, twenty thousand ton of haddock overboard a week that's dead, and it's not goin' to any use at all.

If you catch over your quota for the week, when you come ashore you can be fined a thousand dollars because you got a hundred pounds over your quota. Therefore, if you make a tow and you took five thousand pounds of fish more than your quota, what're you gonna do? You're gonna throw them overboard. They're countin' the fish. This is one regulation that doesn't work at all, it's nonsense, and most of the fishermen has even suggested to the government, 'Look, if we got the fish, rather than throw them away, okay, give us our quota, we get forty thousand pounds a week, we got our quota, I got sixty thousand pounds aboard the boat, you take the other twenty thousand pounds, you process it and sell it, do whatever you're gonna do with it and whatever money that that brings back in, put it into our fishery. Give us a patrol-boat, give us something for the money that we're wasting instead of throwing it overboard and lettin' the gulls eat it. That's what's doin'.''

WHEREVER YOU LOOK   "One time you'd go fishin', fishin' was fishin', you went fishin' and that's all you know, you didn't talk politics, you didn't talk to a fishery officer. And that was it, you just went fishin'. Now, you can't talk to fishermen without talkin' politics. Every damn thing is politics. And wherever you look, there's a fishery officer, you know."

SEVENTY-TWO CONSECUTIVE YEARS   "He never lost a year of fishing till they put the ban on our salmon-fishin' in the Bay of Fundy, when Jack Davis put a ban on commercial fishin' in the Bay of Fundy. That old gentleman told me before he died, he says that, 'I've had seventy-two consecutive years, I never missed a year in the Bay of Fundy until that dirty Jack Davis put the ban on her, and now I can't even get a fish to eat.' ''

A FRUSTRATED SALMON FISHERMAN   "Well, in 1968, which was a good year for me, I had fourteen hundred salmon. I averaged over thirty salmon a day for the eight weeks of the season, an average of twelve pound apiece. From the small and the big, we take only a general average to that and it would be twelve pound. In that year, I had around twelve thousand dollars' worth of fish and I was only gettin' fifty-eight cents a pound for them, that's the price, and I landed twelve thousand dollars' worth of fish. With today's prices, at two dollars a pound, which they're paying for them today, you could just imagine what kind of a season you could have. If you got a year like that it would be no trouble to run yourself twenty-five, thirty thousand dollars for the eight-week season — and this is actually what we should be doing because there's certainly enough fish to support a good commercial fishery in the Bay of Fundy, because at the present time we won't have over thirty boats fishin' in the whole river, bay, the whole works, will be no more than thirty fishermen. And now it's illegal for us as commercial fishermen to take a fish."

JOE BLOW, THE FISHERY OFFICER   "Why is there a ban on salmon? Because there were too many people fishing it, the sustainable yield was going too fast. When they reach a certain level of yield, then the regulations will be relaxed again. When a regulation is proposed, if it's proposed in headquarters, it does not pass until it comes down to the Maritimes, and the officer, Joe Blow, on the spot looks at it and he says, 'This is good,' or 'It's no good.' He's the guy that makes the decision, then it goes back to Ottawa and it's kicked around again. Now, the scientists might scream and holler that it's not the right idea, but Joe Blow down on the shore, the fishery officer, will have a very great influence in what goes into those regulations, and entirely from the point of view of local knowledge. Now, this may fly right into the face of what the scientists or the biologists or other people want. However, this is the way it will go. Most regulations, amendments to regulations, comes directly from the field to Ottawa.

The fisherman loves to give the fishery officer a hard time — that's part of the fun.'

A FACT OF LIFE   "It's got almost to the point where there's more lobster fishermen than lobsters, and it's got a little ridiculous. It used to be in the old days a fellow could go out and in the course of a week get several thousand pounds of lobster and make a good living at it; no longer can he do this because there's too many others trying to catch the same lobster, with the result that he only catches several hundred pounds, and therefore is not making a good living, and is therefore complaining.

So who's to blame? The government and the regulations, but the regulations are saying we'll only issue so many licences. We'll only license so many boats; we'll only permit so many traps. Now all this is to conserve the population of lobsters, so they can only be cropping the sustainable yield, which is getting less because of the pressure of fishers. So, because it's getting less, you've got to clamp down and say there will be less fishing, and this hurts the fishermen and you hear all kinds of complaints about it, but it's a fact of life."

TWENTY-SIX

New Frontiers

*A New Frontier... Pushing into the Unknown... An Oceanographer
Speaks... Charting... The World of 1696... An Impression of the Society
... From the Apothecary's Cupboard... Surveying on a Sealer... A
Scholarly Look at the Language of the Sea... Not Ships, Boats...
Canada's Newest Fishery... Buffalo Fish... Out of the Dustbowl... The
Great Oyster Transplant... Catholic Fish... The Fur-Trader's Cigar...
Communities on the Sea Floor*

T he oceans cover seventy-one per cent of the earth's surface,
and contain life forces and natural energies that are alien
to land surfaces. In the coldest water, under the deepest ice,
there is life. Currents and earthquakes, immense trenches and
mountains that ring the earth, are all to be found beneath the
oceans. In the salt waters that encircle the globe (and even in the
fresh-water lakes and streams that cross our land), there are
numberless secrets and treasures that oceanographers and marine archaeologists and other scientists are just beginning to discover and are learning more about through careful but very time-
consuming research.

This chapter is about the people who work on the water ad-
vancing our knowledge of these new frontiers. I find it a very
exciting one, and hope you will too.

A NEW FRONTIER "I started in the underwater business here
in Canada in the early sixties, and I got into it by a peculiar method. You see, if you run into an architect, for example, and you ask
him how he got to be an architect, he went to school. I became an

underwater archaeologist because a committee decided that they needed a museum archaeologist to go out in the field and do something that needed doing, and they said, 'Walter, you're an archaeologist, so gird up your loins, or whatever archaeologists use when they're diving, and go and do us some underwater archaeology.' I was rather stunned but I was also intrigued. You see, to cut a long story short, in Northern Minnesota, right on the river between Minnesota and Ontario, they had started diving to discover stuff that the fur-traders used. And they had approached the Royal Ontario Museum, and they in turn appointed me to work with Bob Wheeler, the man from the Minnesota Historical Society.

Bob Wheeler turned out to be one of the nicest chaps to work with that I ever saw. So he and I together decided to ignore geographers and politicians. Our job was to search the boundary waters between Ontario and Minnesota, this portion of the fur-trade route. We decided that the boundary waters logically should have extended from Montreal to the mouth of the Mackenzie, so we searched the whole damned country — Quetico Park, James Bay, the Churchill River in Northern Saskatchewan, the Mackenzie, all over. When we started it we had to learn by doing, because no one had ever thought to search the old canoe routes, until this chap in Minnesota, Davis, did so. Diving at that time was a salt-water operation, started, of course, by Cousteau in the Mediterranean. People had picked it up and were doing it off Florida. But the idea that you could learn some history in the murky, bumpy waters of the French and Mattawa rivers, or in the Churchill or Ottawa — nobody had ever thought of before.

This was a brand-new frontier in archaeology. This was something that had never been tried before, and we had to fly blind. We had to train people to work in fast water, we had to train people to work by feel, because normally in the waters we were working in you had a visibility of about six inches on a clear, sunny day with a good tail wind. We continued it, Wheeler and I, for an even ten summers, doing a little bit here and a little bit there, because we were mostly working with sports divers, who had other jobs. We worked across Manitoba and across Saskatchewan and got up into Aklavik. That was the last time I saw Bob, at the mouth end of the Mackenzie River. And we stood there looking at that muddy water and said, 'To hell with it.'

The waters that we were diving in would vary from a couple of feet sometimes to forty feet. The deepest we ever got into was forty feet, and that was at the bottom of the Persian Rapids. It's a strange rapids, a beautiful rapids on the French River south of North Bay in Ontario, and it's still Parisien — it's a French community. But the natives and I usually refer to it as Persian Rapids.

There was a hole there forty feet deep, and Don Hughson and Jimmy Sheppard, the divers from Sudbury, got in there and they found at the bottom of this hole 108 iron axes, beautiful superb specimens which we still have here in the museum. And there are some of those in Minnesota, of course. They found musket-balls, thousands of them. Musket-balls tend to look one very much like another, unless you're a musket-ballologist, if there is such a thing. But you want to measure them, weigh them, you count them, and you draw graphs. You see, they were handmade in moulds and they weren't working to modern specifications, so you measure a whole heap of them and take a central tendency. They cluster around sixty-eight one-hundredths of an inch. So you say they were probably made for a 68-calibre musket. And then you find a musket and you saw off the barrel and you clean off the rust and you measure the bore of the musket with a micrometer, and you build up pictures of what happened in the old days by these meticulous details.

The moral of the story is that, if you want to do it, you need the largest heap of musket-balls you can get. So the boys came up and reported that there, and later on another group said that on the Winnipeg River, the place was loaded with musket-balls. So I said, 'Get these Javex bottles, fill them full of water, they'll sink and you can drop these musket-balls in them.' So the boys sat there in cold water, picking up musket-balls one at a time and dropping them into a Javex bottle. They'd tie a rope to it, pull the rope, and (I'm sitting up in a boat) I would pull it up. It was nice for me, I'm sitting up there with loons and birds around, in lovely country. But this poor guy is in the dark down there, in freezing water. It's not a congenial occupation. But they did it.

The best areas we ran into were unquestionably the French

River that goes south of Lake Nipissing down to Georgian Bay, because everything that went west of there had to go through that. That was the main channel. The fur-traders would start in Montreal or Lachine, some place there, and they'd get in canoes up the Ottawa, turn left on the Mattawa through a little muskeg there and into Lake Nipissing, cross that and down the French.

Now, you don't get into trouble when you're paddling upstream. You run into trouble when you get a heavily laden canoe and are over the divide and are going downstream and you want to shoot the rapids.

These fur-traders were experts. They were superb canoeists, no question about it, but they would have an eighteen- or twenty- or up to thirty-six-foot canoe, the big North canoe, that would carry up to three tons of gear. Nobody in their right mind wanted to unload this stuff at a portage. You see, you couldn't bang your birchbark canoe up on the gravel or up against the rock as we do and hang on until you unloaded it. You had to leap out in the shallow water — or not so shallow water — at the foot of the rapids, hold it off while it was unloaded, and then carry three thousand pounds of stuff over a portage, a mushy muskeg area. You carry two pieces, as they call it — that's 180 pounds on your shoulders — and then you go trotting off at a nice brisk trot through a muskeg. With that amount of weight you can only go one way and that's straight down into the mud.

The men, as a result, always wanted to run through the rapids because it was much easier. They were professional paddlers, these boys, and the icing on their cake was the excitement and drama of running the rapids. So they would do it — and then they would upset every once in a while.

So we learned that the place to look was at the foot of rapids, when they are going not loaded with furs, because furs will float, a bale will float and they'll go off in another canoe and pick it up, but with a bale of axes, that will go straight down. The only time they had axes and the heavy goods that would sink to the bottom was on the way west. So you would go to the height of land and work west, downstream somewhere where they were shooting.

I think the mother lode for the Quetico Underwater Research project was at a place called Boundary Falls on the Winnipeg Riv-

er, at the boundary between Ontario and Manitoba. The fur-traders would come out of Lake of the Woods, paddle north, and
swing west to Boundary Falls. We went there because we knew
from a journal there had been an accident there.

We read that on August 9, 1800, about nine in the morning,
Alexander Henry the Younger was heading west with a bunch of
trade goods for the fur-trade post and he upset a canoe in the
north channel at Boundary Falls. He left us a list of what was in
there. He had muskets, musket-balls, iron axes, powder, high
wine — I've forgotten the details. And a couple of cases of hardware and he didn't tell us what kind of hardware, for which I'll
never forgive him.

We went there and we stood on an island in the middle of the
falls, looking it over. We'd had many years of experience by then,
we'd both read the journal, and we said, 'It could be here, but it's
more likely over beyond that little reef, that little channel there.'
So we sent the divers over there and Wheeler and I each in our
own canoe went up into a little cove and dropped our anchors
there. Bob smoked and I lit a cigar and we admired the scenery. I
just got my cigar nicely going when a diver came up, Claus
Breede, a young Dane with a beard. He looked for all the world
like a soggy Viking emerging from the water, and in his hand he
had an axe, a beautiful trade axe, and he said, 'Interested?' and
Bob and I both made proper professorial comments — 'You're damn
right!' or something profound like that, and Claus said 'There's
a whole bunch of them down there, looks like a case of them.'

Now, Claus was a superb diver but he was also a very good
artist, so we handed him some waterproof paper and a normal
lead pencil he used for writing at the bottom and we said, 'Go
down there and draw us a picture.' Claus did it and brought it up
— beautiful. He had it from the end and both sides. Then we sent
divers down to see if they could lift the thing as a unit, and they
went down and squiggled underneath it. The iron with the rust in
the water tends to fuse them together, and we got out this whole
case of iron axes, got it into a gunny sack, heaved it aboard the
Royal Ontario Museum fleet, that is to say, an eighteen-foot
canoe, peeled back the burlap, and there it sat. And this was the
case of Alexander Henry's axes. And I'm just admiring them, it's

all cruddy, needs a lot of washing and soaking, on the edge is something that we think are files or ice chisels or both, this is a beautiful, magnificent find, so we're just admiring it when another diver comes up and says, 'There's an awful hell of a mess of musket-balls down there, boss, what do we do?' I says, 'Nip over there and get a few Javex bottles and drop them in there.' He says, 'You mean you want all of them?' I says, 'Every damn one of them. They might look all the same to you, but it's very important you get them all up.' He says, 'There's also birdshot.' I told him to put the birdshot into a different bottle and when one gets full just bring it up, and I'll give him another one.

So he heads off for Javex bottles and another chap says, 'There's a bunch of these wooden things down there, they don't look natural to me.' They surely didn't look natural. As soon as I saw them I knew they were the handles of an old French-eared knife, an early form of jack-knife. I recognized this thing when I saw it — the blade was all rusty but the form was still there, and I recognized the form and I said to Bob, 'This is the first time in all my life that I ever knew what kind of a handle they had on this thing. I knew that they were a clasp knife, but what they were mounted in I never found — and neither did anybody else in the world.' We were sitting there looking at the first damned one that had ever seen the light of day for a couple of hundred years. He said, 'There's a whole nest down there, do you want them all?' And again we said, 'Every damn one of them.'

By this time we were bright enough to say, 'Gather them up but leave them there, put them all together and put a marker.' So you take a Javex bottle, put the cap on — underwater archaeology wasn't possible at all until plastic bottles were invented, you use them for markers for everything. We put markers on these, made a rough map of the position of these things. And we found that what we had was a long line of stuff. Obviously, a canoe had upset upstream and the heavy stuff sank first. We spent three days there, three of the most exciting damn days of my life. My wife Eva was there. My daughters Diane and Christine were there, little babies at the time. We set up an open kitchen on the island at Boundary Falls and Eva did the cooking, millions of flapjacks and corned-beef sandwiches for the whole herd of divers. We had about twenty of them there and we ended up with what must have been the mother lode of underwater Canadian archaeology.

We found whole herds of gunflints, several muskets, repeat muskets, several broken ones, we found musket-balls, we found birdshot, we found a bale seal there that says 'Isaac Whieldon, London'. One of the chaps came up with something that looked for all the world like a little silver dish. He was kicking for shore and holding this in his hand, and he said, 'There's some more down there.' I said, 'Mark the position and bring them up.' He brought up eighteen in three different sizes. He turned them over and we were cleaning the crud off them and we noticed the stamp on the bottom. I couldn't clean it up well enough then, but when we got it back to the museum, we had the technicians peel it off, and there's the stamp of a London pewterer. It is a beautiful, beautiful find. They were pannikins, little tin dishes. These obviously weren't for the fur trade because none had ever turned up at any other sites, and I'd never seen or heard of such a thing before.

Back at the museum, when the technicians were cleaning it and I was back at my desk, where I think profound thoughts and write them down and read books, by chance I was looking for something in Kane's book *The Wanderings of an Artist*. The place where I opened the book was the spot where he was returning from Edmonton or some place in Alberta and it was Christmas, and he tells how they sat down to the finest meal he'd seen for months. And he sat there and admired the table loaded with this and that, *and the beautiful tin dishes*. That was it! What I had here were tin dishes, the kind that had graced the table of the Factor.

Most of the kettles were damaged, but we found many in mint condition, and other people I know — when I wasn't around — did hang them over the fire and brewed a dish of tea in them.

If I put the whole heap together, ten years'work, it would weigh in the hundreds of pounds. This is not the sort of work where you find a lot of stuff, mind you. Most places we dived we found nothing. If I laid it out on a table, say three feet wide, the table would be a block long. You see, I've got about a quarter of an acre of musket-balls and an eighth of an acre of birdshot. We have doz-

ens of old flintlock muskets, side plates, which were lock plates
for the muskets, hundreds and hundreds of gunflints, dozens of
knife handles, dozens of butcher-knife handles and various items
made out of wood.

I had no problems with my divers, except for the fact that I
overworked them. On the French River one of them came to me
and said, 'Walter, you've never been down there, you don't know
what it's like.' He said, 'I'm not complaining for me, but I'm more
experienced and younger and healthier than most of these guys.
You're working them too hard.' So I learned.

But I had no trouble with them. They used to con me at first
that because of the special physiology required for underwater
work they needed a special diet. Who was I to argue? So, instead
of the Kraft spaghetti dinners I was wont to feed them, they
conned me into buying large amounts of T-bone steaks, which
had to be washed down, of course, with Burgundy because there
was something special in the grapes of Burgundy that aided their
digestion. It took me a remarkably long time to realize I was being
conned. Then, when I did, I let them get away with it half the
time. They worked beautifully.

We stopped this work, not because we got everything from the
rivers, but we got the bulk of it. We hit the obvious places. We
realized that if we went out and got more it would add very little
to the story. We had the information we wanted. About 1972, Bob
said, 'Let's go on to bigger and better things.' And I asked him, as I
recall, 'Do you have her phone number?' "

PUSHING INTO THE UNKNOWN   "I've been going to sea on
scientific oceanographic expeditions every year since 1959, with
the exception of two years ago. At sea we collect observations on
the ocean bottom, its structure, geological history, composition,
and how it got there and what it's potential might be. We do this
by means of very sophisticated electronic instruments. I personally don't go down in submersive boats, although I have taken a
lot of deep-sea photographs.

I have often thought about my attitude to the sea. I have looked
at it long enough and often enough and I have wondered, how do
I feel with respect to the sea. There it is, rolling around and it

always looks the same and yet is always different. And regrettably I have come to the conclusion that I have no attitude towards the sea. I don't love it, I don't hate it. I'm really not elated by it, but what I love is work at sea.

I love being on board ships. One reason is the ship is a very self-contained and very self-reliant community. I always felt that on board ship, with the other sixty-seven people around you, you can get anything done. It doesn't matter what it is, they will fashion it out of rope and canvas and a piece of wood and a piece of metal and make it, whereas on land you have to fill out purchase requisitions and get approval for this and that and so on, and it never gets done.

The water obviously affects and shapes the sea bottom, but it's not so much the weight of the water that affects it as the movement of the water. It's quite abrasive, you know, and it becomes even more abrasive when it picks up a bit of sediment, in fact it's one of the strongest shaping forces on the earth, the movement of water, both on the earth that the sea has exposed and the earth beneath the sea that we don't see. It has a sandpapering effect. It sandpapers here and deposits over there, so that the bottom of the deep ocean is a grand depository for material that has been eroded from rockies and high mountains, Laurentians, Appalachians. Rivers bring the sediments in, and this all gets deposited in the middle of the ocean. In addition to sandpapering, it's also depositing in other places, so it's more a moving company rather than just a destroying agent.

If you were sitting on the moon, and there was no ocean on the earth, the most prominent feature that you would see on the earth would not be any of the features that we know from the land, no Himalayas or any of the other mountain chains. The most prominent thing that a moon man would see on the earth would be a chain of mountains called the mid-ocean ridge. This chain of mountains is a continuous chain which starts somewhere in the Arctic Ocean, close to the North Pole. It goes then between Greenland and Europe with a few places sticking out above the sea water, for example Iceland, through the central Atlantic, around South Africa, into the Indian Ocean, with Mauritius again outcropping on it. One branch in the Indian Ocean goes north into the Red Sea, the other branch swings south of Australia, crosses all of the Pacific, and goes into the Gulf of California. This chain of mountains, one continuous chain of mountains, is over seventy thousand kilometres long, and the height of this chain of mountains is comparable to very high mountains on land, in places it could be higher than the Rockies or the Alps. But by and large it is not so much its height that would impress you in looking from the distance, but the mere fact that it just girdles the earth all around its length and its breadth, as if somebody had taken a big balloon and a brush and painted one long line from one end of the balloon all around it to the other.

In scientific work at sea, a very high proportion of all conclusions and discoveries occur at the time when the observation is coming in. You might be on the midnight watch and you're looking at some instruments and all of a sudden the needle flickers and you say: 'Gee, this must be interesting — and this is probably why it happened.' And I've found that in all my scientific work the really interesting scientific ideas have all come out like that. And then you spend the next five years analysing, and doing computations and so on, just to get the last little bit of confirmation of your idea.

I'm quite sure that what we are doing today will look just as exciting and challenging in two hundred years as the voyages of *Beagle* look to us right now. I'm quite aware that every time we sail we are on an expedition to the unknown, and that we are just as much exploring the unknown now as they did one hundred, two hundred, five hundred years ago. It's just that our limits are wider. The boundaries of science are much wider than they were even a few dozen years ago, so that any individual can work only on a smaller section of this larger boundary. But that still doesn't mean that we are not pushing into the unknown."

AN OCEANOGRAPHER SPEAKS "Any oceanographer who goes to sea and spends a considerable amount of his life at sea — and some oceanographers do, they're at sea for up to three months at a time — you go through storms, you go through calm periods, you go through warm periods, you go through sunny periods, and you can't help but be influenced by these changes which are always appearing when you are at sea.

I don't think this makes the scientist quite take on the personality of the ocean, but I think that working on the ocean makes the scientist be very patient because he had many failures. I've always felt that if somebody is going to be successful as a scientist studying the earth, they have to be very patient and they have to be very persistent, and I think that's the ocean's chief appeal to scientists. So even though we have got into rough storms, quite bad storms at times, I only felt the sort of challenge of work in weather which is rough. And we have worked in quite strong storms, and we do know that the peak of the storm in which you can't work is just going to blow itself out in a matter of a few days at the most.

But I don't think I ever could say that I've been in a situation where I would prefer to be back home. I think there have been times when I've been away long enough, I just want to get home. But after you've been at sea for quite a while, you get used to the pitching and tossing. You just get used to it and work with it."

CHARTING   "My prime responsibility is to direct a program of charting all the navigable waters of Eastern Canada. Well, actually I would say of charting about forty per cent of Canada's waters out to the edge of the Continental Shelf. There are estimates that it will take one hundred years to complete the initial charting of Canada's navigable waters. It is a very tedious and costly method of mapping Canada, because we have no system by which to penetrate the waters yet, so it means we must go out on the water. Every precaution that is possible is taken, and while the master of the ship has the final word, the hydrographer in charge can discuss the program and try to convince the captain to take his ship into the area. But the captain has the final word on the safety of the ship and personnel, including the hydrographer in charge. The hydrographer must use a great deal of tact, and the captain of the ship must have a great deal of interest in what is being done. Normally, the hydrographer and the captain will get their heads together and look at the program and the captain will advise the hydrographer in charge what he will do or what he will

attempt to do. If the area is dicey at all, a launch will be put over
the side, or possibly two launches, and these will go well in
advance of the ship, so that the ship will have time to stop if the
echo-sounder on one of the launches has found something, and of
course this ship is in constant radio contact with the launches.

Normally this works out very well, but three or four years ago
we lost one of our chartered ships, the *Minna*, in the sub-Arctic,
Resolution Island. We had been extending the survey up through
the Labrador Sea from Canada across to Greenland and it was
necessary to put another transmitter station ashore, so we had
pre-selected a site on Resolution Island and the ship had gone into
this very small anchorage in a cove on Resolution Island, and
unfortunately she was very light and the wind caught her and carried her over a reef and we lost her, and quite a lot of equipment.
Fortunately we didn't lose any people.

Our survey season will start about the 1st of May and terminate
at the end of October. We are certainly interested in the composition of the land from the shoreline. The men go ashore to establish
geodetic control, and we also collect such information as the
heights of cliffs, the composition of cliffs, the composition of the
foreshore, so I would say a hydrographer spends possibly twenty-five per cent of his time ashore during the course of a survey.

To be a hydrographer, you have to be a bit of a pioneer. I've
been a hydrographer for more than thirty years, sixteen of which
were spent in the field, and you have to be a bit of a pioneer; you
have to appreciate what you're doing."

THE WORLD OF 1696 "Marine archaeology is a relatively new
science and there are very few places where formal training in the
discipline can be obtained. Consequently, the main contribution
has been made by experts in other areas moving into the field of
marine archaeology and starting off essentially from scratch and
developing their expertise in this new region. And in Canada
there are, as far as I'm aware, no training programs in this discipline at all. And the archaeologists that are in the marine field are
almost all from other areas.

I've been directly involved in archaeological investigation for
about six years now. Certainly there are thousands and thousands

and thousands of wrecks off any coastline, whether it's in Canada or any part of the world. And the majority of wrecks that are known are usually of the more recent vintage, and by recent I mean 1800 to the present day. The older wrecks of more archaeological and historical importance often haven't been found, or haven't been identified if they have been found. And as far as the serious investigation of these is concerned, I suppose you could say simply in Canada it started about ten years ago. It's quite a recent period of investigation.

The wreck I'd like to describe is H.M.S. *Sapphire*, which was sunk in action in 1696, in Bay Bulls, Newfoundland. This wreck was discovered, as far as we can understand, by divers about fourteen years ago now. A diver was just casually fooling around on the bottom when he came across a mound of pottery items and some number of stones, plus a whole variety of cannon. At the time he didn't know what he'd found, but after a while, of course, the news leaked out. Divers used to regularly visit the site and of course took up a variety of the items that were lying around the bottom. They didn't know what vessel it was, you see, and when we came on the scene and dove on the vessel first in 1970, we realized that it might be a certain age — you can identify cannons, you see, the type of cannon. We didn't know what the vessel was, but we started looking around in the more easily accessible documents, the histories of Newfoundland and things of this sort, Prowse's *History of Newfoundland*, and we came on a ship referred to as the *Zephyre* that was lost in 1694. And then I happened to be visiting England and I was able to visit the Public Record Office in Britain where there are extensive records, particularly of Royal Naval vessels. And very quickly I discovered that the vessel was in fact, or most likely the vessel was, H.M.S. *Sapphire*, which was sunk in action with the French in 1696.

The only way you can identify a vessel is by finding artifacts, items from the ship, which are datable to some degree or other, and datable items can be fitted into the general context of what you think the vessel is. And the most important item found with regard to the *Sapphire* was a pewter spoon handle that was dated 1695, which would be the year before the vessel was actually sunk. The vessel was sunk in 1696 — so it's a very good datable item. The *Sapphire* is in sixty feet of water and on a silty bottom, and so consequently when the vessel settled, it was possible for silt to infiltrate portions of the hull and protect it from being eaten up by the wood-boring worms and bacteria and so on that are present. We think the *Sapphire* would settle down further over a period of time, and also material would be brought in from other parts of the bay and would tend to build up on the ship over a period.

In the case of the *Sapphire*, the first thing that people noticed when they found it were a large number of cannon lying around. Now, as well as the cannon, if you look more closely you start to see portions of the hull, and of course if you're used to diving on old wrecks, this will become one of the most obvious clear features. And you can see things like the ribs projecting out from the silt, and in some cases, with certain vessels, you can make out a whole outline of the ship.

The shape of the wood on the bottom will depend on how much is exposed. If it's well exposed, then it's usually worn down by the movement of sand and gravel and so on, or silt in this case, over the wood. And also, if it's well exposed, wood-borers will get into it. But in this case the wood under the silt is extremely solid — I mean, you'd have to saw it to get a sample of the wood.

You have to conduct a relatively major operation to remove the silt from the vessel because of the sort of pieces of equipment used in cases of this kind. The most commonly used one requires an air compressor and a connection from the surface, and a tube the air can expand up, and as the air expands up the tube it creates the suction at the end by the silt, and this will suck the silt off the vessel and it will be deposited somewhere else.

If you're doing an archaeological investigation, the problem is the matter of time; you have to be extremely careful in getting rid of the silt because at all times you may be exposing artifacts, and they have to be recorded in position, and retrieved and taken to the surface — and usually with some care, so the progress of the operation is quite slow.

We keep note of things like documents that are organic, everything that's wood or leather or cloth, what we determine is organic, and you can get preservation of organic materials other than wood. It depends on the condition of the site. There have been, for example, even pieces of newspaper kept on site. The classic one is in the excavation of Port Royal in Jamaica, where a watch was retrieved by excavators and in the back of the watch was a piece of newspaper that was put there about 1690 by the owner of the original watch, and when the town was sunk into the ocean by the earthquake was the time the watch was lost.

But by and large documents aren't maintained at any state. Occasionally I'd get portions of them; leather remains in remarkably good condition under the water and really doesn't degenerate over a long period of time. So you can pick up fine things like shoes and any leather buckles; things that are made of leather do tend to remain in quite good condition, but other organic items not so well.

One of the problems of any marine archaeological investigation is you have to have proper conservation facilities available. These items would never last in any stage of the removal process whether they are on the surface or whether they are being transported from the site unless the boxes were always kept damp. If they do dry out, of course, they tend to crack and very rapidly will disintegrate."

AN IMPRESSION OF THE SOCIETY   "One of the reasons for doing the marine archaeology is to retrieve information not available from any other source. When the vessel went to the bottom it was a microcosm of the society that was available at that time, and as such would represent a unique collection of items in common usage, a collection that perhaps would not mean anything as individual items, but when the items are collected together in one group, they can give a much more reasonable impression of the society of that particular period.

I mean, for example, in the case of the apothecary's items found on the *Sapphire*, there is very little knowledge really of the sort of things that were carried on board a Royal Navy warship of that period. Did they have standard apothecary's kits? Did they have standard items for treating diseases? We really didn't know — we're beginning to learn a little bit about this.

Another reason for doing marine archaeology is that some

items have been discovered already from shipwreck sites that
were completely unknown before. One of the most famous examples was an incredible computer that was discovered in a
shipwreck in the Mediterranean dated from about the time of
Jesus. And this computer had somewhere in the order of one hundred cogwheels in it which were used for computing certain items
of information about the movement of the planets and the moon
and so on. And there was no conception that the technology was
sufficiently developed at that period to develop a machine of this
sort. And although this is not a relatively recent wreck of the type
we've been working on, I think we should realize there are items
that just do not exist in museums now.

We have an example, in fact, from H.M.S. *Sapphire*, a ceramic
pot which we have been unable to get identified. Nobody has seen
anything like it ever. It was not known to exist, but in our
Sapphire records several have been found, and these are essentially new items that have not been recorded before."

FROM THE APOTHECARY'S CUPBOARD   "In 1974, almost
three hundred artifacts were retrieved from the *Sapphire* which
were, of course, not whole items. They were just fragments in
some instances, but there was quite a number of bottles, wine bottles, the bottoms or the necks intact, and medicine bottles. They're
very clearly of the late 1600s. There were also parts of ointment
jars, which again were very commonly used at that period and
were discontinued going into the 1700s.

One very interesting find was a pewter syringe, which was not
recognized in the beginning because it was all corroded, but then
we were able to study the finds of H.M.S. *Dartmouth*, the sister ship
of the *Sapphire* sunk in 1690, and they had a far less corroded syringe. These were very commonly found in the doctor's or the apothecary's cabinet for the treatment of syphilis or venereal disease.

Obviously on the second site explored in 1974, we were very
close to the area where the apothecary had set up his equipment."

SURVEYING ON A SEALER   "In 1950 we decided to reactivate
the survey of the Arctic and sub-Arctic which had been dormant
for quite a number of years due to the lack of interest or lack of

activity in the Arctic. So that year it was my good fortune to be
appointed to an Arctic survey, and not having any icebreakers or
ice-reinforced vessels of our own, we decided to charter. We
chartered two that year, both of them sealers from Newfoundland. One was the *Terra Nova* and the other was the *Algerine*. It
wasn't a bad little ship but the stench was pretty high. Every time
we ran into a sea, of course, the billows rolled up as high as the
ship, and of course she had been that spring sealing and the hold
and possibly the pump had never been scrubbed down, so the
stink was pretty high. But eventually we got used to this and everybody started smelling the same as the other person, so, no problem.

I was appointed second in command of the party on the *Terra
Nova* and we left Ottawa the latter part of April; we had some
work to do along the Nova Scotia coast and eventually mid-June
the *Terra Nova* arrived at Pictou, where we were to meet it — and
we saw this dirty little steamer come steaming in. It was the best
we had, so we made the best of it. We loaded ship and it took us
about a week to load ship and provision. They only had a small
deep-freeze up forward, and this was supposed to last a group of
men, about twenty-one or twenty-two of us on board ship, it was
supposed to last us for a four months' cruise. So we loaded our
two launches on the ship and the rest of the survey equipment
and set sail.

Our first port of call was halfway up the Labrador coast, at
Hopedale, which is a prominent place there, and it was most
interesting to me, because this was before the white man had
really started to affect the coastal people. So we sailed into the
harbour, and we were the first ship to arrive that year, so the Eskimos got out and met us by first dancing around the flagpole which
was up on a large outcropping of bedrock, and beating hands and
drums, and the dogs were howling and so on. And then they came
down and got into the boats and came out and surrounded the
ship and chattered away amongst themselves. Quite a few of them
could speak English, because fishermen had been running into
Hopedale, English-speaking fishermen, and they could speak
English quite well.

This old gentleman that we called the pilot, he was the individ-

ual that was supposed to bring any strange ship into port, because
of his local knowledge, an old gentleman of about sixty-
five or seventy, I guess. And according to custom, being a good
host and the senior person of the village, he offered his wife to the
visitors. We had to use quite a lot of tact because this chap was
quite insistent that someone take advantage of his offer, so we had
to use tact, you know . . . it's necessary that I be back on the ship,
or it's necessary that I be here, or something like this. I don't know
if anyone did take advantage of his offer or not . . . I don't think
this is a custom we have any more unless one goes to the far, far
north.

So we worked there for about a month and then after we'd been
there about two and a half weeks, it was discovered that all our
fresh provisions had gone bad, so they were throwing the fresh
cabbage, fresh potatoes, and so on over the side with no intention
of bringing in any new supplies. It was most interesting because I
was introduced to various Newfoundland dishes, for instance fish
and brewis, which consists of a mixture of salt cod and pork
scraps and onions and small pieces of very hard bread mixed
together. We were served this Friday mornings for breakfast, and
we'd get up another morning and have a big bowl of stew for
breakfast, you know. We did have fresh meat and we had juices
and this sort of thing, and as long as we had the input of vitamin
C, then we certainly wouldn't get scurvy.

So we sailed from Hopedale up away along the coast and then
we crossed up into Hudson Strait, up off Cape Weggs. We managed to kill a polar bear, so we brought that on board and we
were most happy in our ignorance because the first part we ate of
the polar bear was its liver, and we discovered a bit later on that
you should never eat the liver of a polar bear, it's supposed to be
rank poison, but we had eaten it and no one had suffered any
sickness or anything like that, so we ate some of the polar bear,
and it didn't taste bad.

I think it was a day before we left Coral Harbour to start our
voyage south, the chap who was in the cabin with me — I think
we had about three and a quarter feet of deck space, the rest of
the space was taken up by the two bunks and a small settee in the
corner — he came to me complaining about a pain on the top of

his foot, so I told him, 'Maybe you had your shoe laced too tightly yesterday and maybe you should loosen it.' So he went about his business. And the next morning he told me that his one leg was starting to feel very funny and it seemed to be starting to draw up.

So we left Coral Harbour and started our way south and we were running over to some islands there on the western part of Hudson Strait; and about a half-day out we ran into a real gale coming down Hudson Strait. So this poor character was in his bunk tossing around, by this time he couldn't get out, and this other fellow and myself were holding an electric lamp to his leg and so on. He was in quite a bad way, and of course the ship was piling around at about eight to nine knots, and when we stopped in at Hopedale he was in his bunk and he was getting pretty darn sick and no one knew what was wrong with him, but both legs were starting to pull up and he was having problems straightening them.

At Hopedale we had reached the point where we were living on split-pea soup — that was our main diet three meals a day — so I should imagine we were the only people who bought potatoes from the Eskimos, but we had to buy a couple of bushels of potatoes from the Eskimos to continue on our voyage. So we continued on and south of Hopedale we ran into a storm, and, oh, it was really a terrible storm. The ship was running down the wave and stubbing her nose into the next one, and the green water would go back over the ship. So that was one time that I can truthfully say that I was green from seasickness, and then I can on the other hand say that was the last time that I've ever been seasick.

Well, we nicely got back to Pictou on the 11th day of October and this chap who had the illness, we immediately got a doctor to come down and look at him, and he diagnosed his case on the spot as being rheumatic fever. So he finished up in the Pictou hospital and I think he got back home in Montreal in December and he eventually got back to work the end of February, and he never had any serious effects even though he had taken quite a beating for about two weeks coming down the coast on the vessel.

Yes, I still enjoy split-pea soup, but I did say when I stepped on the jetty at Pictou that that was the last voyage that I would undertake on a vessel such as that. So we didn't recharter it the next year. We headed for the nearest hotel; of course at that time there was only one hotel in Pictou, the Braeside Inn, which is still standing, so we headed there. And I think possibly the first thing some of us did was to buy a bottle of rum and have a few drinks and try to forget about the problems we'd had the previous four months. We had a few drinks, and of course this only added to our appetite, added to our good spirits, so we did go to the dining-room and Lord knows what we ordered, but I should imagine it was fairly substantial, and possibly some of the waitresses still remember our arrival."

A SCHOLARLY LOOK AT THE LANGUAGE OF THE SEA

"On the question of the effect of the sea on language, it's a hard one to talk about in very precise terms, because I guess that you'd find a parallel phenomenon at work, say, in the language of farmers or in traditional mining communities. But there's no question that you can generalize about the characteristic language of fishermen, people who work on the water.

It's always struck me as interesting, for example, that Newfoundlanders comparatively rarely talk about the ocean or the sea. The sea is something over the horizon, almost literally unless you're a deep-sea sailor. You'd use the term 'sea' of a particular wave that swamped your boat, 'a great big sea hove in Long Beach,' or you might say 'there's a big sea on,' but the generic term is 'the water', or 'the salt water', and you find this time and time again.

Usually Newfoundlanders will talk more specifically about the tickle or the bay or the bight or the narrows or the channel strait. Or if they're fishermen, they won't use water terms at all; they'll talk about the shoal or the sunker — that's a barely submerged rock — and this reflects their intimate familiarity with every condition of wind and water and sea bottom and current and shoal which determine, of course, where the fish are. And so they'd have names for underwater features, the trap berths where they place their traps will all have names.

Newfoundlanders will be talking about underwater locations with the same degree of specificity as landsmen will talk about a rock or a field or a meadow."

NOT SHIPS, BOATS   "In Newfoundland we don't use the word ships. In my experience you'd refer either to a boat or a vessel, and a boat would be anything from a small open craft which might be a fairly substantial, you know, twenty-eight to thirty-five feet; a vessel would be a deck vessel, it might be a schooner or something larger. Ship is not used often, but then, of course, you've got hundreds of specific kinds of craft, each with its name, from a Rodney to a skiff to long-liners and schooners. And we find in Newfoundland still, even today, a transfer of nautical usage to land applications, so that you might for example go for a cruise in your car, not a drive, and a traditional name for a front stoop or verandah in front of the house is 'bridge'.

And the language of Newfoundlanders is often marked by a high degree of understatement. For example, you wouldn't often refer to a rope or a cable — the usual term is a line. I remember once my brother and myself were picking up a small vessel we had and we hove to alongside a great big Department of Transport ship, and there were a couple of fellows there working on the deck and we were scrounging a bit of gear and we said, 'I don't suppose you'd happen to have a spare piece of line?' And they didn't even look at one another, but disappeared, and a minute later they came back and lowered down the most bloody big cable, about a ten-inch cable, and gave us our line."

CANADA'S NEWEST FISHERY   "Say a farmer has a fifty-five-acre slough in his backyard off his back forty. For that body of water he'd buy approximately five thousand trout fingerlings. In those days, in 1970, when the Saskatchewan aquaculture scheme started, they were worth two and a half cents apiece. He puts them into the water as soon as the ice goes out at the end of April, the first part of May. He doesn't have to feed 'em, with these minute organisms in the water, especially fresh-water shrimp. They go from two or three ounces to ten to twelve ounces in October and November and they're left there until after the ice forms, you get three inches of ice and then they harvest the fish exactly the same as they'd do any fish with the gill-net under the ice.

That year was the start. In 1970 they harvested eight thousand pounds of fish and they sold it dressed for sixty to seventy-five cents a pound.

In 1977 they harvested 164,300 pounds of dressed rainbow trout and it sold for two to two dollars and a half."

BUFFALO FISH "We have what we call a rough fish-removal operation in the Qu'Appelle Lakes where they take carp and buffalo fish out. They take almost two million pounds a year at least of these out.

The buffalo fish are a rough fish, an undesirable species, and the idea is to take them out of these lakes to improve the environment for the other species, the desirable species.

To me a buffalo fish is just a big over-sized carp. But they are fished yearly, taken out of the Qu'Appelle Lakes and out of Last Mountain Lake and shipped down to the poorer markets in the United States, that will buy this cheap fish product because of the fact that it is cheap."

OUT OF THE DUSTBOWL "We have a lake that's called Last Mountain Lake, to the local inhabitants it's called Long Lake. It's ninety-seven miles long, approximately four and a half miles wide, and it's located forty miles north and slightly west of Regina. It's right in the dustbowl of Saskatchewan. It produces two hundred and fifty thousand pounds of whitefish each December — commercial. And immediately following that you have anywhere from two to three hundred fishermen that are allowed to have a domestic fishery of a hundred pounds per fisherman. Then in January, February, March, up till approximately three years ago, there was either between one and two million pounds of tullibee taken off the lake. In the summer months they take between a million and a million and three-quarters pounds of carp and buffalo fish out of there. Okay, then on that lake itself you have five beaches, you have one, two provincial parks and the sports fishery. I think it was approximately five years ago the largest pickerel was caught in that lake one New Year's Day.

Well, the sum total is that you've got a lake there in the dustbowl of Saskatchewan that's producing more fish per acre of water than any lake in the world."

THE GREAT OYSTER TRANSPLANT "When it was found in 1952 that the oyster disease had spread to the waters of New Brunswick and Nova Scotia, we arranged a plan whereby ten thousand barrels of P.E.I. disease-immune oysters were transplanted to the devastated waters of New Brunswick and Nova Scotia. And this planting or transplanting, or whatever you want to call it, was a rather tricky operation, because we wanted as little transplant mortality as possible. So the whole thing had to be done quickly, that is, once the oysters were out of the water, they had to be transported immediately across the strait and spread on the beds of New Brunswick and Nova Scotia.

We had a large patrol-vessel, a former navy Bangor minesweeper, about two hundred feet long, and we loaded her with all she could carry, and she would cross the strait and we had a fleet of ten or fifteen smaller patrol vessels would take the oysters from her in boxes and immediately spread them. These oysters were right out of the water, right on the deck in the boxes, and the boxes held a bushel and a half. We had to keep them and keep them in good condition. They had to be soaked down with salt water all the time that they were being carried if it was a very bright, sunny day. It was quite a trick to get them across."

CATHOLIC FISH "There are the two basic religions, and it's wonderful when you go into an outport today, you'll find the sharp division. One outport along the eastern part of the Great Northern Peninsula was typical. You went into a bay, one side of the bay was settled, so was the other side, one side was Catholic, one side was Protestant.

Now, we were attempting to develop the fish-handling process by the fishermen, to get away from the old unhygienic way that they used to make fish, and when I say 'make fish', I mean salting and drying their fish. We were proposing the use of the community stage, and the federal government was sponsoring this and putting up these stages. This one wasn't working too well. So I had to go out and find why.

And I soon found why — because this community was definitely divided by religion. Unfortunately we had established the community stage on the Protestant side of the thing, you see, so that there was some difficulty in the Catholics using this. They wouldn't meet on shore, but they were congenial people and they fished together out on the Atlantic, so they liked to meet and chat in the evening. So where did they meet? They'd meet on what they call the middle ground. Now this was the middle of the harbour, and they all got into their dories and came out from each side and they all sat around in their dories and they chatted in the middle ground.

Now, I had tried to get a meeting going, but I couldn't get a meeting, I'd either get all Catholic or all Protestant. So there was a meeting right made to order, out in the middle ground. So I just jumped in a dory and I sculled out there and I had a meeting. We didn't relocate the stage but we did get a working agreement, and one of the fellows said, 'Well, I don't rightly know as how we can make Catholic fish on that there stage.' And I said, 'I've got news for you, my son, the fish haven't got the message yet — they don't know they're Catholic, so it's not going to make any difference to them.'

Well, of course, we all had a big laugh out of this, and it was realized that there was a little bit of prejudice here, and things loosened up and the thing finally worked."

THE FUR-TRADER'S CIGAR   "The rarest item we found has no significance whatever. History would have remained exactly the same if we hadn't found it. But one of the kids at Boundary Falls brought up a thing and said, 'What's this queer chunk of wood?' And it looked like a knot that you see weathered out of an old pine stump and it was about the size of the end of a cigar, and when I cleaned it up I realized that's exactly what I had. I had the end of the cigar.

You could see where he had bitten it on one end, slightly tapered, and the fire here, and also where he had butted it out, because it was splayed out at the end like a butted cigarette. It was the end of a role of twist tobacco which appears in all the literature I had read and written about for years and years, but tobacco doesn't survive. This one did because it was mixed up with a bunch of iron.

And I took it to a cigar expert, a botanist at the University of

Toronto. He peered at it and said, 'This is the end of a role of twist tobacco,' and then he said, 'The man who lit it had been smoking it for quite a while and it was glowing nicely.' How he told this from one battered cigar butt I don't know. He said, 'Something happened, he did not reach over and put it in an ashtray, he butted it accidentally.' This was to me a priceless bit of totally useless knowledge. It showed me that the end of one of these pieces of twist tobacco had been smoked as a cigar. He had it nicely drawing, was very pleased with himself when the damned canoe hit the rapids and upset and he had the cigar in his hand and he grabbed for the gunwales. The thing went down and got mixed up with the iron.

I peer at it once in a while. And I think this is a nice thing to find."

COMMUNITIES ON THE SEA FLOOR "I'm sure that one of these days we're going to have communities living on the sea floor. This is not quite Star Wars — although they might be at war — but one of my pet ideas has been that as the over-population of the earth increases, we will have to start looking at the next available real estate, which is under the sea water."

TWENTY-SEVEN

The Moon on the Water

*The Moon on the Water... A Little Chill Up My Spine... It's a Disease...
Out of Lunenburg... No One Fishin' Below... On Great Slave Lake...
Very Romantic... Keep Working... Man with Big Canoe... The Lovely
Part... Good Money... The Average Wage... The End of Kingston...
Engineers in White... Inshore, Offshore... A Job on Shore... That One
Big Fish... A Matter of Votes... Stuck with the Fish-Draggin'... Leaving
the Bank... What in the Hell Did I Give Up?... The Best Part of Your Life
... An Old Sailor's Hobby... The Tusket Islands... Slowly Dying*

It seems unfair to talk at length about fishermen, and have
them recollecting their engrossing and often extraordinary
lives at sea, without paying much attention to the object of all
their efforts: fish.

Fish are amazing. Every part of a fish is used. A fish's head
ends up as glue, fertilizer, and animal feed. Its scales are made
into artificial pearls. The air bladder becomes gelatin used in jelly, beer, wine, and cement. The bones, fins, and entrails end up
as fertilizer and animal feed. The entrails are also used in the
production of vitamins, medicinal oil, amino acids, insulin, hor-
mones, and enzymes. Oils from the bodies of fish become part of
soap, paint, tanning, lubricants, printing ink, metal-plating, steel-
tempering, and shortening. Poultry and livestock feed is made
from the flesh. Need I add that, by eating fish ourselves, we ob-
tain protein, minerals, and vitamins. And fish tastes damned
good!

Five years ago, it looked as if the Atlantic fisheries were all but
finished. Haddock and redfish were just about gone, and cod,
"the beef of the ocean", was threatened. However, with limits
and regulations, the old tradional stocks came back, and new
discoveries were made of great shrimp resources off the coast of
Labrador and a whole new snow-crab fishery around Cape Breton. The best years ever for fishermen have been the last five.

The factory ships, the floating frozen-fish plants, will mean the end for most small fishermen. Even now, the big fish-processors dictate to many fishermen. Les Stoodley told me: "Fishermen no longer have the sense of independence, the kind of freedom they used to have, when, if they wanted to go fishing, they could. The enjoyment is gone, because a fish-plant operator says, 'You will be there at seven o'clock in the morning to set sail for the Grand Banks.' They can't go the way they used to. That kind of lifestyle robs them of the familiarity and the kinship of the sea they had."

Nevertheless, in my ramblings along the east and west coasts and in inland Canada, I talked to many and many a fisherman who had his own boat, and perhaps a partner, and was out at sea before dawn broke and was still at it when night fell, that day, and perhaps the next and the next, until he scarcely knew the sea from the sky.

And all of the men who worked on the water in other jobs — towing barges, piloting ships into harbour, guiding tourists down a river — agreed that life on the water is a hard, demanding one. But they love it, it's in their blood. An old Newfoundland fisherman summed it up for me, "What's easy in this world? What's easy somehow?"

THE MOON ON THE WATER   "On the sea, you know, you see pictures that no artist could paint. You see some of the loveliest sunsets and some of the loveliest nights, the moonlight nights with the glitter of the moon on the water and the ripples, and you see beautiful sunrises in the morning. And then you'll see some grey dawns that look very bleak, very bad-looking, but you don't draw on the bad-looking ones, you always think about the nice ones.

And this is one thing I miss very much about not being able to go salmon-fishing in the Bay of Fundy in the summer now, is that I used to see lovely sunrises, the lovely daylights and the lovely sunsets. You would be out there fishing and you'd see these things

and you would sit and look at them and know right in your heart
that there's no artist under the sun could ever paint those scenes
that you see when you're on the water.

In the wintertime you'll get the aurora borealis and the northern
lights flashing through the sky, and millions of stars in the skies,
and really some pictures that on the land, if you're a landlubber
working on the land, who never went to sea, these things wouldn't
mean a thing to you."

A LITTLE CHILL UP MY SPINE   "Sometimes when you're sitting by yourself at some of these abandoned homesteaders'
cabins, there's one particular place along the river, it's called Williams' Creek, and they had a beautiful home there, and when you
sit there you can just picture the family and the kids running
around.

And this fall we were sitting there, this was later on in the evening, we just went down ourselves for quiet time on the river and
there were two owls hooting back and forth to one another across
the river. It was almost like a song, and I got a little chill up my
spine. I was thinking about the family that lived there and I
thought this was a woman singing at first, you know."

IT'S A DISEASE   "It's a disease, that's all it is really, you know.
When you're out there you wonder what you're doing there and
when you get ashore you want to go back. I don't think anyone
loves the sea that's been on it, because they know what it can do,
but you can't get away from it and you miss it and you go back
again. It gets in your blood when you go so long. It's in your blood
that it's right to get out there.

You know, when I retired from sailin' boats I was home here
one spring, that was in '68, and I called my brother, who was
swordfishin', I said, 'If you want anybody to go along with you
when you come in, I'll go.' And I had to wait about a month and I
said to my wife. 'I think I must go to the doctor, I don't feel good.'
A couple of days after that my brother come in and he called me.
He said, 'Are you ready to go?'

Look, when I took my togs out there I felt like a chicken, aboard
the boat. I felt right at home till the seine boat docked. But while I

was walkin' around not doin' anything, I felt terrible. So, it's like they say, a sickness. It gets in your blood or something, it won't get out."

OUT OF LUNENBURG "Lunenburg is not as active now, due to the fact so many schooners have all gone. We don't have any salt-fish-curing plants in town any more, the boats are still here but the plants are not.

Boats operating out of Lunenburg today are probably about thirty-five to forty scallop boats and fourteen, fifteen stern trawlers out of National Sea Products. At Riverport, which is counted in this area, there's probably about ten or twelve scallop boats and ten or twelve stern draggers. So in the whole area you probably have about sixty or seventy boats working where at one time it was salt fishing and you had a hundred and forty to a hundred and fifty schooners going out of Lunenburg alone."

NO ONE FISHIN' BELOW "They's gettin' no young fellas to go at it, no more, not on this part of the coast anyway. They're all going to work somewhere else.

There's no one fishes below where I live now. At one time there was thirty or thirty-five dories fished below where I live now, and there's no one fishin' below at all."

ON GREAT SLAVE LAKE "No, the fishing at Great Slave Lake is starting to get poor. Gary Johnson was the first man up there, and the first year he was there he got two hundred and ten thousand pounds of fish, trout and whitefish. And when him and I quit we were only getting about sixty-five, seventy-five thousand pounds, and it wasn't enough to make good money on."

VERY ROMANTIC "A lot of holiday fishermen really are not there to catch fish. They'd like to catch a few fish, but their big thing is the experience, the total immersion in the wilderness, in that kind of life. It looks very romantic from the outside, and I guess from the inside, too. I've seen both sides of living in the city, living on the farm, and living where we do now, on the water. I much prefer the last."

KEEP WORKING "The idea is to keep working. The man that retires and says, 'I've done enough now, I've done my share, I'll set down and retire,' that's only another way of sayin', 'I'll sit down and wait for death.' And, it'll come very rapid sometimes. Keep goin', keep your work as long as you're able to work and you can enjoy your life better. Nobody enjoys sitting down and doin' nothing.

I'll be ninety in October. I got good health, good heart, perfect blood pressure, feel all right, there's no reason why I can't go fishin' or do anythin' else for that matter. Can you see any reason?"

MAN WITH BIG CANOE "We're working harder now, really, on these boats than we did with the smaller boats. Years ago with a smaller boat, out of every dollar you probably took seventy-five per cent of that home, maybe even eighty per cent of it all home. Now, we maybe take twenty per cent of the dollar home, the rest is going for expenses.

Two years ago I had this boat up in Port Everett and I was packing the cross-tree off her to get the aerials fixed on the thing. It weighs quite heavy, it's made of iron, and I passed an old native there and he said to me, 'You know, the Indians have an old saying, "Man with big canoe has to work a lot harder,"' and I thought that was very, very apt, and this is true. You know, as you go along, 'cause you have a big boat doesn't always say your life is that much easier."

THE LOVELY PART "The season would begin late March, probably April 1, and go up until Christmas. They'd tie up for three months. Last year most crews shared seventeen thousand, that's a crew. This year you're looking probably twenty, twenty-two thousand. In the three months they're off they're drawing unemployment at about, this year it will be one hundred and sixty-three bucks a week. So Yarmouth County is probably the most prolific and productive fishing area on the east coast. There's big money here. Always has been, probably always will be because of the diversity of species. We don't just depend on the cod. We have the herring, the mackerel, the lobster, the scallop.

There's no ice problems. We're close to the Boston market, which is eighty per cent of our market. So, this is the lovely part. If you're a fisherman, move down here."

GOOD MONEY "I would say that today the low one would probably make twenty-five thousand as a crew member on a boat — and you go on from there. I know one dragger here, his crew share last year was forty-two thousand dollars. As for a captain, there's so many different deals, you know, the way the share agreement in the companies work, it's hard to say, but a top-flight fisherman I guess he's up in the seventy, eighty thousand dollars, for his own personal share. And if he owns the boat and the net and all the rest of the stuff, he's getting another twenty, thirty per cent on top of that."

THE AVERAGE WAGE "Back when I started in the forties I would say that in fishing we would work maybe seven or eight months of the year for about four thousand dollars. That was working on deck as a share, you know, just a deck-hand. And at that time here in Port Dover an ordinary person working, say, construction, for somebody else would be working for about two thousand dollars, back in 1945. Very, very poor wages at that time. I would say that the fishermen in 1945 would double the ordinary average worker around here.

Today, I would say, we have to work real hard to make the average wage with the ordinary fishing. But after thirty-five years you're not going to go work for somebody else."

THE END OF KINGSTON "The difference has all taken place since the Seaway opened and it cut Kingston off as a port. The ships travel the deep-water channels. There was no deep-water channels on this side of the island, Wolfe Island. Before the Seaway went in we averaged some six hundred foreign vessels a year, and that's in an eight-month period, coming through. That's twelve hundred vessels coming up and down, changing pilots during the season. Now it's very rare we see any ships through this side, they're all on the American side some twelve miles away."

ENGINEERS IN WHITE   "In an engine-room on a tugboat of about five hundred or six hundred horsepower, there'd be one man on watch. Sometimes you'd have an oiler with you and you have a second engineer that takes over when you go to bed at midnight or two. It was sort of warm down there as long as you didn't get under the ventilators to get some fresh air into you and if the door was open and all that. The temperature would be seventy-five.

Nowadays it's much different because everything is wheel-house-controlled. You know, the engineer is usually in bed or having coffee and you're working handling the controls up in the wheelhouse. The engineer is there now to oil the engine. That's about it nowadays. Mind you, he has to know what he's doin' because if he has to make a fast repair or somethin', he has to do it, but the engine-rooms are so hot nowadays with high-speed engines, over a hundred degrees on some of these, that an engineer couldn't stay down in the engine-room continuously.

There's generally too much power jammed into too small a space. And nowadays, you see, with the high speed there's noise. You've gotta have, an engineer has ear-muffs on him. In the old days there was quite a bit of noise but you could persevere with it. That's what told you how the engine was running, the rhythm of the engine. But today it's too much noise. You see, it all depends where you wanna start in the old days. Steam was very quiet, steam was beautiful. It's all diesel now.

In the old days the engineer usually had a rag in his back pocket and he wiped his hands on it and kept everything clean. That's the way it went. Every hour or so or every half-hour he'd go around and inspect everything with the oil can, and if it required a little bit of rough oil he'd go and put it on and hope to gosh it'd stay that way, that somethin' didn't seize up.

But today the engineer is just as clean as the captain. You have a lot of 'em now in white."

INSHORE, OFFSHORE   "I believe the inshore fishery will survive, and that the individual boat-owner will survive. There's no indication that the man working the craft boat is in any sense disappearing. He's making a good living, too.

But the offshore fishery is, of course, almost all collectivized. You have to put a lot of capital into offshore fishing, and it's not something that the single individual or the family can do any more. There was a time when a single family could own a banker, a banker being a schooner that fished the Banks. Well, now a single family can't own one of those beam trawlers or stern trawlers ... or one of the more complicated things, factory ships, which are the common thing now. There's no way a single family can own this sort of thing. It can only be done by large corporations or by co-operatives, and this is why the offshore will certainly be totally collective — it's practically totally collective already."

A JOB ON SHORE "I want my son to go out and make a trip fishing as soon as he is old enough to be safe at sea, say sixteen, seventeen, because I want him to see that life and see how hard a life it would be to earn this great money. 'Cause all young boys look at it now and say, 'Oh gee, I'm goin' fishin', look at the money.' So I want him to make a trip.

I'm not going to say, 'Don't you ever go out to sea,' because I would never stop him if he wanted to go to sea. I would rather see him have a job on shore, but I'd like to see him make a trip just to learn from it because, believe me, I'll never forget what I learned from the trip I made and I'd never want to go back, no way."

THAT ONE BIG FISH "I think if you like the water, you stay with it. You enjoy its various moods. And, of course, there's always that one big fish somewhere that'll make your name for you, and all the little ones in between."

A MATTER OF VOTES "I think there's actually about 150 boats that fish on the north shore of Lake Erie. We're not only fighting to make a living now but it's got to a point in the last four or five years where we're even fighting to keep fishing. I mean, the government is against us right down the line. I read this *Out of Doors* and magazines like that and all you've got to do is read these articles of these sportswriters, and a sportswriter and a bunch of anglers can meet with the Minister of Natural Resources, they can meet with Premier Davis. With a phone call, half a dozen of them can go to him and meet with him and tell him what they want. Well, two years ago when they were putting on some laws that you could hardly live with, a few of us fellas went and tried to meet with the Minister, and the day that they said we could meet with the Minister we got to Toronto and he'd flown out to New Brunswick to meet with somebody out there. This is the kind of run-around we've got right down the line. The Ontario Hunters and Anglers, they claim they've got seventeen thousand votes or something if things go their way, you know, and they're poking at the government all the time about how many votes they've got. Well, right now we've got a minority government and if they can get rid of us and get those anglers to vote for them the next round, maybe it won't be a minority government. I think that's all it boils down to right now. All they can hear is the anglers hollerin', 'We don't need them commercial fishermen.' "

STUCK WITH THE FISH-DRAGGIN'   "If I had it to do over again I wouldn't be fishing. Well, there's no life to it, not for the man and his family, eh? You're gone twelve days and you're home, too, whereas the way I see it, I envy the fellow that's workin' eight to five, which I had my chance to do and I just chose to go fishin', that's all. But if I would've went through college and got an education, why, I could've done the same as that. But I'm stuck, I'm stuck with the fish-draggin', so that's what I've gotta do. You know, it's the only thing I know to do."

LEAVING THE BANK   "May of 1968, I was sitting in the office in the bank one morning. I managed a bank for the Toronto-Dominion, and it appeared that I had a very bright future ahead. But the sunshine outside was even brighter, and I closed the door to the office, and decided that I would leave the bank.

And I subsequently handed in my resignation and looked for and found a tourist resort that I thought I'd like to run — a fishing camp. I was married at that time, had four children to support, and really very little substance to lean back on, other than of course my experience. Now most of my days are spent on the water, guiding, looking after our fishermen.

Oh, I put very little money down. The lodge was in reasonably good shape, as far as Northern Ontario lodges go. Over the past twelve years, we have added something in the neighbourhood of two hundred thousand dollars' worth of buildings, boats, and motors, and we've torn down five of the older buildings and replaced them, re-vamped the store completely, rebuilt all the boats, rebuilt all the docks, and we now have a nice operation. Well, in the summertime, I'm on the water now from six o'clock in the morning till sometimes eleven, twelve o'clock at night for the months of May, June, July, part of August, most of September, and some of October. I like Lake Temagami."

WHAT IN THE HELL DID I GIVE UP? "I was talking to an engineering technician one day and he was getting close to retiring and his big dream was to get himself a small boat and be able to cruise the Pacific coast fjords, the islands and the inlets of our west coast. And I all of a sudden thought, well, for God's sake, what in the hell did I give up? Then I just wanted to get back to it. I did work for the government for, well, like 1962 to about 1966, and then I went back fishing."

THE BEST PART OF YOUR LIFE "My father was a fisherman, my grandfather was a fisherman, and that's the way we were brought up, in boats. And I go down every Sunday morning to the harbour front now, every Sunday morning, and lots of times the wife and I will go out Marine Drive. I love being able to live alongside of the water and hear the sea breaking up against the rocks. The way I feel about it now is that my time is runned out, because that is the way we were used to.

Let's see, I've only been ashore on the land for twenty years, I'm sixty-five; forty-five years of my early life I spent going to sea — and that is the best part of your life."

AN OLD SAILOR'S HOBBY "I miss the sea. I still work at my little hobby, puttin' ships in bottles. I sell them for twenty dollars. It takes maybe eight, nine days to put one in a bottle, that is, if I work from scratch, but I don't do it that way. I make about a dozen hulls, half a dozen or so sets of masts, put sails on them, and then I got to paint all them, three or four coats of paint inside the bottle.

There's eighty-odd threads for riggin' and they all hang out the neck of the bottle and I got them tagged. I know the names: foremast, mainmast, mizzenmast, main guys, main shrouds. And I got them all marked, port and starboard side. So, if I look at my bottle port side and see the shrouds are loose, I pull these threads, and when I'm all finished I cut the threads inside."

THE TUSKET ISLANDS "I know a man, for example, he's seventy years old, he's had three major operations in his intestines, he was a fisherman for about sixty of those seventy years, and whenever I talk to him he talks about the islands, the Tusket Islands. When the lobster season opens they have shanties and they move in there for the whole week and they only come home on the weekend. They do this for, oh, I'd say, about two months, at the start of the season, and they go back in the spring.

And that man would move here today, you know, if his wife would let him, and I mean he literally has tears in his eyes when he talks about the days on the island.

And when you look at it, it was bloody hard work, you know. We used to get up at four and work late and eat and go to sleep. But, you know, everything about it, the smell, everything, you never hear him say a bad thing about it, although you'd think, my God, they'd literally work themselves to death."

SLOWLY DYING "How in God's name can you feel any kinship with the sea when you're eighty feet in the air on a steel long-liner or a trawler instead of being two feet away in a twenty-five-foot dory?

But the dories have gone to firewood, they got burnt in stoves or beach parties or God knows what. A lot of them just rotted on the flakes and the beaches and the rocks, and the people that lived in them, that loved them, because they provided a living that mellowed with the years, they've accepted the change. And what really is tragic, there isn't anybody to replace them, nobody. The flakes have gone, they go to work in the fish plant now, these same people. Somebody dictates that they punch a clock, and I hear these glowing stories of how things have changed for the better, and I keep asking myself, have they really? Or do I remember what was pleasant about it and forget the hard times?

But for me the kind of Newfoundland, the kind of Grand Bank that I grew up in, is dead, is gone, and all the colour and the character is slowly, slowly dying. When men like my father die, Phil Riggs and Morgan Francis and Traps Rose, it will be dead."

The Storytellers

The wonderful men and women who graciously spent time with me to pass along their stories are recorded here, chapter by chapter, story by story.

Chapter 1: Something Different Every Day
Killer Whales: Captain Jack Hann, Coal Harbour, B.C.
Up Over the Bow: Leonard Wilson, Lorneville, N.B.
Swordfish Attack: Cyril Henneberry, Sambro, N.S.
To Hell With It: Captain Gilles Pintal, Montreal, Que.
Good, Clean Rivalry: Ray Barrett, Old Perlican, Nfld.
Don't Show Your Hand: Fred Kohse, Vancouver, B.C.
An Early Launch: Thomas Gallant, Stanley Bridge, P.E.I.
An Eventful Trip for Mr. Jennings: Captain Clem Phillipson, Prince Rupert, B.C.
The Biter Bit: J. Foster Sharp, East Bideford, P.E.I.
Just Push It Through: Gib Lauzon, Alliston, Ont.
The Proper Light Touch: Tom Black, Lunenburg, N.S.
God Help Me!: George Brown, Grand Manan, N.B.
An Alberta Cash Crop: Charlie Scott, Edmonton, Alta.
Highliner Fish: Murray Laffin, Lunenburg, N.S.
Hope It's Going To Miss You: Captain William Evans, Saanichton, B.C.
My God, That's a Woman!: Doreen Noseworthy, Portugal Cove, Nfld.
Man Overboard, Man Overboard!: Bruce Hunter, Edmonton, Alta.
Respect for the Sea: Joe Bauer, Steveston, B.C.
Excuse Me, Is the Lady of the Cabin at Home?: Captain Stanley Mortensen, Vancouver, B.C.
In the Shoes of the Fisherman: Jack Powell, Port Dover, Ont.
The Hooks Caught Him: Cyril Henneberry, Lorneville, N.B.
The Case of the Stunned Halibut: Captain Clem Phillipson, Prince Rupert, B.C.
Creaking: Lunenburg, N.S.
All Part of the Eel Business: Michel Thuot, St. Jean, Que.
Go Out and Make Yourself a Livin': Leonard Wilson, Lorneville, N.B.
All Those Shallow Areas: George Sandell, Port Dover, Ont.
Something Different Every Day: Cameron Cook, North Head, Grand Manan, N.B.

Chapter 2: Characters
A Retired Fisherman: Captain Robert Power, Halifax, N.S.
Uncle Cy: Les Stoodley, Grand Bank, Nfld.
The Russian Steward: Captain Claude Deroy, Montreal, Que.
Noah Fished in the Summer: Les Stoodley, Grand Bank, Nfld.

A Family Affair: Ray Barrett, Old Perlican, Trinity Bay, Nfld.
On the Labrador: Captain Albert Blackwood, Safe Harbour, Nfld.
Still Hanging On: Leonard Wilson, Lorneville, N.B.
Octopus Weather: Jack Critchley, Minstrel Island, B.C.
The Canadian Merchant Marine: Paddy McKee, Montreal, Que.
Half the Village: Tom Black, Lunenburg, N.S.
Closing Up the Outports: Joseph Smallwood, St. John's, Nfld.
No More to Safe Harbour: Nina Blackwood, Safe Harbour, Nfld.

Chapter 5: Hard Work, Long Hours
Just Working, Working: Fred Kohse, Vancouver, B.C.
Keep At It, Boy: Murray Laffin, Lunenburg, N.S.
Nobody Slept: Lunenburg, N.S.
Drifting Off to Sleep: Leonard Wilson, Lorneville, N.B.
Night and Day: Leonard Wilson, Lorneville, N.B.
Long Hours: James Patterson, New Westminster, B.C.
Making Lobster Traps: Cyril Henneberry, Sambro, N.S.
Hauling Traps: J. Foster Sharp, East Bideford, P.E.I.
Everybody Had Rowboats: Fred Kohse, Vancouver, B.C.
Working for the Cannery: James Patterson, New Westminster, B.C.
Bait for the Halibut: Hazel Patterson, New Westminster, B.C.
The Survival of the Fittest: Frank Nishii, Steveston, B.C.
Building a Net: Jack Powell, Port Dover, Ont.
Oiled Nets: James Patterson, New Westminster, B.C.
Some Cold: Cyril Henneberry, Sambro, N.S.
The Night My Daughter Was Born: Wellington Halliday, Digby, N.S.
Late for School: Ray Barrett, Old Perlican, Nfld.
Double Your Money: Lunenburg, N.S.

Chapter 6: Strange Sights and Superstitions
There's No Rocks Here: Jack Critchley, Minstrel Island, B.C.
Paddy Parr's Light: Nina Blackwood, Safe Harbour, Nfld.
That Ship Is There: J. Foster Sharp, East Bideford, P.E.I.
In San Mateo Bay: Joe Bauer, Steveston, B.C.
Ghost Ship: Leonard Wilson, Lorneville, N.B.
In God's Pocket: Joe Bauer, Steveston, B.C.
Piles of Rock: Captain Lewis Orr, Kingston, Ont.
Superstition and Mythology: Dick Found, St. John's, Nfld.
These Old Fellows: Captain Albert Blackwood, Safe Harbour, Nfld.
Mirages: Jack Critchley, Minstrel Island, B.C.
Not Alone on the Sea: Doreen Noseworthy, Portugal Cove, Nfld.
Superstitions and Bibles: Captain Albert Crouse, Peter Davidson, and Captain
    Colin Mosher, Lunenburg, N.S.
Don't Whistle: Murray Laffin, Lunenburg, N.S.
Just Flapping Around: Captain Albert Blackwood, Safe Harbour, Nfld.
A Forty-Ton Shark: Leonard Wilson, Lorneville, N.B.
Death of a Whale: Reg Hazelton, Digby, N.S.
A Big Sea Lion: Fred Kohse, Vancouver, B.C.
A Load of Herring: Captain Clem Phillipson, Prince Rupert, B.C.
Dolphin's Wake: Captain Clem Phillipson, Prince Rupert, B.C.

Some Queer Serpent-Like Creature: Jack Critchley, Minstrel Island, B.C.
The Ogopogo: Captain D. K. (Kip) Powick, Kelowna, B.C., and Halifax, N.S.

Chapter 7: Skippers and Men
Able To Catch Fish: Alain Meuse, Yarmouth, N.S.
Intuition: James Patterson, New Westminster, B.C.
To Keep the Men in Their Place: Murray Laffin, Lunenburg, N.S.
Tight Boots: Captain Albert Crouse, Lunenburg, N.S.
All Hands on Deck!: Murray Laffin, Lunenburg, N.S.
The Foremost Man: Captain Albert Blackwood, Safe Harbour, Nfld.
Afraid of the Old Man: Cassie Brown, Rose Blanche, Nfld.
From St. John's: Captain Albert Blackwood, Nfld.
It Wears You Out: Cyril Henneberry, Sambro, N.S.
A Bad Egg in Every Crew: Captain Colin Mosher, Lunenburg, N.S.
Through the Lower Decks: Murray Barnard, Halifax, N.S.
Good-Living Fellows: Captain Albert Blackwood, Safe Harbour, Nfld.
No Problems with a Quart a Day: Captains Ernest Symes, Matthew Mitchell,
     and Albert Crouse, Lunenburg, N.S.
Give and Take: Captain Clem Phillipson, Prince Rupert, B.C.
Somebody'll Git Hurt: Reg Hazelton, Digby, N.S.
A Little Squirrelly: Captain William Evans, Vancouver, B.C.
Onion Thief!: Russ Melanson, Dartmouth, N.S.
Hook, Line, and Sink: Captain Clem Phillipson, Prince Rupert, B.C.
Punishment at Sea: Wellington Halliday, Digby, N.S.
Other Fellows Depending on You: Captain Clem Phillipson, Prince Rupert, B.C.

Chapter 8: Ice
Ten Miles Out: Svein Sigfusson, Winnipeg, Man.
A Cold Life: Charlie Scott, Lesser Slave Lake, Alta.
The Marvellous Jigger: Charlie Scott, Lesser Slave Lake, Alta.
The Saskatchewan Fishery: Hough Nordland, Prince Albert, Sask.
Warmer Than on the Prairie: Carl Christenson, Prince Albert, Sask.
Time for Tea: Albert Holm, Gimli, Man.
Winter Fishing: George Greening, Prince Albert, Sask.
Good Sports at Lesser Slave: Charlie Scott, Lesser Slave Lake, Alta.
Early Break-up: Charlie Scott, Lesser Slave Lake, Alta.
Mouth to Mouth: Dori Holm, Gimli, Man.
Fishing by Dog Team: Charlie Scott, Lesser Slave Lake, Alta.
Cat Train over the Ice: Carl Christenson, Prince Albert, Sask.
The Ice Was Starting To Candle: Peter Lazarenko, Winnipeg, Man.
Casting Whitefish on the Waters: Charlie Scott, Lesser Slave Lake, Alta.
When the Ice Goes Out: Bruce Hunter, Edmonton, Alta.
Riding the Spring Break-up: Stoney Thorsteinson, Selkirk, Man.
In the Arctic's Grip: Captain Stan Mortensen, Vancouver, B.C.
Icebreaker: Captain Paul Fournier, Musquodoboit Harbour, N.S.
Ice Fields and Icebergs: Captain Paul Fournier, Musquodoboit Harbour, N.S.

Chapter 9: You're a Fisherman
You're a Fisherman: Ray Barrett, Old Perlican, Nfld.
The Salt of the Earth: Grace Young, Lunenburg, N.S.

All Afire: Reg Hazelton, Digby, N.S.
She Burned for Days: Paddy McKee, Montreal, Que.
A Good Tight Cabin Floor: Leonard Wilson, Lorneville, N.B.
An Hour in Lake Erie: Jack Powell, Port Dover, Ont.
Caught By a Stern Dragger: Gailyn Risser, Lunenburg, N.S.
The Blue Wave: Les Stoodley, Grand Bank, Nfld.

Chapter 12: Partners to the Men

Partners to the Men: Ray Barrett, Old Perlican, Nfld.
Enough Crying: Grace Young, Lunenburg, N.S.
I'd Just Lay There and Shiver: Nina Blackwood, Safe Harbour, Nfld.
You Just Know the Boat's Out There: Gailyn Risser, Lunenburg, N.S.
Spyglasses on the Hill: Captain Albert Blackwood, Safe Harbour, Nfld.
My Mother Ran the House: Les Stoodley, Grand Bank, Nfld.
Days Alone: Vi Sparrow, Delta, B.C.
Pure Hell: Gailyn Risser, Lunenburg, N.S.
It Bothered Her: Peter Lazarenko, Winnipeg, Man.
Their Father Is Away So Much: Gailyn Risser, Lunenburg, N.S.
The Fisherman's Daughter: Gailyn Risser, Lunenburg, N.S.
The Boat My Husband's On: Gailyn Risser, Lunenburg, N.S.
A Deaf Ear Around the House: Leonard Wilson, Lorneville, N.B.
Good for Both of Them: Lunenburg, N.S.
Good To Have Him Home, And . . . : Audrey Holm, Gimli, Man.
A Big Drastic Change: Murray Laffin, Lunenburg, N.S.
Sticking By Their Men: Joe Bauer, Steveston, B.C.
Playing Around: Captain Clem Phillipson, Prince Rupert, B.C.
Laying Around: Gailyn Risser, Lunenburg, N.S.
Six Months Married: Eli Tucker, Quidi Vidi, Nfld.
A Girl in Every Port: Leonard Wilson, Lorneville, N.B.

Chapter 13: Towing and Being Towed

A Tugboat Master: William Stewart, Sambro, N.S.
Pushing Down the Mackenzie: Captain Stanley Mortensen, Vancouver, B.C.
Sandbars on the Athabasca: Roy Schlader, Athabasca River, Alta.
Everybody Was Working: Captain Alex Rogers, Victoria, B.C.
Anything Can Happen Aboard Here: William Stewart, Sambro, N.S.
Towing Coal: Captain Stan Fraser, Victoria, B.C.
Surging on the Line: Captain William Evans, Saanichton, B.C.
The Island Sovereign and the Sudbury II: Captain Evan D. Jones, Sidney, B.C.
Davis Rafts in the Hecate Straits: Captain William Evans, Saanichton, B.C.
Breaking Up: Captain Evan D. Jones, Sidney, B.C.
Holding Up for Weather: Captain William Evans, Saanichton, B.C.
Torpedoes from a Log Boom: Frank Nishii, Steveston, B.C.
A Barge on the Rampage: James Patterson, New Westminster, B.C.
In the Beachcombing Business: James Patterson, New Westminster, B.C.
Sinking the Barge: Bill Cook, Winnipeg, Man.
Being Towed—and Not Being Towed: Jack Critchley, Minstrel Island, B.C.
Tugs Versus Nets: Captain Stan Fraser, Victoria, B.C.
Towboat Men and Fishermen: James Patterson, New Westminster, B.C.
Shotgun: Captain Alex Rogers, Victoria, B.C.

Kazba Lake Trout: Doug Hill, Kazba Lake, Northwest Territories.
Camp Fires from the River: Gib Lauzon, Alliston, Ont.
Trout in the North: Bill Cook, Gimli, Man.
White Water on the Ottawa: Joe Kowalski, Pembroke, Ont.
Niagara—the Dream River: Joe Kowalski, Pembroke, Ont.
The Yukon River Fan-belt: Gus Karpes, Whitehorse, Yukon.
She's Come Awful Close: Gus Karpes, Whitehorse, Yukon.
The Travelling Restaurant: Gus Karpes, Whitehorse, Yukon.
The Back of the Boat: Irene Pugh, Whitehorse, Yukon.
Gib's Gotcha: Gib Lauzon, Alliston, Ont.
You've Got a Fish!: Gib Lauzon, Alliston, Ont.

Chapter 20: Great Seaplane Country
Great Seaplane Country: John Davids, Edmonton, Alta.
Fishing from a Plane: Sam McKnight, Prince Albert, Sask.
The Face of a Mountain: Captain Mark Goostrey, Vancouver, B.C.
Vancouver to Victoria: Captain Mark Goostrey, Vancouver, B.C.
Amazing Aircraft: Captain Mark Goostrey, Vancouver, B.C.
Mercy Flights: John Davids, Edmonton, Alta.
Searching: George Greening, Big River, Sask.
Skis on the Lakes: Sam McKnight, Prince Albert, Sask.
Bringing Home the Bacon: George Greening, Big River, Sask.
Just Testing: Sam McKnight, Prince Albert, Sask.
What the Hell's the Matter with the Water?: George Greening, Big River, Sask.

Chapter 21: In and Out of the Harbour
A Pilot's Life: Captain Robert Power, Halifax, N.S.
To Take That Ship Out: Captains Stan Fraser and Alex Rogers, Victoria, B.C.
Forty Minutes To Get To Know a Ship: Captain Robert Power, Halifax, N.S.
Even the Best Pilots: Captain Claude Deroy, Montreal, Que.
An Apartment House Coming Straight at You: Captain Robert Power, Halifax, N.S.
The Queen's Escort: William Stewart, Sambro, N.S.
No Steering: Captain Gilles Pintal, Montreal, Que.
A St. Lawrence Pilot: Captain George Downey, Kingston, Ont.
Fire in Toronto Harbour: Gordon Sandell, Port Dover, Ont.
Who Stole My Ship?: John Low, Montreal, Que.
Christmas Icing: Gordon Sandell, Port Dover, Ont.
A Narrow Escape for Saint John: Leonard Wilson, Lorneville, N.B.
A Whale of an Explosion: Prince Edward Island.
Tragedy in the Vancouver Harbour: Fred Clegg, Vancouver, B.C.

Chapter 22: Booze
Away You'd Go for the American Coast: Captain Albert Crouse, Lunenburg, N.S.
To Cuba and Back in Eight Hours: Niagara-on-the-Lake, Ont.
Big Money: Captain Albert Crouse, Lunenburg, N.S.
Up Goes a Rocket: Captain Albert Crouse, Lunenburg, N.S.
Gone Fishin': Captain Albert Crouse, Lunenburg, N.S.
Good Old Rum: Tom Black, Lunenburg, N.S.
Out of Their System: Captain Clem Phillipson, Prince Rupert, B.C.
No Booze on the Boat: Alain Meuse, Yarmouth, N.S.

Runs Like a Bird: Carl Christenson, Prince Albert, Sask.
Looking After the Eskimos: Captain Paul Fournier, Musquodoboit Harbour, N.S.

Chapter 25: Poachers, Bureaucrats, and Other Troublemakers
Oyster Poachers: Leonard Burleigh, East Bideford Narrows, P.E.I.
Poached Oysters and Potted Lobster: Dick Found, St. John's, Nfld.
A Stake-out: Jim White, Ponoka, Alta.
Poached Eggs: Jack Critchley, Minstrel Island, B.C.
Cinders and Other Refuse: Gil Wardell, Port Dover, Ont.
Mostly Sharks: Cyril Henneberry, Sambro, N.S.
A Rustler in the Sturgeon Corral: Peter Lazarenko, Winnipeg, Man.
The End of the Herring: Gil Wardell, Port Dover, Ont.
A Licence for Everything: Avard (Bubby) Pyne, Yarmouth, N.S.
Haywire Bureaucracy: Leonard Wilson, Lorneville, N.B.
Wherever You Look: Yarmouth, N.S.
Seventy-two Consecutive Years: Leonard Wilson, Lorneville, N.B.
A Frustrated Salmon Fisherman: Leonard Wilson, Lorneville, N.B.
Joe Blow, the Fishery Officer: Dick Found, St. John's, Nfld.
A Fact of Life: Dick Found, St. John's, Nfld.

Chapter 26: New Frontiers
A New Frontier: Walter Kenyon, Toronto, Ont.
Pushing into the Unknown: Dr. Bosco Loncarevic, Dartmouth, N.S.
An Oceanographer Speaks: Dr. Cedric Mann, Dartmouth, N.S.
Charting: Russ Melanson, Dartmouth, N.S.
The World of 1696: Dr. Vernon Barber, St. John's, Nfld.
An Impression of the Society: Dr. Vernon Barber, St. John's, Nfld.
From the Apothecary's Cupboard: Dr. Janette Barber, St. John's, Nfld.
Surveying on a Sealer: Russ Melanson, Dartmouth, N.S.
A Scholarly Look at the Language of the Sea: Dr. G. M. Story, St. John's, Nfld.
Not Ships, Boats: Dr. G. M. Story, St. John's, Nfld.
Canada's Newest Fishery: Bill Lovitt, Prince Albert, Sask.
Buffalo Fish: Hough Nordland and Cecil Oliver, Prince Albert, Sask.
Out of the Dustbowl: Bill Lovitt, Prince Albert, Sask.
The Great Oyster Transplant: Dick Found, St. John's, Nfld.
Catholic Fish: Dick Found, St. John's, Nfld.
The Fur-Trader's Cigar: Walter Kenyon, Toronto, Ont.
Communities on the Sea Floor: Dr. Bosco Loncarevic, Dartmouth, N.S.

Chapter 27: The Moon on the Water
The Moon on the Water: Leonard Wilson, Lorneville, N.B.
A Little Chill Up My Spine: Gus Karpes, Whitehorse, Yukon.
It's a Disease: Captains Ernest Symes and Albert Crouse, Lunenburg, N.S.
Out of Lunenburg: Tom Black, Lunenburg, N.S.
No One Fishin' Below: Witless Bay, Nfld.
On Great Slave Lake: Bill Cook, Gimli, Man.
Very Romantic: Bob Brown, Lake Temagami, Ont.
Keep Working: Beecher Court, Rustico, P.E.I.
Man with Big Canoe: Fred Kohse, Vancouver, B.C.
The Lovely Part: Alain Meuse, Yarmouth, N.S.

Good Money: Captain Clem Phillipson, Prince Rupert, B.C.
The Average Wage: Jack Powell, Port Dover, Ont.
The End of Kingston: Henry Black, Kingston, Ont.
Engineers in White: John Shaw, Victoria, B.C.
Inshore, Offshore: Harold Horwood, Beachy Cove, Nfld.
A Job on Shore: Gailyn Risser, Lunenburg, N.S.
That One Big Fish: Bob Brown, Lake Temagami, Ont.
A Matter of Votes: Jack Powell, Port Dover, Ont.
Stuck with the Fish-Draggin': Lunenburg, N.S.
Leaving the Bank: Bob Brown, Lake Temagami, Ont.
What in the Hell Did I Give Up?: Joe Bauer, Steveston, B.C.
The Best Part of Your Life: Captain Albert Blackwood, Safe Harbour, Nfld.
An Old Sailor's Hobby: Paddy McKee, Montreal, Que.
The Tusket Islands: Alain Meuse, Yarmouth, N.S.
Slowly Dying: Les Stoodley, Grand Bank, Nfld., and Halifax, N.S.